Ireland 1170-1509,
Society and History

Ireland 1170-1509, Society and History

Desmond Keenan

To order additional copies of this book, contact:
Xlibris Corporation
0-800-644-6988
www.xlibrispublishing.co.uk
orders@xlibrispublishing.co.uk
301049

Contents

Part 2

England in the Twelfth Century

Part 3
Irish Society 1170 to 1513

Part 4

History of Ireland 1170 to 1509

Veritas vel silentio consumiter vel mendacia. Ammian
Truth is destroyed by either silence or a lie.
To the great reforming popes of the 20th century, Pius XII, John
XXIII, and Paul VI.

Introduction

The Writing of Irish History

Irish nationalist history was propaganda, selecting and omitting episodes to suit a political purpose. It is as easy to distort history by what is omitted as by what is put in. A historian must school himself to remove every trace of prejudice from his mind. This is as true of the dogmas and distortions of Irish nationalism as it is of Bolshevism or Nazism, and it is not easy. Romanticism too must be purged. A romantic view of the Middle Ages such as that expressed in the novels of Sir Walter Scott pervaded British and Irish culture in the 19th century. We should however recognise that Gaelic chiefs and Norman lords were men of their time, and any of them could have fitted into the ranks of the Gestapo or the Bolsheviks in the 20th century.

In this book it is recognised that Irish society was an integral part of the society of North West Europe subject to regional variations. In particular the Church in Ireland was not a 'Celtic' Church different from that of Rome, but a regional variation like the Church in France. In earlier times the Irish Sea joined lands not separated them. Abandoning the simple verities of ideological history gives the historian a problem: a lack of factual sources. We would love to know many things, the negotiations between Gaelic and Norman families, for example, but nobody bothered to write them down. Was the mystical teaching of

St Bernard not transmitted to Irish monasteries though it is found in England? Again no writings. And so on and so on.

In this book I have avoided the use of the word 'Irish'. I use Gaelic as shorthand for those who spoke the Gaelic language and 'Norman', 'Anglo-Norman' and 'English' for those who spoke those languages but with little cultural implications. Family rivalries were all important and intermarriage common. 'Colonisation' must be understood in the context of the time, where skilled workers were imported into less-developed lands as the Germans were doing east of the Elbe. Gaelic chiefs could have done the same thing but did not. Ireland in the Middle Ages was not backward, buts its economy was less developed than that in England which in turn was behind development on the Continent. Improvement was occurring all over Europe, and Ireland was caught up in the process. I considered writing this book in two parts, one regarding Gaelic Ireland and the other Anglo-Norman Ireland, but as there was about a 95% overlap this plan was abandoned. The general aspects of European society are described in Chapter One.

I begin this book conventionally in Ireland with the coming of the Normans in 1169, as no other turning point suggests itself. When should the period end? Henry VIII who was to inaugurate the policy of establishing royal control became king in 1509 though he did not immediately alter his father's policy. Ireland continued to be dominated by the Great Earl of Kildare until his death in 1513. Therefore I conclude this book at that year.

The book is divided into four sections. The first section gives a general description of life in the Middle Ages. Gaelic society was not an exotic 'Celtic' society. From 90% to 95% of social structures and activities was common with the rest of western Europe. There were of course in Europe some regional differences and these are described in the third section. There was little peculiar about Irish society except that it was often behind the times. The second describes conditions in England in the reign of Henry II. This is important for it was these social structures which were introduced by the Normans and there is usually far more information about them in England than in Ireland. The third and largest section describes Irish society in the Middle Ages as far as we can ascertain. The fourth tries to make some sense of the continual internecine disputes between the lords and chiefs and the Government.

These disputes had started hundreds of years earlier and were to continue throughout the Middle Ages. The English crown made sporadic attempts to intervene and impose some kind of order but often unsuccessfully. I have tried to give an outline of the principal events and trends without going into too much local detail. Local disputes and campaigns were very numerous but beyond noticing their presence there is little point in tracing them in detail. They were important only locally and should more properly be dealt with in local or county histories or monographs or biographies. There was no consistent Gael versus Norman struggle. The families involved were often inter-married and disputes were usually restricted. Such neighbourhood aspects have their place but are only confusing in a general history.

Care must be taken to correctly understand the use of terms. Many words were used in the Middle Ages which we still use today like town, city, sheriff, court, parliament, law, farm, road, king, to give a handful of common examples, but with rather different meanings. In the King James' Bible the little towns in Palestine are called cities and the ruler of the city is called a king. We would describe the 'cities' as defended villages and the 'kings' as mayors or town clerks. Most people have only a very general knowledge of events and institutions in the Middle Ages. For this reason I have devoted a large introductory section to institutions and events in Western Europe. These were not always fully replicated in Ireland, but in general anything in Western Europe found its way eventually to Ireland though possibly in modified form. But even institutions like sheriff, or dean, or army which retain their names could be quite different when originally developed or introduced.

The great work on medieval Ireland is that of Professor Otway-Ruthven which all serious students of the period should possess. However, in her desire to present a detailed account of every turn she did not make her work the easiest book to read or follow. To make this book more readable I have omitted a lot of detail in order to present a general picture and updated the narrative by including the results of more recent studies. It is impossible to find any clear pattern in the events of the three centuries which would make them easier to memorise. In England there were episodes like the Barons' Wars, the Hundred Years War, and the Wars of the Roses to provide focus. The alleged Gaelic renaissance in the 14th century was nothing more than a collection of sordid local events without plot or plan where petty chiefs wasted the lands of the peasants, raped their women, drove out industries, killed the old, and reduced local areas to famine conditions. The one bright spot is that the colonised areas survived all attacks and internal feuding and developed as a modern European society, providing the foundations of modern Ireland.

I provide a firm chronological context based on the reigns of the English monarchs, and provide dates for every important event. This enables the reader to have as far as possible a clear chronological sequence in his head. This hopefully will prevent the reader from slipping from one century to another as is easy enough to do. Events just seem to repeat themselves. Nevertheless there must be some going to and fro as contemporary threads are pursued.

Irish romantic nationalism was as much a distorting ideology as Marxism or National Socialism and I have made every effort to exclude it from this book. It is not so much a question of facts as the interpretation of facts. One has only to peruse the now-dated work of Professor Curtis to see interpretation that depend more on the historical romances of Sir Walter Scott that any dispassionate analysis of the evidence in its context.

With regard to society and the economy I have tried to present them in words intelligible to modern readers. Irish society was not innovative and there was little to distinguish it from any other society in Western Europe. But European societies were never identical so the distinguishing features found in Ireland must be indicated. The basics of farming for example never change, but the details change very much. Towns and trade are very much the same in any age, but again the details vary considerably. I have tried to present all the chief aspects of society in a logical division. The great lacuna concerns the lives of ordinary people, what we call nowadays the working classes. The scribes and clerics were from aristocratic classes, and if they mentioned ordinary workers it was likely to be as objects of ridicule and merriment. But we nowadays want to know how ordinary people lived, but the information was never written down. With regard to English-speaking areas we can draw to some extent on English studies, but there are no comparable studies of Gaelic areas. It will be noticed that often especially with regard to Gaelic society that my conclusions are speculative. I preferred to attempt giving a full picture of Gaelic society rather than ignoring whole aspects just because there are no written records. My assumption is that Gaelic society, given the possibilities of the time, could not have been very different from Anglo-Saxon and Norman societies.

It was once assumed that there were rigorous divisions between the Norse, the Gaels, the Normans, and the English, all keeping themselves segregated in their own areas, speaking their own languages, observing their own customs, and fighting each other. This was implicit in the idea of race and race-struggle. There is no evidence of this and we can assume that they spoke each others languages, and copied each other's customs and techniques. Intermarriage seems to have been the rule. Normally more men than women travelled abroad and they took wives where they settled. Customs varied from manor to manor, but they were all very similar, and founded on the technologies, skills, and possibilities of the times.

One has to ask oneself how society functioned when almost everyone was illiterate. Courts clearly had to be small affairs where people could hear each other. Therefore, access to every court was restricted. There had to be a hierarchy of courts, the lowest being the manorial court or its Gaelic equivalent. The highest courts were the king's courts and those of the great Gaelic and Norman lords. Iron was rare and expensive while wood was common. Therefore most things for most people would have been made of wood. A spear or a dagger used less iron than a sword. Only the very rich could afford armour and swords, not to mention horses. Sufficient land had to provided to support a mounted soldier, whether Gaelic or Norman. And so on. Everything must be interpreted in its context. Irish society, like all other Indo-European societies was a militaristic aristocratic society which treated ordinary working people like cattle whose only function was to provide for the needs of the ruling families who would never lower themselves to doing manual labour.

The fascinating point about this period of Irish history is the reflection of the growth of the great institutions which mark the modern states in the Anglophone, Common Law, and representative parliamentary traditions. In 1066 a feudal system of government was imposed on England on top of an existing county-based Anglo-Saxon administration. Gradually the kings saw the benefits of the county system, and without removing the feudal system moved to take closer control over the county administration through judicial circuits. Oddly neither feudal law nor statute law was imposed in these courts but the judges decided individual cases quite often by quoting precedent. The feudal lords resisted encroachment on their feudal rights and they insisted on establishing limits to arbitrary royal power. The Battle of Bosworth Field in 1485 marked a decisive stage in the transfer of local government from the feudal lords to the shires and counties, and to the circuit courts. (Other battles still had to be fought over the uses of royal prerogative courts like that of the Star Chamber in Tudor and Stuart times.)

It is clear that the English kings, despite what the nationalists asserted, had no particular interest in conquering Ireland, still less despoiling it of its riches. Their aim was to prevent the formation of an independent kingdom by the Norman knights which could then ally itself with France. They wished to prevent that which actually happened in Sicily and Scotland. For the most part they were satisfied if the warring factions neutralised each other. The English Parliament had no intention of paying any money to support the king in Ireland. Ireland was the king's concern not theirs. In Ireland the crown always seemed to be hesitating between county administration and the administration of the hereditary liberties. Though the shock of the Bruce invasions early in the 14th century was successfully countered by the counties of The Pale the trend thereafter seemed to favour hereditary earldoms which could only be regarded as a regressive step. But palatine jurisdictions placed the cost of local defence on the local lord. Eventually, in Tudor times, counties were established everywhere and the local chiefs and lords were appointed sheriffs. It is strange this was not done earlier. But nobody can see a century ahead and decisions were made based on contemporary problems.

In 1170 Ireland was emerging from the Dark Ages. Ireland in 1170 resembled the coasts of east and west Africa in the times of Stanley and Livingstone. By 1470 eastern Ireland at least resembled the new American states west of the Mississippi after the American Civil War. Modern institutions of government, states, counties, towns, trade, and industry were established at least in the eastern half of the island. There was state and county government, with the sheriff, his deputies, and his posses to maintain order. There were judges and lawmen that came to town to deal with crime in a summary manner. There were settled communities and small towns on the favourable land, while Indian tribes and gangs of outlaws and cattle rustlers were in the badlands. These latter raided the settled communities. The local sheriff or the local big farmers dealt with them as best they could, while bodies of the United States cavalry dealt with major incursions. There were no guns however; the arrow was still the preferred weapon. The range was open with few fences except around dwellings.

There is no indication that the feudal lordship or the Gaelic lordships or the towns contributed anything positive to these great developments or indeed to any developments. Neither the feudal lords, the Gaelic chiefs nor the town and county administrations were able to unite with anybody for long for a common purpose. Short-time family interests always prevailed. If any group of them united they could have established an independent Irish kingdom either with or without a nominal recognition of English feudal overlordship. But there is no indication that any group at any time seriously contemplated that. All developments from the 12th century onwards whether religious, secular or academic came from without. Ireland simply was not a society of innovation.

The ruling Gaelic families proved surprisingly resistant to innovation though it is not clear why. For one thing there was a persistent need to grab ever more land to provide support for their numerous children. Primogeniture in Anglo-Norman lands reduced this need. Younger sons had to find employment elsewhere as freelances. There was great resistance to primogeniture in Gaelic lands. The chieftainship was elective within the *derb fine* so there were always several contenders who did not want the system changed. Conservatism was endemic also in the learned classes. The antiquated Brehon Law could easily have been updated by incorporating new judgments as in the Common Law but this was never done. It is also puzzling why towns and ports were not fostered and the old system of dealing with foreign traders over open beaches persisted in. A lot of research needs to be done in these areas.

In fact when we discard the anachronistic 19th century view of Irish history as a *rassenkampf* or race war to disguise their own attempts to gain control of the rackets we struggle to distinguish Gael from Norman. They did speak different languages but then peoples adopt or discard languages as it suits them. The same is true of other aspects of culture like clothing, weapons, housing, and so on. Intermarriage was usual, and there is no need to conclude that this was restricted to the upper classes. Housing and domestic management would have been almost identical so a woman could pass without difficulty from one to another. Fashions in clothing changed slowly and the west of Ireland might be half a century behind England. If an article of Gaelic clothing, the great cloak for example, was useful in particular circumstances, everyone wore it. Attitudes towards the Government were almost identical. It might be assumed that because the kernes were known by a Gaelic name they must all have been of Gaelic stock. A little reflection shows this was unlikely. They were freebooters or mercenaries such as were common in Europe at the time. The Gaelic lords were usually in two minds whether it was more advantageous for themselves to engage with the Government or refuse to. Even when Brehon Law was followed rather than the law of the honorial courts there was perhaps little difference with regard to outcomes. Gaelic lords did not have formally constituted self-governing towns but they did have towns. (Brecon was the town of the castle of Brecon before it received its charter.) There probably is not sufficient documentation to decide this question but we should banish any idea of an incessant racial struggle between Gael and foreigner.

In the three centuries eastern or urbanised Ireland kept more or less in touch with the developments in Western Europe. There were small towns with markets and surrounding farms geared towards producing surpluses for export. There were improved ports, ships, roads, bridges and such like. Financial, legal, and political institutions became better. But these improvements did not reach the vast bulk of the people. By the time the observations of foreign writers were written down in the 16th century the living standard of ordinary people had not improved beyond the standard of the Bronze Age or even the Neolithic Age. Agricultural techniques in the Bronze Age were probably as good as they were in the 15th century. In many parts of Ireland a Neolithic farmer could have been placed on a small farm in 19th century Ireland and just carried on farming. Indeed climatic conditions in the Bronze Age were probably better. The population stuck at survival level. In good times it went up and in bad times it went down. In bad years there was not enough food to feed the whole population until the next harvest so the poorest just died. But where some surplus could be produced for exports there was some kind of cushion. In the Gaelic lordships it would seem that any increase in wealth was absorbed by the ruling families and the working families became more oppressed and more likely to die of famine. The increasing value of hides along with a decreasing population would accentuate the trend towards cattle-raising. (In England the increased value of wool and the reduction of tillage were offset to some extent by migration to the towns.) Raising the standard of living for the bulk of the people as was achieved in the 20th century is a very difficult task indeed.

I would like to express indebtedness to two inspired lecturers on medieval Ireland, Fr Columcille Conway, OCSO, and Professor Lewis Warren of Queen's University, Belfast. Fr Columcille was a 'warts and all' historian who broke ranks with the rather hagiographic tradition of Irish clerical historians who were terrified of giving ammunition to the Protestants. He once humorously quoted an historian who maintained that the whole history of Ireland was an attempt by the Irish to prevent anyone from civilising them. Quite. (It was something to do with the Irish bishops, he himself being more republican than episcopal in sentiment.) Professor Warren brought an outsider's view to 12th century Irish history and was a man of meticulous scholarship. He worked out exactly what Henry II and King John were trying to achieve in the context of their time and not in the context of 20th century nationalism. It will be noted that I have drawn on their work and accepted their conclusions in several places in this book.

Part 1

History and Sociology
1170 to 1513

Chapter 1

The Post-Roman World

The Decline of the Roman Empire

The Roman Empire reached its greatest extent under the emperor Trajan (d. A.D. 117). Though it ceased to expand it remained politically more or less intact for another two centuries. Its culture and influence however never ceased to expand until it covered virtually the entire globe. Christianity was born and established within it at this time. Finding the huge empire increasingly ungovernable, Diocletian in 285 A.D. divided the empire and appointed a co-emperor. His successor, Constantine, around 330 A.D. transferred the main capital from Rome to Byzantium to protect the richer provinces in the East. He also made Christianity the official religion. The western or Latin-speaking half of the empire went into decline. The Roman Empire in the West came to an end in 476 when Odoacer, a mercenary captured Rome. The new rulers in the various kingdoms they founded wanted the recognition of the Empire not its destruction. They adopted Christianity often before they crossed the *limes* or boundary fences. They continued the Roman offices they found. A *dux* (leader, duke) was a commander of a military command of frontier troops; a *comes* (companion, count) was a commander of troops in the interior. The offices speedily became hereditary as most offices were at the time.

The 'Dark Ages'

There is no consensus regard the meaning of the term Middle Ages. I prefer the term Dark Ages for the early part for it emphasises the scarcity of written evidence from the period. It covers from the end of the Roman Empire in the West in 476 A.D until 1000 A.D. It was characterised by the lack of written Latin, demographic decline, limited building activity and material cultural achievements in general but also a lack of contemporary written history. The term High Middle Ages refers to the blossoming of achievements in many spheres between 1000 A.D. and 1500 A.D.

Apart from 'barbarian' invasions Western Europe went into an economic decline in the 6th century and this persisted until the end of the 10th century. It was assailed on all sides by highly mobile groups of raiders, Vikings in the north, the Saracens or Muslims in the south, and Hungarians in the east. The Muslim advance into France was halted at Tours by Charles Martel in 732 A.D. His grandson, Charlemagne put an end to the Merovingian line of kings and started his own and attempted to restore the Western Empire in 800 A.D. Though he succeeded in subduing the local overlords in France, Germany, and Northern Italy, his empire fell apart shortly after his death.

By the end of the 6th century the population of the city of Rome had probably fallen to 50,000 and its administration was in the hands of the pope who received some help from Byzantium. Rome was plundered several times. The population fell further to 30,000. The influence of the Church reached a low ebb following the sack of old St. Peter's Basilica by Saracens in 846 A.D. The Leonine Wall, which defines the medieval city, was constructed from 848 to 852. The papacy fell into the hands of the local Italian warlords who fought among themselves over appointments to the papacy. Much of the city within the Aurelian walls was in ruins, and life continued around the various basilicas, churches, monasteries, and castles of the nobles.

This was the period when the character of Western Europe was forged. What in the Middle Ages was called Christendom was a single body with two aspects defence and religion. Local defence was paramount. But so too was the promotion of religion. The building of stone castles, stone monasteries, stone churches, and stone cathedrals went on apace. As much land was devoted to the development of religion as to the maintenance of the secular powers and external defence. These were accompanied by swarms of clergy. There was no dispute about the necessity of any of these.

Mounted warriors were required to intercept and defeat the raiders. Local strongmen, later called counts, provided defences, built strong points, established a system of land-holding which would support the mounted warriors. Each area collected its own taxes. The best known of these systems was called feudalism. The basic point in feudalism was that the local 'king' was the sole owner of all land in the 'kingdom'. He then assigned large tracts of it to greater lords for which they owed him military service. They in turn parcelled out his land to lesser warriors who owed them military service. For this military service they had to equip themselves with horses, armour, and weapons, one or more assistants or squires with their horses, and a supply of food for the campaign.

In England, the kings of Wessex subdued the other chiefs, and tried to substitute a system of shires with governors appointed by themselves, following the example of Charlemagne. In Wales and Scotland they had to be content with pledges of submission and loyalty. But nothing was ever simple, for every appointment in state or church tended to become hereditary. There were no national boundaries stating that this was England, and this was Scotland or Ireland. A conqueror of any nation went on conquering until he was stopped. The same was true of chiefs in Ireland as it was of kings in Europe.

Large abbeys needed large donations of land to exist, and these grants could only come from the great families, especially those who were successful in warfare and had estates to grant. Large numbers of the aristocratic classes entered monasteries where it was noted that there they had a chance to observe the Ten Commandments. These great landowners regarded the monasteries as their possessions, and were often buried in them. They were useful places for dumping children, legitimate or other wise, who were too weak to fight or too ugly to marry. They could expect to be made abbots or abbesses in due course with a prior or prioress to take actual command. In fact in the richer monasteries all the senior offices would have been reserved to the nobility. This close commingling of Church and State had another effect. The clergy became worldly and their manner of life became indistinguishable from that of the secular nobility. Bishops could lead their troops into battle. There were no rigid dividing lines; an abbot could be a builder, a warrior, a learned man and a trader. Kings fought wars and promoted religion.

The Christian Religion in the Dark Ages

The Church

About the year 500 A.D. there was a veneer of Christianity over most of the Western Empire. By the year 1000 there was a Christian civilization with religious and secular leaders as equal partners in common enterprises. Nobody ever questioned that Church and State should be united. The grades or orders of the clergy grew, and worship was centred on the great basilicas and cathedrals. Clerical orders were divided into eight grades, four minor orders of porter, reader, exorcist, and acolyte, and four major or holy orders, sub-deacon, deacon, priest, and bishop. Lifelong celibacy was not required and a man could abandon minor orders to get married. (The terms clerk and clerk in holy orders were not synonymous.) The pope was the bishop of Rome and became pope simply by being elected to that see. Some ranks like archbishop, cardinal, archdeacon, archpriest, canon or dean merely conferred administrative powers. Cardinals had to be at least in deacon's orders. A patriarch was the bishop of one of the great cities of the Empire, Rome, Alexandria, and Antioch, to which Jerusalem and Byzantium were later added. A cardinal legate was a cardinal sent on a special mission by the pope. A priest was not tied to a parish but he did have to belong to some diocese and be subject to its bishop. He could be on the bishop's staff, or the king's, or establish a school, belong to a university or a monastery. No qualification, no course of studies, not even literacy, was required for ordination to the priesthood or promotion in the Church. He had to be male however, of a certain age, and not forbidden by any canonical irregularity or prohibition, like for example being guilty of murder.

It must be stressed that ideas about religion and Christian salvation were very different in those days from those of Protestants of the post-Reformation period. Salvation was believed to come through the powers that God gave to his Church and his clergy. The power and effects of the mass and the sacraments did not depend on the worthiness or the life style of the minister or priest but on his valid ordination by the Church. People knew that unworthy people were made bishops and archbishops because they were of noble families or were well connected. They knew bishops and even popes promoted their relatives. But this did not matter. All that mattered was that the man should be properly ordained and celebrate the rites in the proper fashion. If you could have a good holy bishop or parish priest that was a bonus but not an essential. If the priest or bishop was in favour or out of favour with the other bishops that did not matter to them. He might even be an outlaw. What did count was that when he came to administer the sacraments that he be validly ordained. That was the certainty of the Christian religion.

Bishops and clergy were to be found in every town and city of the old Empire. The bishops of the largest and richest cities were given responsibility for bishops of lesser towns and were called archbishops and their sees metropolitan sees. The Roman provincial capital Auxerre seems to have been regarded as the metropolitan see of the British and Irish bishops. The manner of celebrating the liturgy, the rite, in the British Isles was derived from the Gallican rite of Gaul, itself a local variation of the Roman rite. In the course of the Dark Ages the Roman rite gradually displaced the Gallican rite in France. St Augustine of Canterbury brought the rite of Rome to the Anglo-Saxons and later the Norman bishops brought their own version of the Roman rite.

Though in the great cities and towns of the Empire great stone churches were built the normal building material north of the Alps was wood. Wooden churches and monasteries were often small and poor. Not every monastery was like Cluny. As a congregation or monastery increased in size larger buildings were erected.

Monasticism

There was another side to religion, that of monasticism. The customary date for the origin of monasticism is during the life of the first Christian hermit, St Paul of Thebes (d. c. 341). Monasticism was not part of the original structure of the Church. Originally there were no rules and in the course of time various abbots wrote their own rules. A person could always put on a monastic habit and call himself a monk and apparently this was done right to the end of the Middle Ages. Saint Benedict (c. 480-c. 547) founded the famous abbey of Monte Cassino near Naples in southern Italy. In his classic **Rule for Monks** he noted that there were in his day, post-Roman Visigothic Italy, hermits, cenobites, sarabaites, and gyrovagues. The eremitical or solitary life he admired but said it was only for experienced monks. Cenobites (common life) were those who lived with other monks in a monastery under a rule and an abbot.

Sarabaites and gyrovagues had either set themselves up as monks or had deserted monasteries. Though they still wore the monastic cowl their life was in no way monastic. It is interesting to find St Benedict's strictures being repeated in the 14th century by the Augustinian friar Jordan of Saxony (Jordan, 68). Doubtless a living could be made with a pretence of religion from the gifts of the credulous. The *Rule for Monks* spread widely in Western Europe (St. Benedict xx). Rules were intended more as spiritual guides, than a strict programme. This same is true of the *Rule of Saint Augustine* which appears to be summaries of colloquies of Saint Augustine of Hippo (354-430) which was also was also widely used (van Bavel). The Eastern *Rule of St. Basil* was rarely used in the West.

St Benedict wrote his *Rule* for a single abbey to be under the care of the local bishop. Few monks were priests. In the later period of reform various attempts were made to ensure a level of discipline over numerous monasteries, and in this way various orders or congregations of monasteries were formed. The most important of these were made at Cluny and Citeaux, both in Burgundy, regarding the *Rule of St Benedict*, and at Arrouaise in Artois in Northern France and Premontré in Picardy also in Northern France, regarding the *Rule of St Augustine*. The Fourth Lateran Council refused to recognise any Rules but the ancient three, but was persuaded to include the new *Rule of Saint Francis*. All further religious orders had to adapt one of the four approved Rules to their needs by means of added 'constitutions'.

Worship

Christian worship was based on the Jewish Psalter, a collection of 150 psalms (from the Greek for a song sung to a harp) which had been translated into Greek and Latin. They were sung to fairly simple recitative tunes. All parts of the public services including the readings from the bible were sung to similar chanted notes. (*Cantus*, chant simply means singing.) Individuals in private also tended to use the psalms. This was especially true of monks, some of the earliest of whom tried to chant the entire psalter every day, taking three or fours hours to do so. St Benedict laid down that the entire psalter was to be chanted in a week, but some psalms were repeated on weekdays and the longest psalm was divided to complete the 56 chanted offices in the week (*Rule* chapters 8-18). The Roman Church, and consequently all other Latin churches followed a similar plan.

The focus of Christian worship was the sung 'high mass' or Eucharist with elaborate ceremonial on Sundays and the greater feast days, and shorter services of readings and psalms at various times during the day which were chiefly of interest to the clergy. As monasteries grew larger the monks started to copy from the cathedrals and the cathedrals in turn from the monasteries. The chants became more elaborate resulting in the body of sacred music now called Gregorian chant. Monastic services, especially at Cluny in the following period became evermore complicated. Places of worship were highly ornamented and coloured and lighted with numerous candles which presented an ever-present fire risk and hastened the development of stone vaults.

The practice of religion for the laity and the parochial clergy in rural parishes was not different from that of the monks or cathedral clergy, though clearly a rural priest might have to make do with a single clerk. The laity attended church for the services on Sundays and holy days. One was not saved by his own efforts but only by God's grace. As St Augustine put it in his teaching against the Pelagians, '*Neque volentis, neque currentis, sed miserentis est Dei* ', Not he who wills, nor he who runs, but only God showing mercy. (The prolonged and acrimonious debates in the post-Reformation period about what exactly St Augustine meant by that were far in the future.) The spirit of the Christian religion was later summed up in the prayer of the Angelus. 'Pour forth, we beseech thee, O Lord, your grace into our hearts, that we to whom the incarnation of Christ, your son, was made known by the message of an angel, may by his passion and cross be brought to the glory of his resurrection'. The work of salvation, first made known by the message of an angel to Mary, is brought about by God's grace poured into the hearts of those who believe the message of the Church, through the merits of the passion and death of Christ and leads all who respond to God's grace to share in Christ's redemption. This was the simple message which was elaborated in the liturgy of the ecclesiastical year. It did not require any great knowledge on the part of the rural clergy or laity.

Lay Society in the High Middle Ages

The Development of Europe

Several events in the middle of the 10th century may be regarded as marking the end of the Dark Ages. In 910 the abbey of Cluny was founded and it grew in importance under impressive abbots. In 911 the dukedom of Normandy was formed. Athelstan (d. 939), became king of all England after the Battle of Brunanburh in 937. In 919 Henry the Fowler became king of Germany and his son Otto routed the Magyar forces at the Battle of Lechfeld (10 August 955) and became Holy Roman Emperor in 962. The German colonisation of the lands to its east began. Around 950 in Burgundy there began an experiment with transverse stone vaults over the nave of the church which was to have great importance in the development of Romanesque architecture (Rice, 197). By the year 1000 the Dark Ages were well and truly ended.

The 'revival' of Western Europe covered all the principal aspects of society, religion, warfare, architecture and craftsmanship and trade. Development was continuous in most fields between 1000 A.D. and 1500 A.D. (The great exceptions were medicine and agriculture where Roman authors were still preferred.) Wealth continued to grow. Pressures on the frontiers dwindled. Religion was reformed. Christianity spread to the Nordic countries, and towards the east in Poland and Hungary. The whole revived system of administration, urbanisation, trading, markets, exchange and banking, literacy and industry spread. German colonisation extended the new developments along the southern shores of the Baltic. Skilled immigrants poured into the eastern lands from the west to increase the population and raise the standard of living. Christian kingdoms were formed across the Rhine and the Danube where the Roman Empire had never spread. The Byzantine Empire was also recovering territory lost to the Turks. The sultanate of the Seljuk Turks had collapsed, and little Latin kingdoms established by the First Crusade (1095-99) in the Levant allowed free access of Christian pilgrims to Jerusalem. The victory of Saladin in 1187 however reduced the Latin kingdom of Jerusalem to a narrow strip on the coast, and the great Third Crusade (1189-92) led by Richard the Lionheart failed to win Jerusalem back. Nevertheless the crusaders left their mark on Western Europe for centuries because the military orders needed lands and money to sustain their fortresses and ships in the Eastern Mediterranean. A notable event was the conquest of Sicily by some Norman knights who established their own independent kingdom there. This conquest made Norman knights famous all over Europe.

One of the earliest reforms was that of the papacy which had become a toy of warring Roman families. It was undertaken by clergymen with the support of the German emperor. Henry III of Germany restored order in Rome in 1049 by getting one of his own clerics Bruno of Egisheim elected pope who took the name of Leo IX. He began the reform of the Church though this is more commonly associated with the name of Hildebrand who was elected pope in 1073 and took the name of Gregory VII. The primary aims were to reduce the influence of lay interests on Church affairs and to encourage clergymen to reduce their worldly pursuits.

A most striking development was in church architecture. For important buildings stone replaced wood, and techniques of building improved from generation to generation. When the rebuilding of the church at Cluny began in the year 1000 A.D. the decision was taken to vault it in stone, something that had not been attempted in Western Europe for 500 years. It had a simple barrel vault. Imitations of it sprang up over Europe. But it was noticed that if pointed arches were used instead of round ones the intersecting arches could be of different widths. The resulting architecture was called Gothic and began with the rebuilding of the church of the monastery of Saint Denis outside Paris about 1140. Stone carving developed.

Ships grew in size, sailing techniques improved. At the beginning, ships were little better than Norse longboats. The open Norse trading boat, little different from the longboats, was being replaced by the cog by the Frisians, though its full development was completed by the Hanseatic League. Sailing out of sight of land was developed. By 1500 Spanish and Portuguese ships had reached America and India. Trade, led by the Italian city states of Milan, Venice, and Genoa was flourishing. Trade over the Alps into northern Europe was resumed on a smaller scale, and was based on Milan in Lombardy. With trade and indeed warfare came banking, money changing and money lending and Italian merchants, especially Florentines, spread their techniques over Europe. Trade was organised in Northern Europe by Flemish merchants whose towns lay at the estuaries of several great rivers including the Rhine. Flanders became the great centre for the manufacture of fine woollens. Another great commodity was fur, which came chiefly from Russia. The fish trade too was important, and there were important fisheries in the Baltic. Fish was an important item for those who could afford it, because it could be eaten on a Friday when meat was forbidden.

Some very important developments concerned the horse. As armour grew heavier so larger horses were bred which could carry a fully armoured knight. This proved useful for agriculture as well. The new horse collar allowed the horse to pull heavy wagons and the great plough. Then came the horseshoe, the stirrup, and the high backed saddle. The shoe allowed horses to be used on stony ground. The stirrup and saddle allowed knights to use a longer lance underarm. Packhorses carried most goods on land, the alternatives being the bullock cart or human carrying. Windmills appeared in Europe. The Roman watermill had been fully perfected in Muslim countries and came into Europe through Spain. Arabic numerals, as developed in Muslim lands, came into Europe through Sicily. Fens, and bogs, and moorlands were reclaimed. Gunpowder was invented, mining and trading improved to get the source materials, and iron manufacture to make guns.

Universities sprung up and became centres of learning in which philosophy and rational theology were the most important subjects. Medicine and law were also studied and these four subjects formed the degree courses in the new universities. Roman law survived to a considerable extent in southern France. Roman traditions survived best in Italy. So too did the influence of the towns.

The troubadours developed both music and literature. They were the first to use a vernacular language to express their feelings, the Langue d'Oc or Provencal. Latin still continued as the language of the Church, of civil administration, of the schools and universities, and also of literature. Even the Carmina Burana were composed in Latin. Poetry was powerfully influenced by the hymnody of the Church.

Structure of Society

The Christian clergy saw to it that Late Latin survived in a common spoken and written form and was still the lingua franca for all Europe as far east as Poland. St Malachi and St Bernard could converse without interpreters. Nevertheless, the pyramidal political structure everywhere was the pre-Roman form common north of the Alps. Society was divided into two: the ruling classes and the ruled.

It is worth remembering that the Gaelic and Norman social pyramids were not very different from each other. The social structures of the Celtic, and Germanic peoples like the Franks were not dissimilar. Charlemagne tried to restore the bureaucratic administration of the Empire, but appointments by the emperors quickly became hereditary and largely reverted to the old Frankish forms. But there was this difference. All the great feudal lords were regarded as tenants-in-chief though lesser lords were often their sub-tenants. There was in Gaelic Ireland however no single source of secular authority though there was of religious authority. In Gaelic Ireland the only subordination was that of power.

Three points have to be distinguished (1) a feudal hierarchy or social pyramid and a non-feudal hierarchy or social pyramid, (2) and the bureaucratic system of political control and the feudal system, and (3) feudal tenure and allodial possession of land.

The distinction between the first two is argued by R.A. Brown in his *Origins of English Feudalism* in which he denies that the military and hierarchic English state before 1066 was feudal. For him feudalism had four essential elements, a military class of knights, vassalic commendation, a fief of land, and a castle. In feudal theory all land was owned by the king who allocated parts of it to knights to rule and defend in the king's name. These swore allegiance to him personally as vassals, and then constructed castles to defend the territory. They were always liable to be called to the court of the king and to supply a specified number of knights and other warriors at the king's ban or call. Brown denies that these essential elements were present in the outwardly similar in the pre-1066 Anglo-Saxon social pyramid. The same conclusion can be reached with regard to pre-Norman Ireland. Feudalism was just a special type of the social pyramid.

There were four basic feudal tenures. Tenure by *serjeanty* was a form of land-holding in return for some specified service, ranking between tenure by *knight-service (enfeoffment)* and tenure in *socage*.

Sergeanty was tenure for the performance of a certain duties other than knight-service, usually the discharge of duties in the household of king or noble. *Socage* was a tenure with the obligation to pay sums of money to the lord periodically. *Frankalmoign* was tenure in free alms in return for saying prayers and masses for the soul of the granter. This was often a tenure granted to religious houses. All without these tenures were technically unfree.

In the 'public' or 'bureaucratic' or 'official' society, the king or emperor divided up his territory into counties and appointed officials to administer them. Each was assigned appropriate duties and powers, to defend the county including the construction of castles, to raise taxation, and to supply a specified number of warriors at the king's call. All owed allegiance directly to the king; all the castles they erected were the king's castles, and they could be recalled from their office at any time. A large part of the history of medieval England and Ireland was taken up with efforts of the king to substitute 'officials' like sheriffs of counties for the tenure of fiefs by barons.

In northern Europe the allodial holding of land was the common one before the rise of feudalism. Feudal holding and allodial holding were contradictory: it had to be one or the other. Each free family owned its own farm. Chiefly families owned their own farm or farms. They paid no rent in money or kind for the land. Non-free families might have to pay a tribute for their land, but this was not a rent. By one way or another allodial holding of land in Ireland seems to have become extinct. When this occurred is not clear. Some free farmers may have survived until the 12th century, but these could have been lesser members of the ruling families (Ó Corráin 44). Feudal or feudal-like tenures of land by money or services seem to have become universal in Ireland.

On top of the pyramidal social structure were the contending classes of the greater and lesser noble and ruling families. Beneath these were the working families. The vast proportion of power, wealth, influence, learning and official offices in church and state was in the hands of the noble families. But gradually over the centuries, members of the towns, the *bourgeoisie*, also accumulated wealth. The members of noble or chiefly families, and they were very numerous, could never descend to toil. They were almost always illiterate. Some could be sent to school to become clerics. But most had to learn to ride, to hunt and to fight. Wars provided a great opportunity to young warriors to get land of their own. Associated with the warrior lords were the upper grades of the clergy and the upper grades of the learned and craftsman classes.

There were grades in the social pyramid. At the top was the king of an independent kingdom. Beneath him were a limited number of great lords. At the bottom were the local lords or chiefs, perhaps one to each parish, and in between were two or three mesne lords, who had lands of their own and received tribute from the lesser lords. All of these collected their own revenues. The real power at any time lay with those who were most effective at collecting their own revenues and were most effective in withholding their contributions from their superiors. In France the power of the king was limited for the great lords, the castellans, were adept at collecting taxes and holding them for themselves. Even in England the taxation of the great lords was not effective before the reign of Henry VII. They held to the terms of their tenure, 40 days of knight service with the king's army in a year.

In Ireland, in the 12th century central government, whether Gaelic or Norman, had the upper hand. The Norman advance broke the ability of any challenger for the 'high kingship' of Ireland to put an overwhelming force into the field and the power of the greater chiefs waned. But towards the end of the Middle Ages, many great chiefs like those of the MacCarthys, the O'Briens, and the O'Neills, the former great provincial rulers seem to have, to a considerable extent, concentrated power into their own hands in the shrunken lands they controlled. On the Anglo-Norman side, after the death of King John, the power of the central monarchy waned. The relative weakness of the English crown was so great that if either the Gaelic chiefs or the Anglo-Norman lords had been able to agree who from among themselves should be king an independent Irish kingdom could have been established.

The vast bulk of the population was formed by the working classes. The free independent farmers with allodial ownership of their land seem to have ceased to exist. Free however was a matter of definition. If, from the 12th century onwards, we define free as meaning the right and duty to attend the honorial court of the tenant-in-chief or that of the chief *(ri)* of a *tuath,* then the working and farming classes were almost all unfree. But they were not slaves or serfs and had a right and duty to attend the court of their immediate lord, knight or *ógláech,* or landholding body, usually called the manor court. In that sense they were free of the lower court and could contribute to discussions and decisions, but women, grown-up children, farm labourers, and whole categories of lesser folk were not free of any court. Their usual title in Anglo-Norman areas was *villein* or *villanus.* They were not slaves or serfs but holders of land by various, usually labour, services and bound to the land. In the absence of a coinage, goods and labour services were used instead. In the Gaelic world the free farmers were reduced to a similar status and were called *biatach* or betagh. Any free Irishman on a Norman feudal estate automatically became a betagh. (In England also after the Conquest the Anglo-Saxon free farmers automatically became villeins.)

At the local level, some time towards the end of the Roman period c. 400 AD the great plough was introduced into northern Europe and it had a great influence on the holding of land. It was a much heavier plough and fitted with a coulter to cut the sod and required a large team of oxen to draw it. As it is not easy to turn an ox team the ground for ploughing was usually about a hundred acres. The word which came into use in Ireland for this area was townland, the land belonging to a 'ton' or 'town' or in Gaelic *baile.* These ploughing units were owned by the extended family of a freeman or nobleman. *Baile mac* (ballymac the townland of the sons of) in Gaelic corresponds to ingham (the town or ham of the sons of) in Anglo-Saxon. This carving up of agricultural land seems to have occurred early in the Dark Ages. The grouping of townlands into manors or cantreds seems to have occurred much later. The area from 60 to 100 acres was also called a hide, carucate or ploughland. These formed the basis for cultivation and taxation. The townlands could be aggregated into what the Normans called manors of sufficient size to support an armed knight and his family besides the families of the cultivators. The manor, not the townland or hide, became the agricultural unit. The townland remained the basis for taxation and tithing, the tax or tithe being levied on the townland not the individual properties. There were similar aggregations used by Welsh and Irish chiefs, though when the Norman-Welsh knights came to Ireland they used the Welsh term cantref. A manor did not necessarily imply the use of the great plough or open fields but could be a focal point for collecting the revenues and dues sufficient to support a knight or his Gaelic equivalent. The use of the light plough and spade cultivation could persist, especially in mountainous areas.

There were always the classes at the bottom of society, outlaws, squatters, and travelling classes who were difficult to find or tax. There were also various kinds of travelling folk like entertainers, minstrels, tumblers, jugglers, jesters who travelled to fairs and to great houses scraping what kind of living they could. The lowest class were slaves, and above them were serfs. As the name serf implies serfs were the descendants of former slaves (*servus*). These were not slaves but they were ***adscripti glebae,*** bound to the manor on which they were born and bound to work on the lord's land for so many days a year. (Though the precise practical distinctions between the various categories mentioned in documents at times eludes us and were not necessarily the same over time or in different places. Uniformity was not a characteristic of the Middle Ages.)

There were two other factors in the social structure in Europe in the Middle Ages, the towns and the Church. The rise of the ***bourgeoisie*** was unstoppable, the word meaning the inhabitants of a burg or town, burghers.

Neither the size of the towns nor the volume of trade was anything like what it was to become in the age of steamships. When the new religious orders of mendicant friars were founded they established themselves in the towns. So too, as universities developed they were situated in the towns, not in the great landed abbeys. Artists and craftsmen also tended to congregate within the walled towns because they were safer than the countryside, and it was where their customers also were. Their towns became rich, and were able to hire mercenary troops to defend their interests, and these well-trained and equipped mercenaries were well able to cope with the feudal levies of the kings, dukes and counts.

Bishops and abbots were also temporal lords and had their own courts. These often survived the suppression of the monasteries. The courts of the lordship of Newry originally granted to a Cistercian abbot survived until the 19th century. Of much greater importance was the fact that the clergy were the literate class and so were used extensively by kings and lords to keep their records and conduct their correspondence. The fact that they spoke and wrote Latin made them useful when a king was travelling or had to send an embassy abroad. The king's clerics were the king's clerks. Normally the king and the bishops worked in harmony. Disputes between them tended to be rare. In Ireland, the traditional learned families were endowed with land and given privileges like the clergy. The chiefs, the clergy, and the learned families formed the privileged classes.

Obligations and Exchanges

All medieval societies were strictly controlled. Every person in every position in society knew his rights and obligations. What anyone could do was limited by their status in society. This was as true for the wife or sons of a lord as it was of the betagh or villein. Great power was placed in the hands of a chief, or in his sphere the father of a family. In the Roman Republic a father who was head of a family had power of life and death over all his family, his freemen workers, and his slaves. More practically, all their food, clothing, weapons and ornaments came through him. This made life irksome for grown-up sons; grown-up women expected nothing else. All spoils from a raid came through the hands of the chief, whether cattle, clothing, ornaments of gold, weapons, slaves or anything else. In modern times this system was only to be found in monasteries, but it was the common one in the Middle Ages. Naturally this meant that everything of real value remained with the chief's immediate family.

In pre-monetary societies most of life was conducted under a system of obligations and exchanges, or alternatively through the gift economy. It is not easy in practice to distinguish them. Contrary to popular conception, there is no evidence of a society or economy that relied primarily on barter. Instead, non-monetary societies operated largely along the principles of gift economics. When barter did in fact occur, it was usually between either complete strangers or would-be enemies. (*Wikipedia* 'Barter') Exchange or barter was the simplest concept. One piece or parcel of goods was exchanged for another piece or parcel with no further obligation on either side. Obligation went much further and permeated almost every aspect of life. As it was put in the United States 'There Ain't No Such Thing As A Free Lunch'. A politician naturally had to reward his chief supporters when he attained public office. It worked both ways. A politician could secure a house, a job, a contract, or a license for someone knowing he could call on the obligations at election time. Many officials derived their sole income from these expected gifts. The gaoler expected a gift both to let a man into his gaol and to let him out. So too did the turnkey.

The Spread of Money

Gradually money was re-introduced especially by merchants who began to prefer coins of fixed and known value to the time-honoured practice of weighing out bits of silver. Coins never became really common. In England, the coin of most use to ordinary people, the farthing was not minted in great quantities. Silver pennies were minted in great quantities in the Anglo-Saxon period, and were used to pay the Danegeld. The annual penny per farm was also selected for Peter's Pence, the sum a farmer with about 100 acres was expected to pay.

The taking of interest on unprofitable loans as opposed to sharing the profit from the loan was called usury and was condemned alike by philosophers and by the Church. The law against usury forbade money lending by Christians but not borrowing by Christians. Jewish law on the other hand allowed money lending at interest to non-Jews. Giving or borrowing for commercial or warlike enterprises, while sharing the profits or losses was legitimate. Clerics rushing to Rome to claim a benefice would borrow against the expected revenues of the benefice. Interest to compensate a lender for the risk of losing his capital, and other things, are what are called extrinsic grounds and were gradually allowed. This explains how the Italian merchants were able to lend money in non-profitable loans. (These extrinsic grounds now form the basis of all borrowing and loans in Western society.)

Banking as we know it nowadays originated in the Middle Ages when merchants would issue notes at one fair redeemable at another fair. Therefore there was no need to carry great quantities of bullion from place to place. If the note was to be redeemed for cash at a later date the amount paid back was greater than the amount paid in and so was a form of interest. The merchants with sufficient quantities of gold coins to lend out were, in the earliest years from the Italian cities. Merchants from Lombardy (Milan) were strongly established in the city of London.

Military Matters and Armies

It was commonly observed that roughly trained cavalry would always beat roughly trained infantry, but no cavalry could defeat well-trained and unbroken infantry. Most infantry in the Middle Ages was poorly trained but standards were rising as it became possible for lords to retain professional fighting men like the Swiss halberdiers, Flemish mercenaries, and Highland gallowglasses. Gunpowder decisively swung the balance in favour of the infantry. Even early in the Middle Ages chiefs and lords were keeping limited bodies of fighting men in their households. In Anglo-Saxon England they were called the housecarls. (The training and drill of modern infantry can be dated to the training and drill of Spanish troops in the 16th century. Infantry tactics before that were variations of the 'Highland' charge.)

In theory all freemen subject to a lord could be called out for defence. But it is not clear if this obligation extended beyond the frontiers of their lord's domain. The obligation of the later militia was confined to their counties. Armies were not large. On the Continent after Charlemagne they were composed mostly of horsemen, the knights, and it was these the vassals were bound to provide. Nevertheless many footmen and servants accompanied the army, and probably these latter were very important in a cattle raid when the pace of the army could not be greater that than of the cows. Even the biggest armies probably did not exceed 2,000 plus their servants, and this was the maximum a route march could have supported (Keen 27).

There was a constant technological battle among the metal workers to devise weapons that could pierce any armour, and on the other hand to devise armour that could withstand any weapon or missile. Towards the end of the Middle Ages, before gunpowder became feasible, a knight clad in plate armour was virtually invulnerable. Horse breeders had to provide a variety of horses. There was the destrier, the heavy warhorse that had to be able to carry a knight in full armour. Even for battles a courser was often preferred. The courser was the preferred horse for the *chevauchée* (Ayton, 191). The rouncey was a general, all-purpose, horse for war which could also be used as a packhorse. Poorer knights, squires, and men-at-arms also used the less expensive rouncey. In

Ireland a smaller horse or pony called a hobby which was similar to a rouncey seems to have been adopted for many purposes connected with war. The horseman, lightly armed with a lance, was called a hobelar. Mounted archers were mounted on hackneys which was much cheaper than the destrier (Ayton 191 ff). Packhorses would carry equipment. Lords and chiefs could have larger horses for purposes of ostentation.

Throughout the Middle Ages strong castles and walled towns were built. Even when not built in stone the motte-and-bailey castle was difficult to capture. Storming a castle or a town with even low walls required specific military skills. These were normally non-existent in Ireland and the scarcity of food for the besiegers normally prevented long sieges. Siege guns did not arrive until Tudor times. There were other forms of defence besides town walls and castles. These involved using the natural defences of rough country especially if the country was well-wooded, and the paths through the woods or bogs were few.

At the centre of wars in the Middle Ages was the knight. The cost of equipping and maintaining a knight meant that they were relatively few in number though prominent in illustrations of the time. He was a professional soldier, trained from his youth to fight on horseback. Horses suitable for cavalry warfare were bred, and rudimentary cavalry tactics were developed. Stirrups and high-backed saddles were used to enable the use of a longer lance which could be used for a direct underarm thrust replacing the downward thrust of the short spear. Training was maintained by means of tournaments where a young knight could gain recognition and make some money. This combination of stirrup, saddle and lance, coupled with a common drill for horsemen produced an unbeatable weapon famed all over Europe and the Middle East. No army could withstand it in the open field. The knights did not charge at a gallop. The effect of such a charge would have been to knock themselves out of the saddle. A strong push by horse and man was what was required. The used of body armour was improved. The principal protection of the body was still being provided by chain mail and a helmet. Smiths had to make the metal parts of the harness, and the horses' shoes besides the weapons and armour (Hyland, passim). But archery too was developed, and from this period onwards missile warfare was to play an increasingly important role.

The bulk of any army was formed by the foot soldiers. There were no permanent armies and the call-out of fighting was just for the summer season. It was recognised that many of those called out were poorly armed and equipped, disliked going outside their own county, and wanted to get home for the harvest. As money became more plentiful, kings preferred to receive money instead and to hire professional soldiers who were normally better equipped and trained. The Irish chiefs too came to rely on professional troops. These were paid in the old fashion with grants of land or else by quartering the soldiers on the farms of the betaghs.

Rarely were pitched battles risked except when there was a succession dispute. The 'hazard of battle' was then all or nothing. A day-long battle might be experienced once in a lifetime. Most military campaigns degenerated into the wholesale wasting of the lands of the enemy, burning and destroying every village, farmhouse, or mill and seizing or burning every crop, the *chevauchée*. Though battles were rare, raiding was not. Profit from a battle might be greater, especially if many nobles could be captured and held for ransom. Profits from a cattle raid might be less but it was good fun for the attackers at least. The raid had to be quick and unexpected, and best conducted when the attention of the intended victim was focussed on his opposite border. Raids were normally conducted on foot, and various retainers on foot were required to round up and drive off the cattle. It was glorified in Ireland as a *tain* (toyn) or cattle raid. The aim was to get in fast, seize as many cows as possible, burn houses and crops, kill as many peasants, men, women and children as possible, and get back home safely. It was bad if you got caught or if another neighbour raided your land in your absence. The wasting could be and was carried out on a greater scale by the greater chiefs. This involved engaging allies who would attack from a different direction and devastate large parts of a province. In the Hundred Year's War in France this was called a *chevauchée*. Edward the Bruce's campaigns in Ireland were large-scale wasting raids.

Ships were frequently used in warfare, primarily to transport the fighting men to the point of attack and recover them afterwards. The Viking raids were largely conducted on foot, but their ships could silently transport them to any point. Cavalry was developed chiefly to counter this threat by either finding where the boats were hidden, or catching up with the retreating raiders. Ships were growing larger and by 1170 were well-equipped to transport numerous cavalry horses to Ireland. There were no specialised warships. Kings and chiefs just commandeered the local merchant fleets. As sails gradually replaced oars it was easy for shipbuilders to add wooden castles at the bow and stern for defence against pirates and in warfare. They could have a complement of archers and later gunners. The chief object in a sea battle was to board and capture an enemy ship (Fernandes-Armesto 230 ff, Hyland, 91).

Castles and Castellans

Castles became virtually impregnable. Jean Dubabin gives an interesting picture of the development of France between the partitioning of Charlemagne's empire by the Treaty of Verdun in 843 until the accession of Philip Augustus in 1180. Charlemagne tried to rule his huge empire by appointing officials called counts. The position became known as an honour which the king conferred in return for an oath of loyalty. He was then given a *beneficium* of land to enable him to carry out his numerous duties. He was also made responsible for the defence of his county, to call out troops and build castles for its defence. He also had to send to the king the assigned number of troops, cavalry and infantry when the king issued a ban, and this he had to attend in person. But as local defence became more important during the Viking raids the ban was called less often.

One of his most important duties was to preside over the county court to which all the leading men in the county were bound to attend. Officials called *scabini* declared what particular kind of law, local or personal custom, applied in each case, and also when royal capitularies applied. The count also had to send judges to lesser courts within the county where the affairs of lesser freemen which did not come before honorial courts were heard.

He was also authorised to collect the royal revenues for these purposes. There were taxes from freemen whose services the king did not require and fines from the courts. He was empowered to collect royal taxes like tolls on rivers, bridges, and highways, and on markets enjoying privileges. He could also enjoy the royal right of hospitality from the king's estates, from some towns, and from abbeys under royal protection. He could also, in the king's name, impose a local tax in times of emergency. But the 10th century in France the count had largely become a tax collector, and his own share of the taxes rose markedly. The king might try to limit his power by granting exemptions to abbeys and bishoprics.

The count in turn had to attend the royal court. The office soon became hereditary though the duties the count carried out were those imposed by the king. Any castle he might build was a royal castle (Dunbabin, 6 ff). A castle differed from other defensive buildings in that it was a fortified residence (Brown 30). Brown maintains that there were no proper castles in England before 1066, but merely fortifications that might be occupied in times of invasion. Counts controlled the royal castles, and built their own. They also divided up their districts into viscounties and each of these had a castle. The castle became the focal point for local administration (Dunbabin, 144). Though details might differ this was the way the Norman kings of England and Ireland exercised their authority at local level.

The castle as a fortified residence had a dual role. It was the principal defence of its neighbourhood, and it was the means of dominating the local population. Besides the king, lords and bishops might have residential castles. In the enclosed courtyard of the castle they held their courts. From the end of the 10th century recognisable castles existed. They were characterised by a considerable external wall, a large space within these left empty for security, and a group of buildings within a second wall in the middle. The castellan lived in the central tower, while around were buildings to house the men-at-arms and servants. These were not necessarily built of stone. Normally, the first structures were made of wood, and the simplest form was the motte-and-bailey castle. The motte was a mound on top of which was placed a wall. This could be used as a look-out point and as a point of defence of last resort. At the foot of the mound was an enclosure where the lord or knight had his hall, housing for retainers, offices like store rooms and brew houses, and with sufficient space for some animals. Later the wooden constructions could be replaced by masonry ones. They were surprisingly effective. As the castellan's income increased, the wooden structures would be replaced by stone walls which were less likely to be burned. Even a wooden castle was difficult to capture by those who lacked the necessary skills.

The central monarchy in France, for various reasons grew weak, and so the powers of the castellans, the custodians of the castles grew. Like most other offices that of castellan became hereditary and the castellans adopted surnames, by adding the name of their castle, like Hugh de Lusignan. The castellans became noted for the extortionate demands they imposed on those under their protection. They extorted all the old taxes and added new ones, the duty to use only the lord's oven and mills, fines for leaving the area, and taxes on fishing and wood-cutting. The only remedy was an appeal to the castellan's own court. Though they did protect from other extortionists (Dunbabin, 146).

Courts and Courtyards

In pre-literate times the normal way in which public business was conducted was by holding a meeting. The superior, king, sheriff, bishop, abbot, lord of a manor, or free farmer called an assembly of those subject to them to present matters appropriate to the jurisdiction. The superior could attend in person, or send a deputy, a judge or steward, to deputise for him. Monks under the Benedictine Rule were summoned once a day before the abbot, or in his absence the prior, to receive instruction, to receive penances for their faults, and appointments for their daily tasks. The pope's assembly of his cardinals was called a consistory.

For each meeting there were certain grades of people who were said to be free of that court and were bound to attend. These were called freemen and later in feudal times, freeholders. Only the head of a family was a freeman; his sons were not though the family was free. The reason for this was that obligations like days of labour, military service, or money in lieu were placed on the family holding. The obligations of the feudal lord to the feudal overlord in as much as they affected the freemen of the court would also be explained. It was an age when almost everyone except clerics were illiterate so all communications had to be verbal.

The law in these courts was the custom of the court; this was particularly true of manorial courts. In most countries there were some royal enactments, but most matters were dealt with under customary laws. There were also collections of judgements which gave guidance. It was of the nature of such collections that some of the judgments might be contradictory or only partially applicable, so there were specialist advisors in the count's courts to advise on precedent. At the start of the Middle Ages each local lord was the judge in his own court, and he appointed other men, perhaps successful soldiers or tax collectors as judges. In time many courts had some literate clerics to keep records of judgments. They could also advise on precedents. In England, reliance was placed on a jury of local freemen who testified from their own knowledge about whether a crime was committed, where lay a particular boundary, or what was the customary law of that hundred. A jury was just a representative selection of men free of that court.

It was a feature of the Middle Ages that the law and the courts were constantly developing. The practice of law became fragmented, and different courts were established to deal with different matters. Laws were collected and harmonised. In Ireland the collection of laws was called the Brehon Code, and in England Common Law. Places where the law could be studied were established. Roman Law, Canon Law, and international law (*ius gentium*) were studied in universities. Common lawyers set up their 'Inns of Court' but largely common lawyers were just apprenticed or articled to a practicing common lawyer of repute.

It was an age of autocracy and summary justice. The king or lord, or a justice appointed by him, took his seat or bench in the courtyard and addressed the crowd. Until the 19th century judges and bishops read out a charge calling attention to some matters which the court desired those assembled to pay due attention. The cases, both civil and criminal were called before the court. In either type of case the accuser spoke first and the defendant replied. The judge put the case to the jury who gave their decision on the spot. A case of murder could be completed in half an hour.

Colonisation

From the 11th century onwards colonisation became a feature of Western European societies which continued until the 20th century by which time most of the globe was colonised by them. What was distinctive about colonisation was that the incoming ruler proceeded to develop a hitherto backward economy. New techniques of agriculture, mining, manufacture and trading were developed. Numerous workmen and craftsman, who were skilled in those matters, had to be imported as well. They had to be lodged in defended towns. Weaving fine broadcloths required first the importation of several new skills. To sell these widely traders who had knowledge of shipping and trading places had to be imported. They then had to construct towns and manage town life. Ships had to be built on the most modern principles, and fitted with the most modern means of defence, and these required shipbuilders. More advanced agricultural skills had to be imported.

The great place for colonisation was in the Slavic and Baltic lands to the east of the Holy Roman Empire where German-speaking colonies developed the fertile plains of Poland into a granary for cities in the west (Barraclough, 249; Dunbabin, 141-3). It was essential to develop natural resources for the benefit of a growing population. Existing but rather backward kingdoms like England or Denmark could entice in those with the skills they wished to adopt and usually did so. At the beginning of the Middle Ages all of England's foreign trade was in the hands of foreigners, but gradually the English learned the techniques of trade. There was much internal colonisation. Places within a region which were thinly occupied were made suitable for cultivation, whether by draining bogs or swamps, or by clearing woodland, and the most recent techniques used to make them support a larger population.

The Economy, Cities and Trade

All kinds of manufactured goods were being produced and traded. These goods were of course still manufactured by hand, but surpluses were being produced for trading. Trade developed extensively especially in Italy. The water-powered fulling mill was developed. This was one of the first applications of machinery to an industrial process. The windmill was introduced from the Near East and gradually became common where waterpower was not available. Trading too developed in northern Europe and developments there had a more direct effect on Ireland. Trans-alpine trading was also very important. Like warfare, long distance trade was confined to the warmer half of the year. Alpine passes were closed in the winter. The routes over the Alps were re-opened and mule trains started north as soon as the snows cleared from the Mont Cenis Pass between Italy and France. Lombard trade with the North re-commenced with great consequences for travel to Rome.

The most important development as far as England was concerned, and at one remove Ireland, was the development of the cloth industry and the wool and cloth trades in Flanders in modern Belgium. The Flemish weavers bought the famous English fine wool, and from their strength in this trade, gradually came to control the entire trade of the region. As spinning, weaving, and finishing processes became ever more refined, so too did the demand for fine clothes. The Flemish weavers found a great outlet for their goods in the fairs of Champagne which linked the merchants and bankers of Italy with the North. Woollen and linen cloth and furs from the north were traded with Mediterranean. Lombard moneychangers, soon to be called bankers, dominated the trade.

Improved metal work was also in demand, especially for armour and weapons. This led to a counter demand by the towns for the metal ores or roughly smelted metals. Besides iron, copper, lead, silver and tin had to be mined and traded. A secondary market in wool developed. As England exported its fine wool to Flanders it had to import coarser wools from places like Ireland. Thick rough woollen cloth with little of its natural oils removed was useful for keeping out the rain. Dried fish was an important traded commodity as it could be eaten on days when meat was forbidden for religious reasons. Leather, which was used for so many purposes, stimulated a demand for hides.

It was possible to travel from Champagne to Florence in twenty days. Reaching Rome from Ireland was not particularly difficult, perhaps if the winds were favourable taking not more than six weeks. A cleric could get to Rome, conduct his business and return in one summer, the Lombard bankers advancing the cash. They were more likely to travel in one summer and return the next. No travel in the Middle

Ages was without danger, so merchants, pilgrims, clerics, and official couriers always travelled in groups with an armed escort, going from one walled town to the next in the course of a day. Towns were walled and strangers who could not account for themselves were expelled at nightfall especially if they were from neighbouring areas. Every ship was fully armed. A ship's company that could not defend itself could easily be plundered, not necessarily by pirates. A king or chief could thus easily assemble a fleet for war. London became the great centre of England's trade, but Bristol too from the 10th century onwards was a growing port. It had close connections with Ireland, dealing mainly in wool.

Cities and Towns

Roman cities and towns in most of Europe shrank but survived. In Ireland and countries beyond the Rhine there were no Roman towns. In England, some shrunken Roman towns may have continued. Settlements called wick or *wic* may have grown up around markets. Town (ton) and ham both mean farmstead. A *villa* or house on a large Roman estate would have had a collection of buildings or huts nearby to house the servants, farm workers, slaves, craftsmen, etc and their families. In the Dark Ages, similar collections of huts grew up around churches, especially cathedrals, large monasteries, and castles, as they were necessary to provide goods and services. Some of these grew to be independent towns, but at first they were mere adjuncts to the main building. In Ireland there were quite large settlements about the great monasteries. Traders would come to them and the monastery's or chief's compound.

Nowadays, the concepts of trade and self-government are regarded as the essential constituent of a town. It must have at least a market. Viking towns, though tiny were organised for trade. The government of such towns was no different from that of the petty states around them.

The chief of the warband was also the chief of his town. Nevertheless, as the revenue from customs on traded goods grew, kings began to grant 'charters of exemption' to towns who undertook to pay the revenues direct to the king, and he allowed them to have their own courts exempt from the court of the local shire or hundred. It was not until 1191 that the concept of a community of a town was recognised as a corporate body with a charter.

Political Events in the Twelfth Century

Crusading was one of the great religious enthusiasms of the Middle Ages, like building cathedrals and going on pilgrimage. The crusades had their origin in a phenomenon which arose on the great dry steppes of central Asia. A pastoral culture like that in Gaelic Ireland and east Africa developed on the steppes the home of the horse. The climate and vegetation favoured horse-rearing and because the vegetation was fairly sparse the culture was nomadic, namely the flocks and herds had to be constantly moved from place to place within each group's territory. As was common with pastoralists from the time of Abraham there were endless disputes, usually over water. The density of population was necessarily low but the area was vast. The phenomenon which arose was the ability of chiefs to mobilise vast armies of men with some training in warfare. They are generally divided on a linguistic basis into Turks, Tatars, and Mongols, but the culture was essentially the same. The Tatars plagued Russia until the time of Peter the Great (1682-1725) who turned the tide. The Mongols attacked China, while Turkish-speakers attacked the Byzantine and Persian empires. Their advance was eventually stopped by John III Sobieski the Polish king at the gates of Vienna in 1683. In the time of Richard I they were not particularly important being mercenaries in the armies of the Arab caliphate, but they had in Saladin a gifted general. What led to the intervention of the west European chiefs in the First Crusade in 1098 was the habit of Turkish marauders robbing and killing Christian pilgrims though this was not part of Arab interpretation of Islam. A military Order, the Templars, was founded by knights who vowed to devote their lives to protecting the routes to the Holy Land. Another Order, the Knights Hospitallers, was founded to provide safe hostels for the pilgrims and they too became a military order. If an individual knight wanted to go on crusade with his lord's permission he would have to mortgage his estate to the Jews for several years to raise the cash.

The First Crusade (1095-1100) was successful largely because of divisions among the Seljuk Turks. The knights established various small states along the eastern Mediterranean. The only crusade in this century that had much affect on Ireland was the Third Crusade that was launched following the capture of Jerusalem by the Kurdish Muslim Saladin who ruled in Syria. Among the kings who went was Richard I Lionheart, king of England, who left his younger brother Prince John in charge in his absence.

The Capetian kings in France after the accession of Philip Augustus in 1180 were gradually gaining control over the great lords. In England there was a relatively strong centralised monarchy which also included the original lands in Normandy. Besides England and Normandy, Henry II was feudal overlord of the whole of western France from Normandy to Gascony. Louis VII of France in theory was overlord of eastern France from Flanders to the Pyrenees, except in parts claimed by the Holy Roman Emperor. But after the death of Henry II in 1189 and the accession of Philip Augustus in France in 1180 the relative fortunes of the two countries were reversed.

Leisure, Sport and Recreation

A large number of days were devoted to rest, and also in the long evenings people had to provide their own entertainment. Eating and drinking formed a large part of these entertainments, whether banquets of the great or lowlier feasts of the peasantry and villagers.

We know more about the recreations and sports of the noble classes than we do about those of ordinary people. Reading especially in English was quite a common pursuit principally among women of the upper classes (Leyser 240 ff). Noblewomen were expected to be patrons of artists and to appreciate literature. As the Middle Ages advanced books became cheaper even before the invention of printing. Ladies patronised the troubadours who sang of courtly love. Other noblewomen's recreations were complicated love affairs, playing chess, flying hawks, training young squires in the art love and polite society, and queening it at tournaments (Power, 35f).

Noblemen were devoted to martial events, wars, tournaments, and the next best thing, hunting. In border areas, the cattle raid was a popular diversion. Horse racing was also popular. At banquets music was always popular and story telling. There were professional entertainers, often travellers, like harpers, jugglers, fools, jesters and acrobats. These could perform in the halls of the rich or at fairs. Dancing was discouraged by the Church. Little is known about it in this period. Some dances may have been brought back from the crusades, and to have come first into Italy, but dancing was known before that. Though men and women danced it is not clear if there was mixed dancing.

With regard to the leisure activities of the lower classes, in England at least football was popular. It was a rough sport often played between all the menfolk of two parishes. Football may have developed among the trade guilds in the towns, but it may be that there it was first recorded. Running and jumping were natural contests to see who could run fastest or jump highest. Wrestling and archery were popular. Contests could be held between towns or parishes. Much time was spent in taverns (Lydon, Ireland in the Later Middle Ages 20f).

Theatre however seems to have developed in the towns. It was an easy step singing the history of the passion of Jesus in church using several voices to putting on entire religious plays. These were put on by the guilds of the various trades or 'mysteries' and so are commonly called mystery plays. It was not until the Renaissance that secular theatre developed.

Music

Music played an important role in medieval society. As it was not written we have little idea what it was like. Religious music, the so-called Gregorian chant, was the first to be given a theoretic description. It was based on eight 'modes' each of which had its own characteristics. Musical notation was devised by Guido of Arrezzo, a Benedictine monk from Arrezzo in Italy about 1025. But as early as the beginning of the 10th century efforts with being made to improve the music by singing in two different pitches, fourths or fifths above. There could be and was endless development of this, in particular in the cathedral of Notre Dame in Paris.

Popular music also developed especially by the troubadours. Medieval music instruments were played, including, recorders, horns, trumpets, whistles, bells, and drums. (www.medieval-life.net/music. htm). See also 'the sound of the cornet, flute, harp, sackbut, psaltery, dulcimer, and all kinds of music' (**Book of Daniel** 3.5). Heroic tales and legends were sung as chansons. These had their equivalents in Ireland.

Architecture, Crafts and Art

The Middle Ages is famous for its Romanesque and Gothic churches, cathedrals and castles, but these were the exception. Most building was done in wood as it was across all northern Eurasia from the Atlantic to Japan. On the other hand substantial stone and brick buildings were built from Spain and North Africa, across the Middle East as far as India.

From its perishable nature, either from rot or fire, few wooden buildings survive. Other building materials like earth are equally perishable. Some buildings, like the mud-walled cabins built by the poor in pre-Famine Ireland were never intended to be permanent. The local young men could build small cabins with low walls of mud, make a roof from a structure of branches, and cover it with sods all on the day before the wedding. Life was lived in the open. The more prosperous peasants could build houses of wattle (interlaced rods and twigs) and daub (a mixture of clay, lime and chopped straw), roofed with thatch, with overhanging eaves to protect the walls. Larger structures still, like churches and halls of chiefs and bishops, could be made of a timber frame with infilling for the walls. The hall was a long building not a round one. Medieval craftsmen became as adept at joining small pieces of wood, as stone masons became in joining small blocks of stone. Slating or tiling was first enforced in towns because of the danger of fire spreading.

Fortifications in the early Middle Ages were built of wood. They usually consisted of a palisade with some halls within. As these were very vulnerable to attack by fire they were made more secure by building a mound (motte) of earth, with a building (keep) on top, surrounded by an outer palisade surrounding a yard (bailey). Wooden mottes and baileys were commonly first built, with the wood gradually being replaced by stone. The keep too grew in size, became a defensible dwelling place built of stone and became known as a castle. It was much more expensive to build in stone and the buildings were expensive to maintain. When towns were surrounded with stone walls repairs were often neglected until a threat arose. Until the end of the Middle Ages most town dwellings were of wood.

Churches could be roofed with timber. Stone vaults, though much more expensive to construct, were less liable to be destroyed by fire. The engineering problem of how to construct a simple barrel vault was not difficult. A stone vault could weigh thousands of tons but various devices were developed such as intersecting arches and groin vaults, rib vaults, buttresses and flying buttresses to make the vaults higher, the walls thinner and the windows larger and the whole structure lighter. The use of the pointed arch gave greater flexibility for it meant that the space covered did not have to be square. The appearance was enhanced by carving the stone to make a smooth surface to the walls or to decorate pillars. All buildings, even Cistercian ones were brightly painted.

The Church in the High Middle Ages

Organisation, the Hierarchical system

The Church was a very powerful body numerically, socially, organisationally, and politically. Its structures covered the whole of Europe. In a more restricted sense by Church was often meant clergy *(clericatus),* namely those who had been ordained to official offices of the Church. Clergy came to include all those who had been given the tonsure, or shearing of the hair. The tonsured person got all the immunities of the Church including immunity from military service, an essential point if a man wished to study. The clergy wrote and spoke the common international language, Latin. In English the words clerk and cleric came to have the same meaning, and when mention is made of the king's clerks it does not necessarily mean more than that they had received the tonsure.

At its simplest there was a structure of pope, archbishop, bishop, and parish priest. The central figure in the hierarchy figure was the bishop who was in charge of a diocese. For administrative reasons, the Church is divided into provinces at whose head are archbishops. The pope had great authority over the whole Church especially in the matter of appeals from lower ecclesiastical courts. Each bishop, archbishop, and the pope had a court which was as informal as secular courts of the time. The papal court and archbishop's courts were largely appellate courts. The pope could 'provide' i.e. appoint a bishop of any nationality to any see. The great problem in the Middle Ages was the by-passing of the simple structure of appeals from one court to the one above. Anyone at any level could appeal directly to the pope. This was very profitable to the papal clerks and officials for there were fees to be paid at every stage of the appeals process.

Like all public figures the bishop, the archbishop, and the pope had their courts, and an informal body of canon law, being largely collections of decrees of various councils grew up. Unlike the Brehon and Common Law codes, these were collections of enactments not collections of judgments. Often bishops had civil jurisdictions as well, and abbots had manorial and even civil jurisdiction over their own lands. The penalties that could be imposed by strictly religious courts were of a religious nature, deprivation of office or suspension from office, excommunication from church services and interdict, the prohibition of holding any official public service like the chanting of mass or the administration of the sacraments in a given diocese or country. Only the pope could put a whole country under interdict.

In the Middle Ages the power of the archbishop over the bishops in his province was quite extensive. Of interest is his duty to fix the date of Easter in his province, and to administer a see during a vacancy. English kings claimed this right especially with regard to the temporalities.

A bishop could call a council of all the clergy in his diocese; and archbishop of a province could call a provincial synod, and the pope could call a general or ecumenical council. During the Medieval Period there were several ecumenical councils to which Irish bishops would be summoned: Lateran III (1179), Lateran IV (1215), Lyons I (1245), Lyons II (1274), Vienne (1311), Constance (1414), Basel/Ferrara/ Florence (1431) and Lateran V (1512). The source of doctrine was the teaching authority of the Church, and the test of doctrine was *quod semper, quod ubique, quod ab omnibus,* i.e. what was taught and believed always, everywhere and by all. Hence the need for general councils to establish this.

The Diocesan System

The Diocese

The structure of the diocese at whose head was a bishop was simple. A diocese is the area of jurisdiction of a bishop. It was often attempted to make the boundaries of dioceses coincide with political boundaries. The bishop might divide up his see into rural deaneries presided over by rural deans to whom he gave various powers of administration. He might also give administrative powers to archdeacons who were important officials in the Middle Ages. The dean had to report once a year to the bishop and no doubt bring episcopal dues. He was also the channel of communication between the clergy and the bishop and the instructions of the bishop were transmitted through him. His principal duty was to conduct visitations of the parishes under his care. An instruction would be given, complaints heard, dues collected, disputes resolved, and penalties imposed. Over the centuries great gifts of land were made to dioceses and monasteries. Bishops and abbots were drawn almost exclusively from the governing class, and indeed many of the monks were from that class as well. The bishop conferred orders on those who were presented to him.

The Chapter

The chapter was originally the household of the bishop; the priests, deacons, and minor clerics who helped the bishop with the worship in the cathedral and the administration of the diocese. A semi-monastic rule was devised for them and they were called canons. These cathedral canons were ordinary diocesan priests. Some took monastic vows and were called canons regular. These could be attached to cathedrals or might not. Finally a bishop could install monks like Benedictines in the cathedral to undertake that part of the divine service. There had to be a place close to the cathedral for a hall where the canons could sleep and dine. The canon in charge of the chapter was called the dean, and the second officer was called the archdeacon. Each canon had to be given a farm for his support, which on his death or promotion passed to his successor. Establishing a chapter meant finding a dozen or more farms. The actual course of the day of life of monks, canons regular, and diocesan canons was very similar. They chanted the same offices in church, ate at a common table, and resided in a building. Typical was the chapter of St Patrick's in Dublin where 13 prebendal stalls were provided and the officers named as chancellor, precentor, treasurer and dean. The precentor or cantor led the chants.

The chapter became responsible for the cathedral, it fabric and its activities, whether liturgical, educational, or pastoral. Their best known duty was to elect a new bishop when the old one died. As the lands belonging to the dioceses were in many places feudal tenures, the king wrote to the chapter giving them the right to assemble for the election, and at the same time indicating the person he wanted chosen. This was called the *Congé d'Elire.* Chapters were not bound to follow this direction, but if they did not they might have difficulty in getting the lands of the dioceses released to the new bishop.

Parish clergy, chantries

By the 12th century it would seem that parish boundaries had become fixed, quite often being co-extensive with the manor, and the sources of revenue of the parish rector or village priest designated. Ireland had been an exception to this but the process of determining provinces, bishoprics, deaneries, chapters, and parishes was begum. If the official rector could not discharge the duties personally he appointed a vicar. Frequently the vicar had some of the *glebeland*. The *tithes* or tenths were divided into the 'great tithes' of corn, hay and wood, which went to the rector, and the 'small tithes' of milk, eggs etc which went to the vicar along with altarages, offerings, and burial fees (Bowlt, 29 ff). It was usually the vicar who went impoverished. An altarage was an offering specifically made to the vicar. The right of the clergy to receive tithes in England was conceded by the Anglo-Saxon kings but did acquire a legal force until 1285. They were introduced, in principle at least to Ireland by Henry II's Synod of Cashel in 1171.

At the local level the priest might be from the working class and be virtually illiterate and impoverished. Little thought was given to providing an income for the priest. Occasionally an entire townland or hide might be set aside for his support resulting in the placename Preston. They were paid in other places less than a ploughman. Rich livings normally went to dignitaries from the upper class who had received a university education. Each office or officer in the Church was funded separately. Each parish had to provide and fund its own parish priest. Normally the nomination was left to the local lord or patron of the parish who presented him to the bishop for ordination. The bishop seems just to have accepted these nominations.

Christianity had spread through the towns of the Roman Empire, the clergy belonged to the bishop's household, and he was responsible for teaching them. It is surprising to find that the education or training of the rural clergy was not regarded as a matter of prime importance. Their illiteracy mattered much less in an age when people were used to storing vast amounts of information in their memories. Similarly, nuns could sing the psalms in Latin even if they were entirely ignorant of the language. Priests were supposed to be celibate but there was always difficulty in getting this rule enforced.

There grew up in the Later Middles ages the institution of chantries. A chantry could consist of one or more priests who undertook to chant certain offices, and who received an endowment of land to enable them to do so. They were important for another reason, for they often kept the local Latin school the fees of which helped to support the priests.

Religious Orders

In the 11th century the religious order or congregation of monasteries with the greatest influence was the Benedictine congregation of Cluny. Monasticism thrived especially among the upper classes and was a powerful force from 950 to 1150 after which its secular influence declined as other influences grew (Kidson, 319). In Cluny, to ensure uniformity, it had been decided that there should be only one abbot who would have charge of all Cluniac foundations, with priors in individual houses. The Cistercians tried a different method and from their practices the government of nearly all religious orders is derived. Besides the *Rule* they drew up a more detailed book of customs making the *Rule* of St Benedict more precise. Then each abbey was made responsible for maintaining discipline in all its foundations, and had to make a formal 'visitation' of each of them every year. Then all the abbots had to assemble each year at the mother house of the Order namely Citeaux for a general court or chapter where all matters regarding discipline could be discussed. Their general provisions were admired by the Holy See and all other monasteries were obliged to adopt them or something similar. The Cistercians too sought out the best masters and most authentic manuscripts of Gregorian chant such as existed at the time to bring a rare and religious beauty to the divine services. Attempts were also made to find the best manuscripts of the bible and the most authentic copies of the Roman rituals and missals and chants to purge out local abuses (Merton, *Waters of Siloe*, 3-16). As monasteries and cathedrals got extensive grants of land at distance and in distant places it became necessary to organise them into manageable units which were called granges. The early Cistercians employed only laybrothers to work these granges each of which was provided with a small set of monastic buildings including a chapel. These were likely to be built of wood.

From the 11th century onwards there arose a profusion of religious orders for different purposes. The Vallumbrosans, the Camaldolese, and the Carthusians were eremitic orders, the Knights Templars, the Knights Hospitallers of St John, the Knights of Calatrava (Spain) and the Teutonic Knights (Germany) were military orders. From the 13th century the newly-formed mendicant orders proved to have greater popular appeal than the old monastic orders. The Dominicans, the Franciscans, the Carmelites, and the Augustinian friars were preaching orders, often called mendicant (begging) orders. The Brothers of St Anthony, and the Knights Hospitallers were nursing orders. The Trinitarians and Mercedarians were established to raise funds for the redemption of captives from the Moors of North Africa. Towards the end of the Middle Ages there arose in the Low Countries the Brethren of the Common Life. These were laymen without vows who lived a life in common, strove to cultivate a spirit of prayer, and devoted themselves to good works like education. Their ideas and spirit are enshrined in the *Imitation of Christ* by Thomas *a Kempis* (from Kempen in Germany).

The Financial Basis of the Church

Every Church or religious organisation must have a system of financial support. This meant that they had to be supported directly from the land. A change came with the mendicant friars whose endowment of land was very small, namely ground for a monastery and church. These had to be built and supported by the voluntary offerings of the local people so initially all friaries, as they were called, were in towns. The best time to found a monastery was after a successful war for then the lord had plenty of somebody else's land to distribute, and from piety some of it would have to go to the Church. In Ireland Norman and Gael were equally assiduous in this respect.

The diocesan clergy also had to be supported and with grants of land appropriate to their status, which, where the lands were extensive, involved the grantee in feudal obligations. Lands had to be provided for bishops, for members of the chapter, and for the parochial clergy. The revenues from these lands, together with others revenues from the office like tithes and altarages were called a living. The larger livings became very important for the support of sons of the nobility. Little thought was given to the parochial clergy though in some areas some acres of land called a glebe with the tithes could provide a modest but stable income. One of the great problems which faced the Church reformers in Ireland in the 12th century was how to get enough land to endow the diocesan clergy, as much of the available land had already been given to monasteries. (Only the Cistercians could survive on waste land.)

The revenues of these rich monasteries were often given by the pope *in commendam* to another cleric, usually to the great detriment of the monastery. Later in the Middle Ages rival Popes dispensed them freely to their supporters. Grants and endowments for monasteries of friars were much cheaper than for abbeys because initially the friars needed only a patch of land in a town on which to build their church and monastery. The burden of supporting the friars and the building fell on the townspeople as a whole.

The Papacy and the Lay Lords in the High Middle Ages

In the Dark Ages, bishops with their extensive estates had to take on a proportionate share of the costs of defence against the raids of the barbarians, and so they became, and remained, great feudal lords called to the king's Council and to Parliament. So the main point the reform of Gregory VII (Hildebrand) who became pope in 1073 was to re-balance the powers of the bishops vis-à-vis the kings. This was a reform of the clergy and not directly a reform of the morals of the laity. Reforms were aimed chiefly against simony, the buying and selling of spiritual offices and investiture, which was the control by laymen over Church offices through their feudal control of ecclesiastical lands. Usurped Church revenues were reclaimed. For reasons that are not obvious, the reformers began to insist on the celibacy of the clergy and to insist that the clergy should devote their time to religious matters rather than secular.

The papacy grew in moral esteem and the popes established a system of collections of offerings for the support of the pope. Anglo-Saxon England was among the earliest kingdoms to levy a penny a year on all households with an annual income of 30 pennies or more to be sent to the pope. According to the text of the Bull *Laudabiliter*, Henry II promised the pope one penny per household per year from Ireland also for the support of the pope (Peter's Pence or pennies, collected voluntarily to this day)(*Wikipedia 'Laudabiliter'*).

All through the Middle Ages the kings of England maintained close connections with the papal chancellery. Not only the kings and princes, but also ordinary clergy had recourse to the pope by means of appeal. Papal jurisdiction was normally an appellate one. It appears however that the papal court, both to boost its own importance, and for financial gain, encouraged direct appeals. Officials in Rome could pronounce on the suitability of an abbot or bishop in the west of Ireland when they had no possible way of judging his merits. The Great Western Schism from 1378 to 1417 resulted from the return of the papacy to Rome under Gregory XI in 1376. During its course there were rival popes in Roman and Avignon. The French court naturally supported the pope in Avignon, so the English court equally naturally supported the pope in Rome. From 1409 there was a third pope. At the Council of Constance (1414 to 1418) it was agreed that all three popes should resign or be deposed. Pope Martin V was elected and after some years was universally recognised.

Religion in the Middle Ages

Formal worship as it had developed in Roman times and in the Dark Ages continued. An additional shorter version of the divine office or liturgical chants in honour of the Blessed Virgin, or Our Lady (Notre Dame) as she was called was devised in some monasteries and then was made compulsory in all. This Little Office became a favourite book of devotion of the educated laity, and *Books of Hours* became medieval best-sellers. They are chiefly famous nowadays for their illustrations. They were not formal canonical books, and could vary in content, and individual artists could illustrate them to their heart's content (Harthan, 9). (The official modern approved text can be found at www. officiumdivinum.org.)

Many modern 'devotions' originated during the course of the Middle Ages which were scarcely present at the beginning of the period. The chief one, and indeed earliest one, was a devotion to Mary the Mother of Jesus, *Notre Dame*, Our Lady, especially promoted by St Bernard. A development of the Little Office was the rosary or the recitation of 150 *Pater Nosters* (Our Fathers) in place of the 150 psalms. Gradually *Ave Marias* (Hail Marys) replaced the *Paters,* and beads, usually with fifty beads were used to keep count rather than fingers. The 150 Aves were divided into 15 decades and these decades too were assigned mysteries from the life of Mary for contemplation. Promotion of the saying of the rosary is traditionally associated with the Dominicans. The Franciscans promoted the saying of the *Angelus* thrice a day which concentrates on one mystery, namely the annunciation by the angel Gabriel to Mary in Nazareth that she is to be the mother of God (Luke 1.26). St Francis brought in the nativity and the crib. The devotion of *Corpus Christi*, the body of Christ in the Eucharist, grew in importance. Pilgrimages became a feature of the age.

Most people were illiterate and even many of the clergy were illiterate. Yet a literate priest would be lucky to possess even a single book of the Bible in manuscript.

The centre of religion and worship lay in the liturgical year with its cycle of feasts and ceremonies and above all sacraments. Cathedral worship and monastic worship had come together. Instruction was not separate from liturgy. The liturgy was based around the celebration of the sacraments. Help could be obtained through the communal mass and sacraments and also through contact with holy things, the fabric of the church, the sound of the bells, the use of blessed water, pilgrimages to holy places, burial close to a church or a saint, and above all holy relics. No unnecessary 'servile' work, i.e. work normally done by slaves, could be done on Sundays or holy days. The Gregorian chant, now in its full development, formed the background music to the Middle Ages. It was to be heard in every cathedral, monastery, chantry, convent, and parish church, or churches of friars or the military orders or the hospitals of the sick. It was part of the setting of people's lives from the day they were baptized until the day of their funeral.

An American in the 20th century was extraordinarily impressed when he heard the Gregorian chants sung in a Cistercian monastery. 'But the cold stones of the abbey church ring with a chant that glows with living flame, with clean profound desire. It is an austere warmth, the warmth of Gregorian chant. It is deep beyond ordinary emotion and that is one reason why you never get tired of it. It never wears you out by making a lot of cheap demands on your sensibilities . . . it draws you within where you are lulled in peace and recollection and where you find God' (Merton, *Seven Storey Mountain*, 397.) Priests and monks depended largely on their memories. It was routine to commit the entire Latin psalter and the thousands of Gregorian chants to memory. Teaching of religion was by word of mouth, at times illustrated with simple pictures as are found in manuscripts and carved on crosses. It is strange though that there seems to be no records on the Cistercian attitude to mystical prayer though the first monks in Mellifont were instructed in this by St Bernard himself. In England in the Middle Ages there was a rich body of mystical writings, but none in Ireland (Merton, *Waters of Siloe*, 289).

There were according to Gratian forty one feasts besides Sundays on which mass was celebrated and no work done and no court sessions held (*Catholic Encyclopaedia*, 'Ecclesiastical Feasts'). They were devoted to Our Lady, to the Apostles, John the Baptist, and various martyrs. It was noted that the five-day working week was already in existence in the Middle Ages. The holy day was a day of rest but it was also a day of feasting and recreation. With a religious celebration about twice every week religion was not far from people's minds. There seems to have been little emphasis on morality; if one sinned (and all men sinned) one hoped to confess and be shriven before one died. If anybody wanted to do more, monasteries were founded. Or one could go on a pilgrimage if one's status in society permitted it. Many superstitious practices, often survivals from the old religions, were taken over by the Christian Church and made harmless. So a 'holy well' could be blessed by the Church and dedicated to a saint. Pagan religious festivals could likewise be turned into saints' days.

With regard to religious practice there was no theoretical distinction between monastic and lay spirituality, or between private devotion and public worship. Religion was not centred on the individual relationship with God but by joining one's self to the Church outside of which there was no salvation. The contemplative monk or nun represented the peak of religious practice. Those with worldly duties like canons, religious knights and hospitallers, preachers, and so on adopted as much conventional monastic practices as was suitable to their occupations. Married lay people, peasants, merchants, and serfs followed monastic practice at a distance. Leisured aristocratic ladies had their chapels, and in their devotions followed the monastic hours of prayer closely. A

Book of Hours normally contained an abbreviated office called the Little Office of Our Lady. It is noteworthy however that half of the books owned by Cecily, Duchess of York, were by or about women mystics, the most important of whom was St Bridget of Sweden (Leyser 232f). Again the absence of mystical writings from Ireland is strange. In the 14th and 15th centuries the *Devotio Moderna* (modern devotion) rose whose great monument is The *Imitation of Christ* by St Thomas a Kempis. In the age of Chaucer he had little confidence in the spiritual value of pilgrimages *Qui multum pergrinantur raro sanctificantur*, those who go often on pilgrimages are rarely made holy.

Religion brought great comfort and joy to people. There was none of the gloominess and dullness of the post-Reformation Puritans or Jansenists who considered themselves just and despised others. Life was often harsh but there was hope of a better life to come. A man or a woman did not feel alone. There was a loving God, and Jesus and his mother, and all the saints one could appeal to. Holy days were days of rest and merriment after the religious duties were discharged. The little parish church and even more so the big monasteries and cathedrals were brightly painted, and lit with as many candles as the congregation could afford. One sinned and then one went to the priest for forgiveness. Everyone sinned so all were in the same boat. The sins of the priests and monks and nuns and the local lords would have been a staple of discussion in the local parishes. Purgatory was probably more feared than hell so one made every effort to shorten it. The doctrine of Purgatory, based in part on the text of the Second Book of Maccabees *'sancta ergo et salubris cogitatio pro defunctis exorare ut a peccato solverentur'* (It is a holy and wholesome thought to pray for the dead that they may be loosed from their sin, 2 Maccabees, 12.46, *Vulgate*; *Catholic Encyclopaedia*, 'Purgatory'.)

There is a question which is too big to be discussed here but which should be kept in mind and that was the growth of a moral or ethical sense especially among the middle classes or bourgeoisie. The very poor lived as best they could, honestly or dishonestly. The rich expected morality to be bent to their convenience. The learned and religious classes battened on the rich to survive in comfort. But there did arise ideas of honesty in dealings, in the rule of law, of lack of corruption and cruelty in public officials, of the worth of the common man, and the right to be consulted over taxation and other public issues. 'When Adam delved and Eve span, who was then the gentleman?' dates from this period. Questions like these should be kept in mind when considering the Statutes of Kilkenny for example.

Religious Education and Science

Though a tradition of secular learning survived in some towns in Italy like Bologna and Salerno, the revival of studies in northern Europe in the 12th century was dominated by the clergy. A great stimulus was given by translations of Aristotle from the Arabic. The clerical scholars of Europe followed him and much of the intellectual effort of the Middle Ages centred on incorporating the works of Aristotle into traditional Christian learning. Aristotelianism displaced Platonism and Neo-Platonism as the dominant philosophy. The Franciscan friar Roger Bacon with the encouragement of the pope devoted himself to the study of the natural sciences. Astronomy and mathematics were also studied. Though Ptolemy's theory was largely accepted on the basis of empirical evidence, the possibility for mathematicians to compute the date of Easter a hundred years in advance was endlessly fascinating. A canon Nicholas Copernicus argued that the earth must move round the sun, but characteristically for the period he was more concerned with the perfection of circles, the heavens being supposed to be composed of perfect circles.

Europe began to eclipse all other centres of learning for the study of arts, law, and theology. From monasteries and cathedral schools sprang up institutions which came to be called universities. To avoid feudal military service all students had to enrol themselves temporarily as clerics which meant that masters and students at the universities were all at least nominally clerics. The name university was first applied to the schools of Paris, and later became common. A licence from the chancellor of the diocese to teach was no longer sufficient, but further degrees of bachelor, licentiate, magister (doctor, professor) were coming into use. The university was given papal recognition and was no longer subject to the bishop. The core of a university was one or more colleges endowed with land where masters and students lived in a common hall and dined at a common table. It was not essential for a university to be in a town. Oxford and Cambridge were just placed in manors deep in the countryside. What was essential was that there should be several masters of suitable distinction. The course was composed of lectures by the master and disputations between the students. These early colleges were little different, as far as teaching went, from the traditional bardic, legal or medical schools in Ireland, but their development was to be much different. The least satisfactory was the faculty of medicine which unlike the other faculties made no advances. It is significant that most Irish clerics who went to Oxford to study chose canon law. It was the route to high office either in Church service, royal service or both.

Gradually more and more laymen were able to devote themselves study. Count Giovanni Pico della Mirandola (1463-94) was probably the last man to issue the challenge to debate *de omni re scibili* (all things knowable) religion, philosophy, natural philosophy and magic. After his day there was simply too much to learn and learning became fragmented.

Belief system, fairies, spells, magic, curses.

The educated clergy, and increasingly scholars, were well acquainted with the basics of Greek philosophy. But lay people, from kings downward, knew little of this. The beliefs of the people of Ireland were little different from those of England. Their world was still that of the flat earth, of ghosts, imps and fairies, goblins and hobgoblins, of witchcraft, magic, the evil eye, and evil spells, omens and portents. There was a whole body of folk wisdom regarding these beliefs, and how to counteract hidden influences. One should never start a journey on a Friday, for it was an unlucky day. Demonology was an important topic, how to detect the presence of the devil, and to counteract his evil influence. One thing had disappeared and that was polytheism. People were very credulous with regard to miracles, and all the popular shrines had a saint who worked miraculous cures. It was believed that curses could have an effect, for example that a man or woman could be made childless by a curse. Some religious people like St Benedict of Nursia, St. Columba of Iona, and Muhammad got a reputation for being miracle workers. The shrine of Saint Thomas of Canterbury became a famous place of pilgrimage.

Religion and superstition got thoroughly intertwined and the aim of the Protestant reformers was to strip out the elements they regarded as superstitious and so be left with 'pure' Christianity.

Part 2

England in the Twelfth Century

Chapter 2

The High Middle Ages: England

English practices and customs had a powerful influence on Ireland. Much of what was done in England was transferred to the towns and counties of Ireland as they were brought under the justiciar. There are in addition much more numerous surviving records in England.

The Land

Climatically, the British Isles were in the path of the depressions sweeping in succession from the North Atlantic. There were differences between north and south, and east and west. There was a famous division between the 'Highland Zone' and the 'Lowland Zone'. The lower flatter lands on the east of Britain (the Lowland Zone) were dryer than mountainous areas further north and west (the Highland Zone). But parts of England could be similar to parts of Ireland, Scotland and Wales. Altitude was as much a factor as latitude. With regard to agriculture, in general the west and north concentrated more on animal husbandry, and those to the south and east on tillage, though both were practised in all areas. There were the same kinds of animals, and the same kinds of agricultural tools, techniques and seeds.

History

England, by 1170 was more advanced in the redevelopment than Ireland but not by a great deal. England had some advantages over Ireland. It had been a Roman province with towns and roads. The roads remained passable, even if the wooden bridges had long since decayed. Its river systems allowed easy access to the interior. This was a disadvantage in Viking times, and England had suffered more than Ireland. But when trade revived they proved an advantage. The absence of natural barriers made it easier to achieve a single kingdom in most of Britain. It was closer to the Continent, so the new ideas reached it sooner. Building in stone and the use of glass arrived earlier, as did the revival of learning.

Like most parts of Western Europe, Britain had received immigrants from German lands beyond the Rhine and Danube. There followed a period of dark ages when virtually nothing was committed to writing so it is extremely difficult to work out what was happening. There was however a common culture, just differing in local details, all over the British Isles. Houses were the same, clothing, weapons, systems of agriculture, forms of art, and so on. The big difference was between those regions which adopted the heavy plough, and those which did not. To justify having a great plough which brought up nutrients from deeper down, a piece of tillable land of at least 60 acres was needed, and so was characteristic of the Lowland Zone. Long distance trade had virtually ceased, but local trade continued, and also trade with northern France. The use of Latin as a written and spoken language seems to have been confined to Christian churches and monasteries.

The English Church was fortunate in that a learned Greek priest, Theodore of Tarsus (602-690), was appointed archbishop of Canterbury, and helped to reorganise the Church on the latest lines. Ecclesiastical buildings were increasingly built of brick and stone in the Roman fashion. Stained glass and painted plaster on the walls indicate Frankish influence. In the secular world, though houses and villages were still built of wood, increasing numbers of them were designated as *wics* or markets. The most important wics were Lundenwic (London) and Hamwih (Southampton). These were developed and protected by the Saxon 'kings', for customs duties from time immemorial had been a great source of royal revenue. Coinage was re-introduced, but in quite a large unit, the silver penny, that was suitable only for considerable items like annual taxation, customs dues, and bulk buying. Exchange and barter and days of labour were still used for domestic purposes. *Wics* grew into towns and by the 11th century there were more than a hundred recognised towns (Saul, *passim*).

Britain suffered more from Viking raids and had more Viking settlements than Ireland. There were close connections between the Norse of York and the Norse of Dublin. We have no idea what arrangements they made with the local rulers. The local chiefs in Wales had the most success in preventing Norse settlements, though it is doubtful if this was to their own long-term advantage (Evans, 132). It was from Wessex (South West England) that Alfred began the reconquest.

Under Alfred (d. 899), Edward the Elder (d. 924), Athelstan (d. 939), and especially Edgar the Peaceful (d. 975) the kingdom of England advanced in size, in the enforcement of laws, and the revival of monasticism. The Monastic Reform Movement that restored the Benedictine Rule to England's undisciplined monastic communities peaked during the era of St. Dunstan (d. 988), Aethelwold, and Oswald. England prospered during the peaceful reign of Edward the Confessor (1042-66). He imposed the collection of Peter's Pence in Wessex on every monastery, and every household worth more than thirty pennies per annum (*Catholic Encyclopaedia* 'Apostolic Succession'). England was a relatively large and ordered kingdom.

On Edward's death there was a fierce struggle which was won by the Norman William of Falaise, better known as William the Conqueror who defeated Harold Godwinson at Hastings in 1066. The lands of all who opposed William were confiscated and given to William's followers as tenants-in-chief under feudal law which was imposed in matters concerning the rights of the crown. The Norman conquest of England was much harsher than that of Ireland where most of the major chiefs were allowed to keep most of their lands. William, recognising the importance of towns for taxation and other purposes, kept most of them in the royal demesne, and granted them early forms of charters. William I (d 1078) inherited a kingdom, well organised by the standards of the time. He accepted Anglo-Saxon law of the time as the law of his English kingdom. (This was earlier than Common Law which was Norman in origin.) It was customary at the time not to interfere with local laws and customs most of which were not written down. It was also important to know what laws applied in each court. The rites and practices of the various churches and dioceses (called uses) were reformed. The most important was that of Sarum (Salisbury) copied apparently from Rouen which was adopted in whole or in part in other dioceses. Henry I (d 1135) and Henry II (d. 1189) did much to develop the administration and the execution of justice in the kingdom. (Warren in *Henry II* gives a full picture of England at this time). When England was united with the king, the latter could bring an enormous force to bear against any adversary. Yet, as was common everywhere in the Middle Ages, great vassals proved difficult to keep under control.

From 1066 until 1453 the kings of England were closely involved in the affairs of France. War in France was always popular with the knights for it provided great opportunities for personal advancement and enrichment. The most famous intervention became known as the Hundred Years War, 1337 to 1453. Consequently little attention was given to Scotland, Wales, and Ireland except spasmodically.

All the tenants-in-chief had the right to hold their own courts called honorial courts which were the centres of administration in their lands which were not necessarily contiguous. To defend England against

Welsh and Scottish attacks, special powers were granted to the greater barons and bishops who lived close to the borders. These were called the marcher lords. Royal writ did not run in the marches. The lords built their own castles and held their own courts. Similar jurisdictions called liberties, or palatines, and eventually presidencies were established in Ireland to enable powerful local lords to deal with trouble on the spot.

From the time of Athelstan (d. 939), and especially after the beginning of the second millennium until around 1300 England grew in population, urbanisation, trade, wealth, industry, agriculture and art. The population expanded from around 2 million in 1066 to around 6½ million in 1347. The high point was reached in 1300; there followed several years with poor harvests. Wet summers in 1315, 1316, and 1317 caused a widespread famine. By 1340 much of the land in the midlands was no longer being cultivated, and land reclaimed from the sea was being again invaded. In 1348-9 the Black Death swept away half of the population. There was a rapid decline of population down to around 2¾ million following the Black Death and other plagues and epidemics like measles, tuberculosis, and smallpox. The population had simply grown too large to allow the support of small holders and petty traders through bad years.

No single explanation is satisfactory as to why Western Europe went into reverse for most of the 14th century. Work for the survivors became plentiful; wages went up, the return on land went down. With the scarcity of labour women's work became more valuable; widows especially seized their opportunities. Parliament responded with new labour laws and new taxes like the poll tax. The principal aim of the Peasants' Revolt in 1381 was the removal of serfdom which the landlords were enforcing. Serfdom gradually disappeared over the next hundred years largely by serfs deserting the manors. Enclosures ended the 'open field' system of cultivation. Land was let to individuals. There was greater population mobility, high mortality and low birth rate, and population refused to rise. People moved in and out of towns and villages. The population of the towns fell though few actually disappeared. Investment in sheep farming and manufacture of cloth grew, and cloth replaced wool as the great export. There was an increased demand for meat and wool. The overall wealth of England probably did not decline, but it was distributed differently. Manufactures, principally cloth, replaced raw wool as the principal export. Sheep rearing became more profitable than tillage. This accentuated the decline in the rural population, but on the other hand the increased margin of profitability meant that more could be spent on manufactured and traded goods. England was still backward compared to neighbouring countries on the Continent but was closing the gap (Dyer, 160 ff, Briggs and Jordan, 59 ff). Exports from Ireland were closely linked to economic conditions in England.

By 1170 England was somewhat richer, more powerful, and more advanced than Ireland. The building in stone was more advanced. Towns, markets, and the use of cash encouraged production. Foreign trade, as in Ireland, was in foreign hands, but in the course of the Middle Ages there grew up a great export trade in wool to the weavers in Flanders. Towns, monasteries, and even parishes grew rich on this trade. Whether learning was better in English monasteries and cathedrals than in Irish in 1170 is impossible to say. Ireland later was to fall behind having failed to develop universities.

The Government of Henry II

Government in the Middle Ages was very different from what we have nowadays. States scarcely existed: there were just the personal dominions of kings and lords in various forms of subordination. A great king like Henry II could have several dominions which he ruled variously as count, duke, king or feudal overlord. All of these had their own separate administrations and the superior lord did not interfere in the affairs of the lesser lord unless his own rights were threatened. In England, which provided the model for the Government of Ireland, kings had greater rights of monitoring and controlling counties than feudal fiefdoms. The central affairs of the king, and the officialdom to control them formed the basis of the central government at Westminster. Local affairs were left to the counties which were regularly inspected by the king's judges on circuit. (The administration of Henry's other dominions, Normandy for example, was more feudal). The English form of government was introduced into Ireland, and developed there *pari passu* with that in England.

The Government of England in 1170 was very different from what it was to be in 1470. It was still a personal rule, though the king appointed various officers in counties, and sent out itinerant judges to keep a check on them. The king and his assistants and chancellors, in an age of general illiteracy, might have a record of the names and lands of about 5,000 feudal vassals and appointed officials. Apart from that people knew each others' faces in their own areas. There was not a state as such to which one pledged loyalty. Loyalty was to a person, namely the king and had to be renewed to the next king. In between the death of a king and the coronation of a successor there was actually no state. In post-Conquest England it may be said there was no such a thing as society, only individuals and families (Garnett, 80). Early medieval society was a web of personal loyalties and pledges of fealty.

Henry began to interfere in the honorial courts, to enable cases before them to be transferred to the royal courts. This especially with regard to the tenure of land; the tenant-in-chief (*in capite*) could no longer decide unilaterally against one of his tenants. The writ of right (*breve de recto*) was addressed to the lord of an honorial court. The writ *praecipe* was similarly addressed to sheriffs but similarly dealing with honorial courts. Other royal writs were *Utrum, darreign presentment, novel disseisin, and mort d'ancestor*. Cases could be sent to the assize and the power of the lord to disseize an heir and to claim relief from the heir was severely limited. He laid the basis for Common Law, the law available to all the king's subjects in the itinerant courts all over England.

Henry II's household or court, for the most part, moved round with him. It was necessary that a king, accompanied by a sizeable force, should visit every major vassal. This court was not like it was in Stuart times when noblemen hung around the king's palace. Rather it was a collection of his chief officers, and their assistants, and a lot of personal servants. The principal officers who moved around with the king were the steward, the butler, the constable, the chamberlain, and the chancellor. These were in charge of the food, the wines, the horses, and the clothes and the writing. Most of those in the chancellery would have been clerics who wrote the king's letters (writs) and read those he received. This group, which probably numbered some hundreds, moved from one of the king's manors to the next where they would consume all the food (and filled all the privies) before moving on to the next. It was easier to put the king's garments and other equipment on to the backs of horses and move them, than to carry the food to Westminster. Payment in food was very important in the Middle Ages. This was the second reason why the court was perpetually on the move.

The other meaning of the word court is much the same as yard, and often combined as courtyard. The king's bench was the king's chair, and it was placed in the courtyard when the king was engaged in any of his public activities. The king's court was properly a feudal court where the affairs of vassals were dealt with. He could summon the barons there for a conference, give instructions, give judgments, proclaim laws, meet ambassadors, and receive petitions and so on. Naturally only the barons attended the court yard. He did not have to carry out all these duties personally. He could appoint a leading member of his court to sit in the king's bench and adjudicate in cases among the barons in which the king had an interest, often a financial one. Judging was just one of the facets of ruling any trusted officer could be assigned to do, largely depending on local custom and his common sense. They were like district officers or collectors in the days of the British Empire.

Henry however found it convenient to leave three offices in the palace at Westminster to which the Norman kings had transferred the centre of administration from Winchester. These were Exchequer, the Treasury, and Bench of Common Pleas. The exchequer or checker board was the table on which the barons, and other officers, paid their dues to the crown. Records of what was due were kept by literate clerics. The Treasury was a strong room, with large chests to hold gold and silver coins, and was under the Lord Treasurer. Common pleas were those in which the king was not involved. The king could appoint anyone to hear cases, and remove him again. Any of the king's men could have been sent out as an itinerant judge. They were at first called justices in eyre and later justices in assize (*assise,* sitting). There were no hard and fast rules regarding these offices which were established for administrative convenience. Assize courts were king's courts, not shire or liberty courts, but their sessions were held in the shire courts, the judge not the sheriff presiding. (They were replaced in 1971 by Crown courts.) The justices reported to the Court of Common Pleas and to the Exchequer. There were no exact rules and an official in one might be told to discharge the function of another. When the king was not in England, an official called the justiciar presided over the Treasury, the Exchequer, and the Common Pleas (Warren *op. cit.* 305-7). (Assizes and sessions both mean sittings; kings and judges sat in court.)

Law

Law was the commonly agreed body of customs and indeed statutes accepted in a particular court. A person was tried according to the law of that court. The English system of royal circuit judges was superior to anything in Ireland, but at this period it was just starting. There were no judges as such. Gentlemen or clerics of the king's court were sent out on assizes to the county and shire courts where they discovered local law and custom in addition to the limited Anglo-Saxon written code. They, and their assistants and clerics, learned on the road. As they pooled their experiences a common body of laws and precedents was built up, and they instructed others. The important point was that they were sent out regularly by the king to check local magnates and sheriffs, a point not lost on the Irish bishops.

Common Law was customary law, but gradually the best practice was selected and applied universally. Its corner stone was and remains precedent, namely decisions made earlier in similar cases. It was pragmatic law, and there was no theory of jurisprudence, unlike in Roman and Canon Law. In 1170 there was no agreed body of Common Law. The written work of Henry de Bracton, a cleric from Devon, *De Legibus et Consuetudinibus Angliae* (The Laws and Customs of England), was composed primarily about 1235 gathering together compilations of two other clerical judges as well as his own.

Canon Law had just been codified, or at least harmonised. It was a collection of decrees of earlier councils. It was used in ecclesiastical courts, in all cases involving clerics and in all cases involving marriages and written wills. The Church of England retained the probate of wills until the Probate Act of 1857. The right of clerics to be tried in ecclesiastical courts was called the *privilegium fori*.

There was a fourth body of law which had application in certain cases and was called *ius gentium* (the law of the nations). It was derived from Roman law, and was to develop into international law. It was concerned with conventions regarding the rules of war and truces, and for the trial of pirates. These afterwards were tried in an Admiralty Court. Later judges appointed had to have studied civil (Roman) law in a university not Common Law. Finally there was 'March Law'. It was the customary law of the Marches. The term particularly applies to Anglo-Norman lords in Wales, who had complete jurisdiction over their subjects, without recourse to the king of England. The king only had jurisdiction in treason cases, though the lords each bore personal allegiance to the king, as feudal subjects. Extensive 'palatine' privileges had been granted by William the Conqueror to the great barons with estates along the Welsh borders (*Wikipedia* 'Marcher lord'). Among their rights were to build and maintain castles, make peace or war, establish markets, and appoint sheriffs. They had their own chanceries and courts. They devised laws appropriate to their circumstances. The laws varied from march to march. People living in the Marches were subject to the customs of the March, while those in *pura Wallia* (Unmixed Wales) still adhered to the laws of Hywel Dda (indigenous Welsh law). Among the marcher lords were William FitzOsbern, William Marshal, William de Braose, Gilbert de Clare, Roger Mortimer, and Hugh de Lacy who later had lands in Ireland. This was the system of law which Henry II introduced into Ireland, Norman practice there replacing Gaelic practice. Later developments in England were systematically applied to Ireland in whole or adapted to local needs. Courts and government were synonymous.

Local Government

Almost all government was local. The courts themselves were bound by the immemorial customs of the place. These were ascertained by asking a local jury. Most disputes were probably settled without coming to any court. Yet the men of the parish or manor would ensure that some kind of rough justice prevailed and that there was no oppression of the weak among them. Royal enactments and parliamentary legislation might apply to those who attended the county or honour courts, and charters might give specific permissions to rich merchants, but they were not intended for the bulk of the population. The system of courts was complicated and tried to cover every eventuality. The county council Acts in the late 19th century were marvels of simplification.

It is doubtful however if the full complexity and diversity of English local government was ever imported into Ireland or the American colonies.

A court or courtyard was as its name implies a space out of doors where matters could be discussed, orders given, disputes settled, grievances aired, new methods or arrangements introduced, and indeed judgements given. Administrative government and judicial processes were functions of the same court or assembly. The court was formed by the convenor of the court and those summoned to it. There were courts of sheriffs, coroners, escheators, and royal bailiffs; courts of liberties, counties, hundreds, boroughs, baronies, vills and manors, and ecclesiastical courts of archbishops, archbishops, and even archdeacons. Only those who were free of a particular court attended that court. The lowest grades, the vast bulk of the population, attended the manor courts. The most important courts were the sheriff's or county court, the lord's (baron's) court, and the bishop's court.

The powers of local courts and officers were very extensive. They comprised everything that was not reserved to the crown. In England the crown reserved such matters as the making of war and peace, the construction and maintenance of castles, and the 'pleas of the crown' such as murder, killing the king's deer, and highway robbery. The king could interfere at times in such matters as the protection of heirs and heiresses, the claiming of treasure trove, granting charters to towns or protection to monasteries. In fact, because in feudal theory the king owned all the land rights, some, such as those over fisheries or wrecks, could be given to local lords or religious houses. But in practice the local lord or sheriff was supreme in his own dominion and the king sought some measure of periodical control by sending out his own justices on commission.

Anglo-Saxon England had had a comprehensive system of courts. The country was divided into counties of shires which have survived more or less the same until the present day. Each was ruled over by an ealdorman or earl appointed from the local noble families. In each there was a royal official, the sheriff whose principal duty was to keep an eye on the king's interests especially his financial ones. The total defeat of the Anglo-Saxon earls after 1066 and the parcelling out of their lands meant that their hereditary jurisdictions were brought to an end. William the Conqueror came from Normandy where they did not have shires and sheriffs and just imposed the Norman honorial courts or castellan courts. To avoid local concentrations of power a fiefdom could consist of several properties in different counties. But William's successors recognised the value of a counter weight to the power of the lords and re-instated sheriffs in the county courts but not the earls. When the Normans re-instated the honorific title of count/earl for particular important barons they was not in charge of a counties but their lands might be spread over several counties.

Norman honorial lordships were an earlier and feudal form of government in which the king or emperor entrusted the rule of a particular tract of land, for example a county, to a noble man as tenant-in-chief. So long as he discharged his feudal duties, the king did not interfere with the internal affairs of the county or earldom as it was called in England. When the lord died his heir expected to succeed him, but had to petition the king in order to do so. Honorial courts of their nature tended to become hereditary, and to exclude the writs of the king's courts. Palatine jurisdictions were grander versions of honorial courts given to some powerful local figures to defend the borders with forces on the spot. The kings from Henry II onwards extended royal control over the honorial or baronial courts, which did not please the barons. They issued writs removing cases from the honorial to the king's courts (Garnett, 90). The most common of the prerogative writs are *quo warranto, prohibito, mandamus, procedendo*, and *certiorari*. These writs allowed appeals from any court to a royal court. They put an end to subinfeudation as regards knight's service. Also the king used his prerogative rights to transfer cases from any court into his own courts. As Warren points out the county courts hedged in the signeurial courts (Warren, *Henry II*, 372).

The establishment of a county court did not extinguish the rights of a lordship or honorial court. The two systems overlapped. Sheriff's courts in the castle in the county town were responsible for a particular piece of territory, the county, and it was more convenient for most people. Honorial courts were attended by the vassals of the lord no matter what county they lived in. There was no system of appeal from such courts. Their powers and procedures were virtually identical. As all local government was notoriously corrupt the king established various devices to keep an eye on the affairs in counties. During the reign of Stephen there was little difference between an honorial court and a sheriff's court. Both were fairly arbitrary, brutal, corrupt, and summary. The unfree were subject to manor courts only and their cases were never transferred to the king's courts.

The first duty of the early sheriffs was to ensure the royal revenue from the counties. The king through the itinerant justices tried to keep control of the county officials. Though these justices sat in the county courts they sat in the king's name and dispensed the king's justice. Their assizes were therefore royal courts and came to be held twice a year. When they were not present the sheriff presided in the county courts. The kings also insisted that the appointment of sheriffs remained with themselves from a list prepared by the county court. Another royal officer, the coroner was appointed to investigate suspicious deaths especially of those detained by the sheriff. The sheriff too was the military governor of his county and was responsible for its defence. Though formal Commissions of Array to sheriffs did not antedate the reign of Edward I, the duty of every freeman to defend his county was established in Anglo-Saxon times. When a county was shired this duty of providing the array of the county would have devolved on the sheriff. The array would have existed also in the Norman lordships in addition to the quota of knights they had to provide for the king's wars whether these were in England, Scotland, or France.

Perhaps the most complete and logical was the county structure of the Anglo-Saxon kings. For financial and military purposes every man in a county had to belong to a tithing of ten men who were mutually responsible for each other's conduct. They were the basic peace-keeping unit in the village. Tithings were grouped into hundreds and hundreds into counties. Though overlain in Norman times by honorial and manorial courts they persisted throughout the Middle Ages. In Norman times, tithings were administered in the manorial courts and had to give an account of themselves twice a year at the court of frankpledge. In the Middle Ages kings made great demands for manpower apart from the warriors; woodmen, carpenters, masons and miners being required. The hundred remained the basis for the militia system until the 19th century. Taxation was however based on the hide or townland except in the cases of poll tax which was on the individual.

As far as most people were concerned government meant local government. Local might mean their county, their bailiwick, or their manor. The affairs of the king concerned few people personally. For most freemen the most important court was not the shire or honorial court but that of the hundred, which corresponded to a barony in Ireland. The hundred was a division of land of sufficient size to support a hundred households though it is not clear how those households were defined, but seemingly it was equal to 100 hides, the 100 acre farm of the free farmers. The term in Wales was the cantref (a hundred dwelling places), and this term was introduced into Ireland by the Normans as the cantred. A cantref had to support two knights. The only court most men could to attend was the manor court or that of the immediate landowner. The affairs of a manor court were largely concerned with matters of tillage and grazing and common rights or rights over the common lands. This was complicated by statuses of freemen, unfree men and clerics.

Manorial courts were not finally abolished until the Probate Court Act of 1859 though most of them had by then long fallen into disuse.

The Economy

The English economy by continental standards was quite backward. Its industries were the cottage industries of the peasants. Its foreign trade was in foreign ships and depended on the credit of foreign bankers. If anyone wanted to travel abroad, to Calais, Rome, or Jerusalem, he had to go to a foreign banker, either Jewish or Lombard, to get the gold coins with repayment charged on his rents. England was a primary producer. Tin was abundant in Cornwall and in Spain, but not elsewhere. There was plenty of fish in the seas, but the international markets seem to have been controlled by foreigners. It had one great export commodity, fine wool. As the industrialisation of Europe commenced with the weaving of ever finer textiles, and the wool of English sheep was particularly prized, many counties, towns, and monasteries in England grew rich on the production of wool. The coarser Irish wool was imported into England to make up for the shortfall caused by the export of the fine wool.

The economy of England like that of almost everywhere in Europe was overwhelmingly a rural one. Most were supported directly by agriculture, but the wastes, forests, marshes, rivers and lakes all supplied goods to support human life. Towns were small and were supported by the produce of the countryside. Agriculture has traditionally been divided into pastoral (livestock rearing) and tillage (cultivating fields to grow crops). But it is doubtful if pure example ever existed. Tillage reached its greatest extent in the 13th century, and in the following century it declined. It was not until the early 19th century that tillage reached the extent it did in the 13th century. The decline was probably partly caused by the deterioration of climate that occurred in the 14th century, and was accelerated by the fall in population caused by the

Black Death. The greater profitability of sheep's wool caused further decline in the rural population. Yet it is likely that the disposable income and standards of living of the survivors kept rising.

Certain parts of England and Ireland, like many parts of Western Europe, adopted the three open-field system of tillage in the early Middle Ages. In England, in Anglo-Saxon times there were three systems of tillage. In the south east, especially Kent, the Roman system persisted. In a belt in the middle, 'champion' or 'champagne' country a system of three open fields was adopted. In most of the Highland Zone, the 'Celtic' system survived. In parts of south Wales, after the Norman invasion, a hybrid system seems to have been developed. The importance of this lies in the fact that when Norman lords developed their manors in Ireland and imported colonists they were likely to bring the system of tillage prevailing in their areas of origin.

The English Manor

The manorial system was by and large introduced in the Lowland zone, the most productive part of England. It is often confused with the feudal system, but it was only the bottom rung of the feudal ladder. Its chief purpose was to provide cavalry for the king's army. The lord of a manor, whether a person or an institution like a monastery or church, often had several manors. To each he appointed a bailiff whose duty was to manage the manor and secure its revenues and dues. Over the bailiffs was a steward or seneschal. The holders elected an officer called the reeve who was a kind of foreman of the villeins. On him devolved the daily duty of managing the agriculture on the land. All had to attend the manorial court, or court baron. The precise powers of the manorial court varied according to the grant of the feudal overlord. Many also enjoyed rights of justice over their free tenants through a grant of 'franchise' from the king, though certain serious crimes, such as murder, killing the king's deer, and highway robbery, were known as 'pleas of the Crown' and were almost always heard in royal courts. If a lord like a Cistercian abbot had extensive civil and criminal jurisdiction his courts were presided over by himself or by the steward or seneschal when required. He did not necessarily visit every manor, and most courts in most manors would have been concerned merely with local issues.

It is commonly agreed that manors each consisted of up to three classes of land: demesne, the part directly controlled by the lord and used for the benefit of his household and dependents; serf or villein holdings carrying the obligation that the peasant household supply the lord with specified labour services or a part of its output subject to the custom of the manor; and free peasant land owing money rent fixed at the time of the lease, without such obligations but otherwise subject to manorial jurisdiction and custom. Villeins could have holdings of up to 30 acres and so had most of the strips. The thirty acres were not a compact unit but a package of strips in the various ploughed fields in the manor, the strip being a certain number of furrows. (An acre could be 22 yards wide or 44 furrows.) They usually had to work three days a week on the demesne land of the lord. Those whose tenancy was from the lord of the manor were called copyholders. (This was called copyhold as distinct from the socage of those higher up the social scale. It seems to have been usual in the later Middle Ages to change villeinage into copyhold, doubtless accompanied by a fine.) Beneath these were cottagers or cottars (*cotarius* in the Domesday Book) who lived in cottages, cultivated a small garden and worked as day labourers on other people's land. Then there were servants, male and female of all kinds, indoor and outdoor, herdsmen, fishermen, wildfowlers, farm labourers, and so on.

Tenants of the same manor assembled in manorial court or court baron, of which they were the judges. Enforcement of decisions rested on the officials appointed by the court. Where the lord of the manor had a demesne farm, the manor court appointed a reeve to supervise the farming activities, using labour services and collecting rents. Usually at Michaelmas the reeve presented an annual account to the seneschal. This was an account of all who had discharged their obligations (or had not), changes of ownership, successions, disputes, fires, depredations, and such like. Additional sources of income for the lord included charges for use of his mill, bakery or wine-press, or for the right to hunt or to let pigs feed in his woodland, as well as court revenues and single payments on each change of tenant (*Wikipedia* 'Manorialism', Hinde, *The Domesday Book* 16-17). The villeins in places seem to have attended the manor court and formed part of a jury. The villeins were by far the most numerous of the land holders, and it is likely they were the free tenants in pre-Norman day who had their status reduced when feudalism was introduced as happened also in Ireland. They were unfree only in the sense that they could not attend the hundred, county, or honorial courts.

In open field areas the tenants lived in a common village, which usually held the parish church, a tiny building. Each tenant was allocated a number of strips in accordance with the size of his holding in such a manner that each got his share of the good and bad land. The use of other lands, wastes, woods and waters was also allocated in proportion. The number of cows, pigs, geese etc. each family was allowed to have on the common land, or common was decided. In manor courts, the local lord or his steward dealt with disputes among those who were free of his manor court. Practical matters like the days of labour owed to the lord, and when they were due were explained at these courts. So too, in the three-field system of cultivation, the allocation of strips, the choice and rotation of crops, the charges at the mill, the fallowing of a field, and the multifarious duties of the manor were dealt with. This agricultural structure was probably in place before the coming of the Normans, and they found it very useful (Dyer 'Economy and Society' 144). It was left to the lord of the manor to provide the village church and priest.

By the end of the Middle Ages the openfield farming system was in decline. Money rents were becoming common. The distinctions between copyholder, villein, serf and slave virtually disappeared. Enclosures and consolidation of holdings became frequent with consequent loss of pasture, pannage, turbary, and such like. The large farmers or strong farmers became known in history as yeoman farmers. Many others were reduced to the status of hired labour either on the larger farms or in the towns. Hired labour and cash rents were preferred to days of labour.

Where the manor was not divided into open fields with villages as in the Highland zone the manorial court functioned in a similar fashion and all rents and dues were collected in a similar fashion. A picture comes from the earldom of Ulster. The lands of the manor were not necessarily in the one place. The manor was a fiscal centre where the tenants went to pay their dues. Locally, there would have been vills which consisted of wooden hall situated on a defensible motte. The mill of the manor would have been fairly close to the vill which was not a village but a unit of land in the manorial system more of less corresponding to an ecclesiastical parish. (See further on cantref below.) Only the ground corn would have been taken to the lord's own house. The demesne land was let out to individual tenants who paid their rents and dues in kind. The manors (a Norman term) seem to have been taken over from the earlier Gaelic local lord unchanged (McNeill 88-89). Those who worked the lands were in many cases betaghs who were taken over and re-settled (McNeill, 98). (On the pattern of agriculture in Wales see G.R.G Jones 'Patterns of Settlement'.)

The Normans of the Marches

Around 1066, the Welsh chiefs like their Irish counterparts were warring among themselves. Apparently, neither Harold Godwinson nor

William the Conqueror had any plans to subdue Wales, but only to prevent the emergence of a powerful single chief or prince who could carry on more aggressively Welsh attacks on English counties (Evans, 156, Kearney, 62). William, following the pattern of Charlemagne, established three earldoms with quasi regal delegated powers to block Welsh attacks. Among the powers was one to build castles, and another to make war without having to refer to the king for permission. The king might be in Normandy. On the death of the strong chief Gruff *ap* Llywelyn in 1063 south Wales was again split among weak local rulers, and the Normans were ready to take advantage. To the south in 1091 Robert Fitzhamon advanced as far as Cardiff. By 1093 Bernard of Newmarch had established himself in Brecon.

In the marches and in other parts of the Highland Zone the unit of landholding and administration was not the manor but the more ancient *cantref*. It was this system rather than the manorial system that the Normans introduced into Ireland where it was called a cantred. A cantref nominally consisted of a hundred vills, i.e. groupings of hamlets and homesteads. The vills were interdependent and intercommoned, sharing pasturing rights, fishing rights, and access to woodland in other districts of the cantref, and rendering food rents, to the lord of the cantred, his nobles and officials. It was possible to halve a cantref for it was comprised of two commotes. It was possible also to assign the renders of a vill or a number of scattered vills to individuals. It was possible to assign a package of rights and services drawn from the scattered parts of the whole. It was not readily possible to divide it by carving it up into self-contained economic units or manors without destroying its complex social and economic structure (Warren 'King John and Ireland', 36). (It is probably right to assume that this system was used all over England before the open-field system was adopted.)

Part 3

Irish Society 1170 to 1513

Chapter 3

Ireland in the Twelfth Century

General

Source material on the social aspects of life is better for this period that for the preceding one. Unfortunately most of it comes from the Norman/English-speaking regions. English social historians have vastly greater sources of information from surviving records. With regard to the Gaelic areas, we have the earlier law codes, genealogies and annals, and also descriptions in English from Elizabethan times. The Brehon Law codes had fossilised. When researching for my earlier book, *The True Origins of Irish Society*, I founded it very difficult to get an exact idea of how the society actually functioned. We have more information on English-speaking areas, and this information can be supplemented from English sources.

Documentary evidence regarding most aspects of social organisation in Ireland is normally lacking. I therefore make some assumptions. If some piece of technology or some form of social organisation was in any part of Ireland we can assume that it was *known* about in all parts of Ireland. It might not be *adopted* or not adopted immediately. If we know from Norman sources about the organisation of manors, given the possibilities of the time, there must have been an equivalent structure in Gaelic areas. Usually, the Anglo-Norman lords and their successors had more up-to-date and efficient versions of something. If the Gaelic lords saw a point in adopting it in their own circumstances they did.

While it is fairly easy to construct a general outline of the history of Ireland and the structure of the central Government in Dublin in the Middle Ages it is more difficult to determine what was happening in the Norman lordships, and often nigh impossible to discover what was happening within the Gaelic lordships especially at local level. (Though the infighting of the various chiefs and who won is usually scrupulously recorded.) The kinds of records which enable English historians to reconstruct life in England simply were not kept, or if kept were not prized and preserved. Those who wrote things down were not interested in the common people or their affairs. Local chiefs kept their courts but no records were kept. The legal corpus was never updated, still less modernised. Genealogists were engrossed in the claims, real or manufactured, to property and status of their employers and nobody else. Annalists were haphazard in what they recorded.

Besides these earlier native records there are various descriptions of the Irish in Tudor times by English observers. That these descriptions were often hostile and prejudiced does not invalidate them. They are a useful check on what can be gleaned from other sources. Clothing, food, weapons, lordships, courts, markets towns, ships etc. etc. were basically the same. Political and social organisation did not differ greatly between Normandy, England, Scotland, Ireland and Wales. Forms of warfare were limited by the technology of the time, and the cost and availability of materials. Administration was circumscribed by the fact that few laymen could read and write. Effective groups were limited to a size where the individuals could recognise each other and communicate with each other by speech.

Still a considerable amount of information is available even about even Gaelic life in the Middle Ages. Records were kept about quite a number of things concerning the central government and its relations with England. Some information is available about the internal affairs of some of the Norman lordships. It is fairly easy to reconstruct what the external affairs of the chiefs of the major Gaelic families were about. But about the internal affairs of their lordships there is virtually nothing.

It is possible to place Irish society in the 12th century within the general development of Europe. Some things in Ireland had remained virtually unchanged in some respects from the Early Iron Age up to the 19th century. For example, many aspects of agriculture in the spade-using plots in the mountains and boggy part of Ireland had scarcely changed. Also, the rural character of Irish society based on the local 'big house' of the local ruling family was unchanged. Warfare was in many ways unchanged from the Iron Age or Bronze Age. Weapons of war were edged weapons like swords, knives, or spears in their various shapes and forms which might have changes in fashion but remained essentially the same. Military tactics were primitive, the wild charge, the attacking and battering with sword, spear and shield like at a 19th century faction fight, until one side broke and fled, usually after a short encounter. Wars came and went, but it is difficult to determine how often a particular parish was affected. Armies were small but the passage of either a friendly or unfriendly army was likely to be equally disastrous, except that the friendly army might not burn so many houses.

Houses, even of the rich, changed very little. The hall (*aula*) of the local chief or lords was a long low thatched house of wood and wattle, usually with a loft for sleeping of a kind still found at the end of the 18th century. The hall was probably surrounded by a fence like an African kraal, though the chief did not live in a village as we would understand the word. His kraal or *lios* would however house numerous families of servants, cooks, tradesmen, washerwomen and so on. The custom of surrounding the hall with an earthen bank which has left traces of so many 'ringforts' in Ireland seems to have died out after 1000 AD. There were no towns properly so-called but the enclosures of the monasteries and greater chiefs would have been larger and included wattle-and-daub huts for hundreds of people, some of whom were professional soldiers. The lowest rank of lord or chief, the *ógláech* would have had about 1,000 acres to support him by the end of the Middle Ages. By that time the allodial land possession of the farmers had passed to the chiefs, so the organisation of the *ógláech*'s estate would have been more or less identical with that of a knight, his equivalent in rank, with its rents, food renders, and days of service. Most people would have lived within 2 or 3 miles of the 'big house' and it would have formed the centre of their lives. The place where they lived would have been the equivalent of the modern parish. They would have paid their rents or dues to the seneschal or steward. The lives of those who lived in the big house would have been like that described by Sir Jonah Barrington in the 18th century, hunting, shooting, drinking, and joining any war that happened to be going on. The phases of the moon were always important for if there was no moon there was no light at night.

There were of course changes. The use of the horse in warfare, with weapons and tactics, suitable for horse warfare was coming in. So too was the use of mail for those who could afford it. In agriculture, the ox team and the great plough changed the agricultural scene in many places, though in other places the old ways remained. Apart from ecclesiastical or defensive building the use of stone was rare. Only at the end of the Middle Ages did Gaelic chiefs start building castles. In many places the building of boats with a leather skin over a wicker frame was to continue until the 19th century.

It should be kept in mind that there was no such a thing as a struggle by the 'native' Irish against the 'foreign overlord'. Such was completely contrary to the mentality of the age, even if any of the clans could have afforded it. A list is given of the leading Gaelic families in Ireland. Every one of these was engaged in a constant struggle with its immediate neighbours to gain land or to protect land. Life was taken up with manoeuvring for advantage. The stronger clans won and increased their land, while the lesser ones disappeared from history. Every war until the end of the Tudor period was a local war. Only one of the great Norman lords, the Earl of Desmond, seems to have entertained the idea of establishing himself as an independent king of Ireland after the example of Scotland. He lacked ruthlessness of Robert the Bruce and quickly abandoned the idea.

The Dark Ages in Ireland (432-1169)

There was an Early Medieval Warm phase, c.750-1200 when conditions were relatively clement in Europe and North America, allowing settlement in inhospitable parts of Greenland, reducing the problems of ice on the coast of Iceland, and allowing widespread cultivation of the vine in England. Irish monks and Viking warriors reached far out into the Atlantic. Cereals could be cultivated in most of Ireland. The Church in Ireland developed in an idiosyncratic manner and in the 12th century it was being brought into line with contemporary norms in the rest of Western Europe. Much of the distortion seems to have been caused by the custom of giving extensive grants of lands to monasteries and not cathedrals with the result that bishoprics were poorly endowed.

Travelling conditions in Ireland closely resembled those regions in East Africa in the nineteenth century which also depended largely on cattle-rearing. The foreign merchants on the coasts, with local guides and supported by friendly chiefs, could travel to the more inhabited inland places. Wine merchants from Gaul, or their native agents, went as far as the great monastery of Clonmacnoise in the centre of Ireland (Ó Corráin 71). At the same time small settlements were to be found in remote spots. We can surmise that these were occupied by weaker groups driven from more fertile areas by stronger groups. Some parts, especially of central Munster seem to have been entirely uninhabited. The settled areas formed only a small part of the total area.

The whole Gaelic system was geared for the benefit of the ruling families in a cattle-rearing society. Tilled crops were very vulnerable to destruction by invading forces, whereas cattle could be driven to hiding places. Deterioration in climate, or a loss of population through plague, could allow the cattle-rearing culture again to triumph. It is quite surprising, having regard to what was happening in much of Europe, there seems to have been very little reclamation of land in the Middle Ages. A distribution of monasteries founded in the period 1100 to 1500 is little different from that of monasteries founded in the period 600 to 1100.

While long distance travel was restricted, and there were no invasions, it must not be imagined that there was no contact with the neighbouring island or the Continent. From 580 onwards Irish monks travelled especially to south Germany just over the former Roman frontier. They would have travelled most of the way on Roman roads. Travel in Merovingian Gaul was not exceptionally hazardous. There is evidence of many contacts, even before the coming of the Vikings. Irish art and Northumbrian art were scarcely distinguishable. Irish art was also strongly influenced by Viking art. Viking weapons had been adopted and rudimentary castle-building had been commenced. The Irish learned to fight on the sea. Irish chiefs from the north of Ireland interfered in Scotland, and some from Leinster in Wales, but military contacts were sporadic. Contacts with Rome had been established. The new calculation of the date of Easter was accepted in 630. Economically Ireland lagged behind England, as did Scotland and Wales. But this was not uniform. Yet almost anyone coming to Ireland from England or North West France or the Low Countries could see obvious room for the latest improvements. Trade between Ireland and the Continent had continued throughout the Dark Ages on a small scale. Every year wine and olive oil had to be imported for religious services, while the chiefs relished wine rather than poor local ale. The traders would come to rendezvous points on the coasts. As the chiefdoms were consolidated from around a hundred to about thirty of medium rank, every chief sought to get a toehold at least on the coast or on a navigable river.

The O'Neills kept all this trade in their own hands in their own territories and would not allow towns. But most of the great chiefs preferred to control the Viking towns. These towns were originally small trading posts established at defensible points on the coasts, and usually in marginal lands not controlled by any of the great chiefs. Though originally raiders, the Vikings became great traders. In their wooden towns, defended with wooden fencing, a considerable variety of goods could be safely stored. Wooden quays and wharfs could be constructed where goods could be landed. Though called Vikings there can be no doubt that by the 12th century most of the inhabitants of the towns were of mixed Viking-Irish stock. When the Normans arrived, Dublin, Waterford, Cork, and Limerick were probably on a par with similar ports on the other side of the Irish Sea.

General Conditions in the Middle Ages

It is essential to purge modern geographic ideas from our minds. There were no real maps of Ireland apart from the coasts. Lydon reproduces an Italian map of 1339 which is a slight improvement on Ptolemy. It indicates the various ports where ships called. It is called Hirlanda, which tells us the name of the island in the Middle Ages. In Latin it was and remained Hibernia (Lydon, *Ireland in the later Middle Ages*, 1). Places mentioned were more numerous on the east and south coasts, less frequent on the west coast, and virtually absent on the north coast. No inland points are noted.

We must too go back in mind to a time when there were no roads, no towns, no permanent fences or boundaries, no clocks, no books, no machinery, no coal or oil, no glass in windows where there were any, almost no literacy, no democracy, mostly no money, few stone buildings, little pottery or metal vessels, almost no metal in everyday use, iron being used almost exclusively for weapons and armour and wood for domestic furniture and vessels. The use of coins was rare, and most workers probably never handled them. Some skills in limited occupations were extremely high, as we see in ornamental metal work, swords, and the illumination of manuscripts. But their products were never used by ordinary people.

In Tudor times, an era of map-making, the Government realised that it needed a map of Ireland. By 1599, when Boazio's map was ready, about three quarters of Ireland was mapped with some accuracy, though far from Ordnance Survey standards. There were many suitable places for ambush. As in France in the 18th century, the merchant, missionary, or traveller went from customs post to customs post as he entered each local *tuath* (barony). (A *tuath*, plural *tuatha*, genitive *tuaithe*, was the original district ruled by the lowest rank of independent chiefs. It might cover an area of about ten miles by twenty miles. Estimates of the number of *tuatha* at any one time vary from 150 to 180.)

Like most of northern Europe at the time, Irish society was rural. Life revolved around the houses of the great and lesser lords, and the monasteries and bishoprics. But landless men could hire land from the owner who might be a lord. He could demand the return in the form of days' labour in his own fields, or in so many days lodging for himself and his retinue. This was called coshering. Clientship involved giving cattle to the client, who returned a percentage of the calves. Its chief purpose apparently was to enrich the lords and to give them status. Other dues and taxes to chiefs took the form of gifts, for gift culture was as prominent in Ireland as elsewhere. The profits from a successful cattle raid or slave raid were distributed by the chief. He and those to whom he distributed the cattle could lease them out to others for a percentage return.

It was surprisingly easy for a society to function without money, and indeed it seems that in many parts of rural Ireland money was rarely used until at least the 18th century. There were commonly recognised equivalent values of goods and services. Many duties could be discharged by days of labour, or by cows. One unit of value was a heifer called a *sét*, and six *séts* equalled a *cumal*, a slave woman, at least according to Brehon Law. Later, as elsewhere, the practice grew of using an ounce of silver divided into 24 parts. (Ó Corráin, 73). There were no common measures for anything, time, distance, weights or measures. An acre or a ploughland was an approximation, and not necessarily the same from district to district.

Between equals, and for smaller amounts, some normally traded articles were probably used as a means of exchange if there was no direct swap. Fish could be swapped for grain. Wool could be swapped for linen. But a piece of woven cloth would be universally acceptable, and relatively permanent. It is more likely the system of gift and obligation applied. The acceptance of several small gifts like quarts of ale could result in a much larger obligation when called in. The system obviously worked satisfactorily in many places. As the smallest coin produced was the silver penny it would have been of little use in everyday transactions such as buying a pot of ale.

Few people could read or write. Such learning as there was committed to memory, and only of use in the courts of chiefs to which ordinary people had no access. Most of the rural clergy were likely to be illiterate and to have committed the services to memory. Customs and verdicts were committed to memory for there were no court records. Genealogies, which were claims to rights real or fictitious, were memorised. This was common in Europe at the time. Boundaries were determined by asking older men under oath to state where they were. Local custom was committed to memory. Counting could be done on fingers and based on the number twelve which was easily divided and multiplied. Only the literate could use Roman numerals. The handy 'Arabic' numerals had not reached the West. Physicians were only for the very rich.

Most skills were rustic. Fields for tillage were small and shifting. Impermanent wattle fences were often to keep animals out, not animals in. Spinning was done with the distaff and spindle. Local weavers produced a rough unfinished cloth. Grain was ground with the quern. Most cooking, in the absence of metal or pottery vessels, was perhaps done using a hay box. Brewing was primitive. Tools and utensils were made of wood. By the twelfth century most houses would have used thin ash or hazel poles in the roof which was then covered with thatch. Boats had a basket-like frame covered with hides, rough but sea-worthy, and which could sail only with the wind. Fishing boats seem to have catered only for their own local needs. The skills of foreign masons as displayed in Mellifont Abbey, the 'great monastery', were set off by garish colours. There was little or no internal trade, each district producing what it needed. Some local trade was to develop around market towns. No doubt similar local markets were to be found in the neighbourhood of monastic towns, or the *lios* or *rath* of a chief.

Ireland, unlike Scotland, never produced a university or any school of higher education, throughout the Middle Ages, though it is not obvious why not. The numbers of proficient Latin scholars were probably equal in both countries. All scholars had to go abroad for higher education after acquiring the necessary proficiency in Latin. But without universities to systematically train young men in the higher branches of learning there were probably few really learned men. Systematic training of the parochial clergy did not antedate the Reformation. Nor did the theology of the Medieval Church require it. Literacy and the availability of books and records are different things. A library (*bibliotheca*) could be merely a large box. Increasingly, all clerics and more and more laymen could read, perhaps letters or parts of the bible.

Like elsewhere in Europe merchants banded together and armed themselves, travelling in compact groups from walled town to walled town by daylight only. Packhorses had to be used so traded goods had to be relatively compact and expensive and relatively close to a small local port. The merchant families were foreigners, and all trade was in the hands of foreigners, and limited to the needs of chiefs and monasteries. Such towns as existed were tiny, and at the beginning all of them were ports. They were often as far upstream as a shallow-draught boat could sail, and where a ford crossed the river. They had to have a sheltered body of water, where the boats could be safely kept in the winter-time. They had to be small enough to be defensible, with tiny houses within them, and with only a handful of short streets. Finally, they had to have fields outside the walls, for growing crops, and keeping animals. The houses in both towns and countryside were almost invariably of wood, or wood and wattle, and roofed with thatch. They were easily burned in time of war. This was typical of North European towns, though the Irish towns were smaller than most.

Ireland too at the time was not a political entity. To adapt a well-known comment about Italy, it was 'a geographical expression'. The idea of nation was used in the university of Paris for organisational purposes, the English being lumped with the Germans (Hindley, 11). What local customs there were in each *tuath,* what local weights and measures were used in each of them, or what local prices for goods or labour were we have no idea. It would be extraordinary if Ireland had a common set of these when nobody else in Europe had. Many chiefs strove to establish a permanent 'high kingship' over the whole of Ireland, but none successfully for long. Two attempts were made in the 12th century to establish a hierarchy, and resulted in the establishment of four equal provinces under four archbishops.

The problem with Ireland, as with Wales and Scotland, was geographical. There were five or six areas of population and cultivation where the top grade of chief, the *ri ruirech* or provincial or paramount chief could emerge. The boundaries of these provinces were marked mountains, bogs, and forests. Though great efforts were made by five of the provincial families to establish an overlord (*ard ri*) over the whole of Ireland, none was successful for long. Ireland as an entity to defend, to fight and die for, did not exist. Such concepts did not exist. There were hierarchies of families each one striving to better itself, or to avoid being swallowed up. These families, whether they spoke Gaelic, French, or English or Norse freely intermarried. The use of the Gaelic language was not necessarily an obstacle. Languages are adopted or dropped whenever there is an advantage for change.

A characteristic of medieval society was its sheer brutality and cruelty. It was observed that the Ten Commandments were observed only in monasteries, if there. Raiding, including slave-raiding was commonplace. Torture of prisoners and blinding of rivals and the execution of hostages were customary. Nobody expected justice from the more powerful except it was in the interest of the powerful man. Coveting and seizing of land was what all the powerful families did. Wives were moved around, sent back or got rid off when no longer useful. Extortion from the poor was the norm. This was true of Gaelic and Norman lords and sheriffs of counties. Gifts of alms and gifts to churches were intended to offset these offences. The more successful the warrior the more land he had to give to the Church, a noted fact among both Gaelic and Norman lords. Thieves, robbers and outlaws abounded so that towns provided themselves with walls and merchants travelled in armed groups. In these aspects Ireland was no different from the rest of Western Europe.

The Land: Geographical Aspects

Ireland is an island in the Atlantic off the northwest flank of the European Continent. The island is 300 miles in length on its northeast-southwest axis, and 185 miles in breadth at its widest point. Surface drainage was often poor, and where the underlying rocks came close to the surface, almost impossible. Ireland was described as a land of woods, bogs and lakes (Nichols, 5). There are about 4,000 lakes in Ireland most of them quite small. The land surrounding them was usually badly drained. Almost everywhere in Ireland drainage was essential for tillage. This was true with regard to the great Central Plain. In such places Ireland's famous bog lands formed. Towards the north of Ireland the clay had been moulded into small steep-sided hills usually described as resembling the surface of a basket of eggs. This is the drumlin belt. Drainage, and so communications, was poor in this area, and it was one of the last in which agriculture improved. In the west the rainfall over much of the region is so high and leaching of the soil so great that bogs form the natural surface cover of even limestone soils provided the slope is not too great. Ireland proved to be poor in minerals. Considerable efforts were made to find them and to develop mining, but the pockets located were invariably small, and often quickly exhausted (Freeman; Keenan, *Pre-Famine Ireland*).

With great areas of fairly low but barren hills, extensive bogs, swampy river basins and extensive forests Ireland was naturally suited militarily for defence. Even small clans could hold out for centuries in their own defensive spot against predatory neighbours. Meath was probably the largest and richest region of good agricultural land with the greatest density of population yet this could not be translated into military supremacy. On the other hand, the Northern *Ui Neill* from the poorest province were probably the most successful military family, but neither could they establish permanent military overlordship.

The rivers tend to flow outwards towards the sea, and are mostly quite short. (The Shannon however, at 240 miles, is the longest river in the British Isles. Lough Neagh at 151 square miles is the largest lake in the British Isles.) They may have insufficient water for navigation or power in dry summers (Freeman, 53). There would have been flooding in winter time along the banks of most rivers and lakes. Oats, and grass and later potatoes, cope better with the climate than wheat or barley. On the other hand, as waterpower was developed, the swiftly flowing rivers provided many sites for mills near the coast

Almost the whole of the country is covered with glacial drift or till, deep in some parts but shallow in others. In some places the drift has weathered to soils exceedingly fertile and suitable for ploughing; in other places the shallow soils over the moisture-soaked clays produce very good grass, but are unsuitable for tillage. The soils are often infertile podzolic in structure, but acid brown soils are found in the east and boggy soils in the west. These soils promote the growth of bogs (Bellamy). In some areas west of the Shannon the drift was thin over the porous limestone rock and provided excellent grazing for sheep. They corresponded in this respect to the chalk downs in England. Soils suitable for tillage are to be found in every part of Ireland but more abundantly in the eastern half. But tiny patches of good soil can be found everywhere even in the midst of bogs and mountains.

Climate, Soil and Vegetation

The climate of Ireland is typical of a large part of North Western Europe and was commonly described as equable without any great extremes. Climatologists, using various techniques, have studied the history of the variations in earth's climate. Towards the end of the last Ice Age, about 30000 years BC the earth began to warm, and caused the Ice Age to end. By 15000 BC the Ice Age was considered to be over, but the warming continued until around 5000 BC, the post-glacial climatic optimum, at an average annual temperature of around 16 degrees. In the later-Roman period the temperature may have fallen, but a warming phase was in force from 900 AD to 1300 AD, the medieval optimum (Pretty, 12; Bellamy, 125-8). It was followed by the Neoglacial Period (Little Ice Age) of glacier growth which started about 550 years ago with a return to colder climatic conditions c. 1400 to c. 1890, during which valley glaciers re-advanced in the Alps, and Swedish Lapland. The decline in the later Middle Ages is well attested notably by the difficulty the Danes had in getting to their settlements on the coast of

Greenland which were wiped out (Pretty, 'Sustainable Agriculture in the Middle Ages: The English Manor').

According to Pretty the all-year wet and cold conditions in the late 7th century began to give way to drier and warmer summers and markedly colder winters. The difference in temperature between 800 A.D, and 1300 A.D. is estimated to be about 1 degree, while rainfall fell by about 10%, and also shifted from summer to the rest of the year, so that summers during 1250-1300 were some ten per cent drier than during the late Anglo-Saxon era. Analysing date from 14 manors of the bishop of Winchester in the south of England, he showed considerable variation according to the times of year the rain fell. It is fair assumption that similar variations were to be found all over the British Isles. Differences however in the tillage belt of eastern Ireland, from county Down, through Meath and Kildare as far as Limerick and north Kerry are not likely to be great. Bellamy notes that west of a line down the middle of Ireland, where rainfall exceeds the capacity to run off bogs are likely to develop, the open-field system was never introduced (Bellamy, 127).

The rainfall is abundant, but not excessive. It is fairly equally distributed throughout the year, and the drying of the soil in summer is to be attributed to increased evaporation. Rainfall forms a gradient from west to east with from 30-40 inches in the east, 40-50 inches in the centre, and 50-70 inches in the west. Snow is fairly rare and in many winters there is no snow. In a typical year snow might fall on between 10 and 20 days in the year, and would rarely lie for more than a few days. The variability of the rainfall, especially excessive precipitation during the autumn in some years, imposes restrictions on tillage. (Trade, pilgrimages, and warfare normally had to cease in wintertime.) There would have been flooding in winter time along the banks of most rivers and lakes. As noted above, the warmer dryer summers of the early Middle Ages permitted the cultivation of cereals further west and north, and further up the mountains than in the 20th century. On the other hand, as waterpower was developed, the swiftly flowing rivers provided many sites for mills near the coast. Ireland later tended to be more developed in the maritime counties than in the inland ones, but this does not seem to have been the case in the early Middle Ages when the great chiefdoms were mostly inland. Lesser, often tiny, chiefdoms were to be found along the coasts.

Like most of Western Europe Ireland belongs climatically to the temperate Atlantic province whose natural covering is oak and birch forests. Though grass grows well the natural cover is woodland and uncultivated land is rapidly covered in scrub. Over large parts of Ireland, particularly in the wetter western areas, but on the mountains everywhere with a heavy rainfall and not too steep slopes, the immediate vegetation cover was bog plants, especially mosses, rushes and heathers (Bellamy 58). Even in the 12th century much of the country was still covered by either forests or bogs. Forests were extensive even in western regions where nowadays only widespread bogs are found. Around the settled areas in much of the woodland all the better timber had probably been removed for fuel and house building, though in parts of Munster and in Wicklow great oak woods stood until the end of the Middle Ages. In a cattle-raiding society woods were necessary to hide cattle in time of invasion. The timber too could be plashed across the tracks to baulk the invaders. Defences of even small *tuatha* could be very effective. Everywhere there were places, at times very small, where some tillage was possible, and where scrubland and half regenerated forests could support cattle. Cattle-grazing, especially by the great herds of the chiefs, should be regarded as taking place in semi-open woodland.

Forests covered large parts of Ireland even in the west which today are covered with bogs. Woods were to be found along rivers, on the margins of bogs, and even on the mountains in the west. In south Leinster there was a great wood filled with wild pigs, red deer, and wolves. There were almost no hedges or walls (Nichols, 5). As the population grows woodlands get cut back. By 1170 much of the woodland was cleared from Meath, and by the end of the Middle Ages much of The Pale was virtually treeless. There was less clearance of woods in the Gaelic areas but heavy overgrazing prevents the natural regeneration of timber. The great destruction of Irish woods commenced in the 17th century. The temperate broad-leaved deciduous forest once removed naturally regenerates to its primitive state with the widespread exception that in the wetter boggier areas it turns to bog plants. When fields were abandoned after being exhausted by several years of cropping they quickly reverted to scrub which could be browsed by animals. This provides a rich environment for birds and animals, especially even-toed (cloven hoofed) ruminants like cattle, sheep, pigs and deer, that browse the leaves of shrubs, forest plants, and grasses. Pollen analysis shows the use and abandonment of sites over longer terms (Bellamy 126-7). In many places, as elsewhere in Europe, when the primitive woods were cleared by early farmers, the forests could not regenerate, but formed bogs or heaths (Bellamy 93). Though grass grows well it is not the natural cover for Ireland.

Tillage, and in particular the cultivation of cereals provides more food per acre than pastoralism. Pastoral societies tend to be less dense than tillage-based ones. But cattle, pigs, sheep and goats can thrive on mast from forest trees, grasses and shrubs unsuitable for human consumption. The Normans, after they arrived, realised that much of eastern Ireland could be turned over to tillage without great difficulty. Norman expansion of modern methods was limited by climate. Ireland was on the limit for the profitable cultivation of wheat, taking bad years with good. Indeed, it has been since the Middle Ages at the limit of profitable tillage. It was noted that the Anglo-Norman families occupied only those parts of Ireland suitable for their system of tillage. In the earldom of Ulster all the manors and associated parishes were below the 500 foot contour, though there is some evidence of cultivation up to 800 feet (McNeill, 83).

Communications

When Henry Morton Stanley set out from Zanzibar in 1871 in the direction of the Great Lakes there were numerous trading posts, Arab and Portuguese, along the coast. But inland there were no roads, nor bridges, nor navigable rivers. There were tracks known to local guides and used by traders and slave raiders. The whole land was filled with warring tribes. The tracks led from one fording point on a river to the next. At all times a strong armed guard was required and gifts had to be given to every chief through whose territory the expedition passed. Malaria and other diseases were rife. In the wet season when the rivers were high travel was impossible. A traveller travelled from ford to ford and stopped when the river was high. In Ireland with similar conditions the tracks were almost impassable in winter. Oddly, across the Central Plain from Dublin to the Shannon, a region of bogs and poor drainage, terminal moraines called eskers left by the Ice Age form raised ridges of gravel which facilitate travel. North of these lies the drumlin belt of small rounded hills about 500 yards long by 250 yards wide, the spaces between them being boggy. Apparently most foreign merchants rarely ventured inland and their maps just showed coastal settlements (Lydon, *Ireland*, 1)

When a new justiciar or Lord Deputy arrived in Dublin he would find a port not very different from Chester or Bristol. Nor would the sea journey of about 100 miles mostly in sight of land on one side or the other be difficult in summer. The castle of Dublin was like any other castle and Dublin like any other town. But with regard to the rest of the country he would have to ask his officials. They would know roughly in what direction the great chiefdoms lay, their estimated military force, how many days' journey it would take to reach them, and the principal monasteries in each direction. Distances were measured in times not miles. From merchants too he would glean information about the various ports and landing places around the coasts and which chieftains dealt at each port. Inland traders would provide him with information about inland routes and their difficulties at various times of the year. They could tell him too whether particular routes could support large armies and for how long.

There were several well-known long distance routes in Ireland. Calling them roads is misleading. The main route from Dublin to Munster followed roughly the line of the railway from Dublin to Cork and Limerick through Laois and north Tipperary. When this route became unsafe in the later Middle Ages an alternative route was found down the Barrow valley through and Kilkenny into Tipperary. Travel between Ulster and Meath was virtually restricted to two routes, one to the east and one to the west, though local pathways through the bogs and woods in-between did exist and were known to local guides. From Donegal the chief route led into north Connaught and was the scene of constant warfare. As late as 1690 there was only one route from Carrickfergus and Belfast into North Leinster with few wide places between the woods where an army could deploy. Travel was virtually impossible in winter time. The great advantage of monastic cloisters was that it allowed the monks to go dryfoot from one part of the monastery to another, and especially into the church.

For local journeys stretches of various rivers and lakes were used. But the systems of rivers and lakes were not joined together. The Shannon and its tributaries were navigable at certain times of the year, but in other the waters were either too high and fast or too low. The same was true of rivers flowing into Lough Neagh. A much greater problem lies in the fact that the rivers fall off the edge of the central plateau quite close to the coast, and so are of little use for navigation and commerce. River transport was not available for sea going ships, so imports and exports would have to be trans-shipped after a portage. River craft were often light coracles and were probably used in very shallow water

It is however notable that five of the six counties of Northern Ireland touch Lough Neagh, though the frontage of County Down is nowadays reduced to a tiny amount between Antrim and Armagh. Donegal too manages to get a tiny toehold on Lough Erne, which would seem to indicate that an opening on to inland waterways was valued. The long lakes could be used for trade or military purposes. The O'Neills of Tyrone too managed to secure a few miles of the shore of Carlingford Lough between County Down and County Louth. The Boyne in county Meath was an exception. Dublin, which had a poor harbour, and poor connections with the interior however emerged as the largest port.

Population, Growth and Constraints

With the trade routes re-opened, and much of eastern Ireland suitable for modernisation in the military, economic, and commercial senses, there came at last a great flood of nett immigration of farmers, craftsmen, and traders, the small people that nobody in the Middle Ages bothered to record. It is not clear why this modernisation had not proceeded earlier, but it may have depended on conditions in England which was then prepared to accept imports of wheat, leather, or flour. The results, economically, where recorded were spectacular. The income of single parishes in Ulster became greater than whole Irish dioceses. Still in those areas where it was successful a market economy was established, and there was more to trade than mere 'fruits of the forest' chiefly furs.

It is estimated that the population of Ireland in the 12th century was around half a million, which was also the estimate for Roman times, but it could have been considerably less, and also varied a great deal from diseases famines and migrations both inwards and outwards. The population may have peaked at over a million or a million and a half around 1300 A.D. as did the British population. In these centuries of colonisation there was a great inflow of immigrants from Britain. These were concentrated along the east coast, but were quite few in Ulster (McNeill, 122). As all the towns were in this region of colonisation, it is supposed that the Black Death caused greater mortality than in the more dispersed populations of the rural areas. The Great European Famine of 1315-17, coinciding as it did with the widespread devastation of the Bruce invasions, probably caused a greater reduction in population than the Black Death itself. There were also repeated epidemics in the second half of the 14th century. The population may have fallen back to as little as half a million again (Clarke 'Population' *Medieval Ireland*; Barry, *Archaeology of Medieval Ireland*, 177). Probably half the population was in English-speaking areas by that time, though they covered only a third of the whole country. Gaelic areas were under-populated and indeed, some borderlands between great chiefdoms may have lost the bulk of their populations through the systematic wasting of their lands (Duffy, P. J. 'Geographical perspectives', 15).

Irish Society: Social Structure

The culture of Ireland and its social structure, when the Normans arrived, bore an extraordinary resemblance to those of the cattle-rearing cultures of Sub-Saharan Africa in the 19th century. There were trading settlements all along the coast. There were no roads, only tracks. The people dwelt in huts in round kraals. The kraal of a chief was only a bit more imposing than ordinary kraals. The chief was guarded by a body of warriors carrying spears. He also had his religious advisors whom the Europeans called 'witchdoctors'. The chief, perhaps with lesser chiefs near him, conducted his business in the open air. All traders had to present their goods before him first, accompanied with a suitable 'gift'. There were local chiefs and paramount chiefs and somewhere a local 'king'. Wealth was counted in cattle, and the chief occupation of the chiefs was to raid other chiefs to steal their cattle. This gave an opportunity to 'blood' young warriors against the time they were needed in a real battle. Craftsmen were able to produce extraordinary art with the most primitive equipment.

Irish society was constantly changing and the kind of society described in the Brehon Law lasted only a short time. The chief of the local *tuath (ri tuaithe)* was no longer the pivotal person, but the chief of the province *(ri ruirech)*. By the twelfth century these latter had gathered most of the powers into their own hands. They claimed the right within their own province to appoint and depose rulers, and to seize and dispose of lands. As Ó Corráin noted (32) the developments which gave rise to feudalism in Europe occurred in Ireland too. By the end on the Middle Ages, this situation was modified in various ways. Much of eastern Ireland had improved tracks and many rivers had bridges. Port facilities were improved. Chiefs, now called lords, began to live in castles. Possession of land began to be more prized than possession of cattle, and chiefs, like the Normans, were trying to get it into the exclusive possession of their immediate families. Warfare changed as chiefs like the English came to depend chiefly on mercenaries. English weapons, following the invention of gunpowder were adopted. Guns and gunpowder had to be imported and so cash became more important than cattle. For the chiefs cattle ceased to be a status symbol and became a source of cash.

By the 12th century the structure of Gaelic society was not very different from that of English or Norman society. Indeed they were virtually identical. All three had their origin in the Indo-European warrior culture of the Iron Age. In each there was a hereditary ruling class. These formed the warrior class and were bound to provide troops and ancillary workmen when their superior lord commanded them. Associated with them were the clergy, the learned classes and some valued craftsmen who were exempt from the hosting or ban. In the Norman feudal structure there was a strictly subordinated hierarchy, from the feudal overlord to mesne lords to local lords who were the equivalent of knights. Each controlled an extent of property proportionate to his position, and each was obliged to attend the court of his immediate lord. The lowest level in Norman areas was called a manor. The manors were also the parishes which remained as the civil parishes. But Norman manors were often pre-existing Gaelic tribute units assigned to Norman knights or freemen. Sometimes, especially if colonists were plentiful, the lords restructured the unit like an English manor and village. In other places the existing cultivators were left in place. The senior clergy and professionals were assimilated to this class.

The structure of Gaelic society was similar. Ó Corráin cites an example of the territory of a *ruiri* named O'Driscoll in Cork, diocese of Ross. He would have been under a provincial chief, a *ri ruirech*, like MacCarthy. He controlled six lordships originally *tuatha*. The chief of the *tuath* was no longer called *ri* but *tuisech* or leader. Within the *tuath* there were from five to fifteen lesser lords called an *ógláech* (young warrior) a title that clearly corresponds to *miles* (knight or *knecht*). (*Ógláech* strictly speaking meant a soldier as in *gall oglaech*, a foreign soldier.) These were obviously the successors of the lower degrees of lords such as the *aire desa* or *aire echta* (Keenan, *True Origins*, 185). There were thirty-six of these in O'Driscoll's territories. These lords would have owned several family farms or townlands, and allowed the original cultivators to remain in possession subject to heavy duties of coshering and other contributions (Ó Corráin, 171-2). As provision of lands had also to be made for the free classes, the clergy, the learned and highly skilled craftsmen like smiths and carpenters, the top heavy nature of society becomes evident.

The *ri tuaithe* ceased to be a significant figure but the *tuatha* however survived, usually ruled by the chiefs of septs who were from lesser branches of a superior ruling family. Most of them seem to have been renamed baronies in the sixteenth century and remained as administrative units until the 19th century. It is clear that boundaries were rarely permanent, and a modern barony may not correspond closely with an earlier cantred or *tuath* though they occupied roughly the same area.

We know that during the Composition of Connaught in the 16th century the commissioners proceeded in their evaluations 'barony' by 'barony'. In the non-feudalised Gaelic areas they may have proceeded cantred by cantred. (The name cantred or cantref may have been applied to existing units, parts of existing units or multiples of existing units were stitched together.) The likes of Dermot MacMurrough, Hugh de Lacy or King John did not send out survey teams: they used existing units of land division. The old *tuatha* survived as administrative and taxation units midway between the county-sized chiefdoms and the local townland or farm which was the basic taxation unit. It corresponded in size with the English hundred. It is fair to assume too that the head of the family or sept still exercised locally most of the functions (including the superstitions) of the *ri tuaithe* (king of the *tuath*). By the end of the Middle Ages some of the lesser families or septs might not have controlled areas larger than a manor or parish, the same as a knight. The present boundaries of the parish of Ballymascanlon in County Louth seem largely identical with the lands given to Mellifont Abbey by Hugh de Lacy, in itself obviously a pre-existing unit (Columcille, *History of Mellifont* 120-121). With regard to nobility it must be remembered that there could be seven degrees of lordship within a *tuath* no greater in size than 20 miles by 10 with a population of less than 5,000. It was a rank with an honour price, and did not in itself imply wealth.

The power and influence of overlords was often less than it seemed. After they had conquered a neighbouring *tuath* the loyalty of the subordinate chief was by no means assured. Subjection only remained as long as it could be enforced.

The Normans never intended to be a separate ruling class. Their aim at first was to marry into the ruling Gaelic families in their area. The Gaelic rulers also wanted to marry into the Norman families. Differences of language did not necessarily imply differences of customs or practices. As far as the ruling families went, apart from the great English lords whose main estates were elsewhere, the ruling families were inter-married. The Gaelicization that occurred in places in the later Middle Ages may have been largely linguistic though minor Gaelic families, especially in Leinster did increase their power. Or it perhaps brought to the fore in Norman areas practices which had been there from the beginning.

Beside the distinction between the old ruling families and those which had arrived more recently, there was another important distinction, that between the 'free classes' and the 'unfree classes' and there was little dissimilarity in this regard between Old and New Irish. Indeed it seems to have been found everywhere in Indo-European culture. The free classes were the various degrees of 'lords' and also the free farmers and their families, and free craftsmen and their families. This 'freedom' was the right to attend the court, or leet, or *aonach* of the local chief, and technically also freedom from various rents, dues or taxes payable by the villeins or betaghs. In Norman areas a freeman was one who held land by feudal tenure. They could attend the honour court and county court. Those who could not were called unfree. There were also ancient servile classes descended from slaves who were called serfs. Originally they were their master's property and could be bought and sold. But in the Middle Ages they differed little from villeins or betaghs.

The great bulk of the population, whether free or unfree attended their local manor court or Gaelic equivalent. The independent free farmer had disappeared, being reduced in status to the non-free classes. The free farmer had owned his own land and did not pay rent for it, though he might have renders to the chief on other grounds such as clientship, and also had to make a return on the cattle lent to him by the chief. Cattle—rearing was the principal source of support. But the chiefs and their advisors were able to heap dues and obligations, eventually crippling, on the free and unfree classes. It was in the interest of the ruling classes to get as much of the land of the free farmers into their own hands to provide for their sons.

Another point to remember was that unfree persons, i.e. anyone who was not a full freeman, did not bear arms. Shane O'Neill in the 16th century shocked the Gaelic world when he recruited people like *betaghs* into his army. But betaghs were not serfs though treated everywhere as such. Actual fighting was confined to the 'noble' classes. Again this was not peculiar to Ireland. The other people, free and unfree, assisted in warfare with goods and services with forced labour.

In the Old Irish part the free farmer, the *boaire*, whose farm was around a hundred acres, had virtually disappeared and was being replaced by the betagh, an 'unfree' farmer who held his land by an equivalent of villeinage, i.e. as a tenant in return for services. The *boaire* could easily become a betagh by getting hopelessly into debt to a 'lord'. Brehon Law was loaded heavily in favour of the ruling families, for they allocated the number of cows a free farmer could have on the common grazing lands, woods, bogs, moorlands or meadows. The lord then provided the cattle. As every lord had a lifelong obligation to provide lands to support his numerous sons the easiest way to do this was to turn a *boaire* into a betagh, whenever, in a bad season he could not make the legal return of cattle to the lord. The son then occupied the farm and the betagh's family did the work. The betagh corresponded to the Norman villein and was equally bound to the farm. Serfs were the ancient slaves though their obligations were lightened and were equally *adscripti glebae*, bound to the land. Despite the differences in terminology, there was little difference between the various branches of Indo-European societies.

There is little doubt that in Anglo-Norman Ireland especially after the depopulation caused by the Black Death there arose again, as in England, the class of non-noble free farmer or forty shilling freeholder who attended the hustings in the sheriff's court to return members to parliament.

Newcomers to the scene were the peoples of the towns. The burghers of the towns got charters of freedom from the king or the local lord, in return for an annual fixed sum of rents and other dues. They were only to be found in the Anglo-Norman part of Ireland. They were not exempt from military service. Though not numerous, they became responsible for a major split in Irish society which came into the open in the Statutes of Kilkenny. These brought the prejudices of the towns against the lawless Gaelic chiefs and Anglo-Norman lords into the open.

Irish Polity in the Twelfth Century

In the twelfth century when the first Norman adventurers came to Ireland there was very little difference between their respective societies. Their chief motivation was personal or family enrichment. The 'king' or provincial chief of Leinster, Dermot MacMurrough and Richard de Clare, Earl of Pembroke were entirely comparable, though it was an advance in wealth and status for the earl to marry the daughter of a provincial chief. (These provincial chiefs would have had a status equal to that of 'kings' of Wessex or Mercia.) Those who were merely knights stood to gain by marrying into chiefly families, and these chiefs were only too anxious to have them as sons-in-law because of their military skills. When the various knights or freelances came to Ireland, their first concern was to marry into the local ruling families. So it would seem, within a century there was a single mixed-race ruling class in Ireland.

The balance was somewhat upset when Henry II landed and claimed to be feudal overlord in virtue of a papal grant. His aim was to prevent his feudal vassals in England and Wales acquiring powerful lordships of their own outside his control. Accordingly, he formed feudal fiefdoms and conferred them on trusted vassals just as his predecessors had done along the Welsh and Scottish marches or borderlands. The fiefs were roughly equal in size to strong provincial chiefdoms. They could keep a check on each other and on the local chiefs. Further fiefdoms were created as occasion arose. Henry's vassals were richer and more powerful men from richer parts of England or Normandy and could afford to develop their new fiefdoms economically. This they did by introducing colonists, those skilled in the various arts and crafts, to reproduce the practices of English manors in Ireland. They were also able to develop trade and it would seem that temporarily at least had a commercial as well as a military advantage over the Gaelic lords.

No Irish chief had managed to establish a monarchy in Ireland for his family. Henry II of England was largely accepted as a feudal overlord by the principal chiefs. In practice they paid as much or as little respect to their feudal overlord as did any of the powerful lords in Europe in the Middle Ages. The greater and lesser chiefs were perpetually at war with each other. The constant search for land for the ever-increasing branches of their families lay at the base of much of the incessant warfare. They would submit to the central authority as long as the central authority had power to compel them. Control over the frontier areas had to be indirect, and with as little interference with local affairs as possible. Cattle raids and corresponding black rents for 'protection' are common in such societies. Those on the coasts indulged in piracy and the corresponding 'protection'. Life could be good for the well-armed and well-mounted warriors.

The ruling families of the newcomers in the 12th century have been traditionally been called Normans, but few of them had direct links with that province of France. The earliest military adventurers were the 'brood of Nesta' a Norman-Welsh family, whose mother Nesta, was from a Welsh ruling family in South Wales. Others were Flemings; indeed they could have come from anywhere in Henry of Anjou's vast domains.

The exact number of small local ruling Gaelic families may perhaps never be counted, but the figure of a hundred gives an idea of scale. Or one might prefer the estimated 330 baronies as a better indicator. (In the 18th and 19th centuries they were called county families or near-county families because of their importance and influence in their own counties.) There were about 30 major chiefs corresponding to the similar numbers of dioceses based on the chiefdoms. But there were only four major families who could attempt to exercise power outside their own province, to which the ecclesiastical provinces corresponded, and to advance claims to be the overall ruler of Ireland. These were the O'Briens in Munster, the MacLoughlins/O'Neills in Ulster, the O'Connors in Connaught, and the MacMurroughs in Leinster. The fifth family, the O'Mellaghlins in Meath, once one of the most formidable, had gone into decline, while the MacCarthys in Munster never really matched to O'Briens. Henry II himself took over Meath, and appointed his own vassal barons, to provide himself with adequate military power, and to prevent anyone else seizing it.

With regard to the feudal overlord, the king of England, the chief preoccupation of the king and his Council in England was to prevent any of his feudal subjects setting up an independent kingdom in Ireland. This was precisely what the feudal knights succeeded in doing in Scotland and resulted in periodic wars right down to the 18th century. The knights appointed by the king then owed him feudal military service, especially in France where they would be most needed. With a proper revenue established various financial subventions to the royal treasury could also be expected.

Ruling Families

The basic political unit in Ireland was the *tuath*. The bulk of the people in a *tuath* belonged to the lower or working families not to the ruling families. The amount of land owned by the chiefs and their ever-expanding families went on increasing. The Middle Ages was the period of the great territorial expansion of the leading Gaelic clans whose chiefs systematically plundered and conquered the lands of the lesser neighbouring clans, seized their lands and distributed them among their followers, and to the Church. One way or another, the chiefs were getting more and more control of the land in Ireland, and became an increasing proportion of the population. Increasingly too, the landowners were relatives of the chiefs. In two parishes in Clogher in 1659, there were 112 MacMahons, 91 McKennas, 69 O'Duffys, and 56 O'Connollys (M'Kenna, 244). Ó Corráin notes that in the twelfth century there were 200 families belonging to the *Dal Cais* in east Clare where there had been none four centuries earlier.

In the course of the Middle Ages the practice of having a fixed family surname arose. Any family in the grades of nobility adopted either Ó, from *Ua,* denoting grandson, or *Mac,* a son. The more recent, and lesser families, were given Mac, while the older ones favoured Ó. When the city of Galway refused to admit a *Mac* or an Ó did they intend to exclude humble people just coming to the market? It is unlikely. Among the other classes the practice, common elsewhere in Europe, of giving the father's name in the genitive case survived in Gaelic areas until recently. Even when a surname like O'Connor was adopted the actual father's name was added as is common still in some European countries like Russia. Though at times a nickname was preferred especially by the O'Neills.

Norman and British Families

Dennis Walsh, in his website, gives a partial list of about 200 leading families who came to Ireland in the Middle Ages Though it does not pretend to be either complete or scientific the names gave a good idea of the extent of colonisation, i.e. the settling of outsiders and the places where it occurred. Ulster (8,952 sq. miles) had the fewest names, 12 in all, mostly in Co. Down. Leinster (7,634 sq. miles) had the most with 135 different names, and 115 of these were in five counties, Louth, Meath, Dublin, Wexford and Kilkenny. Wicklow had 2, Carlow 2, Laois and Offaly 1 each. Kildare had 8 and Westmeath 6. Munster (15,290 sq. miles), twice the size of Leinster, had 83 different surnames, widely dispersed over the five counties. Waterford had 14, Cork 23, Kerry 10, Limerick 15, Tipperary 14 and Clare 7. Connaught had 25 of which 13 were in Galway and 12 in Mayo. These names to be recorded would have been those of substantial land-holders, (http://www.rootsweb.ancestry.com/~irlkik/ihm/index.htm.

Although there was a great concentration in the area, subsequently called The Pale, the idea that Anglo-Irish culture was confined to The Pale is misleading. The great ports of Wexford/New Ross, Waterford, Cork, Limerick, and Galway with their hinterlands were always strongholds of the Common Law and commercial culture. Some of the frontier families like the Condons, and Roches in Cork, the de Verdons and Bellews in Louth, the Plunketts in Meath, and the Nugents, Tuites, and Tyrells in Westmeath who had the military strength of English barons, held the line. Much of the losses in the period of Gaelicization in the 14th century were suffered by the great earldoms of Ulster, Ormonde, Kildare, and Desmond. Apart from towns like Galway and Athenry, the Anglo-Norman lords in Connaught adopted Gaelic customs when they were fashionable, and reverted to English ways when it suited them.

It is clear that most of Ireland in the 12th and 13th centuries never received a sufficient volume of colonisers to develop agriculture and the industries. Even in the earldom of Ulster, in county Down and county Antrim, colonisation faded out within 20 miles from the coast even when the earls had semi-feudal control over the eastern half of the province. But the areas reasonably well colonised in the 12th and 13th centuries formed the bases for the waves of modernisation in the 16th and 17th centuries. It was from these families that modern Ireland arose.

Leading Gaelic Families

By Tudor times there were about a hundred recognised 'chiefs of their name' or 'chiefs of their nation', both Gaelic-speaking and English-speaking. At the top were the five principal Gaelic families, the O'Neills of Ulster, the O'Connors of Connaught, the O'Briens of North Munster, the MacCarthys of South Munster, and the MacMurroughs of Leinster. There were then about 30 secondary families, about one to each county. In the third rank there were at least a 330 notable families (later called county families) corresponding to the 330 baronies. Beneath these were about 1,000 local names, about one to a modern Catholic parish, who was the most important man in the parish with a rank later in England called squire. Within the barony which might measure twenty miles by thirty there were other families whose head had formerly been called 'lord' *(aire)* who were bound to supply a certain number of armed warriors to their local chief, as we have seen in the case of O'Driscoll above. These sons of 'gentlemen' would have formed the basis of the fighting force of the great provincial families. They were often lords of manors when a manor was equated with a parish and village. (For a list of local families in the Middle Ages see www.rootsweb.ancestry. com/~irlkik/ihm/index.htm 'Surnames, Gaelic and Norman'.)

These families formed the basis of the political, military, and social structure of Ireland throughout the Middle Ages and Tudor times, and were only destroyed by the great plantations and land appropriations of Stuart time. Politically, Ireland resembled present day Afghanistan or Somalia. The territories controlled by these families or clans were the building blocks of Ireland. Many of these ruling families did not survive, but the territory they controlled did not disappear: it was simply taken over by a rival family, usually an offshoot of the dominant clan. The concept of a centrally-controlled bureaucratic administration simply did not exist in Gaelic areas. There was only the pyramidal subordination of chiefdoms.

ULSTER (*Ultonia, Ulidia, Ulaid,* the land of the *Voluntii?*)

Chief families and Sub groups: Lands in

Ui Neill (Hy Niall) : Donegal
Cenel Eogain : North Donegal, esp. Inishowen
Clan Connor (Fir Maighe Itha) : Derry

Cenel Binnig (Binny) : Derry, W. of Bann
Cenel Conaill : North Donegal,
Cenel Enna : North Donegal
Cenel Feredaig (Ferady) : East Donegal

Clan Connor (Fir Magh Ithe/O'Cahan) and *Clan Binnig* were early offshoots of *Cenel Eogain.* There were numerous other sub-divisions as time went on. The dominant four generation family or *derb fine Cenel Eogain* was later called the *Ui Neill* (after a different Niall, Niall *Glundubh* d. 919) and by the end of the Middle Ages was itself split into three families O'Neill of Tullaghogue (the Great O'Neill), O'Neill of Clandeboy (*Clann Aodha Buidhe*) and the O'Neills of the Fews (*na Feadha*) besides lesser branches. (See Burke's *Peerage and Baronetage* 'O'Neill' for the full story.)

Oirgialla (Oriel): Most of Ulster, Louth
Fir Li : Derry
Ui Tuirtre : E. Tyrone north of Blackwater
Ui Fiachrach : W. Tyrone around Strabane
Ui Cremthainn : N.E, of Lough Erne
Fir Rois : Monaghan, around Carrickmacross
Ui Meith : Monaghan, Omeath in Co. Louth
Dartraige (Dartry) : barony of Dartree, Monaghan, Cavan
Fernmag (Farney) : barony of Farney, Monaghan
Oirthir (Orior) : barony of Orior, East Armagh
Mugdorna (Mourne) : barony of Cremorne, Monaghan (later Mourne S. Down)
Fir Managh : Fermanagh
Ulaid (**Ulidians**) : Ulidia, i.e. East of Bann; later Earldom of Ulster
Ui Eachach Choba : baronies of Iveagh or diocese of Dromore in Co. Down
Dal nAraide : Diocese of Connor in Co. Antrim

Dal Fiatach : Diocese of Down in Down and S. Antrim

Others

Dal Riata (Route) : Between Bush and Bann in Antrim

Cianacht (Keenacht) : barony of Keenacht

Cuailgne : Cooley peninsula, North Louth

Connaille : Mid Louth

Fir Arda Cianachta : barony of Ferrard in South Louth

Ui Niallain : barony of Oneilland South of Lough Neagh

Ui Bresail Macha : S.E of Lough Neagh

Fotharta (Faughart) : at Faughart near Dundalk.

It would seem that the *Oirghialla* were not a single family with its offshoots as was common elsewhere but a group of local *tuatha* who were subject, or subjected themselves to a mesne lord. This overlordship was not in the hands of a particular *tuath* but could have come for any of the *tuatha*. Not until 1273 did the MacMahon family get a secure grip on the title which they never relinquished. The individual *tuatha* were picked off one by one by the O'Neills except the MacMahon heartland in Monaghan and the O'Hanlons and the *Ui Bresail* in east Armagh. The following were still identified by Baptista Boazio in 1599: *Cenel Conaill* (O'Donnell, O'Doherty, MacSwiney), *Cenel Eogain* (various O'Neills, O'Gormley, and Clandeboy), *Ui Eachach Choba* (Magennis), Oriel (MacMahon), *Oirthir* (O'Hanlon), The Route (Sorley Boy MacDonnell), *Fir Maighe Itha* (O'Cahan), *Ui Bresail* (Terlough Brazilio).

Dal nAraide and *Dal Fiatach* were swallowed up in the earldom of Ulster, and much of it was later re-conquered by Clandeboy, MacGuinness, and the Scots. The lands of the *Cianacht* were taken over by the O'Cahans (Clan Connor). The *Ui Meith* of Louth, the *Cualigne*, the *Connaille*, and the *Fir Arda Cianachta* were easily absorbed into County Louth. The *Ui Eachach Choba* (Iveagh, MacGuinness), *Oirthir* (O'Hanlon), and *Ui Bresail* (Terlough Brazilio) survived in difficult and rough country. By the 17th century the O'Hanlon chief was little more than a rapparee, a cattle rustler.

By the Tudor period the *Ui Niall* had conquered and occupied more than half of Ulster. Most of the conquered lands passed into the hands of the *Cenel Eogain*. The main line was the three branches of the O'Neills. Its offshoots were the O'Kanes, O'Mullans, O'Mellons, O'Gormleys, McCawells, MacLoughlins, O'Devlins, McCloskeys, O'Carolans, O'Duddies, O'Quins, O'Donnellys, O'Hagans, O'Toners, O'Hamills, O'Brollys who parcelled out the conquered lands among themselves (Mullin and Mullan, 21). At each generation of the ruling *derb fine* the outermost branches were shed, and each had to take a new clan name. The *Cenel Feredaig* (MacCawells) moved towards the south and partially displaced the *Ui Cremthainn* from the lands north of Clogher. The barony of Clogher is now in the diocese of Clogher, but in the county of Tyrone (the land of the *Cenel Eogain*). The *Cenel Conaill*, once the equal of the *Cenel Eogain*, got bottled up in the area now called Donegal. The O'Donnells emerged as the ruling family. They had a success in wrenching Inishowen, the ancestral lands of the *Cenel Eogain* from them when the latter were concentrating on greater opportunities in mid-Ulster. The *Cenel Conaill's* expansion eastward, was blocked by the *Cenel Feradaig*, so throughout the Middle Ages they made repeated attempts to establish an overlordship in North Connaught. In any quarrel they normally took the opposite side to the O'Neills, so when the latter opposed the Government the O'Donnells supported it. Not until 1598 did O'Neill, O'Donnell, and Maguire combine against the Government.

Similarly the medieval kingdom of the *Oirgialla*. The name is interpreted 'tribute-paying' families. Such were common all over Ireland. They may originally have paid tribute to the *Ulaid* but later to the *Ui Neill* who steadily encroached on their territories. At some point too, probably in the mid-twelfth century, they got a common mesne lord. The chief of *Fern Magh*, Donnchad Ó Cerbaill (Donough O'Carroll, an excellent warrior, succeeded in establishing the mesne chiefdom of *Oirgialla* (Oriel) in extent corresponding to the present diocese of Clogher plus County Louth. He is famous for donating lands for the founding of the great abbey of Mellifont. The lands presumably were seized from the *Fir Arda Cianachta* in south Louth. Though these were *Cianacht* we are told they marched with the *Oirgialla* in the hosting of O'Carroll or Murtagh MacLoughlin of the *Cenel Eogain* their common overlord. Oriel had at its greatest extent in the twelfth century under the O'Carrolls who had swallowed up most of the lesser *Oirgialla* families. The O'Carrolls seem originally to have been *Ui Cremthainn*, but to have moved eastward to control the territory of the *Fernmag (Farney)* and to establish their suzerainty as mesne lords of the lesser ruling families in the difficult border area. Later in the Middle Ages, the mesne chiefdom of Clogher split into two parts. The O'Carrolls were replaced by the MacMahons in the eastern half, while a family called Maguire become lords of the western half as vassals of the O'Donnells. The hold of the mesne lords over the subject lords was often tenuous. Maguire was probably either *Fir Monagh* or *Ui Cremthainn*. The Maguires controlled Fermanagh, and the MacMahons Monaghan, while Louth had been shired. By the end of the Middle Ages, the Maguire chiefs had managed to transfer three quarters of the land of Fermanagh into their own hands, at the expense of lesser families (Nicholls, 12). The part of Oriel in Leinster (Co Louth) came rapidly into Norman hands early in the Middle Ages. The remainder survived until the 16th century under the MacMahons. The *Ulaid* remained a strong kingdom, increasingly under a single ruler, until conquered by the Normans and made into the earldom of Ulster. Iveagh however re-established itself. The lands conquered by the early Normans were basically those of the *Ulaid*, but they managed to conquer and briefly hold along the north coast lands recently conquered by the *Ui Neill*. At their greatest expansion at the death of the Brown Earl in 1333 the lands adjoined the Norman lands in county Louth, but subsequently the route was cut.

MEATH (*Mide*, the Centre?)

Chief families and Sub groups : Lands in

Hy Niall (Ui Neill) : Meath, Westmeath, Longford, etc
Sil nAedo Slaine : Brega in East of Meath, barony of Skreen
Clan Cholmain : around Lough Ennel in Westmeath
Caille Follamain : Killallon in W. of Meath
Sil Ardgal : west of Tara a minor free family
Sil Laegaire : west of Tara a minor free family

Others
Cianacht Brega : Brega in east of Meath, barony of Duleek
Gailenga : North Meath, Cavan, Dublin, barony of Moregallion
Luigne : Meath/Dublin borders
Saithne : Dublin
Deisi Brega South Meath, baronies of Deece

Subject to **Clann Cholmain** but possibly *Ui Neill*
Cairpre : in Tethba, co. Longford
Maine : along the Shannon, S. of Tethba
Fir Chell : N. of Birr, S. of Maine.
Other subject families
Cuircne : E. of Lough Ree
Delbna : barony of Delvin in Westmeath
Delbna Ethra : E. of Clonmacnoise on Shannon

Meath and Westmeath were the great centres of the Southern *Ui Neill* and several of the subordinate families may have been early offshoots of the dominant family. The different formation of the clan names has been noted but not explained. By the 12th century, all were paying tribute to the chief of *Clann Cholmain* who had managed to exclude the *Sil nAedo Slaine* from the overlordship. In their heyday the latter had exacted tribute from the neighbouring families, and expelled the *Cianacht Brega* from the fertile lands in the barony of Duleek. They took refuge in the heavy clay lands in South Louth, which became the *Fir Arda Cianachta*. As was common the *Sil nAedo Slaine* split into contesting factions. At one point it seemed that *Clan Cholmain* would achieve the kingship of all Ireland, but the family became weakened by internal strife. It survived as a tiny subject family to appear in Boazio's map of 1599. Meath was the most fertile, richest, and most advanced province, and numerous small subject families survived, and indeed could be prominent locally for centuries. As in the North there were constant attempts at seizing neighbouring territories for their followers. By the twelfth century the strong upstart kingdoms of O'Rourke and O'Carroll were making inroads into the lands of the families subject to *Sil nAedo Slaine*. By that time too the sub kingdom of *Cairpre* seems to have extended to the extent of the diocese of Ardagh, and lasted under the name of Annaly (O'Farrell) covering co Longford until the 16th cent.

The territory subject to *Clan Cholmain* (O'Mellaghlin) were granted to Hugh de Lacy and parcelled out among his followers, Tyrrells, Nugents, and Plunkets etc. In Boazio's map the following are still listed: *Tethba* (Annaly, O'Farrell, O'Farrelly), and O'Mellaghlin (a tiny territory). What was not seized of *Clan Cholmain* territory by the Normans was seized by the *Ui Failge* of the *Laigin*.

LEINSTER (Lagenia, *Laighin*, the land of the *Laigin* or Lageni)

Chief families ad sub-groups : Lands in

Ui Dunlainge : South and West of Dublin
Ui Dunchada : plain of the Liffey
Ui Faelain : Northern Kildare

Ui Muredaig : east of River Barrow
Ui Chennselaig : Co Wexford
Ui Drona (Idrone) : barony of Idrone in Carlow

Others
Ui Failge (Offaly) : Leix/Kildare borders
Loigse (Leix, Laois) : between Slieve Bloom and Barrow
Fotharta : places in Wexford and Carlow
Dal Mesin Corb : east of Wicklow Mts.
Ui Mail : Imaal, west of Wicklow Mts.
Ui Garrchon : East Wicklow
Ui Enechglaiss : East Wicklow

There were other minor families especially along the coast.

The original ruling family, the *Laigin,* had their centre along the Liffey and the plain of Kildare. They gave their name to the province and probably to the Lleyn peninsula in Wales. The lands they ruled in Meath were progressively captured by the *Ui Neill.* They may at one time have been overlords of the whole of Leinster but in historic times they were confined south of the Liffey. The original ruling family the *Ui Dunlainge* were displaced in the 12th century from the provincial overlordship by the *Ui Chennselaig* (MacMurrough). Dermot MacMurrough's grants of lands to Strongbow and his followers were largely those of the conquered *Ui Dunlainge.*

The *Loigse* and *Ui Failge* expanded the areas under their control in the later Middle Ages but not reaching the size of the present counties of Laois and Offaly. The *Loigse* appear in Boazio's map as the newly planted Queen's County, and the *Ui Failge* as King's County, and also as O'More and O'Dempsey. Idrone is given as O Drone. The *Ui Chennselaig* (O'Kinsella) apparently represented by O'Morough. The O'Byrnes and O'Tooles of Wicklow were originally in Kildare but after the Norman (or possibly O'Phelan) seizure of their lands, settled in Wicklow and survived as robber barons in the hills for the rest of the Middle Ages. The O'Tooles seem to have been originally the *Ui Mail*. The Normans occupied a fertile strip from Kildare in the north to Wexford in the south, and this always provided a route of communication between Dublin and Munster. It goes without saying that these lesser clans throughout the Middle Ages increased their local power and family possessions at the expense of their still weaker neighbours like the *Ui Garrchon*, and *Ui Enechglaiss*, *Ui Mail*, and *Dal Messin Corb*. The *Loigse* and *Ui Failge* (O'Mores and O'Connors) were equally ruthless in seizing other people's lands.

MUNSTER (Momonia, origin unknown)

Chief families and Sub groups : Lands in

Eoganacht : North and west Munster
E. Locha Lein : around Killarney
E. Raithlind : around Bandon (baronies of Kinelea and Kinelmeaky)
E. Glendamnach : around Galsworthy in N. Cork
E. Airthir Cliach : around Donohill in Tipperary
E. Aine : around Knockainy in Limerick
E. Caisil : around Cashel

Other major families
Ui Fidgente : county Limerick
Osraige : county Kilkenny
Ciarraige Luachra : North Kerry
Deisi Mumain : baronies of Decies, co. Waterford
Deisi Tuaiscirt or Dal Cais : county Clare around Bunratty
Muscraige (Muskerry) : baronies of Muskerry in Cork and Tipperary

Minor families

Eli : barony of Eliogarty north Tipperary
Corcu Duibne : barony of Corkaguiny, Kerry
Corcu Baiscind : west Clare
Corcu Modruad : Clare
Corcu Loegde : South Cork (Ross)
Benntraige : around Bantry, Cork
Fir Maige : around Fermoy, Cork

The *Dal Cais* (O'Briens) under Brian *Boru* (d. 1014) had broken the power of the former provincial overlords the *Eoganacht Caisil* (MacCarthy) and driven them from their stronghold at Cashel in north Munster. (Cashel however was retained as the centre of an archdiocese.) As in the other provinces land grabbing was endemic, the bigger families seizing the land of the lesser, or driving them out. By this time too some branches of the former overlords, the *Eoganacht* had dwindled into insignificance. The O'Briens were apparently unable to occupy and control the lands of the *Eoganacht Caisil* in North Munster, so they were allocated to various Norman lords. The MacCarthys in turn seized what land they could from the families in South Munster and re-established themselves as a powerful force. The *Ui Fidgente*, like *Clan Cholmain* further north, were riven by disputes, and the *Dal Cais* and the *Eoganacht* tried to seize the territories they controlled. As further north, this was a sufficient excuse for the new feudal overlord to transfer the lands into his own hands. (In 1111 it was still sufficiently a political unit to be given its own diocese, Mungret attached to the Norse city of Limerick which was controlled by the O'Briens).

The situation was changing all through the Middle Ages. In Boazio's time the following can still be identified: *Eoganacht Caisil* (MacCarthy families, O'Sullivan families), *Dal Cais* (O'Brien, O'Kennedy), *Osraige*

(Fitzpatrick), *Eile* (O'Carroll), *Corcu Loegde* (Carbery, O'Driscoll). The Normans settled the fertile areas in a wide band across the centre of the Province, in the area where the *Eoganacht* had been dominant before being subdued by the O'Briens and their lands given to the diocese of Cashel. The Gaelic families survived to north and south of this band. The name *Muscraige* (Muskerry) survived as a place name and the name of a barony though their lands had been seized by the *Eoganacht* MacCarthy family. The name *Ciarraige* (Kerry) survived in the earldom of Desmond, but the ruling families disappeared from the county. *Eoganacht* families were the various branches of the MacCarthys, the O'Sullivans, O'Kirbys, O'Moriartys, O'Cahills, O'Carrolls, O'Flynns, O'Donoughues, O'Mahonys, O'Callaghans, and O'Keefes.

CONNACHT (Connacia, land of the people of Conn, from whom allegedly *Ui Briuin* and *Ui Neill*)

Chief families and sub groups : Lands in
Ui Briuin Ai : Roscommon (Elphin)
Ui Briuin Seola : E. of Lough Corrib (Annaghdown)
Ui Briuin Breifne (Breffney) : South Lower Lough Erne (Kilmore)
Ui Fiachrach Muaide : N. Mayo and Sligo (Killala, Tireragh)
Ui Fiachrach Aidne : S.W. of Co. Galway (Kilmacduagh)

Others
Ui Maine : East Co. Galway (Clonfert)
Minor families
Umall : around Clew Bay
Conmaicne : scattered in several places Connemara
Ciarraige : various local spots
Partraige : Partry Mts
Luigne and Gailenga : Leyney in Sligo, Gallen in Mayo

The eastern part of Connaught has the best land, and it was held by the most powerful families especially the O'Connors of *Ui Briuin Ai*. It was also the land granted to the Normans, but was never properly colonised. The O'Connors however retained their ancestral lands of the *Sil Muredaig* (Shilmorthy). There was an extraordinary collection of minor or broken families whose land was readily available for the greater chiefs who lost land to the Normans. The Partry Mountains were to become notorious in the Great Irish Famine, but before the advent of the potato, the population would have been tiny.

Surviving until Boazio's time were *Ui Briuin Ai* (O'Connors, MacDermotts), *Ui Briuin Seola* (O'Flaherty), *Ui Briuin Breifne* (O'Rourke), *Ui Maine* (O'Kelly, O'Madden). Two families of the *Ui Fiachrach Aidne* the O'Haynes and the O'Shaughnessys remained as tenants to the Burkes until the 17th century. The chiefs of *Ui Fiachrach Muaide* became the O'Dowds. The *Umaill* survived under the name O'Malley. They seem to have shared an ancestor with *Ui Briuin*. The O'Haras and the O'Garas were derived from the *Luigne*. With the MacDonoughs they are listed as erechholders (urraghs).

Chapter 4

Government

Central Government

The Feudal Overlordship

Charlemagne wished to restore the bureaucratic administration in the Western half of the Roman Empire, what was to be called the Holy Roman Empire, but did not succeed. After his death the offices of the officials he appointed became hereditary. The emperor or the king of France simply lacked the power to refuse to instate the heirs of the local lords. England was never part of Charlemagne's empire and so never came under its feudal structure. The Anglo-Saxon monarchs of England had begun to 'shire' parts of England appointing shire reeves who were not part of the local aristocracy to maintain royal interests in those shires. This system was taken over by the Normans who brought the feudal structure along with them in addition. This combined system was what Henry II brought to Ireland. Throughout the Middle Ages there was a long struggle by the crown to establish its authority over the hereditary feudal nobles (called barons) and to make the royal courts and the shire courts the principal instruments of rule.

The primary objective Henry had in coming to Ireland was to ensure that none of his liege subjects could establish there an independent kingdom as knights from Normandy had done in Sicily (Warren, *Henry II*, 114). It was not to conquer Ireland and to take the land of the Irish chiefs to give to his feudal followers. Nor was it his policy to allow Norman knights to seize lands from the Gaelic chiefs for this would have become swordland outside the feudal system. Given the meagre resources of any medieval government there was no possibility of central government interfering in local affairs. Gradually however Henry's successors were drawn in to keep the peace.

For 200 years the system worked as intended. The Irish fiefdom was a source of knights and other troops for the king's wars and a source of revenue. These declined in the later Middle Ages and the fiefdom became a cause of expense. It was however never abandoned. The original reason, to prevent the emergence of an independent state which would, like the Scots, side with the French, survived. It was not until late in the reign of Elizabeth I, after attempts of some Gaelic lords to establish a Catholic kingdom subject to Catholic Spain, was an outright war of total conquest commenced. It was only then too that an English monarchy could afford the cost of the war.

Feudal society in Henry's time was still a personal thing, not one of structures of government, though these were beginning to be established in England. The state and the king were the same thing. Government was the personal relation between the king and the 'vassals' who did homage to receive their lands. It was different from swearing 'fealty' (fidelity, faithfulness) to him (Dunbabin, 111-7). The king dealt in person or through his justiciar with his great feudal vassals, his tenants-in-chief. In Ireland he seems to have dealt directly with the heads of the five great provincial chiefs of the 'Five Bloods'. In Henry's day in Ireland there were probably not more than a dozen or score of vassals who dealt directly with the king. But as the scope of government increased and justices sent on assize, and as subinfeudation was phased out, the number of those who could attend any of the king's courts rose substantially.

Strongbow surrendered the lands he controlled as lord of Leinster to Henry and got them back as a fief, thereby establishing the royal right to them. Henry also took control of the broken and fragmented chiefdom of Meath over which Dermot MacMurrough and others had claimed lordship when the O'Mellaghlins were driven out, and gave it as a fief to Hugh de Lacy ensuring the royal right to it. From Rory O'Connor and the other Gaelic chiefs he asked for no more than an oath of fidelity and the tribute such as Gaelic chiefs normally paid to their superior chief. O'Connor was to collect the tribute from the other chiefs (Warren, *op. cit.*, 200-1). This O'Connor was unable to do, least of all from the O'Briens of Munster. All the great Gaelic families eventually recognised the overlordship of the king of England. At various times in the Middle Ages some Gaelic lords sought to hold their lands from the king directly as tenant-in-chief. In 1461, when Edward IV came to the throne and became also Earl of Ulster, the O'Neills of Tyrone became tenants-in-chief, a status they had long sought (Simms, 'The King's Friend', 214-5). In 1449 the Duke of York, Earl of March and of Ulster was greeted for the last time in Irish history by the mass submission of the Irish chiefs, but in fact they sent very little in the form of actual tribute (*op. cit.* 222).

Only when O'Connor failed did Henry take Munster into his own hands, and divided it into feudal fiefs, once again to prevent a Sicilian situation. He also took the largest of the Viking towns into his own hands. The Gaelic chiefs were allowed to keep their lands; the Brehon Law was to remain in their domains. Henry though regarded himself as the feudal lord over the whole of Ireland by papal award and the consent of the lords spiritual and temporal of Ireland and thus able to make feudal grants of land when occasions demanded them. Henry seems to have regarded himself as the high king of Ireland from the time of the abdication of Rory O'Connor in 1183 (Warren, 'King John and Ireland',

26). (The lands left with the Gaelic lords were not changed into feudal fiefs and the Gaelic lords retained them for their *derb fine* until the time of the Tudor policy of surrender and regrant.) Henry appointed John 'lord' of Ireland in 1174 apparently as a step to becoming king of Ireland (Warren, *Henry II*, 206; 'King John and Ireland', 26). Ireland was intended to be a separate kingdom, each new king presumably doing homage to the king of England his feudal overlord, before ascending the throne. The kings of Scotland were feudal vassals of the kings of England who rarely interfered. It was this homage that was rejected by John Balliol.

As Henry could not remain in Ireland he appointed a justiciar to act in his name, to keep feudal control of the fiefdoms and the royal towns, and deal with the Irish chiefs. Common Law, as understood at the time, was to apply in these areas with the justiciar's court as the chief court. When other solutions failed, either because of problems with the Norman knights or the Gaelic chiefs, he appointed his son John as lord of Ireland. (This also meant that Prince John 'Lackland' could have lands and revenues for his own household like his brothers.) John began a policy of giving grants to Norman knights as fiefdoms. Henry's policy with regard to Ireland failed because he refused to allow the Norman knights to conquer the whole of Ireland when that was still possible. If the knights had conquered parts, as John de Courci did in co Down, they would have held it as swordland and not as vassals (Warren, 206). The royal demesne in Ireland, from which the king drew direct revenue, at the time of the death of Henry II consisted of Dublin and Waterford with some land around them. John added the counties of Desmond and Munster. Unfortunately for Ireland Richard I died without issue and John became king of England, retaining his title as lord of Ireland, titles retained by successive monarchs.

John, when he became king, devoted adequate time and resources to the problem of Ireland. His policy was to gain control of the marchlands between the provinces, the debateable lands which none of the provincial

Gaelic chiefs had ever succeeded in holding securely, by making grants to various knights (Warren, 'King John and Ireland', 27). This seems to have been done with the consent of the various provincial chiefs who had failed to control them. These small marginal chiefdoms, like the later O'Byrnes and O'Tooles in the Wicklow Mountains, survived largely by pillaging their neighbours. (There were Highland clans along the Highland Line like the MacGregors who lived in a similar fashion.) Cathal *Crovderg* O'Connor after a civil war in Connaught agreed with John to hold one third of Connaught *per baroniam,* i.e. as a feudal fief. This would guarantee that they would remain in *Crovderg*'s family (against Brehon Law) while he would have to provide 'knights' to the royal army when called upon.

John's successors had little time to devote to Ireland, and the promise of John's lordship was lost. But the system he established was so successful that it was 200 years before another English king had personally to visit Ireland (Empy, 'The Settlement of England', 1). His son Henry III retained John's title as Lord of Ireland (though there was no 'Lordship of Ireland' as a specific title) and in 1274 he attached it permanently to the kingship of England which had not been Henry II's intention.

The lords and barons of England, in parliament or out, did not regard Ireland as an English problem, but as a royal one, and they often objected to paying for English troops to be sent to Ireland. The barons were happier to contribute to and join royal expeditions to France where the pickings were richer. The kings had to assemble forces as best they could (Connolly, 'The Financing of English Expeditions to Ireland').

The Irish or Dublin Government

General Observations

We can only attempt to give, in this section especially, some general indications of what central and local government was like. Firstly there was no one pattern in force everywhere, and secondly, institutions were constantly changing and developing. With regard to the central Government we can have a fairly good idea regarding the state of the institutions in England in the time of Henry II, and also of the state of those institutions in the time of Henry VIII. Consequently, we can have a reasonable idea of the state of the corresponding Irish institutions at any given time. The same can be said to a lesser degree regarding local government in the counties and shires though we are hampered by the fact that there was not a single universal model of local government, and much depended on the local customs of the English places from whence the feudal lords came, the conditions of their charters, and Irish local customs which they felt necessary to accommodate. With regard to the Gaelic lordships, though there was constant change, we have little contemporary written evidence regarding what conditions were like at the beginning and the end of the period, or how conditions differed in the various lordships. The archaic code of Brehon Law is unreliable evidence even if it ever had been applied universally. However we can make conjectures based on medieval practice elsewhere and also from the practices of similar warring, cattle-raising tribes in Africa.

What we call kingdoms had in the Middle Ages certain characteristics which came about in different ways in different countries in a haphazard fashion. The Gaelic word *ri* (ree) was equated with the vague Latin word *rex* and Old English *cyning* (see *Oxford English Dictionary sub voce*). This latter is understood as the chief of a local group or people, kin. A more appropriate translation of *ri* is chief, though in this book I often use the word lord as fairly equivalent to the various grades of Norman lords.

Brian *Boru* (meaning doubtful) around the year 1000 had managed to conquer all the provincial chiefs and exact tribute from them. He did not manage to establish a dynasty. After his death in 1014 successive chiefs of three of the provinces, Ulster, Munster, and Connaught tried to emulate his feat, and some succeeded briefly for some years. They became known as high kings with opposition. These high kings could exact tribute, command attendance at their hostings, interfere in the succession in other provinces, divide provinces, or remove parts of their territories. They could reserve judgments to their own courts. It could scarcely be called a Government of Ireland. It is no wonder that Irish ecclesiastics welcomed Henry II.

The Government which Henry II established in Dublin was modelled on that in force in England during his reign when Henry was absent in France. Most of England was under the control of the officers of the counties, and of the cities and towns. More than one of these, like the sheriff and the coroner, were appointed so they could keep a check on each other. In border districts, where there was a need for a powerful local lord, marches or palatine counties were established, giving to the local lord or indeed bishop much greater power and authority than was usual. In Ireland these were called liberties. Royal writs could not be served in a liberty. The complaint that the royal writ did not run outside The Pale is therefore misleading. Care was taken by successive kings to place men they personally knew and trusted in positions of importance in Ireland. They were perfectly aware that knights like John de Courci could accept invitations to intervene in local wars and carve out independent chiefdoms for themselves. There was always a close connection between the monarchy and the leading lords in Ireland who were often great barons and earls in England as well.

Purpose and Policies of the Irish Government

In the heyday of Irish nationalism this question would never be asked. Everyone then knew its purpose was to conquer Ireland and to hold the 'native' Irish in chains. But this view does not stand even the slightest examination. There is simply no comparison with the army of knights, foot soldiers and clerics that Duke William of Falaise brought with him to England in 1066. The continued stubborn resistance of the Anglo-Saxon nobles allowed William to declare their lands forfeit and to share them among his followers. Doubtless many who followed Henry II to Ireland had similar expectations, but he made only two grants, one to Hugh de Lacy in Meath and one to Richard de Clare in Leinster. For the rest he recognised Rory O'Connor as lord of the remainder of Ireland.

The original purpose of the justiciar's court was to regulate the affairs of these three and settle disputes between them. When the first justiciars were appointed their duties were very limited, being largely concerned with dealing with the affairs of the two tenants in chief and the Gaelic high king Rory O'Connor. There was no Irish army; the feudal tenants-in-chief would provide the knights and other soldiers in summer time when called on by the king or justiciar. The justiciar's court, staff, and household were tiny. It probably included a seneschal or steward in charge of the food. A handful of noblemen in the justiciar's court could perform all the tasks required of a butler in charge of drinks, a chamberlain in charge of the bedroom, a marshal in charge of the horses, a cleric (chancellor) in charge of writing and sealing letters, etc, and a treasurer in charge of the big chest in the king's bedroom. (They of course had servants or junior officers who did the actual work.) The revenues of Dublin, Waterford, Cork and Limerick and some lands around them were apparently all that was required initially to support them. The lands around Dublin were initially quite small, much of the future county Dublin being allocated to de Lacy. Against this, constables with small garrisons had to be maintained in the towns. The retention of the ports was not made for financial reasons but to prevent them falling into the hands of local chiefs. There was also to be a tribute from the Irish chiefs which Rory O'Connor was to collect, but it is doubtful if much of it was ever paid.

There was no policy of conquest or suppression. Neither were there policies of economic exploitation or subjugation. Local lords were responsible for all local affairs including defence and justice. But when the experiment of allowing Rory O'Connor to continue as 'high king' of Ireland broke down as it rapidly did, the justiciar became more and more involved in local disputes.

The actions too of the local Gaelic lords and Norman knights became more complicated. Both parties had in interest in getting other people's land and were prepared to collude with each other. The king then took the opportunity to exercise the feudal overlordship and take disputed lands into the royal hands. This was particularly marked in John's reign as he tried to construct strong Norman lordships in a semi-circle around the lordships of Leinster and Meath. The other policy was to grant feudal lordships to Norman knights they could not otherwise control. Such was the case with John de Courci in Ulster. It had been Rory O'Connor's duty to expel him, but he failed in the attempt. As in the original case of Strongbow, it prevented a feudal knight getting a non-feudal lordship independent of the king. It has been observed that if the justiciars had been less scrupulous with regard to the lands of the Gaelic chiefs in the 13th century when the Normans were strong, the Normans could have taken over all the land of Ireland as they did in England. As it was, the role of the justiciar for much of the later Middle Ages was largely that of a fire-fighter just trying to deal with outbreaks of violence as they arose. But in the 15th century, the Great Earl of Kildare as Lord Lieutenant restored the power of the king's lieutenant to what it had been at the beginning of the 13th century.

Structure and Officials

When considering officers and officials it is a mistake to assume that they knew much about their job, or that they were energetic and honest in the discharge of their duties. Indeed one should make the contrary assumption. No training or aptitude was required for any job nearly all of which were filled by patronage. Loyalty was normally the first requisite. On the other hand, those making appointments generally tried to get a person with some efficiency and skills to do some of the work, often as the deputy or assistant of the office-holder. Especially in the later Middle Ages English officials had a poor opinion of the quality of Irish office-holders. One should assume that bribery and the exaction of fees was normal.

The name justiciar was given to the chief official who was charged with running the government of one of the king's dominions when he could not be present in person. Such an officer was commonly appointed in England when the king was in France or abroad as was often the case until 1215. On the Continent the officer was usually called the seneschal. These could take decisions without waiting for express instructions from the king. The king had satisfactory methods of accounting and control, and had devised standard procedures for routine matters (Warren, *Henry II*, 294). Later in the Middle Ages the term justiciar went out of fashion and was replaced by lieutenant, usually referred to as the Lord Lieutenant for the office holder was invariably a nobleman. If the Lieutenant did not go to Ireland a deputy for him was appointed, referred to as the Lord Deputy.

The powers and duties of the justiciars when they were first appointed were to carry out the duties of the king, as the king would do if he himself were present in person. Gradually, both in England and in Ireland, other officers were appointed with specific duties, with regard to the courts and the revenue for example. Later in the Middle Ages the powers of the Lord Lieutenant or Lord Deputy were listed in their commissions (Otway-Ruthven, 145). Though instruments of central government were put in place, and some parts of Ireland were shired, and given sheriffs and shire courts, the government of Ireland until the end of the Middle ages remained essential feudal. The justiciar governed much of Ireland through the great feudal lords. At first, the justiciar was allowed £500 for his household which included 20 men at arms. Later it became necessary to make fixed contracts so that he could maintain larger forces of men at arms and archers.

The justiciar always acted with a council. Neither in the Norman system or in the Gaelic system was the king an absolute monarch. In the Gaelic system the leading members of the ruling family chose the chief or lord and acted as a check on him. In the Norman system, though primogeniture was the rule, the chief barons in council gave their assent. This was not necessarily the heir apparent who could be set aside as Henry I and Stephen showed. The king governed with a council of leading lords and made legislation with their consent. It is not clear who belonged to this council but certainly the great lords and ecclesiastics who formed the king's court did. The same was true of the justiciar's court.

The line between a council and a parliament was far from well defined and the same assembly might be called by either name. The term Council in itself was a term of vague significance, being applied alike to the Privy Council, a permanent body composed of sworn members who held the position either in right of their rank as prelates or magnates, or by virtue of special summons, the Great Council, consisting of the prelates, higher clergy and that vague body the baronage, or the Common Council, similarly constituted but with the addition of 4 representatives of the commonalty. The term Parliament, again, was used for sessions of any of these three councils, and it was only after the Common Council had become properly representative of the three estates that the term gradually became narrowed down to imply the national representative assembly (Salzman, 208f, Otway-Ruthven 148). The Council developed largely under Edward I; it then consisted of the king's chief officials, Chancellor, Treasurer, and Keeper of the Privy Seal; it became the centre of late medieval government; the Chancellor always seems to have been the most important figure in it (Underhill, 31, Chrimes' book *An Introduction to the Administrative History of Medieval England* is recommended. A smaller council known as the Privy Council dates from Tudor times).

In Ireland the justiciar had his council and he too appointed various members to the new offices as they were formed. The office of the justiciar (king's lieutenant, lord deputy) was by far the most important. In fact it can be said to be the government of Ireland as the king and his council were the government of England. The justiciar was commander-in-chief of the army, the head of the civil administration, and the supreme judge. He could summon armies from the feudal lords (or scutage in lieu of service) and lead these armies anywhere in Ireland at his own discretion. He was responsible for collecting the royal dues and taxes. He appointed the various officials to the chief offices, and his patronage extended to other lesser offices like constables of castles. At first he appointed sheriffs to the counties, but this duty was later given to the treasurer and the barons of the exchequer. When keepers of the peace were formed in the various counties they were appointed by the justiciar. The council, or part of it, travelled around the country with the justiciar for they formed his court. It was a simple affair unlike the viceregal courts of the 18th and 19th centuries.

In England the king's personal curia or court was gradually split up into distinct offices, perhaps chiefly at first for record keeping, though individual officers could move from one office to another. An office (*officium*) was an official duty. The office holder would be given a small room or chamber (*camera*, what we call an office) in which to carry out his duties. It would have had some boxes in which to keep the records. The chancery would have had also attached a somewhat larger room or scriptorium or perhaps a part screened off with *cancelli* (screens). Medieval government was tiny, the king being content if most of the revenue came in, that the lords did not fight each other, and some sort of justice was executed on the worst criminals. The king's foremost concern as always was to be ready for war, whether sought or unsought. The justiciar's establishment with all the officers and courts was very small though it grew slightly in the course of the Middle Ages. Nor did it need to be large. Probably fewer than a few hundred people or institutions had any business in its courts. Like all courts at the time both sides just presented their cases and a judgment was either made or deferred.

One officer the justiciar had to have to hand in 1171 was the Chancellor, usually a literate cleric who had under him several literate clerics to conduct the justiciar's correspondence. Most laymen at the time were illiterate so the clergy had to be intimately involved in government. A formal Chancery Office for correspondence, almost invariably in Latin, was established in 1232 under a chancellor even though the justiciar already had his clerks who performed this. All written documents had to be sealed with an official seal or great seal which was kept by the chancellor. (The seal or *sigilla*, a small figure indicating the king, was a stamp impressed on wax attached to a string attached to an official document. Different colours of wax could be used.) In time too the chancery took on judicial functions. In the courts there was no hard and fast distinction between justice and administration. The chancellor was to become the second most important official after the justiciar.

The Court of Exchequer in Ireland was established around 1200. It had two duties, to collect Irish revenues and to maintain the king's fiscal rights. The clerks were normally literate clerics and those making or disputing payments were illiterate. For business a table with a chequerboard cloth was kept and accounts were kept with split tally sticks, one half for the man to keep and the other for the cleric. (The tally sticks remained in use until 1724 but were maintained as records until 1824 when famously burning them in the heating system in the House of Commons set the whole house on fire.) The chief cleric was appointed treasurer in 1217. The treasurer at first was the chief official after the justiciar and had a seat on the council. Later another cleric was given the title of chancellor of the exchequer to keep a check on the treasurer. The chancellor of the exchequer who later prepared the budget remained a judge in the exchequer court until the office was abolished in 1817 when the two exchequers were merged. The remembrancers were in charge of keeping the rolls on which the various records were kept. On the court side of the exchequer various officers were appointed as barons of the exchequer but the judges who formed permanent barons of the exchequer were not appointed in Ireland until 1272.

A chamberlain whose duty was to look after the affairs of the king's chamber *(camera)* or private room was appointed. The powers of this office grew in the Middle Ages because the chamberlain had daily contact with the king. The escheator's office was very important, and early in the Middle Ages he was a member of the council as important as the treasurer. He was in charge of lands which came into the king's hands for various reasons. These could be forfeiture of lands of tenants-in-chief, such lands during the minority of the heir, and the lands of bishoprics and abbey during vacancies. The skills or qualities of those appointed to these offices seem in general not to have been high (Frame, 'English Policies and Anglo Irish Attitudes in the Crisis of 1341-42'; Johnston, 'The Interim Years: Richard II and Ireland, 1395-1399', 184; Harbison, 'William of Windsor, the Court Party, and the Administration of Ireland', 163).

When any branch of government emerged or was developed in England a similar branch was, sooner or later, developed in Ireland. (One suspects that in many cases offices were established in Dublin because there was one in London but without any local pressing need for it.) Coats of arms and the other paraphernalia of heraldry developed in Norman Ireland as in England. To distinguish helmeted knights in battle or in tournaments devices were painted on their shields. There was no law about the matter and any knight could adopt any emblem. As a general rule, the simpler the device the more ancient it is. In accordance with the theory that the king is the font of all honour nobody could make himself a knight and so could not give himself a coat of arms. Richard II appointed an Ireland King of Arms in 1382 but no steps were apparently made to give him jurisdiction in Ireland. At the same time Irish chiefs began awarding themselves coats of arms and other heraldic devices. Several well-known devices emerged at this period, the Irish harp, the red hand of Ulster, and *azure, three crowns or* (blue field with three golden crowns) granted as an augmentation to the Earl of Oxford and Duke of Ireland in 1386 (Fox-Davies, 462). Heraldry in Ireland with the proper heraldic conventions dates from Tudor times.

Finances

A primary aim of any government at any level is to extract as much revenue as it can from its subjects. This has been true since the earliest records of trade in the Middle East and it applied at all levels of government. The welfare of the subjects was not a matter of concern except in so far as it might affect revenue. The revenues of a medieval government came from six sources. There was the income from the king's feudal rights, mostly collected by the escheator. There were the rents of assize, the rents of the king's demesne land and the farm of rents from towns in royal hands. There were the profits of the county or sheriff's courts and the profits of justice in the royal courts. From the reign of Edward I there were the customs collected at the ports. Finally, in the later Middle Ages was direct taxation (Otway-Ruthven, 162). This direct taxation, such as poll taxes were presented by the king as requests for subventions for particular reasons like the expenses of the marriage of the king's daughter.

As a general rule in the Middle Ages all income came from the land. However, as trade increased it was possible to tax transactions of merchants and many ways were devised to collect these taxes most of them local, for example port taxes, road taxes, and bridge taxes. When other transactions developed, for example in the law courts, it was possible to charge fees for example for writing out documents or by charging fines. Some went to the crown and some to the office holder. Nevertheless it was usually necessary to provide institutions with an endowment of land specific to that institution. So lands had to given for the support of bishops, of the chapters, of archdeacons, of monasteries, schools, universities, and of parish priests, and these were not transferable between one and other. There was no wealth of the Church as such, only the wealth of individual institutions within it.

Before cash became common most revenue was exacted in kind, in goods and services. These might include the provision of food or forced hospitality. Medieval finances were extraordinarily complex, almost a policy 'If it moves tax it; if it does not move tax it'. There was no idea of a consolidated fund into which all taxes were paid and out of which all payments were made. Every office and institution was self-financing. An office was the income of its occupant and it was up to him to collect the fees and dues attached to the office. Every office holder took part of the income or whole of it for his own support. The gaoler collected fees from his prisoners, a custom abolished in the 19th century. The turnkey had to be paid for opening the door, both going in and out. Captains of soldiers were given money to feed and clothe their troops and were allowed to keep part of it. Lords charged with supplying the army made great personal fortunes out of it. So too did commissioners of revenue. Sources of revenue varied as much as the places that were taxed. Places on the seashore paid fees that were not applicable elsewhere. Justice paid its own cost and the cost of supporting all lawyers. Writs for example, had to be paid for. The man who composed the writ, the judge who authorised it, and the clerk who wrote it out, all got their cut. The payment of salaries to public officials from the public taxes became the general practice only in the 19th century.

Sources of royal revenue which the sheriff had to account for were the royal manors in each county, receipts for encroachments, profits of royal justice, portions of special levies, danegelds, scutages, and aids. Other people who had to send in accounts were bailiffs or stewards of honours, reeves of towns, custodians of the temporalities of vacant bishoprics and abbeys, and of escheated baronies and fiefs (Chrimes, 58.) Royal levies, subsidies paid by a levy on the county, were put forward by Edward in his writ for the Model Parliament 1295. As late as 1294, when the knights of the shire consented to a subsidy of a tenth being levied from the counties, special arrangements had to be made with the towns for a subsidy of a sixth (Salzman, 211).

Royal prerogative rights were fines for homage, livery of lands and reliefs, wardships, escheats, and episcopal temporalities. 'Casualties' in exchequer terminology fluctuated considerably. There were also profits from justice, mints operating periodically, and two thirds of the profits from absentee's lands. Most judicial profit came from the Court of Exchequer. Eventually royal customs dues were imposed at ports and made up much of the justiciar's revenue. Later too there was the opportunity to hold ecclesiastical and seigniorial lands in the king's hands for periods of time. The two major items of expenditure were defence and officials' salaries (Ellis, *Tudor Ireland*, 172). These were collectable in theory. That very much was collected from most of Ireland is doubtful. Many of them could be and were assigned away to private individuals.

Treasure trove, which Adam Smith noted provided no small part of a monarch's revenue, came under the responsibility of the coroner not the sheriff. Another source of income was wrecks of the sea (*wreccum maris*) though these were often given to the local lord. They also came under the coroner. Whales and sturgeons were royal fish. These rights were derived from the royal prerogative, the authority innate in monarchy to decide anything. The same is true of all unmarked swans.

Warren notes that the king (Henry II) was open to financial offers for offices, the wardship of a minor, the marriage of an heiress, a service of his court, and even his good will (Warren, Henry II, 269; Lydon, England and Ireland 54). Rather striking in Ireland is the absence of a large royal demesne, lands held in the king's own hand to provide goods, services and money for the maintenance of the court, or in Ireland the justiciar's court.

(In England William I had reserved 1,400 manors as a royal demesne, made more profitable by erecting towns on them.). Henry II did not see fit to retain such lands, nor did John though both had opportunities to do so. They may have felt that the revenues of the ports the king held would be sufficient for the tiny justiciar's court of their time, and any military activity required could be met by the feudal levy. It meant that the justiciar was very constrained when conditions grew more difficult in the later Middle Ages. Subventions from England became increasingly necessary especially after trade from government-controlled ports declined. The crown lands in Ireland were very meagre. These in 1470 (20 manors in the Pale) could have yielded £1,200 but were usually used instead for purposes of patronage. By resumption and reversion the number of manors increased and output was improved. So eventually the total revenue from this source was c. £500. The royal demesne in Oriel, the barony of Ardee and parts of Monaghan probably returned nothing (Smith 'Medieval Border' 44; Ellis, 171).

The regular royal revenues of the county were valued at a certain sum which as called the farm of the county, and the sheriff was responsible for paying this sum into the exchequer. The items which made up the farm varied from county to county; royal manors and boroughs; revenues from the shire and hundred courts; in some counties the sheriff collected an annual tax called sheriff's aid at a fixed sum per hide; where the frankpledge system existed the sheriff collected the fees; the sums had been set at the time of Henry II and had not been changed (Painter, 89). Warren too notes the great diversity of dues from each county, though presumably in Ireland they were more uniform as counties were formed on an established pattern (Warren, *op.cit*, 268). As elsewhere in the Middle Ages various fees and dues were compounded into a fixed farm, (*fee farm* or *foedum firmum*) or annual sum. The farm of the county meant that the sheriff had compounded for a fixed annual sum to be paid to the crown. He then kept all that remained from the various charges, not to mention bribes. He therefore strove the more strenuously to collect what was due. In the 19th century it was noted that a sheriff had a right to 43 different fees and the speed with which a writ was executed corresponded with the promptness with which the fee was paid. A salary from the county cess was made payable in 1836.

Another source in wartime was scutage, the payment from the holder of a knight's fee, or part of it, in lieu of actual knight's service. A man who was entitled to be a knight could be fined if he did not take the opportunity. The king got money out of him one way or another. Scutage was an important part of the Irish revenue. The profits of justice from the courts were important at first but they declined. They included fees for writs, fines, and the confiscated chattels of felons (Otway-Ruthven, 164).

The revenues of the Government in the early days were good, rising to between £5,600 to £6,000 a year in the years from 1278 to 1284. This was to decline to around £2,400 between 1413 and 1423. After that it rose steadily to around £5,000 by 1500. The crisis of Irish finances was caused by (1) financial inefficiency and corruption (2) the devastation and occupation of royal lands by Irish chiefs (3) the granting out of royal estates to favoured individuals (4) a structural shortage of coin in the lordship. Where the royal courts could not function there was no profits from them. Where the sheriff was no longer effective no revenue came from him. Trade declined and so did the customs collected at the ports. By and large the Government's revenue Ireland fell to about a third of what it had been at its peak. Otway-Ruthven summarises the various ways in which the royal revenue had melted away. Returns from the royal manors declined or could not be collected. The customs revenue had been granted away. The profits from the counties virtually vanished. No mention was made of any returns from the king's feudal rights. The profits of the courts were spent on the fees of their officials. Fees from the Hanaper Office went to the Lord Chancellor. The king had to resort to other forms of taxation in the form of assessments on the lords, the clergy, and the counties and boroughs which resulted in the beginnings of parliaments (p 166).

As in England, subsidies voted by Parliament came to play an important role. These subsidies were at first assessed on counties but later on townlands with cultivated land. These came to be called taxation from the setting of the tax rate, for example two shillings on each ploughland. This was called a carrucage or plough tax. It was a property tax (Ellis, *Ireland in the Later Middle Ages*, 37; *Tudor Ireland* 60).). This was changed to an annual subsidy most of which was not collected. On the other hand many subsidies were collected locally. Rulers had always systematically taxed traders coming into or leaving their territories. So it was not surprising that a custom on the export of wool, wool fells (sheepskins), and hides was imposed on a regular basis under Edward I in England and Ireland. This was an important source of revenue in his reign but later declined. Later, as in England, a tax called poundage was levied on goods entering or leaving the country. Such taxes were easy to collect in the major ports but caused widespread evasion through smuggling. By the end of the Middle Ages there were three port taxes; the great custom, a duty on the exports of wool; the little custom, a levy on all foreigners trading in Ireland; and poundage, an *ad valorem* duty on all exports and imports. (The duty on the import of wine was called tonnage.) The prisage of wines (called butlerage) was granted to the Butler family by Edward I who collected it for the king. The prisage of wine or levy of one cask in ten, and the taking of one-tenth or one-fifteenth of other commodities were in force. Attempts to impose additional dues were forbidden by Article 41 of Magna Charta which recognized the ancient and just customs (*Wikipedia* 'History of the English fiscal system').

To mount a summer expedition, the justiciar called on those with feudal obligations to serve at their own cost for 40 days. Those not needed for the fighting were required to pay an equivalent sum in cash namely a scutage. The justiciar then drew on the royal revenues of Ireland, or that part of it which was not consumed by those collecting it, his own salary, and finally grants from the council in England when he could get them.

Mints and Coinage

In 1210 John ordered the establishment of royal mints in several Irish towns to produce English coinage for use in Ireland. A mint was a small workshop in which small discs of silver were struck with the king's image by hammer and dye. These seem to have belonged to Italian merchants who were engaged in Irish trade and increasingly in banking and money-lending. Mints were established in Dublin, Carlingford, Drogheda, Waterford, Limerick, and Cork which indicates where money was most needed. The coins were identical with those in use in England. In the middle of the 15th century it was decided to reduce slightly the value of Irish silver coins and a copper coinage was issued in Ireland (Burke, 29). Reducing the silver content would reduce their value as bullion below the face value and prevent the export and reduction of coins. The illicit forging of debased coinage by melting it down, adding cheaper metals to the silver and re-minting it remained a perpetual problem throughout the Middle Ages.

Consultation, Parliament and Legislation

We must begin by noting that parliament in the Middle Ages meant something very different to what we know nowadays. Parliament was not supreme; it was just an enlarged council or court which the king summoned, usually when he needed money. Kings normally consulted the great lords, the tenants in chief, and the greater bishops and abbots in council. They normally promulgated new statutes to meetings of the council. For important issues the council was afforced, i.e. more individuals of importance were summoned to it. Councils were summoned by the king. Those summoned were bound to attend, and could not depart until given leave to do so. Lords came to be defined as barons (and later viscounts, earls and dukes). As chartered towns became financially important and the balance shifted from lordship courts to county or sheriff's courts the king began to invite members of the 'commonalty', i.e. not noblemen or clerics, to his councils. Subsidies to the king were assessed on counties. The enlarged council or parliament as it was now beginning to be called was comprised of three 'estates' (statuses), the nobility, the clergy, and the commons. The representatives of the counties and cities gave assent to the assessment of their county and reported back to the sheriff and county court the assessed sum. The estates met separately and voted as separate 'houses'. Numerous Cistercian abbots and heads of houses of Canons Regular were called at first. But afterwards only three Cistercian abbots, those of Mellifont, St. Mary's Abbey, Dublin, and Baltinglass were called. The third estate, very much the lesser one, was to be called the House of Commons, though of course there were no houses at first or even a regular place to meet. The lords sitting in council could act as a court, and in fact the House of Lords remained the highest court until 2009. They reserved the trial of peers to themselves in accordance with the provisions of the Magna Charta.

The third estate differed from the others in being composed of representatives; two knights of each shire or county were to be selected by each county court attended by the whole body of freeholders of the county to represent them. Up to 1430 A. D. knights were elected in the open shire court, but the franchise was then restricted to forty-shilling freeholders. Their expenses were to be paid by a levy on the county. The guiding principal, 'that that which touches all shall be approved by all', was put forward by Edward I in his writ for the Model Parliament of 1295. Parliament was then made complete by the return of two representatives from each city and borough. In 1371 proctors (*procurator*, financial agent) from the lower clergy, two elected from each diocese, were also summoned and became a regular part of parliament. The clerical proctors formed a separate house (Salzman 211; Otway-Ruthven, 170).

The role of the commons was strictly limited. They were to approve the king's levy on the boroughs and counties, and churches and to report back to them the king's reasons for the levy. (There were no newspapers in those days.) They could approve of the king's ordnances, but it did not matter if they did or not. Their consent to legislation was not required. Nor could they initiate legislation. They could petition the king for a particular piece of legislation, their petition beginning with 'Whereas' followed by a recitation of the reasons for the proposed legislation.

When regular summonses were made for two knights of the shire to be sent to the king's parliament, the writ was sent to the sheriff who duly summoned a court of the county to elect the two representatives and to collect a sum to defray their expenses. Not all sheriffs were conscientious or honest in the discharge of this duty (Prestwich, 17). On the reception of a writ from the Lord Chancellor, the sheriffs and mayors summoned county and borough courts to choose their representatives. The distinction between hustings and polling did not arise until later. At the hustings or court for the election candidates were selected by show of hands. If some were dissatisfied a recorded poll of individual freeholders was called and held on a later date (Keenan, *Ireland 1800-1850*, 190). The elections in boroughs though technically free were in practice fixed. A statute of 1490 also provided for election by a simple majority of the voters (Hindley, 76-80).

In 1264 following the battle of Lewes in the Second Baron's War, the first of the new-style Irish parliaments was held at Castledermot. In it the great lords who formed the council were joined by the other great lords without whom the country could not be governed, Geoffrey de Joinille acting as justiciar. A decree that land titles obtaining in 1264 would be respected was obtained (Dolley, 156). Attendance at parliament was not great and was declining. The Gaelic lords were not summoned, presumably because they paid no taxes. Nor did they have an assembly of their own as the institution of high king such as it was had collapsed. Gaelic bishops, who in theory were feudal subjects, were summoned but did not attend. Those bodies which did not send representatives when summoned were likely to be amerced, what we call fined nowadays, which provided a useful record. Attendance at parliament, which in practice was an assent to taxes, was regarded as a burden to be avoided and was never great. There were only 14 counties or liberties eligible to send knights and only 12 towns eligible to send burgesses. At the start of the Middle Ages large monasteries like those of the Cistercians and Canon's Regular were seen as better sources for subsidies, but their wealth declined later.

Parliaments usually met annually. They began to deal with various matters that could have been done in the courts, but this was stopped by Poyning's Law in 1494. Most of the legislation which resulted from petitions was trivial and local, it being assumed that the king would pass the essential legislation in Westminster. The great exception was the Statutes of Kilkenny in 1366 which were aimed at stopping the progressive gaelicization of Ireland. However English legislation would have to be promulgated in Ireland, as Ireland had no representatives in Westminster. This appears to have been done at irregular intervals (see Ellis, 'Parliament and Community in Yorkist and Tudor Ireland'). Legislation was devised by the royal council on the basis of petitions from the Commons which however could be re-worded in the Lords. The statutes themselves often received their final form from the judiciary when the session was over.

The English Parliament did not pass special legislation for Ireland. The Irish lordship was just included in the general legislation for England where applicable. Nobody objected to this and Ireland benefited from it as its statute legislation was automatically updated at no cost. Throughout the 13th and 14th centuries English legislation was applied to Ireland without the approval of the Irish parliament. There were examples of English legislation applied to Ireland simply on the order of the king. As late as 1411 the English statutes against papal provision were 'simply dispatched to Ireland with a royal command that they be observed there'. No mention was made of the Irish Parliament, it being simply ordered that they enrolled in the records of the Irish Chancery and Courts, and that they be publicly proclaimed in the several cities, boroughs, market towns and other places within the said land (Cosgrove, 'Parliament and the Anglo-Irish Community: the Declaration of 1460', 29.)

The Commons were summoned largely to vote supplies. The English parliament could not impose taxation on Ireland because it did not include Irish representatives who could consent to such an imposition. In Ireland as in England since the 13th cent it was recognised that legitimate taxation required local consent. There was however no connection between the right to consent to taxes and the right to legislate (Cosgrove *loc. cit.*).

It was a feature of English government from Anglo-Saxon times, and reinforced by the Norman kings that the monarch should issue statutes and ordinances for the whole kingdom, that is for all freemen. This was statute law as distinct from Common Law which was closer to Brehon Law being more or less a collection of decisions in the king's itinerant courts. These statutes, normally with the concurrence of the Council, were proclaimed in meetings of the Council. They were often cited by the first words of the statute, for example *Quia emptores* (Because the buyers) of Edward I in 1290 which ended subinfeudation. Others were referred to by the meeting of the Council at which they were proclaimed, like the Assize of Arms (1181) or the place where the Council met like the Statute of Gloucester or the Statute of Winchester. Edward III had numerous statutes, of Praemunire, of Provisors, of Mortmain and of Treasons.

Government Military Forces

It comes as no surprise that the forces at the disposal of the justiciar were very small; usually was there no need for great armies. Henry II demanded the services of 50 knights from Meath. The total number of knights that could be summoned from Ireland did not exceed 425. Castles had quite small garrisons. Besides knights there would also be foot soldiers or men at arms, and quite a large number of squires and retainers. In theory all freemen could be called to the hosting at least for defensive warfare. Towns were expected to provide for their own defence. Later on the less wealthy gentlemen were expected to have pony or hobby suitable for war.

A campaign in 1353 shows that the justiciar Thomas Rokeby, had 1,012 men of whom 41 were men-at-arms, 351 were hobelars, 16 were mounted archers, and 604 were foot soldiers (Frame. 'Defence of the English Lordship', 85). In 1369 William of Windsor was told to maintain 200 men-at-arms and 300 archers to be reduced to 80 men-at-arms and 150 archers (Connolly, 111). His actual forces would be larger as he could call on local forces but would have to pay for them. Men-at-arms were professional soldiers like knights but not of the nobility. They were not likely to be villeins or peasants, but members of junior branches of the knightly families. They were often retained by lords and knights. The foot soldiers probably carried bills or spears which were later replaced by firearms. The hobelars had their hobbies or ponies and were very useful in pursuit of a fleeing enemy. If the local lords added their forces, the justiciar might have 2,000 fighting men (Frame, 92). The opposition was not likely to be great either. The greatest of the individual lords could possibly muster and even arm 2,000 fighting men, but at least half of them would have to be left to guard their own districts. There never was combined resistance to the justiciar. Pikemen and archers were seemingly drawn from the lesser families not the aristocracy. However physical strength and aptitude for fighting may have also been taken into consideration. But social divisions were wider in the Middle Ages than even in Victorian Britain. Social and economic factors led a change over to infantry with firearms. Their furnishing for war was much cheaper, and their wages much lower. These men however still had to be free, not villeins or betaghs.

At first the justiciar called on the tenants-in-chief to send men to his hosting for summer campaigns, but later kings and justiciars preferred if they sent money in place of military service. Cash to pay a small number of skilled professionals was much preferred to a general call out of a mob that had to be trained and fed. Also it was not possible, and less and less possible as the Middle Ages advanced, to strip each district of its fighting men. When they returned they would have found their lands ravaged by their neighbours. Kings and justiciars found it necessary to ask for subsidies from the lords, the counties and the boroughs. This in turn led eventually to parliamentary control over taxation. The justiciar had another method of raising funds for campaigns and this was called purveyance. Purveyance was the right of the Crown to requisition goods and services for royal use. The primary problem with the system was that it was open to abuse from corrupt officials, who would often requisition goods and sell them for profit, or use extortion and other means to obtain items or money that was not passed on or divulged to the king. The official set the price he was prepared to pay and it was always below the market price. This led to great resentment (Lydon, *Ireland in the later Middle Ages*, 65).

The justiciar had to maintain a stock of siege equipment which was an essential component of medieval armies as were the craftsmen to make and maintain them. It is likely that any siege engines brought from England lay in Dublin Castle unused. The Gaelic lords had no walled towns and no skill in siege warfare, nor indeed any desire to tie down their troops in sieges. Sieges using guns commenced in the last decades of the 15th century. Earlier methods could involve tunnelling, the use of scaling ladders, and engines like trebuchets. Axes to cut plashed timber were probably the most in demand. Ships, if needed for any campaign, were just requisitioned from the ports.

At times, when the Lord Lieutenant or Lord Deputy was an Irish magnate much larger armies could be raised in the short term in the old ways. What was probably the greatest battle in Ireland in the Middle

Ages was the result of a dispute between the Earl of Kildare and the chief of Clanrickard when each side gathered an army of thousands by calling out their supporters. This was the battle of Knockdoe in 1504 (Hayes-McCoy, 53).

Local Government

Nature of Local Government

In Anglo-Saxon England, Gaelic Ireland, and Normandy there was a similar 'feudal' social structure. Feudalism was a particular example of the general structure. In England there were the grades of noblemen and freemen (Brown), in Ireland similar grades of noblemen and freemen (Ó Corráin 171).

This chapter concerns relations with the crown and royal policy. Local administration will be dealt with in a later chapter. Local government in the Middle Ages was very different from what we call local government today. However, then as now, it was conducted in counties and cities and their equivalents. Like the royal courts relatively few people attended the county courts. The vast bulk of the people attended only their manor court or equivalent. Two aspects of local government must be considered, the courts at their various levels where decisions, administrative or judicial, were made, and the permanent officers corresponding to each grade of court. As noted earlier the crown always paid close attention to who was exercising power in Ireland. Great feudal grants were given to those close to the king at the time. The quite frequent occurrence of lords dying and leaving only minors or daughters as heirs gave the crown chances to maintain some kind of control.

The chief executive officer in a county was called the sheriff, and his opposite number in the Norman honorial courts came to be called the seneschal. The Gaelic lordships to the end retained a more primitive structure. There were few officers in the Gaelic lord's court who had influence over the affairs of lesser courts. The leading officers in a chiefdom or lordship exercised their powers over the lesser or mesne chiefs to secure their tributes, rents, dues, warriors and men. These lesser chiefs, the urraghs, in turn put pressure on their subordinates, and so on until the very bottom.

Business, whether administrative or judicial, was conducted in these in much the same way, through the open courts of the lord, sheriff, or mayor. These courts were not of course public courts but were only open to those who had the right and duty to attend them. The court of the county could also be described as the assembly of the most important people in the county. The Gaelic princes mostly and nominally accepted the overlordship of the king of England, but they were governed by their own laws in their own courts. The sheriffs of the counties and the lords of the liberties were restricted by the conditions in the royal grants establishing them and were bound to attend a Great Council or Parliament when the king or justiciar summoned it. It should be noted that for the most part writs of the royal courts in Dublin did not run in the liberties which were subject only to their own courts. The later complaint that the king's writ did not run except in the counties within The Pale is misleading for most of them never ran in liberties. Only the king or justiciar could issue an instruction to the lord of a liberty. Obviously a writ summoning a Council or Parliament was sent to the lords of liberties.

The pyramidal structure of government was more or less the same within counties, Norman lordships, and Gaelic chiefdoms which became more or less lordships in the later Middle Ages. We can be sure that a similar system existed in the Gaelic and Norman lordships to ensure that everyman was accounted for in time of war and every source of revenue taxed. The same was true of the various levels of Gaelic chiefs. Even the lowest grades of Gaelic lords had to have their courts for that was the way business was conducted in the Middle Ages. We have no record of any of these courts but we can safely assume that they closely resembled manor courts.

County, Liberty and Borough Administrations

Counties

As far as the lives of most freemen were concerned, the county court and the baronial court were the most important ones and they rarely would have any business in the royal courts. The shire was originally a West Saxon territorial unit used as basis for the assessment of taxation and the computation of military service that developed within the kingdom of Wessex during the eighth century. Shiring was applied to Mercia when the kings of Wessex took control and was thereafter gradually applied to the rest of the country in line with the growth of the authority of the rulers of Wessex. The formation of the English shires is therefore a process that took centuries and it is generally speaking, impossible to give a precise date for the creation of any particular shire. The Norman kings preferred the bureaucratic administration of counties over which they could exercise closer control to the honorial courts over which they had less influence. But in Ireland, and in England along the Welsh and Scottish borders, they had to rely very heavily on the feudal jurisdictions of feudal lords. These in theory had more wealth and more knights and men-at-arms on the spot to deal with local incursions. In Ireland, dealing with local incursions was a problem in most parts down to Stuart times.

The kings, as occasion arose, introduced the **county** as the basis of local government. This was not always successful and some counties were made palatine counties or liberties. The first district to be shired was Dublin, the only one in the 12th century. Under John counties were formed in Waterford, Cork, Munster (Tipperary and Limerick). The lands of Strongbow in Leinster, de Lacy in Meath, and de Courci in

Ulster remained honorial jurisdictions under their lords. These ample jurisdictions were called liberties though they were liable to be called back into the king's hand. Louth was broken off from Ulster in 1233 and given its own sheriff. In the same year a separate county of Kerry was carved out of Munster, and then Limerick and Tipperary were formed into separate counties. Later still Connaught and Roscommon were made into shires under sheriffs, but the powers the sheriffs could exercise there dwindled almost to nothing. In Leinster, which had been divided between four heiresses, Kildare and Carlow became counties, while Kilkenny and Wexford remained liberties. Carlow, then larger than today, and extending to and including coastal *Arklow*, probably dates from around 1306. A county, based on Kells, was formed in Meath, and a liberty remained based on Trim. So by the time of the death of Edward I (1307) the Anglo-Norman lands in Ireland consisted of 12 counties and 4 liberties (Otway-Ruthven, 174). In the 14th century, Counties of the Cross emerged, consisting of scattered areas of church land within the existing divisions. Unlike the secular counties (or liberties), the counties of the cross were administered by royally-appointed sheriffs.

The government of the county seems in practice to have been in the hands of the magnates of the county or 'county families', though jury service was imposed on all freemen. This would have been normal practice too in the Gaelic and Norman lordships. Later, the gentlemen of the counties, or lords of the Pale, had to elect the sheriff from among their number and were formally constituted as the governing body of the county though they were summoned by the sheriff only four times a year. (In England, the bench of justices of the peace was made the governing body of the county.)

The principal officer in the county was the sheriff. He was at first appointed by the crown, then by the Treasurer and the Barons of the Exchequer. In 1355 it was ordered that he should be elected each year by the court of the county. His principal duties originally fell under two headings, fiscal and judicial, but gradually in the course of the

Middle Ages the feudal levy was discontinued, the tax of scutage was imposed, and the sheriff, together with keepers of the peace, was made responsible for the muster of his county (Frame, 'Defence of the English Lordship', 80). There is no doubt however the sheriff was responsible for the muster of the county even before the formal statute of Edward I. There was in Anglo-Saxon England an obligation on all free men to serve in the army when called on. Men were not numbered individually but the obligation was placed on the land of every free farmer. His hide became the unit of military assessment and of all taxation. The townland remained the basis of assessment for taxes and tithes until the 19th century. In England and France military service of footmen was reduced to one man from every five hides, the other four paying his costs (Brown, 47-50).

These particular taxes were not the ordinary revenue of the crown, but levies for particular occasions such as a war, or for marrying the king's daughter, and it could be under the Norman kings several shillings per townland. The sheriff was responsible for collecting the sums. For this his officers had to have a list of all the farms in their several bailiwicks. The assessment was simple; every townland paid the same and the assessment never changed. No enumeration of Irish manors or townlands seems to have been made when the counties were established, so presumably the existing Gaelic units were just used. To make it easier, as was commonly done in the Middle Ages, an estimate was made of what each county, and each lordship, monastery and bishopric, should pay and the sheriff undertook to gather that sum. This was called the farm of the county; whatever he collected over and above that figure went into his own pocket, ensuring he was not slow to exert himself. The office of sheriff was one of financial speculation for the revenues collectable exceeded those payable. This naturally led to extortion and King John wished to see the system abolished. The sheriff had annually to bring the money he had collected to the Court of Exchequer.

The sheriff was the general factotum in his county and remained so until the 19th century. Some of his duties were assigned to other county officials but he remained the chief executive officer of the county. The sheriff had to pay particular expenses, repair the king's castles and hunting lodges, hire troops for the castles, keep order in the countryside, provide supplies to the court, and for these he received credits. The sheriff was also obliged to see that people who owed money to the crown appeared at the exchequer sessions. This involved serving the writs of the Court of Exchequer. He collected the juries, arrested criminals, kept a prison, and collected the penalties imposed by the courts. He presided over the courts of the shire and the hundred, and acted as judge in minor cases, was custodian of the royal castles and was often in charge of escheated castles (Painter, 89 ff). Later in the Middle Ages in Ireland much of the revenue of the county had to be held back locally as raids from petty Gaelic chiefs became more frequent. An important duty was to organize the sessions of the assize judges, to have the cases prepared for them to hear, and to carry out the execution of judgment, which often meant the execution of the guilty. There was no sentence of imprisonment. Gaol was where prisoners were held until trial and one of the commissions given to the king's judges was general gaol delivery. This meant that every gaol should be empty after an assize. This was an important freedom for arbitrary detention was illegal. (The exception was imprisonment for debt for the prisoners could be detained until the debt was paid.) The sheriff might have to publicise royal announcements such as the making of peace, but his function was not to carry out instructions from the king and Council in England. His duties were laid down by law and custom. The usual announcements were likely to be that the king wanted more money.

The sheriff had various assistants (*servientes*) or serjeants to assist him as well as special officers like gaolers and clerks. If necessary he summoned a *posse comitatus* to deal with more dangerous criminals, a body which still exists in American counties, as does the sheriff himself.

The other principal officer of the county was the *coroner* who acted as a check on the sheriff. He kept a record of all crimes in which the crown had an interest, and so it was difficult for the sheriff to accept bribes not to prosecute in such cases. He also investigated all unexplained deaths even those in the custody of the sheriffs. The itinerant justices also looked at cases of interest to themselves, and kept a general watch on what was happening in counties. Later *keepers of the peace* (justices of the peace) were appointed to deal with defence and public order. In particular they had to ensure that the manors and townlands had sufficient trained men and sufficient arms to be ready for an array or muster. But it was the duty of the sheriff himself to lead a body of armed men against raiders (Otway-Ruthven, 180).

Baronies

In Ireland the counties were divided into bailiwicks or baronies and it was the duty of the sheriff to proceed to each of these in turn and hold a court there for lesser offences or to settle local claims or disputes. Presumably these more or less corresponded with the present-day baronies. In Ireland a barony was the equivalent of an English hundred. Each had a chief constable, and in Petty's time numbered 252. The baronies seem to have been formed on the submission of the chief of each *tuath*. The government of the baronies followed the same pattern as that of the counties. The sheriff summoned a court from among the magnates of the barony or vice-county. As these baronies were constructed from local *tuatha* there may have been more local feeling or sense of identity in the baronial courts. They presumably had criminal jurisdiction like the corresponding courts in the liberties, though most likely capital offences were reserved to the county court or the assizes. They continued to function until 1898. In the 18th century an attempt was made to establish police forces based on the baronies, the baronial constabulary. They retained the right of setting a baronial cess, and could give guarantees for light railways in their district. (In the 19th century, as administrative units of local government they were superseded by the Poor Law Unions which were constructed from townlands on rational principles.) Barony was a manor amounting to 13 and a third knight's fees.

Liberties

Liberties in the second half of the Middle Ages were really glorified counties and were established wherever the crown felt that there was need for a strong local centre. The fate of the earldom of Ulster demonstrated what could happen when a strong family with local interests was not resident. But England in 1166 was very different from England in 1066 and the power and the administrative skills of the crown were much greater. Like William I Henry II was willing to allow considerable Norman comital or marcher privileges to the great tenants-in-chief. Only one of them, John de Courci, for no very clear reasons was made an earl, though Strongbow was an English earl if not a very important one and other tenants-in-chief already had English titles. But by 1317 it was considered necessary to create more local earls with palatine powers. Regular reporting to the crown was required though not to the same extent as in counties.

As was common, later grants were more specific than those in the honorial or comital jurisdictions granted to the original tenants-in-chief. Reserved to the king were the pleas of the crown, jurisdiction in error, and church lands. The pleas of the crown were arson, rape, treasure trove, and forestall (highway robbery). The writ of error meant that any case in a liberty could be summoned to a royal court. This was not the case with the marcher lords in Wales. The exemption of church lands meant that in a vacancy they with their revenues came into the hands of the king not the lord. From the 13th century royal writs with regard to actions which arose elsewhere had to be accepted. Irish liberties, unlike the English ones, were subject to royal taxation (i.e. the intermittent demands for supplementary revenue), and the appointment of a seneschal had to be notified to the Exchequer (Otway-Ruthven, 184).

The chief officer of a liberty was the seneschal who was, like the justiciar, responsible for all the management of the liberty and for its courts. His duties were military, administrative, judicial and financial. He accounted to the exchequer in Dublin for all the financial obligations of the liberty, not only of the lord, but any which arose within the liberty. The administration of the liberty grew in parallel with that of Dublin with similar officers, marshal, chancellor, and escheators, sheriffs, serjeants, gaolers and so on (Otway-Ruthven 183-187; McNeill, *Anglo-Norman Ulster*, 63). One of the chief duties of the seneschal was to preside over the court of the liberty in the absence of the lord. The seneschal, the sheriffs, and the constables of castles were responsible for the ever-embattled earldom. For most practical purposes the duties of a seneschal were the same as those of the sheriffs of counties, though the lord of the liberty was the formal equivalent.

Below the central court in the earldom of Ulster, which covered most of the present counties of Antrim and Down, there were five bailiwicks or 'counties' presumably under bailiffs but who later were called sheriffs or seneschals. Each held a court for those leading tenants who held by suit of the court. This court had criminal jurisdiction, with appeal to the earl's court in Carrickfergus. The lowest courts were the fortnightly manorial courts which dealt with the collection of rents on behalf of the earl's treasurer and other local issues. They were presided over at times by the sheriff of the 'county'. There were perhaps 120 vills in the earldom dependent on the manors of the chief tenants, but the lands were not farmed on the English manorial system but rented out. The day-to-day business of the working farmers was conducted at these vills (McNeill, 88). McNeill notes that in liberties in south-east Ireland the structure might have been simpler.

It is not exactly clear what exactly was the position of great **ecclesiastical lords**, with vast holdings of land in more than one county, like the abbot of Mellifont. The civil rights of the lordship of Newry, i.e. of the Cistercian abbey of Newry, survived until the early 19th century. The manorial court in Newry was allowed by James I to hear cases up to 100 marks, which presumable was the practice earlier. Monasteries had a right to their own gaols, and every Cistercian abbey had to have one. The abbot of Mellifont had a gallows, tumbrel and a pillory in their towns (Columcille, 83, 106). They had criminal jurisdiction to deal with thieves.

Towns

It should be noted that early in the Middle Ages towns, though important for purposes of trade and wealth-creation, were essentially peripheral to society and government. Kings, and indeed archbishops, needed to control towns, but they did not reside in them. On the contrary they had their halls or palaces, often with a castle, with their manorial grounds outside towns. The government of English kings was not centred on the Tower of London but outside the city at the palace of Westminster. The palace of Woodstock in Oxfordshire was more important, and in any case the court was peripatetic. Westminster became more important administratively than the city of London, and remains so to this day. (Westminster palace and Westminster abbey were built side by side by Edward the Confessor before 1066. Later in the Middle Ages it became the king's principal residence. St Stephen's Chapel, or royal chapel in the palace of Westminster, was in Tudor times allocated to the House of Commons and remains their meeting place to this day, though twice rebuilt.)

Towns were established by bodies of merchants for the exclusive purposes of trade and manufacture. They required a defensible place with easy access and a duly constituted group of merchants to manage their own affairs. Often, when first established, as with Brecon in Wales, the town was just outside the walls of the castle and was completely under the control of the lord of the castle and paid their dues to him like everyone else. Usually, in the 12th century, they sought a charter from their lord which was an agreement regarding their respective rights. It could for example be simply a right to act as a corporate legal body distinct from the court of the lord. What these customs were we do not know for no charters have survived. But they were notable for offering generous burgage plots, low amercements and fines, and permission was granted to take timber from the woods of the local lord for building or fuel. Feudal lords were competing for settlers to occupy their towns that would pay market tolls and burgage rents and supply food for the castle. From such charters emerged the medieval town (Pounds, N. J. G., *The Medieval City*).

By their charters the government of the largest towns was in the hands of the guilds that consequently organised their affairs for the benefit of the merchants and master craftsmen. The local lords became accustomed to receiving a fixed annual sum or farm, the *firma burghi* (Latin *firma, ferme,* stable, constant or fixed) instead of a proportion of profits. Such towns were not originally independent of the lord's officials; in fact the seneschal or castellan controlled the town and the town's court was his court. But successive charters could be sought or bought giving extra liberties. They could be given their own court with their own officials, and allowed to pay a fixed sum or farm annually instead of the market tolls and burgage rents. Perhaps only civil cases could be heard, and the lord could include various restrictions such as a prise on ale. A town could be given a monopoly of trade in the lordship. They could establish a merchant guild to regulate trade and all who did not belong to the guild could be excluded. They could be allowed to hold fairs and try capital offences themselves during the period of the fairs. Highly valued was the privilege of being tried in their own court (Thomas, 17-19).

Like the towns in England, Irish towns grew in importance and got increasing powers of self-regulation in the course of the Middle Ages. As they elected the government of the town they controlled the markets, set the price of bread and wheat, and examined fish and meat stalls for rotten goods. Where guilds did not exist the court of the burgesses exercised these functions, those attending these courts did not have to attend the court of the local lord where they could be outvoted by other interests. As usual the common affairs were dealt with in the guild court and the guild might construct a guildhall. A civic body called a corporation could be established, usually from members of the merchant guild, with its own officers and court, which normally at first dealt only with civil cases. Some of the large towns had a court of *pie poudre* to deal expeditiously (within three tides) with cases brought by or against foreign merchants.

As was customary in the Middle Ages the guilds were careful to preserve their local monopolies of trading. Therefore they routinely excluded others from trading in their towns and this meant excluding local Gaelic craftsmen or traders. Occasionally Gaelic settlements grew up outside the walls (called Irishtown) presumably with the consent of the town authorities or the local lord. Oxmantown or Ostmantown on the opposite bank of the Liffey from Dublin was formed by the Dublin Vikings after their expulsion by the Normans.

Sligo in the north west became quite an important port in the later Middle Ages. It was founded fairly late by Maurice Fitzgerald, 2nd Baron Offaly who built a castle and founded the town and a Dominican friary. It was captured by the O'Donnells in one of their many forays into Connaught and was occupied by the family of O'Connor Sligo who acknowledged the O'Donnells as overlords. It was called a *sradbhaile*; meaning a village or town not defended by an enclosure or wall, and consisting of one street. Dundalk was counted as a minor Ulster port. Its trade was much less than that of Drogheda. It consisted of three separate parts, Castletown, Seatown and *sradbhaile* which combined into one and the settlement around the de Verdon castle became unimportant. We may assume that the Cistercian abbey of Newry traded on its own account and also dealt with the local Gaelic chiefs. Quite early a small town had grown up beside the abbey or close to the Norman castle and it was burned by an expedition from Connaught in 1238. It did not become a customs town so its trade must have been smuggled.

A town did not need a formal charter to function as a town. At first all burgesses would have been given the terms of their holdings by the lord, but the affairs of the town remained controlled by the manor or lordship court. Charters could be bought, usually from a needy lord (Briggs and Jordan, 43-54; Lydon, *Ireland in the Later Middle Ages*, 14-17). Charters were usually based on those of Breteuil which were made generous to attract settlers. These charters did not affect trade or manufacture directly; they were concerned with the relations between the burgesses and the local lord. Apparently the first of the new charters given was that given by Henry II in 1171 to the merchants of Bristol.

Occasionally the king could issue a royal charter as he did in Dublin when he re-peopled the city with merchants from Bristol. In 1192 John confirmed the charter and allowed the formation of a guild of merchants. It is assumed that these merchants were already trading with Dublin and that the charter resembled the charter of Bristol at that date. The right to have its own officers, excluding the royal officers, and to pay a fixed farm rent was granted to Dublin in 1215. Town charters were easiest to obtain on crown land and most difficult on Church land. The chief privileges conferred were the *firma burghi*, the right to elect their own magistrates, the right to hold a municipal court, the right to hold a market, the right to hold corporate property, and often to form a guild of merchants. *Firma burghi* (farm of the town) was the right to collect the king's dues and to pay him a fixed annual sum. This freed the town from the sheriff and other royal officers, and the market could be held free of the tolls and control of the lord. The rich merchants controlled the towns (Briggs and Jordan,

41). The market tolls paid by those who attended the fairs and markets were originally paid to the lord, but usually at a later date the tolls were farmed, i.e. the burgesses paid a fixed sum each year, the *firma burghi*. In return the lord provided protection within his lordship. The larger towns had mayors and sheriffs, but smaller ones a bailiff or provost was in charge. The native Irish were never formally excluded from the towns, but opportunities for exclusion arose when guilds of merchants was formed (Otway-Ruthven, 123 ff). A guild was a closed shop. If you did not belong to it you had no right to trade in the town's shops or markets.

Though towns were separate from the seats of government in castles and from cathedrals yet often all three are found close together. This was partly for reasons of convenience, and partly for defence, though the rationale for the siting of each was rarely the same. Towns normally in the Middle Ages had to provide for their own defences against opportunistic raiders, whether bandits or neighbouring chiefs or lords. The early defences were of earth and timber as with the motte-and-bailey castles. The larger and more prosperous towns replaced these with stone walls in the 13th century. Most Irish towns were within striking distance of a raid from a Gaelic clan lurking in the local hills, woods or bogs. These had neither the time nor the skills to mount a siege, so fairly simple devices like ramparts surmounted with a palisade sufficed, as in the case of the motte-and-bailey castles. Most towns provided themselves with stone walls which were probably a status symbol as much as anything else. The defended area in a town was very small, the walls were not very high, nor very thick or strong; nothing more was required in the days of arrows and spears. The walls were built from local stone and lime mortar as simply as possible. Larger stones bedded in mortar formed the outer faces, while the interior was filled with rubble and mortar. But as we know, a murage tax was required for repairing the walls. However the neglect of the walls seems to imply that attacks on towns were not normally expected.

Towns were tiny, stinking, filthy, noisy, raucous, plague-prone, lively, brightly-painted, fun-loving places celebrating all the feasts of the Church. Medieval towns were small, over-crowded and disease-ridden, kept in existence only by a constant inflow of people from the countryside. Animals like pigs were kept, slaughtered, and the meat sold in much the same place. Buildings were of wood, and the whole town could easily burn down. Yet they were lively raucous places and frequented on market days. Gradually, the merchants began to keep a supply of stock, perhaps of wines, or silks, or rich foreign cloths so that even Gaelic chiefs like the O'Neills could come to them especially when an Italian ship had failed to call at their shores. The O'Neills at least by Tudor times could go either to Carrickfergus or Dundalk. Towns were to be found in areas of Anglo-Norman settlement and the distribution of towns gives an indication of the density of colonisation.

By Tudor times there were 43 mostly small walled towns surviving. All but five of these towns were south and east of a line drawn from Carrickfergus in Antrim to Dingle in Kerry. The exceptions were Galway, Athenry, Roscommon, Sligo, and Coleraine (Freeman, 92). Galway, Athenry, and Roscommon along with Athlone form a group linking Connaught with the midlands and Dublin. Sligo was isolated in the North West. There was a large blank space in the south part of the midlands between the Shannon and a line of towns Naas, Kildare, Athy, Carlow, and Kilkenny that marked the route into Munster. The tiny and isolated town of Nenagh survived throughout the Middle Ages. Another line of towns led from the Kilkenny/Waterford area across north Munster to Limerick and Kerry, and another followed the coast down to Cork and Kinsale. North of Dublin there was another line of coastal towns which reached Carlingford. The route into the earldom was across Carlingford Lough to Greencastle on the other side. There were no towns in the part of south Munster controlled by the MacCarthys. Indeed roads did not reach into much of this area, and into large parts of Connaught before government schemes of roadbuilding were started in the 19th century.

The largest town in the earldom of Ulster was Carrickfergus with a population of around 1,000, perhaps 200 families. Bigger towns like Dublin, Waterford, and Limerick might have populations two or three times that size. The total urban population perhaps did not exceed 50,000 out of perhaps 1,500,000 (3%) and was probably less than the accumulations of dwellers surrounding the houses of the lords and the monasteries.

Of the inland towns, Trim, the town of the Lords of Meath, was the more important until the earls of Ormond made Kilkenny their centre of power. Dublin was already the largest city. Munster had three large ports, Cork, Waterford, and Limerick as well as many smaller ones. There was only one large town and port in Ulster, Carrickfergus, while there were two in Connaught, Galway and Sligo. Among inland towns, which were local market centres and administrative centres were Ardee, Armagh, Athboy, Clonmel, Fethard, Kilmallock, Mullingar, Naas, Trim, Navan, and New Ross. Though described as local market centres they traded with Gaelic centres and probably quite a lot of exports and imports of the Gaelic areas were channelled through them. They could be important in other ways. The abbot of Mellifont changed the grange of Collon into a town with a market and the centre of a manor. It was to become a frontier defence post of The Pale between Ardee in county Louth and Slane in county Meath. Collon, being the head of a subordinate manor, had its own gallows and pillory (Columcille, 78, 106, 131). All of these towns, if they did not have stone walls, would have had earthen embankments surmounted with a palisade for defence and would have served as a refuge when the Gaelic raiders arrived, as they were prone to do in the later Middle Ages. Town walls were ubiquitous in Europe at that time.

The most heavily urbanised (modern) counties were Louth, Dublin, Kildare/Carlow and Kilkenny. The other great area of urbanisation was Waterford, Tipperary, Cork and Limerick. Though these were outside The Pale, they were in the area controlled and settled by the

Anglo-Norman lords, in particular the earls of Ormonde and Desmond. A lighter band of towns spread westward from Meath into Galway in the great de Burgh lordship. Sligo town remained isolated in the north west but surprisingly maintained itself (Barry, *Archaeology* 118-9). In Ulster all the towns were on the coast.

There remains the question of towns in Gaelic areas. It remains a mystery why the Gaelic lords did not immediately copy the practice and establish their own towns and in particular their own ports and get their own revenues. The mystery is less why they did not develop in Gaelic areas but why, with rare exceptions, they did not survive the destruction of the castle or monastery around which they grew up. As legal entities Anglo-Norman towns gained a separate existence and accumulated powers and privileges in the course of the Middle Ages. It is undeniable that towns not separate from monasteries existed in pre-Norman Ireland with a population of artificers to supply the needs of the monastery, and no doubt of the surrounding area. Traders would come to these monasteries and may even have settled in some of them. The same would be true of the compounds of the Gaelic lords. When the mendicant orders came to Ireland they went to towns from which they could get their sustenance from alms. Later in the Middle Ages numerous small friaries were founded close to Gaelic castles for the same reason. Yet Cavan is one of the very few towns that came from this source. As so little was put down in writing in the Gaelic areas it is unlikely we will ever know much about them. Yet with few exceptions they did not grow into recognisable towns in the Middle Ages. Kells and Armagh are examples of monastic settlements which became towns, though Armagh was not recognised as a proper town in the Middle Ages. It is strange, but very few towns arose in Gaelic areas. Cavan town seems to be one of the few exceptions. Sligo was a Norman foundation but survived under Gaelic lords. The O'Neills were notoriously opposed to towns and none were formed in their territories until their overthrow.

The Norman Lordships

Though the courts and administration of the county, liberty and boroughs was essentially the same, some observations must be made about the Norman and Gaelic lordships. It is clear that when various Irish chiefs or English monarch gave grants of land to Normans they used existing divisions of Irish chiefdoms at the time. The unit for a grant was the cantred which is akin to the Welsh *cantref*. This Welsh term, which means a hundred towns (townlands), seems to be derived from the Anglo-Saxon hundred which had a similar meaning, but whether it was commonly used before or after the Norman invasion is not clear. The English hundred was a division of a county, and had its own hundred court. The cantref in Wales was divided into commotes. Each cantref had its own court. Each Irish cantref or barony had its own baronial court. (Baronial courts survived in Ireland until 1898.) The Welsh *cantref* imported by the Anglo-Normans almost certainly had some connection with the *tuaithe*, perhaps some joined or divided. Thus Theobald Walter was granted 5½ cantreds in Munster in 1185. He subsequently used them to determine the shape of his seigniorial manors. Because both the county and diocesan administrative systems were created concurrently, the cantred and rural deanery frequently encompassed the same area (Empey, 'The Settlement of the Kingdom of Limerick', 3 ff; Otway-Ruthven, 176)).

The original grants made by Dermot MacMurrough were quite small; the one made by Henry II to Hugh de Lacy of all the lands in Meath formerly subject to **Clan Cholmain** was probably the largest ever given, and was to act as a counterbalance to the power of Strongbow in Leinster. In turn de Lacy divided the land among his barons. Hugh Tyrrell obtained Castleknock; Gilbert de Angulo (aka Nangle), who became Baron of Navan; Jocelin, son of above; William de Missett; Adam Feipo (aka Phepoe); Gilbert FitzThomas; Hugh de Hose, Hussey; Thomas Fleming; Adam Dullard (aka Dollard); Gilbert de Nugent;

Risteárd de Tiúit received land in Westmeath and Longford; later Barony of Moyashell, in Westmeath.; Robert de Lacy; Jeoffrey de Constantine; William Petit; Myler Fitzhenry; Richard de Lachapelle. One of the privileges of a Count Palatine such as de Lacy was that he could create barons or inferior lords (*Wikipedia*, 'Hugh de Lacy, Lord of Meath').

There was no single description of a Norman lordship, for each was dependent on the powers and conditions attached by the feudal overlord to his grants. They were continually changing over time. It was also the policy of the kings to substitute county government for feudal government whenever it was feasible. For much of the Middle Ages powers were granted to some of the great lords in Ireland equivalent to the palatine jurisdictions given to some of the marcher lords on the Welsh and Scottish borders. Maximum power had to be devolved to a great lord on the spot to deal with Welsh or Scottish incursions. It should be noted that, like bishoprics in the north of England, great abbeys were often feudal lordships with the same duties and powers of secular lords.

The tenant-in-chief received from the king feudal titles to lands of which he would be the feudal overlord normally in multiples of a knight's fee, quite often 50. He was expected to build and maintain a castle on his land. Demesne manors, knight's fees, boroughs, fairs, and markets were important elements in a barony, but owning a castle was virtually essential (Painter, *Reign of King John*, 77). He then recruited followers fit to be knights to whom he allocated parcels of land of sufficient size to maintain a knight, his household and retainers and horses for himself and his followers. This might be 600 acres (5 hides or townlands) of good land or 1,200 acres of poorer land. This would then constitute a manor. The lands were held as knight's fees on the condition of rendering certain services to the lord, the chief of which was 40 days military service a year and castleguard. And it is sometimes said that the most common formula was that for every 5 hides of land granted to a lord, one knight was required by the king.

The knight's fee was the common base unit of denomination. The amount of knight service for a given piece of land was fairly arbitrary (Brown, 61). The knight's fee in Ulster was approximately 2 square miles or 1300 acres (McNeill, *Anglo-Norman Ulster*, 79). Knight's fees were estimated in England at five hides. In County Dublin 10 ploughlands were accounted a knight's fee, but in Meath 20 or even 30 became the norm. This is more likely to reflect lower rents than greater danger. In the earldom of Ulster, the equivalent of 10 hides or ploughlands seems to have been the norm (McNeill, *Anglo-Norman Ulster* 79). The tenant-in-chief could increase the number of knight's fees if he felt it necessary. Meath actually had 120 knight's fees though held for 50. This allocation was known as subinfeudation. Subinfeudation, in English law, is the practice by which tenants, holding land under the king or other superior lord, carved out in their turn by sub-letting or alienating a part of their lands, new and distinct tenures. The tenants were termed mesne-lords, with regard to those holding from them, the immediate tenant being tenant *in capite*. The lowest tenant of all was the freeholder, or, as he was sometimes termed *tenant paravail*. The Crown, who in theory owned all lands, was *lord paramount* (*Wikipedia*, 'Subinfeudation'). But it became the policy of the crown that each knight should be directly subject to the crown and not to his own lord. The practice of subinfeudation was ended by the statute *Quia Emptores* of Edward I in 1290. Very quickly service was commuted to scutage at a rate of 40 shillings for a knight's fee (Otway-Ruthven, 105-7). Heirs to a knight's fee who were minors became wards of the Crown, which took control of the land, or granted it to another, until they were of age.

It is not clear by what means or on what basis the tenant-in-chief selected the lands for the knight's fees. Some place obviously had to be selected for the motte-and-bailey castle, and presumably some existing holders had to be displaced. This would normally be members of the family of the local Gaelic chief. These could either accept downgrading in status or flee elsewhere and displace lesser families in turn. This was normal Gaelic practice. When the MacCarthys of Cashel (*Eoganacht Caisil*) were displaced by the O'Briens they relocated themselves to the remoter parts of Cork and Kerry. The O'Carrolls of *Eile* moved into the Slieve Bloom Mountains to await their opportunity to return. In parts of Meath and Leinster which were under populated, colonists were brought in from England bringing new skills and they formed a large part of the population of The Pale. But in many parts, the existing Gaelic cultivators remained in place. Hugh de Lacy displaced Irish lords only when necessity compelled him and encouraged Gaelic cultivators to remain. This seems to have been the intention of Henry II. But other Normans, including King John, were not so scrupulous (Warren, *Henry II*, 205). We can assume to begin with that de Lacy had free disposal of the lands of the *derb fine* of the O'Mellaghlins, the exiled former rulers, but not of the lands of their subject chiefs. Gilbert de Angulo seems to have received lands of the *Gailenga* (barony of Moregallion (*Wikipedia*, 'Gilbert de Angulo'.) But these lands were not necessarily in the places where a castle would be required, against incursions from the O'Rourkes for example who also had designs on O'Mellaghlin lands. As in England there was a French-speaking upper class, and a lower class speaking the local vernacular. In both England and Ireland in the later Middle Ages French died out. The Earl of Ormond spoke Irish and translated for Richard II.

Otway-Ruthven points out that the original grants to de Lacy and de Clare seem to have been intended to convey to them the same rights which a Gaelic lord had over the lesser lords, and over the Norman knights the same as the king had over them. Royal officials were excluded from liberties. They were what were called a palatine jurisdiction with almost royal delegated power (181 ff). The great Irish lords had a right to build their own castles which they exercised. In the castle was the lord's exchequer which collected his rents and other moneys due to him, and sent them to the lord who might be living in England. In the castle too was the chancellery where the register of writs was kept;

here too was the lord's court; offenders could be executed or held in the dungeons; the castle too held an armoury, and a chapel. The castle might be of the motte-and-bailey type later built in stone (Thomas, **Brecon,** 1 ff). The motte was a mound with a defensive work on top; the bailey was an enclosure in which was the wooden dwelling house or hall, stables, workshops, outhouses etc. Knights normally contented themselves with these latter, and indeed could not construct castles without the permission of their lord or the king.

It is not clear who was summoned to the court of a liberty or what was the legal standing of the lords within those liberties. At first there was considerable harmony between Gaelic and Norman lords with considerable intermarriage. Many Gaelic lords were anxious to get the assistance of Norman knights and men-at-arms in their own local struggles. Despite allegations made by nationalist writers hundreds of years later there is no indication that the Normans were more eager land-grabbers than the Gaelic lords.

In the reign of William I all the great Norman lords were called barons and held their land *per baroniam.* These in turn granted lands to mounted warriors called knights. The Norman kings gradually made some of these whose lands were about equal to a county into counts but they were called earls after nobles of similar rank in Anglo-Saxon England. These, unlike the Anglo-Saxon earls had no strict connection with the county whose name they took. (The wife of an earl was called countess.) Barons became an intermediate rank between earls and knights. The feudal dues of an earl were 1 pound, of a baron 13 shillings and 4 pennies (a mark), and a knight 1 shilling. In parliament barons counted as lords and knights as commoners as it is to this day (Salzman, *Edward I,* 209). (There were 20 shillings in the pound, and this indicates their relative incomes.) But Otway-Ruthven argues that the reason for much subinfeudation was not financial or military but to attract a better quality of tenant (presumably not Gaelic) by giving him a military status (Otway-Ruthven, 104-5).

The great Norman lordships given to the 12th century fell apart half way through the 13th century for lack of male heirs, and were divided among heiresses. In the 14th century earldoms were constructed in the wake of the Bruce invasion and around them affairs in Ireland revolved until the end of Tudor times and even after. The counties under the justiciar coped reasonably well with the invasions of the Bruces and indeed succeeded in defeating the invading army which had not managed to do more than waste the countryside. Nevertheless, the English crown made some attempt to restore liberties. One was Kildare but the liberty was short lived. Later the Earl of Kildare was to become the most powerful lord in Ireland. Carlow was again made a liberty but was often administered by the king because of the absence of the lady heiress Margaret of Brotherton. Louth was made a liberty for John de Bermingham for his life only. More important were the liberties granted in Ormonde (Tipperary) to the Butlers and in Kerry to the Fitzgeralds, earls of Desmond. Several barons were created in the 14th and 15th centuries but it was rather the policy of the crown to restrict titles of nobility. Sir Thomas Preston, Lord Chancellor of Ireland, was created Baron Gormanston in 1370. Another 8 were created in the following 100 years nearly all lords of The Pale. The crown was not as profligate with Irish titles as it later became. The rank of viscount, between earl and baron, was introduced in the 15th century. The title of Viscount Gormanston dates from 1478. The earldom of Ulster conferred on John de Courci in 1181 passed to the crown in 1354.

The Gaelic Lordships

It is a common misconception that family of the Gaelic lords owned all the land of the 'clan', for example that the O'Donnell chief owned the whole county of Donegal and the O'Neill chief the whole of County Tyrone. The clan or *cloinn* or *derb fine* was the four-generation family usual at the time, grandfather, father, son, grandson, and so included second cousins. The mensal lands they had, (usually) conquered, were divided among the members of this ruling family. These mensal lands were originally very restricted. Most of the chief's income came from tributes from conquered families, spoils of raids, taxes on traders and travellers, and above all from loans of cattle to the lower ranks at a high rate of return. When a chief, a great-grandfather, died and was succeeded by a new chief from amonst his sons all the second cousins were removed to be succeeded by a new generation of second cousins. Everyone moved up one place, getting better lands and houses. House moving was not a problem as they had little beyond their personal possessions. There was however this problem called gavelkind by which all the chief's sons, legitimate or otherwise, had a right to equal shares in the mensal land of the *derb fine*. This, with very large families, inevitably led to individual portions getting smaller and smaller causing the *derb fine* to seek ever more lands. The generation that was being removed from the ruling *derb fine also* had to find land of its own, but presumably had long made provision for the eventuality. Some doubtless were more successful in this than others. The offshoots of the O'Neills spread like locusts over Ulster.

Wealth was still measured in cows. The Gaelic lordship was divided into several parts. An area called the mensal land belonged to the chief during his own lifetime. Another area was allotted to the ruling family or *derb fine* from which the lord was elected, and the remaining land was allocated to the chief branches of the name. The remaining land was allocated to sub-chiefs; the proportions of these differed from place to place. It would seem that in earlier times, perhaps in the 5th and 6th centuries when free farmers with allodial possession abounded that relatively little of the land in a *tuath* or county was owned by the ruling family. By the end of the Middle Ages it would seem that virtually the land in a *tuath* or county was in the hands of the ruling family and their offshoots. This did no necessarily mean that the chief himself had to have much land. But in some cases he did. By Tudor times MacCarthy of

Muskerry held half the land as mensal or demesne (MacCurtain, 39). It seems, as was customary in primitive societies, that all wealth in cattle, slaves, or treasures had to pass through the hands of the chief who was supposed to distribute it fairly. If some measure of fairness was not displayed to his most important followers he would not remain chief for very long. Lesser folk nobody worried about. Successful chiefs always had plenty of cattle to lease out to their clients who had to maintain them and pay interest to the chief.

Clientship could be either free or base. The free client received cattle from his lord and was bound to return one cow in three for seven years. The client was a freeholder or a lesser noble, but the lord and the client bound themselves to mutual support. This would be called for at each succession to the chieftainship. Base clientship was more onerous, and could be used to make excessive demands. Though the return in cattle was less (8.5% against 33.3%) food renders, labour services and guestings could make it far more onerous (Ó Corráin, 43). As the Middle Ages advanced so too did the demands of the lords.

The ruling families seem to have got control not only over all the land, but more importantly over all the wasteland, common land, woods, bogs and anywhere cattle, sheep or goats could be grazed. In theory landownership was allodial and was incapable of alienation. But the lord could occupy the land of the debtor until the onerous debt was paid, usually never. Also land conquered in battle became the possession of the conqueror. By Tudor times many of the townlands in Gaelic areas had passed into the hands of the ruling families, the learned families, and the Church. For example, in the barony and parish of Truagh in the reign of James I 38 freeholders named McKenna held tates in free and common *socage*, and not *in capite* from Her Majesty's castle in Monaghan. They held at 20 shillings per tate which was 4 pennies per acre. (If the acres were Irish these would be about 100 statute acres). Of this 7 shillings and 6 pennies went to the queen and 12 shillings and 6 pennies went to the governor of the castle (M'Kenna, 247).

Those granted the freehold by the queen were of course the members of the chief's family actually occupying the land. Minor lordships of pre-Norman times were no longer recorded in the annals as their lands were taken by the ever-expanding sub-families of the great chiefdoms.

In the Middle Ages the administration of a lordship at the top at least began to resemble that of the Norman lordships with officials with similar titles. There never was a question of preserving a distinctive Gaelic culture; the Gaelic lords adapted what suited them to their own needs. Offices in the Gaelic lordships tended to be hereditary. In the Middle Ages families tried to obtain hereditary offices if they could, so that it was kept in the family. This suited the chief as well as he did not have to provide for the family's support. Dermot MacMurrough of Leinster had at his side his counsellor, Maurice Ó Regan. He had his professor or *fear leghlin* (man of learning) Aed MacCriffan. His chief lawyer was called Ó Dorain, and his chaplain, later bishop of Clogher, Aedh Ó Caellighe. His chancellor or scribe was called Florence. The chief executives were the king himself, the hereditary lawyer, and the local bishop (Furlong, 49). Most questions could be decided by Dermot himself personally and his two advisors of Brehon and Church law. In his court, only the affairs of the most important lords would be raised.

The administration of the lordships was minimal; the chief appointed a brehon or judge to decide cases affecting himself or the public interest; his decision was an arbitration to which technically both parties had given prior consent. If the chief had an interest he might compel the losing side to obey. Otherwise the plaintiff had to resort to private distress i.e. seize the defendant's goods or cattle if he were strong enough. There was no criminal law as such; crimes were simply torts which might be composed by paying compensation. The kin of a murderer paid an eric, the Germanic *wergild*. Compensation for thefts was several times the value of the object stolen. It is doubtful if many murders or thefts came to court; matters were usually settled summarily between the participants. If chiefs and judges were known to be venal there was no point in going to court. Occasionally in cases of cattle rustling the rustlers or servants might be burned or hanged. The chief kept kernes to exact his tribute, and a marshal to supervise the quartering of his troops. The household kerne could, if the chief wished, arrest malefactors or collect fines. The greater chiefs had a constable in charge of the gallowglasses. These offices were usually hereditary (Ellis, *Tudor Ireland*, 45f). All of these chief officers would have lived in their own halls in their own compounds on their own lands, being summoned only when the chief required them.

In the Gaelic system in Ireland there were three tiers of chiefs, chiefs who controlled an area corresponding to a province, mesne chiefs, who controlled roughly a county, and local chiefs. In the ecclesiastical reorganisation of the 12th century these were mirrored in provinces, dioceses, and deaneries. At the top were the bigger chiefs like the O'Neills, and MacCarthy Mór; despite claims, the power of the bigger chiefs over the minor chiefs in his area was limited. Below these were lesser but powerful chiefs like the O'Donnells, O'Briens, and O'Flahertys; under the O'Donnells were the MacSweeneys and O'Boyles, and they also claimed tribute in North Connaught where they were being strongly opposed by O'Connor Sligo, who himself controlled the MacDonaghs, O'Haras, O'Garas and the O'Dowds (O'Dowd, 121). On the other hand, powerful sub-branches of leading families like the Clandeboy O'Neills were largely independent of their nominal chief. The O'Cahans (O'Kanes, Ó Cathain) on the other hand were notably loyal.

In the territory of O'Driscoll, the present diocese of Ross (which was never made into a county, but like Louth or Carlow could have been), there was firstly O'Driscoll's personal estates. There were also 36 lords (*oglaech*) whose territory was roughly the extent of a knight's fee (Ó Corráin, 171). It can be regarded as being equivalent in size to a parish though in Gaelic areas they were not necessarily made into parishes. It was of course at the courts of these lords of the lowest grade that the betaghs, and local freemen if any remained, conducted their business.

The O'Brien chiefs were made feudal lords holding in chief by John (Empey, 14). Cathal *Crovderg* O'Connor held some lands from John *per baroniam.* By the end of John's reign the Irish chiefs, even the O'Neills, were paying tribute to John (Warren, 'King John and Ireland' 30, 39). In 1385 80 Irish rulers swore allegiance to Richard II. The problem of most of them was not the king, but the incursions of the greater lords, Gaelic and Norman (Johnston, 178). The Gaelic lords in Ulster became vassals of the Earl of Ulster in the heyday of the Earldom but as, after 1333, the power of the earldom waned it was largely nominal, and O'Neill usurped many of the earl's rights. But after Edward IV became king following the battle of Towton in 1461 the earldom of Ulster was vested in the crown, and so the O'Neills became the direct vassals of the king as they had long desired (Simms, 214).

Gaelic society, like the Norman, was a hierarchical society. Inferior chiefs, urraghs, had to pay tribute to their superior chiefs and provide troops for their summonses in time of war. The Government in Dublin and the king disliked this subinfeudation as it were and wanted the nobility of every rank subject directly to the king. The O'Neill chiefs, especially, clung to their authority over their urraghs for it of course increased their strength and importance. Though his ability to control the greater urraghs would have been limited. The country or extent of rule was not strictly demarcated. Rather it was a complex of rights, tributes and authority (Nichols, 24). Overlordship applied to people not land. The Tudor monarchs demarcated them as they created counties and earldoms.

It was the ambition of every chief to extract as much tribute, or presents, or fines from his inferiors without having to pass any of it on to any superior, Gaelic, Norman, or English. Several of the major chiefs, like those of the O'Briens, O'Neills or MacCarthys seem to have managed this for most of the Middle Ages. Towards the end of the Middle Ages quite a few lesser chiefs like the O'Mores, The O'Connors Faly, and the O'Farrells seem to have achieved this, partly from the weakening of the central Government and partly from the disintegration of the power of the Burkes and O'Connors in Connaught. Indeed it is likely that scarcely anyone from Connaught apart from the de Berminghams paid anything. But this independence had a cost. Feudal and Common Law was in force in the king's courts in two thirds of Ireland. The chiefs were excluded from them and could not access them or benefit from them without recognising the suzerainty of the king. It is clear that many of the chiefs recognised this and realised that the great Anglo-Norman earls did not pay great attention to the king's wishes unless it coincided with their own interests, and that it would be wise to make a nominal submission. They might gain personally, but many in the *derb fine* might feel they would lose. The lands, for example, of the *derb fine* would be handed to the chief as a feudal fief, and would be passed on to his heirs. This problem came to the fore in Tudor times when the policy of 'Surrender and Regrant' was applied, for a new earl would also have to face election to the chieftainship or face a rival. There were problems too over the ownership of land. (Only land surveys from the 17th century onwards went some way to settling this problem.)

Succession in Gaelic chiefdoms was rather antiquated. Succession was in theory confined to the *derb fine* of the deceased chief. Election was made by the free members of the lordship's own lands. But this rule was not always adhered to so that apparently excluded families could get back in. A Gaelic chief was above all a leader of a warband. The one chosen was the one most likely to bring success. Murdering your way to the chiefdom was acceptable if it was successful. Consequently all male children, after their birth, were sent for protection to the *rath* of a powerful sub-chief who was bound to answer for the life of his foster child with his own life. They were awarded lands for this purpose on the basis of appanage, lands for the support and education of a child of a prince or lands held on the condition of appanage, i.e. fostering and educating a child of a prince. Protecting the young man when he came to manhood was more difficult. 39% of the known members of the *Cenel Eogain* died at the hands of kinsmen or in internecine wars between 879 and 1607 (McNeill, *Anglo-Norman Ulster*, 104 quoting J. Hogan).

An over-chief was expected to have at least two client chiefs, as well as his own *tuath* under him; above such an over-chief was the chief of the province; the over-chief was obliged to protect the under-chief, to give military assistance, and to receive tribute. Hostages were usually demanded, and the services required differed from place to place (MacNiocaill). If the under-chief rebelled the hostages, which usually included members of his own family were executed. This inclusion of relatives by no means inhibited the sub-chief. The tribute took the form of military service, food for the overlord and his retinue, agricultural labourers to cultivate his land and to build his castles, lodging for the chief and his followers, animals to carry his belongings. The exactions of labour increased in the 15th cent as the population declined. This explains why so many lords were able to construct tower houses in the later Middle Ages (O'Dowd). Others who held land were those who received grants from the chief, mercenaries, poets, lawyers, and ecclesiastical officials. These might hold the land continuously over several generations in stable lordships. But in unstable ones the holding of land changed hands frequently, the older holders losing land to the dependents of the ruling families (O'Dowd, 121,123).

The document, *The Rights of O'Neill*, (www.maryjones.us/ctexts/oneill.html) dating from the time of Dónal, son of Brian of the battle of Down (c. 1300) states clearly the names of the great chiefs and their named subordinate chiefs who were expected to come with their warriors to O'Neill's hosting, and the number of soldiers at free quarters O'Neill might billet on their lands. Some of the chiefs had to pay a tribute in addition. The O'Neills claimed as their right the overlordship of all the chiefs of Ulster. Some of these like the O'Gormleys (*Cenel Moen*) and the O'Cahans (*Clan Connor* of *Magh Ithe*) were cadet branches of the *Cenel Eogain* but most were conquered clans of the *Oirgialla*. The O'Neills also made claim to overlordship over the O'Donnells of Donegal (the *Cenel Connaill*) which was fiercely resisted and over the remnants of the *Ulaid*, the MacGuinnesses and MacCartans of *Ui Eachach* (Iveagh) and their subordinate chiefs. It is not clear how many warriors were expected at a hosting, perhaps several hundred or a thousand in all, or how many of these were lightly armed kernes, or how many were on horseback. Noteworthy at this date is the insistence of a cash tribute. With a full hosting of his own warriors, and those of the sub-chiefs, and mercenaries O'Neill could put an army of one to two thousand warriors into the field for a short period. This would be rare for many warriors would be retained for defence. The whole force for wasting and burning, holding prisoners and driving cattle, as well as servants, would have been much larger.

The centre of the poet's world, like most people's world in 16th cent Ireland was the local lordship. The strength of the lord depended on how much support he could muster, and it was the poet's duty to increase that support, and especially to legitimize the lord's position, and exalt him as a war leader. Society was war-based and concerned immediately with extending the lands and influence of the lord (Cunningham, 148-9).

In Gaelic areas the local chief's house or hall inside its *lios* or *rath* was the centre of a village or small town as were monasteries. These were the equivalent of the Roman *villa rustica*, the farm-house estate permanently occupied by the servants who had charge generally of the estate (*Wikipedia* 'Roman villa'). Numerous trades were carried on there. Strangely, only in a very few cases did any of these 'towns' or 'cities' survive into the modern age. Cavan seems to be the sole case where a settlement around a chief's house grew into a modern town. Settlements around ecclesiastical houses like Armagh or Kells fared somewhat better. It is strange, though that the Gaelic chiefs did not see the value of towns. Some like the O'Neills were positively hostile to the idea of towns and rooted out all Norse settlements within their territories. They were not hostile to trade, and especially after the invention of gunpowder were obliged to purchase it, and to get their workers to produce marketable surpluses especially of leather to pay for it. In Norman times, the manor house replaced the *lios* or villa, and it too was largely self sufficient even if there were towns nearby. In practice there was often little difference between the domestic establishments of Norman and Gaelic lords.

Late Medieval Lordships

One may give an account of counties and Gaelic and Norman lordships and liberties around the year 1200 but they were very different by 1500. For one thing money made a great difference to the way lords got their revenues. Cash rents and customs on trade became more important than feudal incidents or dues or labour or military services. Law was developing all the time though in Gaelic areas it was not committed systematically to writing, leaving an impression that the Brehon Code was still in full force. Arms, armour, and defensive systems came to resemble each other with Gaelic chiefs depending heavily on mercenaries as was common in Europe at the time. The landowning classes were lords whose followers had become tenants-at-will with few precise rights.

'A Description of the Irish System by Edward Tremaine' paints a picture: an Irish lord rules an area about as big as a county. He is elected from among the close relatives of the former chief. The person who was most mischievous in murdering, spoiling and burning is the one most likely to be elected. He is then followed by all the warlike people of his country, horsemen, gallowglasses, and kerns and with these he does what he likes with the inferior people. He eatheth and spendeth upon them with horse, man and dog. He uses man, woman, and child as an absolute despot, as his personal bondsmen. For he is his own judge. If anyone offends him he is put to death or pardoned as his lord wills (de Paor, *Peoples of Ireland*, 139). De Paor however considered that this was mitigated in practice. There is no doubt however that rule in Gaelic lordships was tending more and more to despotism.

The practice of a chief having many clients continued. In the bloody struggles or the elections to the chieftainship a contender had to have amassed many clients or supporters to have any chance. The chiefs' wealth lay in the farmers under his protection and their cattle. Gaelic society was sharply divided between the landed and the landless, and the latter tended to increase as gavelkind, the lord's exactions, and other economic forces forced holders of tiny plots to alienate their lands. Some tenants however were men of substance. Rent was a form of metayage; one quarter of the produce being payable to the lord. Much of the cultivation was done by the sharecropping churls who were effectively tenants at will without stock, substance or rights, and entirely dependent on the lord. As such their rights were much less than their counterparts in the English speaking areas. The churls were not attached permanently to any one lord but every few years had to seek another lord wherever they could. By Tudor times the bulk of the Gaelic population was in this state. Shane O'Neill was the first to arm the landless labourers; before that the landowners were the only ones who were obliged to follow the lord at the rising out either as horsemen or kerne according to their means. Though it surprised men at the time O'Neill was technically correct, for the landless labourers were descendants of free men. Chiefs however tried to prevent them leaving their lordship as the lords of the Pale and lords in England had also done. By the sixteenth century the chiefs were extending to the lands of the lesser landowners the labour services of ploughing, weeding, and reaping, which their own labourers used to perform, an indication of shortage of labourers.

The exactions of a Gaelic lord from his followers continually increased and continued increasing into Tudor times. They were many and diverse and increasing and were imposed indifferently by Gaelic and Norman lords (Nichols, 35 ff). The Gaelic lesser persons had to purchase protection or slantyacht. One exaction was that the lord, with his retinue, expected to be supported *gratis* by those parts of his country he passed through. They also had to give their time freely to the building and maintenance of their lord's property. They expected to be entertained wherever they went. What came to be called coyne and livery was free quarters for the lord's mercenary soldiers who were just billeted on the people to maintain them at their own expense. Not only the lord's but all the lord's officers had to be supported. The principle of hosting a superior applied widely. A bishop or dean with his retinue making visitations of parishes was supported by the parish. The real abuse was in the enormous size to which a chief's retinue grew. If the client was bankrupted his lands were seized by his lord. When it came to exactions from their inferiors Gaelic and Norman lords vied with each other and copied from each other. Gaelic chiefs exacted heriots (Norman succession fines) from landowners subject to them, and demanded dowries for their daughters. No opportunity to increase their revenue was passed up.

Fr Columcille noted that the Anglo-Norman lords imitated the worst practices of the Gaelic lords, including coyne and livery, and wasting church lands. The problem was ancient. "In 1072, however, the 'Annals' record that 'a forcible refection was taken by Murchadh, son of Conchobar O Maeleachlainn, king of Meath, at Iseal Chiarain, and from the Culdees, so that the superintendent of the poor was killed there, for which Magh Nura was given to the poor.' At that period a refection or entertainment of the king and his followers corresponded to the rent pay-able in later times" (http://en. wikisource.org/wiki/ Page:Dictionary_of_National_Biography_volume_12.djvu/25). Primate Octavian excommunicated all those 'who violently, knowingly and maliciously invade, enter, appropriate, cut down, depopulate, consume, destroy, unjustly occupy and lay waste the lands, possessions, fields, farms, mills, revenues of the house [Mellifont], rights and privileges (of the monks), crops, trees, plantations, woods, thickets, rabbit-warrens, weirs, fisheries and meadows which . . . . to the aforesaid abbot and convent . . . they presume nefariously to extort illegal and detestable exactions, especially those commonly called Coyne and Livery, Foyes [a demand of food for people and horses] and Codhyes [cuddies, *cuid oidche*, hospitality for the night], demanding as their right provision and lodging for themselves, their horses and their servants, food for their men, provender for their horses, fleshmeat, bread, ale, and all kinds of delicacies desired by them or pleasing to them, which they expect to be given and presented to them for nothing after the manner of a compulsory and burdensome imposition, though indeed it may more truly be called an oppression since they extort it from the same tenants and vassals against their will and despite their resistance, by means of threats, terrorism, fury, forcible taking of pledges, savage floggings of men and women, and other devilish and unchristian ways.

And they have even presumed frequently and rashly, with their horses, their followers, their serving lads and their animals, maliciously and occasionally with affected ignorance, to destroy, waste, dilapidate and depopulate, the fences, the ditches, the cornfields, the grazing fields and the pastures of the said abbot and convent and of their tenants and vassals, and they retain and conceal the books, the ornaments (or jewels) and other goods and property of the said monastery of Mellifont which had been lent to them for their use or given to them to hold as a pledge' (Columcille, 148-50).

The Statutes of Kilkenny were aimed precisely at the 'degenerate English' who had copied and made their own the worst abuses of Gaelic society.

Courts

Laws

In the 12th century there was no such thing as all-encompassing legal systems. The law in any place was the custom of the local court.

Laws and courts must be understood in the context of the time. There was no formal place for holding a court, no body of statutes, no civil or criminal codes, no police or other body of officers to seek out evidence, no prosecution service, no schools for training judges in the law, no officers to carry out most punishments. Instead, the chiefs at their various levels resolved disputes brought before them. Normally the king or chief would appoint a senior official, a sheriff or seneschal to arbitrate in most cases, reserving only the most important to himself, and in particular cases where the rights of the king or chief were involved. No king, lord or chief stood aside when his own rights were involved.

Roman law, in particular the written Code of Justinian (*Corpus Juris Civilis*, 529 A.D.) was no longer followed. It had the characteristics we normally associate with law. It consisted of enactments of the ruling person or body, it was written, it applied everywhere in the kingdom or chiefdom, and it was promulgated. Various kings, chiefs, and rulers in the early medieval period promulgated their own local codes of laws, presumably promulgating by edict or decree what was the best of customary local practice and making it the law.

There were five systems of law in Ireland, or six if English statutory law is distinguished from *Common Law* though both are applied in the same courts. Statutes gave more precision to Common Law offences. The relations between the king and his tenants-in-chief followed *Feudal Law* and was taken from Normandy. This was concerned with the relations of lords, vassals, and fiefs. Though by 1170 feudal and Anglo-Saxon law may have been fused into a unity. International *Canon Law* was used in many circumstances all over Ireland. Henry II appointed English Common Law as practised in England since the time of William I to be the law of the Norman districts and this included English statutes. In this he was following the precedent of William the Conqueror who decreed that Anglo-Saxon laws as observed in England in the time of King Edward should continue to be the law of his English-speaking dominions. Gaelic or *Brehon Law* was to be retained as the law in districts ruled by Gaelic chiefs. The study of Roman Law, the *Corpus Juris Civile* re-commenced in the Middle Ages and was the branch of law studied in universities. It had an indirect influence on English law insofar as many senior clerics were familiar with its principles. Matrimonial law was in the province of the Church. International law or the law of the sea was dealt with in admiralty courts and adapted the *Corpus Juris* as a common standard. Admiralty courts were established in 1360 but Admiralty Law was introduced into England by Eleanor of Aquitaine while she was acting as regent for her son, King Richard the Lionheart (*Wikipedia*, 'Admiralty Law'). It was not unusual in Europe to have several systems of law existing at the same time. A case would fail if brought in the wrong court even in the 19th century. With regard to the overlapping jurisdictions of the various courts Warren notes that its complexity defies analysis and local knowledge might be required in particular cases (Warren, *Henry II*, 251).

Both Canon Law and Common Law developed rapidly in the Middle Ages, while Brehon Law, like most things in the Gaelic districts become increasingly archaic and backward-looking. At least the written Law did. In practice the brehons were more pragmatic. All three systems depended on collections of ancient decisions and precedents. The Gaelic laws, or Brehon laws, and the Anglo-Saxon laws were collected and written down most likely by Christian clerics who Christianized them as best they could (Jones, 94). But very few lawyers would have had a full copy. Laws were still committed to memory, and were learned from a master. English Common Law barristers still take pupils.

There were various collections of Church canons and laws. The lengthy Irish collection of canons, compiled in the eighth century, influenced both Gaul and Italy (*Catholic Encyclopaedia*, '*Corpus Juris Canonici*'). The real advance in the collection occurred in the 12th century. It was about 1150 that the Camaldolese monk, Gratian, teacher of theology at the University of Bologna, to obviate the difficulties which beset the study of practical, external theology (*theologia practica externa*), i.e. canon law, composed the work entitled by himself *Concordia discordantium canonum,* but called by others *Nova collectio, Decreta, Corpus Juris canonici,* also *Decretum Gratiani,* the latter being now the commonly accepted name (*op. cit.*). The name *Concordia discordatium canonum* harmonizing conflicting canons, is significant. Gratian's work marked the beginning of the *Corpus Juris Canonici* (the Body of Canon Law) which remained in force until 1917 when it was replaced by the *Codex Juris Canonici,* the Code of Canon Law. By the end of the Middle Ages the *Corpus Juris Canonici* was in force in every Christian country in the Latin Church. It was not a codified system, but a collection of collections of canons and decrees. Some of these, issued by various Popes, had the force of promulgated law. Oddly enough Gratian's *Decretum* was not included, and could be used for interpretation only. The Roman Civil Code (*Corpus Juris Civilis*), or parts of it was being revived in Bologna, and some use seems to have been made of it in Ireland in the later Middle Ages (Nichols, 50). It had a powerful influence on Scots law.

English law was called Common Law. It was largely a collection of judgments made by the judges sent out on circuit. These judges were not lawyers, but among themselves collected customs and judgements and harmonised them, and constantly added to them. It was therefore case law. It was also practical law not theoretical law or the attempted application of Justinian's Law. The king made Common Law courts, record courts so that he and all others could have a record of what was decided. Common Law was thus a record or a selection of records of what had been decided, and judges began to quote precedent, as they do to this day. But then and now they were not bound by precedent. Most ordinary crimes at the time like assault were Common Law offences. A Common Law marriage was one where it was commonly known that a man and woman were living as man and wife though there was no record of their marriage. Before the Norman Conquest in 1066, justice was administered primarily by county courts, presided by the diocesan bishop and the sheriff, exercising both ecclesiastical and civil jurisdiction. Trial by jury began in these courts. It is likely that before this all those assembled in the court decided the verdict. Reducing the number to 12 or 15 or 23 selected men would have simplified the system. (The House of Lords retained the decision of the whole body.) In 1154, Henry II institutionalized Common Law by creating a unified system of law common to the country through incorporating and elevating local custom to the national, ending local control and peculiarities, eliminating arbitrary remedies and reinstating a jury system—citizens sworn on oath to decide without fear or favour criminal accusations and civil claims.

While Canon and Civil Laws joined Theology, Philosophy, and Medicine to form the curriculum of medieval universities, Common Law, like surgery, was taught by apprenticeship, and was much less esteemed and regarded. The status of Common Law judges only rose when they became useful to Henry VIII in establishing the Reformation. If Civil Law little influenced Common Law it was because it practitioners were entirely ignorant of any law but their own (Jones, 96). Henry VIII forbade the study of Canon Law (Jones, 100).

England had also a long tradition of statute law, though most of these enactments were local customary law written down and promulgated by royal authority, the king having taken counsel with wise men. The same practice was continued by the Normans as in the assizes of Henry II. English statutes were normally applied to Ireland by royal command (Cosgrove 'Parliament and the Anglo-Irish Community: the Declaration of 1460', 30).

Brehon Law was given an almost mystical status by Gaelic nationalists as illustrating the superlative justice of the Celtic race. It is difficult to see how it can be described as law in the modern sense. In fact it was a table of tariffs. Brehon law was very similar to Common Law, though differing in detail, and it had a very different history. It was essentially a collection of decisions and precedents, gathered presumably from all over Ireland, and incorporating customs, practices, and decisions derived also presumably from those who introduced the Celtic language. At its heart was a system of statuses and therefore compensations. When a dispute was brought by two disputants the first thing the judge or arbitrator had to do was to ascertain the statuses of the two parties, and these were determined by genealogies. They could determine the social grades of the contestants from the numbers of cattle each owned. They were then able to award compensations; compensation for a slave killed was very different from that for a son killed. Compensation for an eye was different from compensation for a tooth. Some attempts were made to standardize quantities like the bushel for purposes of compensation, but it is unlikely that a national standard was ever adopted. (Weights and measures, were finally standardized as imperial measures for the British Empire in the United Kingdom in 1826, and adopted by the Irish Post Office along with British currency on the same day in the same year. The Ordnance Survey was at the same time standardizing the measurements of land.)

There was no criminal law as such. Every injury had an appropriate compensation. However, in the course of the Middle Ages, English practice was being introduced, such as the hanging of a horse thief. The standard eric (*eraic*) for murder was 105 cows which the murderer or his relatives had to pay to the victim. A thief was obliged to return twice the value of the stolen goods (Nicholls, 59-64).

When it came to be written down, largely presumably by Christian clerics, it was couched in a very archaic dialect which later became almost incomprehensible to later brehons or legal scholars. It was never considered a definitive code, though arbitrators found it convenient to keep referring to it as a great authority. No attempt was made to re-write it in later Irish, or to update it. It is considered that in the medieval period in Gaelic areas it was regarded as little more than window dressing, while legal scholars drew on Roman civil law to update their legal advice (Nichols 50). It was not fixed law and the legal families arbitrated cases exactly as the Common Law judges did. It is a pity no records were kept of their decisions. There were very few enactments written down and published by chiefs, though Irish chiefs controlled areas similar in size to the chiefs of Kent or Wessex. Nor in the Middle Ages did they attempt to enact laws.

One may ask in what courts the Brehon Law was used. We can be certain that it was used in courts of the *tuath* because in these those attending could afford the fees. The point in the parable of the importunate widow was that she pestered the judge to hear her case because she had no money to give him to hear the case (Luke 18.1). But in the courts of the lesser lords and local courts it is doubtful if anyone could afford them. In such cases we can assume that local custom was followed, and local custom was determined by asking the oldest of those attending the court. As was usual in such cases the particular custom which favoured the lord would be remembered.

March Law was a hybrid system which grew up in the Norman lordships in the later Middle Ages. It was customary law and reflected the practices of the honorial courts. Not all historians are happy with the extension of the term march law to cover the adoption of Gaelic practices in the honorial courts and wish the term to be restricted to two features mentioned in legislation (Brand, 'March Law', *Medieval Ireland*; Lydon, *Ireland in the Later Middle Ages*, 45-6). The honorial courts, according to the decree of Henry II, should have been following Common Law.

There was a problem with the apparently clear distinction of Common Law in Norman areas and Brehon Law in Gaelic areas and this was that Gaelic freemen and lords remaining in the Norman districts, and these were often numerous, were not summoned to the honorial, county, or royal courts. This apparently was not intended. At first the language spoken in these courts was French but that was not an obstacle. It is likely that most people spoke both languages. It would appear that the custom grew up of just excluding Irish freemen, chiefs, and their families, leaving them just with their own 'manorial' courts which were of no use in disputes between local minor lords. (The jurisdictions would have over-lapped but that was no problem in the Middle Ages.) A man was normally tried in the court of his lord. But if apprehended for a crime against a man of a different lord he might be tried in that court. The Irish were not actually excluded from the courts, but they could take no action in them. They had to persuade or induce a person with rights in the courts to act for them, and herein the problem seems to lie. (An ordinary freeman in the court of a *tuath* would need a minor lord to back him, so of necessity he would have to become a client of some lord.) The Anglo-Irish lord acting for them gained financially by seeing that those of Gaelic origin on the lands of a feudal fief were excluded, as they would have to give him a 'gift' to represent them. An attempt was made in 1331 to allow all Irishmen except betaghs access to the courts, the betaghs being confined to the manor courts (Otway-Ruthven, 189f). Though Anglo-Irish lords were opposed to demands for access to Common Law courts, but it was possible to purchase the right from the crown (Dolley, *Anglo-Norman Ireland*, 160; Ellis, *Tudor Ireland*, 95). Thomas Fitzgerald, 2nd Earl of Kildare, got a patent allowing his Irish tenants to be subject to English law (*DNB*, Thomas Fitzgerald). The 'Five Bloods' the chiefs of the five principal provincial chiefdoms were never excluded (Curtis, 76).

Lawyers practising in the Irish courts were expected to be familiar with the Common Law. Some travelled to the Inns in London but there were complaints they were being unfairly excluded. Some too sought preparatory instruction from an experienced Irish lawyer before going to London. (the Inns of Court were not teaching institutions but halls of residence where students studied law under the guidance of a senior lawyer and took part in disputations.) By the 15th century, the chief books studied were *The Old Tenures*, Littleton's *Tenures*, and *Natura Brevium*. Tenures clearly were an important subject, while the treatise on the various kinds of writs was highly regarded. Knowledge of the law in Ireland was not considered high in Tudor times (Kenny, 6-11, 21). In 1210 John brought with him a team of able lawyers, who at the instigation of the Irish (*ad instantiam Hiberniensium*) he established that the laws of England were to be kept in Ireland. Most of the lawyers who came with John were experienced lay judges but one was a cleric who had formerly held the position of justiciar. From time to time decrees were issued to achieve uniformity on both sides of the Irish Sea. Attempts by the Irish courts to develop differently were checked.

Courts and Control in General

Society in the Middle Ages was tightly controlled for everyone. The idea of personal liberty, 'I am over 21, and I will do what I want, when I want and as I want' was a concept totally alien to the time. The **Rule of Saint Benedict** as practised in the Middle Ages gives us a good idea how societies were organised. The head of the monastery was the abbot who had full discretion regarding what to do. All food, clothing, medicines etc. were handed out by the abbot. The abbot was however bound in important matters to call the whole community together and ask the opinion of every monk beginning with the most junior. The abbot could appoint a prior to assist him and also deans in large monasteries who were in charge of ten monks each. On lesser matters the abbot could consult only these. There was a strict order of seniority dating from the time of the monk's arrival at the monastery.

Each day the monks went to the chapterhouse, for secular affairs could not be discussed in church. There the abbot, or in his absence the prior, addressed the community on what practical affairs needed to be discussed, appointed or removed officers, received postulants, and gave out the work for the day. Then, if necessary he held the Chapter of Faults where penances were assigned for various offences. All a monk possessed had to be given to him by the abbot.

The situation would have been no different in the household of any strong farmer or *boaire* or the minor relatives of chiefs who replaced them. All food and drink and more importantly clothing would be allocated by the head of the family even to grown up sons and daughters. Everyone's duties and tasks were assigned to them. Nobody had any cash and without cash there was no independence. Any faults, disputes or crimes committed by any of his family, servants or dependents within the family were dealt with by him on the spot. This could involve severe beatings.

With regard to courts in all three systems of law we must banish the idea of learned lawyers, barristers, or attorneys pleading in huge buildings before learned judges drawn from the ranks of the most experienced lawyers. To be made a judge no knowledge of the law was required. A judge was not even required to be honest. A sheriff could be a judge, a bishop could be a judge, the chief of the *tuath* a judge, anyone drawn from the royal retinue. Like lay magistrates in Britain today they were provided with a clerk who was supposed to know something about the law. Many of these could indeed be clerics who, as a class, could read and write. There were no courtrooms. Justice, such as it was, was dispensed in the open, under a tree, or in the porch of a house. (Manorial courts and coroner's courts could be held in recent centuries in the largest room in an inn.) Much has been made of the learning of certain great legal families, but there is no indication that there were learned brehons in each *tuath*, or a learned advocate skilled in Common Law in each barony. Still less in every household.

All courts were variations of a pattern. The lord or chief, in each jurisdiction and at each level, summoned it at regular intervals. An individual could come under several courts for different purposes. There was no distinction between administrative and judicial courts. Administration and judgement were dealt with in the same court. Later some courts became more specialised but still retained some administrative functions. As late as the 19th century assize judges retained some administrative functions. In Gaelic areas there seems to have been little development in the course of the Middle Ages but this appearance may just be the result of our lack of knowledge. We would expect them to follow the practice of the Common Law and ecclesiastical courts fairly closely. There could on the other hand have been inhibiting factors for a change in practice usually means winners and losers. Even in a manor different courts could be called for different purposes, like courts baron, courts leet, and courts of frankpledge (See below 'Manorial and Local Courts'.)

The court or courtyard was where the superior met his immediate inferiors. The meeting was normally held in the open, but religious bodies generally had a special building apart from the church for holding secular meetings. Parish churches however had not the same separation of sacred and profane. Courts were originally all-purpose assemblies and only gradually were specific functions of the original court hived off. An early example was the establishment of an exchequer court with its table cloth painted in black and white like a chequers or draughts board to deal with financial payments and accounting. On farms certain days were still appointed for the payment of rents. The form of a bishop making a visitation of his diocese was just like a judge sent on circuit to visit a county. The leading men or leading clergy were summoned, an address was made to them, and then any affairs could be brought to his attention, and judgments given summarily.

As trial by battle and trial by ordeal were banned, after 1215 they were gradually replaced in the royal courts, including county assizes, with trial by jury. This was followed by the *sub poena* of witnesses who were to bring the accusation. After 1798 in Ireland with its massive intimidation of witnesses by terrorist organisations, the Solicitor General gathered the evidence sworn before magistrates and brought the prosecution himself. An inquisition process was never part of the British justice system and the papal inquisition was not allowed in England. In the 19th century, new civil police forces were given powers of investigation and prosecution.

In both the Gaelic and Norman systems only freemen could attend the courts. In the Norman areas there were, or should have been, manorial courts, the court baron, the court leet, and the court of frankpledge. These courts were held by the lord of the manor or his seneschal, and all the business of the manor was conducted there. By the end of the Middle Ages it would seem that all men with property were freemen, but not their servants. Servants and suchlike, in both systems had to be represented by their masters. Similar courts for issues like small debts were to be found in chartered towns. There seems to have been courts in the Gaelic areas below the level of the *tuath*. Justice, locally, would be left to the *boaire* or free farmer, in his townland, who would adjudicate on disputes within his own extended family and also among those who worked on his land. By the end of the Middle Ages, with the disappearance of the *boaire*, the lowest court would have been that of the *oglaech* (knight) whose holding was about the size of a parish.

In all systems the judge was the lord of the territory, or in the case of shires, the leading men of the county or the assize judges. The king had immediate jurisdiction in all his realms. In the Gaelic system most verdicts were dealt with by brehons, the chief reserving only the most important to himself. In England, the sheriff was not the judge in the county court, but presided over the assembly of the chief men of the shire who took the decisions (Warren, 249-55, 284). The kings began to send out their own justices to supervise sessions (called assizes) in Norman times especially in cases where pleas of the crown were involved which were miscellaneous and numerous. This institution of itinerant royal justices to hear pleas in the county courts was an important development. These justices were not experts in the law, but gentlemen of the royal household who learned their trade on the road as it were.

In Norman times the verdict of a jury became an important method of deciding verdicts. The jury reached its verdict through evaluating common local knowledge, not necessarily through the presentation of evidence, a distinguishing factor from today's civil and criminal court systems (*Wikipedia* 'Common Law'). They were men who were supposed to have some knowledge of the case, for example what were the ancient landmarks, or the ancient custom. They could hear the pleas of the contending parties, believe one side or the other, or substitute their own knowledge, and then swear to the justice of their verdict. Most of these jurymen would have been illiterate, though gradually clerics were appointed to record verdicts. Lawyers might argue from law books, or from what they heard from their teachers, but collections of laws and precedents normally held contradictory precedents as Gratian had noted. The systems were adversarial. The court itself took no action. In the case of a crime like murder, bystanders or witness had to lead the prosecution. It was not until the 19th century that the Government undertook to prosecute in cases where the witnesses were likely to be murdered. Nor did the court carry out the sentence. It was left to the victorious party in civil suits to carry out the sentence if he could. In criminal cases the execution, often literally, was given to the sheriff.

As usual in the Middle Ages when annual salaries were rare officials were paid by fees. They charged a fee for almost everything including being kept in gaol. This meant that bribery would pass unnoticed; the party paying the largest fee getting the verdict. Getting a jury to deliver the verdict made that more difficult. In Gaelic society not all testimony was regarded as equal. Those with a higher honour price could over swear those with a lesser honour price. This gave a great advantage to the rich when it came to disputes over property. It was also unlikely that anyone won a case against a relative of the chief.

Royal Courts

The original, all-purposes, justiciar's court was split into three, Exchequer, King's (Justiciar's) Bench, and Common Pleas. Chancery was only developed as a special equity court much later. The early chancery was purely an administrative office concerned with writs and records and not a court. The specialised courts seem to have been initiated by John who sent out itinerant justices on the English model. As these were presided over by justices of the royal courts in Dublin they were royal courts though held in the counties. There was no particular decision to separate royal courts; this was just done as need arose. They were allocated certain kinds of business but were not restricted to these except in two specific cases. Cases involving royal revenue were confined to the Exchequer, and Common Pleas and Exchequer had no criminal jurisdiction. It must be remembered that the English royal courts were just in their infancy, perhaps consisting of no more than a room, a clerk, and a judge, and in this form they were established in Ireland.

Appointments of chief justices to preside in the justiciar's court seem to have commenced around 1220 an indication that the omni-competent justiciar's court was overloaded, or perhaps to act as a check on his power. (Or perhaps just to provide a remunerative office for someone.) Later the Lord Chief Justice presided in the senior court in Ireland that of the King's Bench. (It was called the justiciar's court until the time of Richard II, and thereafter King's Bench. Its jurisdiction spread to all parts of Ireland held directly from the king. The court met in Dublin, but also accompanied the justiciar around Ireland (Brand, 'Courts', *Medieval Ireland*, 109-10).

The right to hear pleas of the crown was being removed from the liberties. (This of course would increase the fees payable in the Court of King's Bench!) These cases in the royal court or King's Bench were those in which the king had some interest. Pleas of the crown were various. They included such cases like treason or attack on the king's servants which directly involved the crown. But they also include homicide, arson, robbery or breach or royal perquisites like shipwrecks, treasure trove, and beasts of the sea stranded on the coasts (Warren, *Henry II*, 251). The Court of the Exchequer was concerned with financial payments due to the crown. It was the most ancient of the specialized royal courts in Ireland. By a legal fiction it was able to extend its jurisdiction into Common Law and equity cases, but had no criminal jurisdiction (Keenan, *Pre-Famine Ireland,* 307). Later a separate court, the Court of Common Pleas was set aside to hear cases between lords and other persons free of the court in which the king had no interest. Presumably most of the cases would have been concerned with disputes over land. Bishops and abbots spent a lot of their time trying to hold on to their lands. It also had no criminal jurisdiction. The four courts, of Exchequer, of Chancery, of King's Bench, and Common Pleas were to endure a long time and gave their name to a famous building in Dublin. They finally came to an end with the Supreme Court of Judicature (Ireland) Act (1877) when the personnel were transferred to the new logically-separated divisions.

The Court of King's Bench was central to the king's desire to keep a measure of control of the local administration of justice in his own sight. In time the judges sent out on eyre or assize to the county courts were appointed from the ranks of the royal courts. The Court of King's Bench was given the power to summon a case from any lower court into the royal court. Eventually, in the area of Common Law there grew up a right of appeal from the county or liberty court to the king's court. Like everything else, these developments were piecemeal. A Court of Criminal Appeal was not established until 1907 though nationalist M.P's secured that the Act did not apply to Ireland (Keenan, *Post-Famine Ireland,* 241). The Court of Common Pleas in England was given a permanent place in Westminster in 1215, but in Ireland more work was done in the itinerant King's Court until the end of the Middle Ages; lawyers in Ireland were therefore more dispersed unlike in London. As late as the 15th century clerks (clerics) could be made puisne judges, but gradually only those with legal training were being promoted.

Ellis notes, when dealing with the Irish Parliament that much of its work was caused by the amount of administrative and judicial matter which were brought before it. Much of the litigation could have been heard before the ordinary courts; but as in England the Courts of King's Bench and Common Pleas were by the late Middle Ages little more than debt-collecting agencies. Parliament was thus clearing up matters which in an earlier day would have come before the courts. The remedy was to appoint a day in one of the Common Law courts to determine the title of land or whatever; in England the remedy lay in the development of Chancery. It is hard to avoid the impression that courts and gaols, and counties were offices of profit and were run for the benefit of the officeholder not those using or suffering the services.

The assize courts were extensions of the royal courts. The itinerant justices at the assizes were not concerned solely with hearing civil and criminal cases. Magna Charta and the Assize of Clarendon provided for the trial of serious criminal cases on circuit, and the Statute of Westminster II provided in 1285 for trial of fact in civil cases at the local assizes. Certain cases were to be heard in the courts at Westminster unless (*nisi prius*) they had already been heard by justices in assize. They had administrative functions as well and continued to discharge them until the 19th century. They promulgated new legislation. They assessed taxes on towns and royal manors. They reviewed the activities of the lesser courts. They tried to root out crime and local mal-practice (Warren *op. cit.*, 298). As Warren notes, given the difficulties they faced and the lack of resources it is a wonder that the courts functioned at all, but they did (*op. cit.*, 322). The assize courts in the counties and cities were for many freemen the most important courts and remained so until the 20th century.

In 1428 the English Court of King's Bench decided it had no powers to review the acts of the Irish Parliament. After 1441 the trickle of Irish cases which had come before the English Court of King's Bench dried up and the Irish Parliament undertook the job. Some of the work too undertaken by Parliament had apparently been earlier done by the Council; this Irish Council was notoriously faction ridden so the litigants may have preferred Parliament (Ellis, 'Parliament and

Community', 45-6). The English courts remained competent to review Irish decisions of Irish courts. Parliament was itself a court, though appeals from the Irish Court of King's Bench were finally confined to the House of Lords.

The Irish court system grew slowly and in uncertain directions until it finally emerged as a full-blown but very overlapping system. By the 19th century too the judges were incorrupt, something that could not be claimed in earlier days. But practice in the courts bred an order of lawyers who were to play an increasing role in Irish politics.

Shire Courts

After the Conquest there arose in England two overlapping systems of courts, the honorial courts and the shire courts. The differences between shires and fiefs were not great. Both depended on the powers granted to them by the king. In the case of honours and liberties, succession was hereditary, though at each generation dependent of the consent of the king. Shire courts were more closely supervised by the king, largely to protect his own financial interests, than the honorial courts. Shire courts were subject to regular inspections by royal 'justices' while the barons in the Magna Charta secured an agreement that royal judges would only visit them every seven years. In England, shire courts had an advantage over the honour court of a great lord. The latter might have extensive lands scattered over several counties, while the shire court dealt with contiguous lands. If the holding of a lord was small in a particular county his influence might be equally small. In Ireland the extents of liberties and counties was the same and it was to some extent a matter of royal policy whether a county was made a county or a liberty or honour. Though the nature of conquest required that at first great stretches of country had to be granted to great lords, there was always the need to restrain them. The king eventually took power to transfer cases from any court, shire or liberty, to a royal court.

Until that was done there was no appeal from an honorial or liberty court. Writs of *Coram nobis* or writ of error could summon the case before the royal judges.

That being said the vast bulk of administration of the country lay in the shire and liberty courts and remained so until the 20th century. Only the very great and very wealthy had business in the royal courts, though royal justice was available in the county town during the assizes. The standard of justice was not high. Bribes could be accepted. But more importantly, great men in the county or liberty must not be offended. Business was conducted expeditiously, and several hundred cases could be dealt with in a few weeks. Only freemen could attend. The sheriff had to assemble from amongst them a jury or enough men for several juries. These were asked by the judge to attest under oath the facts as they knew them. These had to be honest and respectable freeholders, *liberi, probi et legales*. Later the requirement that they be worth *quadraginta solidi* (forty shillings per annum) was added. Almost certainly jurymen would have been selected from among those of equal rank with the accused. Trial by one's peers (*pares,* equals) was guaranteed by the Magna Charta. On the other hand those of lower rank could too easily be intimidated by those of higher rank. The judge simply accepted their verdict. This was important in cases regarding the possession of land, for very few had written records of their ownership. Monasteries, which usually had charters, were constantly at law defending their properties from grasping local lords (Warren, *Henry II*, 338, 340, and 354). The court proceedings were largely laid down by Henry II. The ordinary people of the county could not attend the county court, but only their manorial or similar court.

Baronial Courts

Little is known of these courts which apparently were not courts of record. They corresponded to the English hundred courts and also to the ecclesiastical deanery courts. They dealt with lesser and more local matters than the shire courts. They were visited by the sheriff in the sheriff's tourn twice a year when he kept himself informed with regard to what was happening in the various districts of his county. Baronial courts survived until the end of the 19th century. They appear to have had some competence to try civil cases of small value, like small claims courts. See also the next section regarding bailiwick courts.

Norman Lordship Courts

The exact structure of administration in the lordships is far from clear and there can be little doubt that it developed in the course of the Middle Ages. In the grant of Meath to Hugh de Lacy to hold by the service of 50 knights there seems to be only two levels of courts, de Lacy's court of the honour, and the knights' manorial courts or whatever they had as the local equivalent of a manor. The first would be the equivalent of the county or diocesan court, and the second the equivalent of manor or parish court. The honorial court was much the same as the county court and the reservation of the royal pleas was the same. The profits of the court went to the lord and not to the king. The seneschal of the lordship presided over the courts like the sheriff in his county. All officials were appointed by the lord of the liberty. In the earldom of Ulster the earl's principal court was at Carrickfergus. John de Courci had a classic 12th century baronial household. He had a steward (seneschal), a constable, a chamberlain, a forester, and at least one clerk. The office of chamberlain was later made into two, a treasurer and a chancellor (McNeill, 63).

There developed intermediate courts on the level of the cantref, barony or deanery. In fact the earldom of Ulster was divided into five bailiwicks. These bailiwicks originally had bailiffs over them who were later called sheriffs or seneschals. Their chief duty was to collect the rents and dues. The bailiffs or sheriffs had twice-yearly sheriff's tourns of the cantreds (baronies). These courts were the main criminal courts, but with appeal to the honour court at Carrickfergus. Local issues were dealt with in the fortnightly manor courts over which the sheriff may have presided. In the earldom there seems to have been an early division into counties, which would later only be reckoned as baronies. We must not expect uniformity for a de Courci or a de Lacy would draw heavily on the local custom in his own part of England.

Gaelic Lordship Courts

There were courts in the Gaelic lordships, presumably at every level, as in the Anglo-Norman areas, but they kept no records, and virtually nothing has been written about them. It is not clear who exactly acted as judge in these courts, whether the brehons acted as judges, or merely gave legal advice or whether the chief or lord presided or a seneschal appointed by him. Everywhere, in the Middle Ages, the king, lord or chief was the final judge and would never hand over judgment against himself to an independent judge. Proceedings, as in Anglo-Saxon courts were adversarial, one person accusing another and the other defending. Decision was not left to an independent sworn jury, but seems to have relied on the weighted testimony of the adversaries. Indeed it is likely that the decision was made by the body of all those attending. The weight of a person's testimony varied with his honour price which was a perfect formula to allow the rich to cheat the poor. The Brehon Law was full of indicators of status and the appropriate honour price. The successful party then enforced the judgment himself, if he felt able. Otherwise he could probably rely on one of the lords who was his patron or on the chief himself to enforce the judgment, or the influence of the Church or the poets could be sought. A satire from a poet was universally feared (Nicholls, 57-9). To force someone to come to court it was lawful to seize some of their property. These courts were held on hilltops or in a rath. Brehons could be hired to state the law. The judge's fee was one twelfth of the sum involved. Gaelic lords were as likely to seize Church property as the Norman lords.

There is little doubt that the lesser Gaelic lords had their own courts where they dealt with the affairs of all the lesser lords and kinsmen, free craftsmen and clerics within their domains. There were also doubtless courts, corresponding to manor courts, which dealt with the affairs of the unfree, the workers who did the work, regarding the patches of lands they held, and the returns expected of them, their days of labour and so on. Holding a court was the way the business of a manor farm was conducted. The rights of grazing in the local woods, what animals could be grazed, and the numbers allowed each year to each family must have been strictly controlled but we do not know how this was done. Putting out too many animals injured the rights and welfare of others. Not that this would weigh too heavily with the chiefs themselves. Though none have left written records we know they must have existed, for that was the way business was done.

Manorial and Local Courts

Most of the evidence we have regarding these comes from England and we have no idea if that evidence is typical. It is important to recognise that every male head of a household was bound to attend some court, and was bound to follow its decisions. There was no such thing as individual freedom. Later in the Middle Ages, when cash rents became common, and with it the ability of the farmer to decide on his own crops, he got a bit more freedom. But he was still bound on all communal issues like access to grazing, water, firewood and such like. The same was true with regard to taxes which were assessed on the county and then split up among the various holdings down to the last townland. County cesses were collected in this way until the 19th century when replaced by the Poor Law valuations.

At this level we can take it for granted in both Gaelic and Norman areas that everyone was illiterate. This would be true whether an expert in Brehon Law or Common Law attended or the local parish priest. It is doubtful if either Brehon Law or Common Law applied at this level. What counted was the custom of the manor or local court. On these everyone was an expert. There was a manor court to which all the heads of the villein families had to attend. This court and not the seneschal largely had control over what was done on the farms of the manor, the adjudication of rights, the allocation of strips, the choice of crops. The seneschal or steward appointed by him would always be present to insist on the lord's rights, the days of labour due, and when they were due. He was not necessarily concerned about who managed the affairs of the tenants between themselves.

Cooperation in the form of common consent was also a principal feature of the manorial courts. These assemblies were convened so that decisions on farming practice could be made, by-laws framed and enforced, manorial officers appointed, and civil actions heard. All tenants, regardless of size of landholding or status, were obliged to attend the manorial court. The labourers and other landless people, though, could not attend and consequently had little voice in village affairs. The court's authority was enforced by a committee or jury of freeholders and villeins, and presided over by the lord's steward. The meeting elected the jury, which judged civil disputes, and manorial officers such as bailiffs, constables, overseers, ale-tasters, and woodwards. These posts were mostly filled by richer tenants. Manorial courts probably had their greatest influence where the openfield system of agriculture was practised for everything had to be decided in the court, the type of crop, the allocation of strips, the days of common labour and so on. Even where this system was not practised, matters like the days on which the lord's fields were tilled, or weeded, or harvested had to be determined. Cheating in such matters as putting more geese on common grazing ground than allocated would have to be controlled. Disputes among neighbours had to be resolved. For these manorial juries were called. These matters have to be determined whenever a group of people live and work together. Punishment was likely to be speedy and brutal. 'The hang the man and flog the woman, who steals a goose from off the common'. Theft of linen cloth spread out for bleaching was probably common and probably horse stealing. The ordinary tenants would have no mercy in such cases which were hard to protect against.

The ordinary farmers and villagers summoned to these courts were probably extremely conservative and opposed to all innovation. Custom, *quod fuit ab initio*, (what was from the beginning) was what they were used to and what they were happy with. Changes did come, but almost certainly at the initiative of the lords who saw means of profit for themselves.

Manors were made into parishes in the 13th century in Norman areas, while in the Gaelic areas smaller *tuatha* were into parishes (Duffy, 'Geographical Perspectives', 16). These courts would have been summoned frequently by a bailiff whose chief duty was to collect rents and determine labour days for the lord's demesne if any. He always picked the best days for the lord, which was one of the reasons productivity was low on the tenants' fields. In the earldom of Ulster, rents were paid in flour, not grain and had to be ground in the lord's mill, and the bailiff would determine times (McNeill, 88).

Courts baron, courts leet and courts of frankpledge survived in places at least until the 18th century (Keenan, *Pre-Famine Ireland*, 313). The court baron had no criminal jurisdiction, but the king could grant further powers. Criminal jurisdiction could, however, be granted to a trusted lord. The most important of these powers was the "view of frankpledge", by which tenants were held responsible for the actions of others within a grouping of ten households. Some time in the later Middle Ages the lord gained the name of leet which was a jurisdiction of a part of a county, hence the franchise was of court leet. The view of frankpledge dealt particularly with tithings in a district. Not all manors had all three courts and indeed English practice may not have been brought into Ireland which had a different past. But as late as the 19th century the manor of Lord Cloncurry had all three, while that of Sir Edward Newenham had a court leet. Some manors could deal with sums up to 40 shillings, while others could deal with sums of a hundred pounds. Some had powers over shipwrecks or the escheated goods of felons, fugitives and outlaws (Keenan, *Pre-Famine Ireland*, 312-3). These courts were gradually replaced by courts of justices of the peace or magistrates. These latter courts gained in authority when groups of magistrates began to act together in petty sessions (*op. cit.* 315). Some towns had small claims courts which survived until the 19th century.

We know virtually nothing of the histories of these courts but they may have persisted as parish councils until the Vestry Act of 1826. Following frequent complaints that the Catholics of the parishes were excluded from voting and yet were compelled to pay the vestry cess to pay for Protestant worship in the parish, the powers of the vestry were restricted but the parish councils, where they still existed, were not abolished.

The concerns of the lord of the manor were far more extensive than just collecting rents, forcing farmers to use his mill, and organising the days for labour services. Canavan gives an interesting list of the privileges given to an Englishman who was granted the lands of the Cistercian abbey of Newry by Edward VI. He was to possess the abbey its lands, and all its civil authority specifically to hold *courtsleet* [manor court where the lord or seneschal sat as judge] and *view of frankpledge* [review of collective tenant responsibility for the tithing and all things which to view of frankpledge appertain, assize and assage of bread, wine, and beer, tolls, customs, wrecks of the sea, chattels, waifs, estrays, chattels of felons and fugitives, felons of themselves outlawed and put in exigent (Canavan, 37).

According to the *Oxford English Dictionary* assize meant the fixing of prices; *assage* not given, presumably assaying quality; *toll* a custom or impost for permission to pass somewhere or do something, or a share in money transactions; a charge for bringing goods to market or setting up a stall; *customs* were customary dues or taxes; duties imposed on goods on the way to market especially those imposed by the king. *Wreck* is that which is cast up by the sea *latwreccum maris,* goods cast overboard or floating ashore from wreck. Originally in Bracton it meant goods washed ashore with no obvious owner; it included anything washed ashore or cast up by the sea like timber, fish, precious stones etc. Wrecks of the sea did not belong to the admiralty court because they did not become wrecks until they reached the shore. The wreck of the sea was a prerogative of the king in his entire realm but was frequently given as a franchise. *Chattel* was the same as cattle from *capitale;* goods meant moveable possessions as opposed to real estate or freehold. *Waif* a piece of property found ownerless which after a due period falls to the lord of the manor. *Estrays* were any beast not wild found within a lordship and not owned by anyone. *Felon* was one who had committed a felony, an act which involved the forfeiture of his fee, and his estate was escheated to his lord. *Fugitives* are those who have fled from duty, an enemy, from justice, or a master. *Outlawed* meant one under sentence of outlawry or outside the protection of the law. *Exigent* meant a writ commanding the sheriff to summon the defendant to appear before the court under pain of outlawry.

Some of these were appropriate to a manor on the sea coast. Assize and assage of bread, wine and beer were appropriate to towns with bakers and brewers. Much brewing was done by women and before the introduction of hops beer was liable to deteriorate after a few days.

By Tudor times the organisation of the territories of the Gaelic lords was virtually identical with that of the Norman lords (O'Dowd, 127-8). In Gaelic areas no system of appeal to a higher court was ever devised, so the judgment of the local court, however unjust was final. Every man for himself, and the noble families had all the advantages.

City and Town courts

Towns usually sought or purchased charters to allow themselves self-government outside the dominion of the sheriff or lord of the liberty. These were comparable to manorial courts, and the cases they could try depended on their charters. Some had criminal as well as civil jurisdiction. In civil cases there was usually a cash limit on the matter in dispute. The mayor and corporation were also responsible for maintaining the walls and ensuring that citizens were exercised in arms. They were also responsible for scavenging, i.e. clearing out rubbish, ensuring the quality of goods in the markets, ensuring a supply of clean water, and pulling down dangerous buildings. The town court might meet as often as once a week. In a city like Dublin the functions of the mayor were equivalent to those of the sheriff or lord of a liberty (Clarke, 'Urban Administration'). They often had full jurisdiction over civil cases within the town.

Ecclesiastical and Admiralty Courts

Civil recognition of the *privilegium fori* (benefit of clergy) dated from the time of Justinian who decreed that disputes between clerics and of laymen against clerics should be heard in **ecclesiastical courts**. This legislation was adopted in Frankish courts. Ecclesiastical courts had no criminal jurisdiction, but synods could degrade a bishop before handing him over to the civil courts. However he could not be put to death or mutilated (Knowles, 83). This was extended to priests and deacons. Gradually clerics got exemption from criminal and civil matters in the civil courts, except in feudal matters. This right was recognised by the Emperor Frederick II in 1139 ('Ecclesiastical Privileges', *Catholic Encyclopaedia*). Civil questions regarding marriage, bastardy, and wills remained in the ecclesiastical courts. Not all monarchs were happy with this and there arose a famous dispute between Henry II of

England and Thomas à Becket regarding 'criminous clerks'. As Warren points out, clerics were very numerous. Many men took the tonsure, the exterior mark of a cleric, simply to avoid military service and to be allowed to attend schools or colleges. One in six of the population may have been clerics engaged in nothing more than writing letters (Warren *Henry II*, 460). Gradually, a working compromise was arrived at between Henry and the pope which gave Henry most of what he had sought to impose at the Assize of Clarendon (*op. cit.*, 539). The dispute was never formally resolved, and the Irish clergy were involved in disputes over the boundaries of the courts until the end of the Middle Ages. Most of the senior clergy like bishops and mitred abbots were also feudal landholders and so had two courts, the honorial court and the ecclesiastical court. They also had to have two separate gaols.

In the diocesan system there was the episcopal court, the archbishop's court, and the papal court with appeals to the higher court. In the later Middle Ages the Popes and anti-Popes accepted appeals from anyone for cash. The first step in seeking a lucrative benefice was to appeal directly to the pope. The major monasteries and mendicant orders approved by Rome usually had exempt jurisdiction and were not subject to the bishop's court but to the courts of their own order. The Cistercian abbots were subject to the general chapter of their order held annually in Citeaux which was the general court for the order.

We can assume that deans and archdeacons who had charge of sections of the clergy would have had their own courts and dealt with routine affairs such as distributing the holy oils. Archdeacons were generally priests, either canons of the cathedral or provosts of the principal (collegiate) churches in small towns. The authority of the archdeacons culminated in the eleventh and twelfth centuries *(Catholic Encyclopaedia* 'Archdeacon'). A bishop who spoke only English rarely needed to venture into Gaelic-speaking areas. It is doubtful if any of them undertook visitations of parishes, which became very important to reforming bishops in Counter-Reformation times. As late as 1455 the archbishops of Armagh were still insisting on the traditional tribute owed to the see of St Patrick (Watt, *The Church in Medieval Ireland,* 204) and it is unlikely that they were the only ones. Nobody ever voluntarily surrendered a source of revenue.

There are few records of ecclesiastical courts. Some survive from Armagh and show testamentary and matrimonial cases prominent (Watt, 175, 207). Testaments requiring probate in the bishop's court were introduced into Ireland by the synod of Cashel (Brand, 'Wills and Testaments'). The ordinary business of the court would have been largely concerned with affairs of the clergy.

Like everything else in the Middle Ages **admiralty courts** were a matter of steady growth. From about 1360 the sea coast of England and Wales was divided into 19 districts, and for each there was a Vice Admiral of the Coast, representing the Lord High Admiral. The admiralty laws which were applied in this court were based upon the Roman civil law-based Law of the Sea, as well as statutory and Common Law additions. The reason this court is associated with ecclesiastical courts is that the proctors who practised there were doctors of laws with university degrees. As Roman civil law and canon law were based on similar principles a proctor could be at home in a probate case and an admiralty case.

Maritime law was introduced in the time of Richard I for cases regarding foreign ships. Then in the 13th century the office or rank of admiral was introduced with his own court. In the time of Richard II these courts were restricted to dealing with maritime matters. Finally, early in the 15th century the office of Lord High Admiral was established, its duties later commonly discharged by an Admiralty Board. Finally the coast of Ireland was divided among four vice-admirals. The High Court of Admiralty of England was the court of the deputy or lieutenant of the admiral. Before that each admiral had his own court.

Crimes

Woodkerne

Woodkerne was the name given to a class of robbers or bandits in Tudor times. Nationalist writers, if they mentioned them at all, liked to pretend they were a 'resistance movement' against British occupiers. They were of course a type found all over the world, mercenary soldiers in time of war and bandits and cattle rustlers in time of peace. The last band of them was mentioned in the 1730's. Agrarian terrorism flared up in the 1760's but it is not clear if there is a connection.

The name kerne (*ceithirne, ceatharnaigh*) meant lightly armed native Irish mercenaries. In Scotland it was pronounced cateran, a freebooter, marauder, or a member of a raiding party, which describes their other side. In Ireland too the word could be translated as bandit or trooper. Similar bands called *diberga* or *fianna* with pagan origins had existed in ancient Ireland describing bands of young unmarried nobles who spent the years between the ending of their fosterage and the inheritance of their father's lands in wandering bands who lived by hunting and looting. The medieval woodkernes were probably mostly younger sons from chiefly or warrior families who had little chance of getting land of their own unless they particularly distinguished themselves in battle. Some may have been from the working classes, perhaps a farm labourer fleeing after a murder. They were notorious for raping any women they came across. They were useful to local chiefs who needed additional warriors in a neighbouring conflict. Ecclesiastical scribes described them as *latrones*, robbers. In the Middle Ages, when the Fenian cycle of legendary tales was being developed the *fianna* were cleaned up and made to be professional soldiers, like the contemporary continental knights in romantic literature. In actuality the kerne specialised in wasting and looting. Kernes and foreign mercenaries had a bad reputation for the devastation of the countryside, plunder of churches and violation of women. The Anglo-Norman knights at least offered compensation for the misdeeds of their followers (Simms, ('Gaelic Warfare in the Middle Ages', 105). The Gaelic chiefs were often unable to restrain the criminal bands on their lands even when it was in their own interest to do so (Smith, 51; James, 46).

During the wars of the 17th century they swarmed over Ireland and were called tories or rapparees. It was difficult to differentiate between bands, often temporary, of cattle rustlers, and small septs who largely survived through cattle-raiding and black rents. Ireland was little different from Scotland. Some historians attribute the acquiescence of some of the Irish chiefs to the land grants to Norman adventurers to their inability to control the woodkerne. One of these grants was in Louth, south Armagh, and Monaghan. The lands in Monaghan and south Armagh proved impossible to hold, and it was in Orior in Armagh that the last of the rapparees held out in the reign of Charles II. The O'Hanlons were chiefs of long standing but reduced to cattle rustling by the loss of their lands.

Ordinary Crime and Penology

That ordinary crime was abundant we cannot doubt, but as the courts either did not keep records or the records are lost it is difficult to get a good picture. Historians tend to dwell on the general social disorder in the late Middle Ages when criminal activities of gangs could scarcely be distinguished from that of lords or chiefs. It was not for nothing that most towns in the Middle Ages were walled. We can assume that ordinary crime was as common then as it is today. Murder, violence, robbery with violence, rape, and, piracy, cheating would have been common. Bribery and extortion by officials were the norm.

In common law, a manor court had a right to a gallows, pillory, and tumbrel (a kind of mediaeval torture device, later associated with a cucking-stool). Much of the evidence comes from the much richer English sources, but there is no reason to suppose that Ireland was different. Throughout the medieval period it was believed that the only way to keep order was to make sure that the people were scared of the punishments given for crimes committed. For this reason all crimes from stealing to murder had harsh punishments. Although there were gaols, they were generally used to hold a prisoner awaiting trial rather than as a means of punishment. Fines, shaming (being placed in stocks), mutilation (cutting off a part of the body) or death were the most common forms of punishment. There was no police force in the medieval period so law-enforcement was in the hands of the community. Thieves had their hands cut off. Women who committed murder were strangled and then burnt. There were very few prisons as they cost money and local communities were not prepared to pay for their upkeep. It was cheaper to execute someone for bad crimes or mutilate them and then let them go. Those sentenced to a period in the stocks were subject to assaults by the public, even stoned, unless they had enough friends to protect them.

The crimes that were committed by chiefs and those who aspired to the chiefdom were quite astonishing. Murder was condoned if it gave proof that the aspirant would be a better leader of the warband. Children were placed with a foster parent who had to guard them with his life to protect them from their uncles. Dermot MacMurrough systematically murdered or blinded those who might threaten his hold on Leinster. He also had the abbess of Kildare raped because she belonged to a rival family (Roche, 27, 30). This conduct was typical of the time.

It was a curiosity of the Brehon Code that the principal punishment was a fine. The fine was assessed partly from the nature of the crime and partly from the status of the person suffering the injury. There is no reason to suppose that punishments of ordinary workers for ordinary crimes were less harsh. Indeed a large fine imposed on a kin group could reduce them to near servitude, and transferring their land to the victorious party. It is not clear what the punishments of the penniless classes were. In England they involved public humiliations and physical abuse in the stocks for example. There must have been an equivalent in Gaelic society probably involving beatings and floggings.

Administration of Justice

There was little public machinery for carrying out the verdicts of the courts. The winning party had to carry out the sentence himself if he could. One exception was the powers given to the sheriff or seneschal to carry out sentences in capital matters such as executing a condemned man. We can assume too that officers like constables in manors and parishes carried out lesser sentences of these courts, like placing in the stocks, or ducking a woman, though they probably had numerous enthusiastic voluntary assistants. It seems likely too that in the Gaelic districts there were minor officials charged with the administration of justice and the keeping of order even if punishments were in fines. It was impossible to enforce a judgement against a social superior unless the plaintiff succeeded in getting the support of a man of similar or greater status.

Military Matters

What military advantages did the Normans have? Warfare in Ireland still followed age-old patterns, consisting mostly of glorified cattle raids. Defence still consisted principally of retreating and dispersing. The Normans came from a far harder school. They developed the compact body of heavy horses with the rider and horse protected with mail and the rider using a long heavy lance held level under arm. It was something few could withstand except in very well prepared positions. The weapon of the light cavalryman was still the light spear held overhead and thrust downwards. The great initial advantage of the Normans, the charge of the heavy cavalry, was a declining asset, for it could be avoided.

Cavalry was now common in Ireland and was to become ever more common up until 1690. But only light cavalry differing little from the auxiliary cavalry units of the Roman army were used. Horsemen had many auxiliary uses but the charge of mailed knights against infantry in broken, boggy, or wooded country was not one of them. Yet there were occasions where the cavalry were clearly decisive.

The fortifications built by the Normans for defensive purposes were simple and effective, being constructed simply of earth and wood. Once again the archers were crucial, for it was their job to keep the attackers at a distance. By placing the wooden stockade on the top of an earthen bank it made it difficult to set fire to, or to place ladders against the stockade even if the Gaelic armies had them. Normal Gaelic warfare involved attacking across bogs and through woods along paths defended as they had been for millennia by palisades and plashed woods. It was soon obvious that small bodies of Normans could not defeat large bodies of Gaelic warriors in the field, nor did the Normans attempt to defend indefensible positions. Their light armour or chain mail afforded some protection but probably very little against a battleaxe.

With regard to foot-soldiers it must not be imagined that the Irish, with experience against the Vikings, were particularly outclassed. It is difficult to determine how many actually fought in any given battle. The figures for the Norman knights, bowmen, and men-at-arms may be accurate, but they were probably always accompanied by a body of Gaelic soldiers. If Hugh de Lacy was to provide a hundred mounted knights from the whole of Meath his total contribution of knights, archers, and men-at-arms probably did not come to more than 500. If one adds in petty Gaelic chiefs and their followers he could rely on we probably come to a total of 1,000 for the whole of Meath. It was estimated that Rory O'Connor in a major hosting could call out 30,000 men (Hayes-McCoy, 31) but even if we reduce this estimate drastically we probably have a figure of 10,000 to oppose the 2,500 Normans with probably an equal number of Leinstermen. But the quality of such massive call-outs was probably not high. In a very poor country like Ireland the problems of maintaining an army of 10,000 men would have limited the time they could stay together as a fighting force. They had to drive all their food along with them, so camp followers, men and women, were probably as numerous as the fighting men, and most or all of the cattle would have been seized from the lands they passed through. We are only guessing, but each *tuath* probably did not supply more than twenty or thirty first-class warriors who could march and fight continuously. Whenever needed, massive numbers of poorly equipped and poorly trained men could be recruited on the understanding that they could go home to reap the harvest.

Rory O'Connor probably had about 2,500 well-armed and experienced fighters to oppose the Normans. As in Anglo-Saxon England, Gaelic forces were made up of those warriors called out by the chiefs and their household troops. These were housecarls or bodyguards, in Gaelic *lucht tighe* which means the same. They had formed the core of Harold's shield wall at the Battle of Hastings (Flanagan, 55). These seasoned troops were professional warriors, men whom the local chiefs kept in their own households and who formed his personal bodyguard not least against his own relatives. But later in the Middle Ages the chiefs relied increasingly on professional soldiers mostly brought over from the Gaelic-Norse of the Highlands and Islands of Scotland. These did not normally live in the chief's house but had lands of their own assigned to them. These were the gallowglasses. Their weapons were the traditional ones, with slashing weapons like battleaxes and swords still the favourites.

Warfare

Irish chiefs and their warriors were not notably inferior to the Norman knights. They were not cut off from Europe. The Vikings had been in Ireland for 300 years. Any young warrior could always go and get experience of fighting in England. They were already using horses in battle, but in the old fashioned war with the old flat saddles and the short down-thrusting spear. They were using ships to move troops about, and making temporary castles in the old meaning of the term not very different from the wooden motte-and-bailey castles which the Normans first built when they occupied land (Flanagan, 71).

Warfare was endemic in Europe in the Middle Ages. It was the chief occupation of the ruling families. Chiefs were leaders of warbands. The grown-up men in every chief's family had no other occupation. From their youth they trained for arms. If they did not like that they had to enter the Church. Before professional mercenary soldiers became common, and means to pay them had been devised, they formed the core of the small local armies, and also of the hostings of the great chiefs. When not at war, hunting at first on foot and, later more commonly on horseback, was a substitute which allowed them to keep up their skills. In theory every freeman was bound to fight, at least when their area was attacked, and many were used on expeditions especially to drive off cattle in a *tain* or cattle raid.

Weapons and Equipment

Armies, both Norman and Gaelic, were divided into horsemen and footmen. The horsemen were always men of higher rank for they had to provide their own horses, equipment, weapons and armour. The army in early feudal times was formed around the mailed and mounted knights commanded by their immediate lord. Each knight brought members of his own household with him to tend his horses and armour but who did not fight in the battles. There was also a body of foot-soldiers the quality of which might vary from excellent to useless. These made up numbers and were useful in other ways like for digging holes or burying stakes to impede the enemy cavalry. But it was axiomatic that the battle was decided by the successful cavalry charge. It is clear that warfare in Ireland in the later Middle Ages required a different composition of forces.

There was nothing unusual in either the Norman or Gaelic armies, both using the weapons common at the time, and adopting the various changes as they developed in the Middle Ages. That is not to say that the Normans were not more experienced in continental warfare and the techniques developed there. There were two points where the techniques of the Normans were clearly superior. One was in the cavalry charge in tight formation with lances held underarm. The attack was not at a gallop as in jousting but at a walking pace with the lance held level and using the strength of the massed horses to break the infantry line. The length of the lance was here important. The other was in siege warfare. Yet these advantages were short-lived. The cavalry charge with the long lance was easily avoided while sieges were relatively unimportant.

There was a basic rule in warfare which held good until the battle of Waterloo in the 19th century and that was that cavalry could never beat well trained and unbroken infantry. (Wellington's infantry repeatedly repulsed charges of the French cavalry.) The front line of infantry could just kneel down and hold their spears at an angle of 45 degrees with the butts on the ground. (At Waterloo fixed bayonets were used in similar fashion.) Cavalry could be used against other cavalry, for scouting and foraging, and above all in pursuit of a broken enemy.

Weapons were constantly changing, or rather the shapes and sizes of various categories of weapons kept changing. Light spears and javelins were used for throwing. Interestingly there was a tendency on all sides later in the Middle Ages to adopt the light javelin perhaps because in Irish woods where the highways were plashed the heavier spear or javelin was less likely to be deflected or had greater penetrative power through hurdles or wicker screens. The Battle of Hastings in 1066 depended not on the cavalry charge which was ineffective but on an arrow loosed off against the English line. The light arrow of the short bow was ineffective against armour. The longbow with its heavier arrow was very effective but required long training. The bolt of the crossbow was effective against most things, but the weapon was slow to use in battle. The crossbow and the long bow were rarely used in Ireland; just the ordinary short bow.

Of hand weapons, apart from the long but unhandy lance of the massed cavalry charge, there was a choice between sword and battleaxe. The battleaxe and the heavy two-handed sword were slashing weapons. The battleaxe especially could do serious damage but the user could not carry a shield and was vulnerable to a thrust when his arms were raised. The Scottish gallowglasses carried battleaxes or claymores (heavy two-handed swords) with a hauberk of mail. The claymore remained popular in Scotland until 1700. The equipment of the Gaelic armies in the 12th century was similar to what was to be found in England at the time. Some at least had protective body armour like breastplates, corselets, shields and helmets. For weapons they had a spear and a sword. There seems to have been a certain number of archers. The ordinary footmen probably preferred the cheaper two-handed axe and not to have used any body armour. Smaller one-handed axes could also have been used (Flanagan, 71).

The Normans had richer lands in England and were usually able to provide themselves with better equipment. The English iron industry out-produced the Irish in terms of armour, arrowheads and crossbow bolts. The knights normally wore chain mail. This is what we see in pictures of William the Conqueror's army and on the late medieval gallowglasses. Though expensive it was much cheaper than the elaborate plate mail of the later Middle Ages. (Plate mail was a response to the crossbow so it is doubtful if it was ever used in Ireland.)

As the Middle Ages advanced the Gaelic and Norman forces became more alike. The cavalry charge with closely packed lances proved unsuitable for Irish conditions, so the Normans adopted the lighter Irish horse. The Gaelic soldiers began to use more armour, most of it probably captured in battle. Lighter leather armour began to be used. At the hard-fought battle of Dysert O'Dea in 1318 was largely fought by foot soldiers, as was the Battle of Athenry in 1316. The Gaelic lords won the former, while the Norman lords won the latter (Hayes-McCoy, 42-3).

The Gaelic lords began to depend on Scottish mercenaries, the gallowglasses. Originally freelances, they were eventually given lands and status. They were protected by chain mail and their preferred weapon was the battleaxe. Each gallowglass was accompanied by two boys, one to carry the armour and the other food. They also each carried three light darts or javelins to hurl at the enemy as the battle commenced. Other Irish chiefs also kept bands of Anglo-Norman or Welsh auxiliaries who were foot soldiers and performed the same function as the Scottish gallowglasses in the North. They were often billeted on the ordinary people (bonnacht). The bonnacht of Ulster of the earls of Ulster amounted to 345 soldiers billeted on the Irish chiefs of Ulster and estimated to amount to £1 a year in food and wages. After the overthrow of the earldom, O'Neill took over the bonnacht. Unlike the kerne the gallowglasses were officered by their own chieftains and were better behaved.

Much of a Gaelic army was made up of lightly armed kernes who were mostly bandits in peace time and ravagers in wartime. They did not wear armour except perhaps a leather jacket. Their principal weapon was a javelin, but they must also have had a short sword, dagger, or hand axe for close quarters. They might hurl their javelins at an opposing army but did not take part in the main battle. They burned houses and ricks, murdered peasants, and drove off cattle. This was in itself an important part of warfare in the Middle Ages (Simms, 'Gaelic Warfare in the Middle Ages', 100 ff). Any campaign right up to the 17th century was followed by bands of bandits who were only interested in raping, looting and burning. To them it did not matter what was the cause of the war (see Woodkerne above). A battle is often as much psychological as physical. Any group suddenly fleeing can trigger a general and precipitate retreat. The sudden loss of a prominent leader can have the same effect. Some elite troops like Harold's housecarls and bands of gallowglasses were trained to stand fast until the last hope of victory is gone, and then to retreat in an orderly fashion. For this reason unreliable troops were kept out of the main battle. Gallowglasses and kernes were mercenary troops, the kernes apparently being paid short term for a particular campaign.

By the end of the Middle Ages the standing army of the Lordship of Ireland was composed of a small band of archers and spearmen or billmen. All were mounted, though the archers dismounted to fight. The spearmen, though often English, were probably armed liked hobelars, or light horsemen, admirable for scouting, patrolling and scouring the country. By this time guns were starting to be employed and the Lord Deputy asked for 60 gunners from England (Hayes-McCoy, 57). The Battle of Knockdoe in 1504 seems to have been the first Irish battle in which guns were used, but not to any effect. The battle was between the Earl of Kildare and Clanrickarde. Both depended heavily on the gallowglasses largely provided by their adherents, though the muster of The Pale had a prominent position in the battle. By this time in the counties the militia or muster of the county was in force to provide local support. The contemporary English bill or billhook which was a slashing weapon not a thrusting one seems to have been the weapon of the county muster. The battle was a straight-forward prolonged slogging match with hand weapons until Clanrickarde's smaller force was weakened and gave way (*op.cit.* 65). Though fought at the very beginning of the 16th century, and apart from the involvement of the county musters of The Pale it was a battle that could have been fought in the previous 7 or 8 hundred years.

Artillery had been brought into Ireland somewhat earlier. A reference was made to the import of a gun in the 14th century. They are hardly mentioned until the royal cannon were used systematically by the Earl of Kildare in 1488 to demolish castles. The first infantry handguns were those brought to Ireland by German mercenaries in 1487 but were for use in England (*op. cit.* 59).

Defensive Measures

Every chief's or nobles dwelling and every town had to have some form of defence, but detailed knowledge is often lacking about them. We have records of various kinds of defence, but none of these were used everywhere and at all times. As usual, records from Gaelic areas are virtually non-existent. The Normans did not introduce the building of castles. Already, in the first half of the twelfth century, Turlough O'Connor was building 'castles' in Connaught. What was called the first castle in Ireland was built at Athlone in 1129 to control the crossing of the river there. This reminds us that the *rath* or *lios* of an Irish chief was not usually heavily defended, though there were exceptions. The 'castles' of O'Connor were probably simplified versions of the motte-and-bailey. For example, by putting a wooden palisade on the top of a bank made it very difficult to assault or to set on fire.

For the defence of the lordship, besides those who owed duty by knight's service, an estimated 425 in all, there was an obligation on all freeholders with lands above a certain value to provide themselves with horses and martial equipment. Even those with quite small estates or farms were obliged to have a horse. Large armies for pitched battles were rarely required. Small forces of light horse mustered locally were far more important in defending against the incessant raiding by small parties. The sheriff, aided by justices of the peace, was responsible for maintaining the muster lists. Forces were called out locally but maintained by a cess on the whole county (Frame, 'Defence of the English Lordship', 80). Much defence was local. The abbot of Mellifont was responsible for maintaining the little town of Collon against any raids from the direction of Cavan or Monaghan. The only time when a large muster was required was during the Bruce invasion when various lords of The Pale undertook to gather an army from their own resources and those of the counties. At first they were unable quite to defeat Bruce in battle though they came close, but Bruce was unable to capture walled towns and contented himself with wasting the country. Forced by famine conditions, partly of his own making, he was forced to retreat and the army of The Pale caught up with him at Faughart in county Louth where he was defeated and killed.

The Lord Deputy was normally given money to maintain small forces in the order of 100 mounted men-at-arms and 150 mounted archers (Connolly, 111). This force was intended to deal with larger incursions such as from the O'Byrnes and O'Tooles who seem, like some of their Highland counterparts, to have supported themselves chiefly by raiding. The Lord Deputy's punitive force would have been supplemented locally in the area being attacked. An expedition against the O'Byrnes in 1353 amounted to 1,012 fighting men of whom 604 were footmen, 351 were hobelars, 41 were armoured men-at-arms, and 16 mounted archers. 408 were thus mounted and were the most use in scouring the mountains and burning everything they came across (Frame, 'Defence of the English Lordship', 85). The whole expedition, counting non-fighting men might have been two or three times that and probably included many women who always followed armies as cooks, washerwomen or prostitutes. Though they would have eaten any cattle they could round up it was clearly impossible to maintain such a force in a barren region for long, and this was what the O'Byrnes counted on. It is clear that there was no serious attack on or rejection of the rule of the king of England as Lord of Ireland in the course of the whole Middle Ages. Edward the Bruce, making a bid for a throne of his own, got little support. All issues were local ones. Even when a great lord like the Earl of Desmond was in rebellion he never made a bid for the throne himself

Many Anglo-Normans built castles on their lands. At first these were quite small and made of wood and often on the motte-and-bailey principle. Some however were on the ringwork principle, scarcely distinguishable from Gael raths. The greater lords could build huge stone castles like that at Trim, the centre of the liberty of Meath, or

Carrickfergus, the centre of the earldom of Ulster. The king himself built large royal castles such as those in Limerick and Carlingford both for internal control and external defence. His Majesty's castle of Dublin has been the centre of the Government of Ireland since the 12th century, though reference to the crown is now dropped. But in many places there are few traces of Norman fortifications even in counties strongly held by the Normans (Barry, *Archaeology*, maps, 39 and 52). Rectangular earthworks and sites with moats are found in counties where mottes and ringworks are scarce (*op. cit.* 86 and 88). The distribution of the later tower houses is also given (*op. cit.* 187).

Earlier, the Gaelic chiefs seem to have depended on the not-inconsiderable defensive power of a well-maintained palisade around the rath like American forts in the mid-West. If a large force approached they could flee to defensive spots in the woods and bogs. Forest paths could be blocked by plashing wood across them and on either side of it. The attackers would have to cut heir way through with axes.

The Gaelic lords were surprisingly reluctant to build castles. Stone castles were not the warmest or most comfortable dwellings. Late in the Middle Ages, tall square tower houses were built in large numbers in some parts of Ireland. These tower houses were a prominent feature of the Anglo-Scottish border. About 3,000 have been identified in Ireland. Like the motte the tower house had an enclosure for animals though the dwelling was now in the tower. A subsidy of £10 was given within the Pale for their construction, but the vast majority of them are in the south of Ireland (Barry, *Archaeology,* 187). Their popularity quickly spread to Gaelic areas. Motives of ostentation and prestige when building a tower house cannot be ruled out. They are not always placed in the best spots for defence (*op. cit.* 188).

The Irish chiefs had by this time adopted the Norse practice of using fleets of ships. The exact shape of the Irish and Norse boats in the twelfth century is a matter of some conjecture, but it is reasonable to assume that both sides used the development of the Norse longboat devised by King Alfred, the dragon boat, with a higher deck amidships to give the fighting men an advantage. Sea fights could occur, but the purpose of a fleet was more to ravage and harry. We hear little about the use of the sea. Control of the northern waters and the links with Scotland obviously remained in Gaelic and Scottish hands. Most of the Irish Sea would have been controlled either from the Lordship itself or from England. Ships were placed in the Irish Sea to forestall Edward the Bruce's invasion, but they were unsuccessful. No serious attempt seems to have been made to root out pirates from the small harbours along the coast of Cork before Stuart times. The Earl of Desmond presumably controlled his own coasts in Kerry and Limerick.

Most Irish castles are tower houses dating from the end of the Middle Ages when they became popular with minor Gaelic and Anglo-Norman lords though there are some great castles on the English or Welsh model. John took over *de* Courci's (*de* Lacy) castles in Carrickfergus, Dundrum and Greencastle. *De* Lacy did not get them back until 1227. The de Lacy's great castle was at Trim, Co. Meath. Maynooth castle was the home of the Fitzgerald's of Kildare. The other great Fitzgerald or Marshal castle was at Lea now in Co. Laois, and was long a target for the O'Mores and O'Dempseys. Dunamase castle, now in Co. Laois was another Marshal castle protecting the fertile plains of Kildare. It was a target for the O'Mores who claimed to be the true owners of the land before it was seized by Dermot MacMurrough. Carlow Castle of William Marshal was strategically important in the Middle Ages when it guarded the narrow strip of land that connected Dublin with the south. Gowran castle in Kilkenny further south had a similar role and became a Butler stronghold. Kilkenny castle in Fitzpatrick territory in Kilkenny was built by William Marshal, but it later became the stronghold of the Butlers of Ormond. Tralee castle in Kerry was once the principal stronghold of the earls of Desmond but later they preferred Askeaton castle in Co. Limerick. The first Desmond castle was at Shanid, Co. Limerick, a motte-and-bailey castle with a stone castle added later. Nenagh castle in Co. Tipperary was the principal residence of the Butler (Ormond) family in the early Middle Ages. As the land around became untenable and unprofitable they moved to Kilkenny. The Butlers did hold on to nearby Roscrea castle. Ardee castle Co Louth was a Pippard castle and remained an important defence throughout the Middle Ages. The de Verdon castle at Dundalk disappeared as the town of Dundalk grew in importance. A great stone castle on the Shannon at Athlone, Co. Westmeath, protected the western border of the Liberty of Meath. It was commenced by the justiciar, John de Grey in 1210 and survived until the siege of Athlone in 1691. Two great castles beyond the Shannon in Roscommon, Ringdown and Roscommon to dominate Connaught had useful lives for less than 100 years. In 1212 by John de Gray, the then Justiciar of Ireland, built the castle of *Caol-uisce*, or Narrow-Water, on Lough Erne in the passage between Donegal and Fermanagh to guard the main western pass of entry into his province. This was to be the western end of a chain.

Organisation for War

When Rory O'Connor was summoning his forces in 1167 he called for ten ships from each of the coastal cantreds. As Flanagan observes this must have been the unit for the assessment of military services. Any existing unit for assessing taxes or labour services could be used for military purposes. Labour services, like the construction of bridges, are known to have been called on. The powers of an Irish chief in the 12th century were clearly the same as those of the Anglo-Saxon kings (Flanagan, 64). For fighting, all the men of military ages in the various ranks of chiefs and lords would be summoned. On the Anglo-Norman side the same was done. Campaigning was confined to the summer months when the ground was hard. Even in the Williamite Wars at the end of the 17th century, standing armies went into winter quarters.

Armies tended to be quite small. While raiding enemies close at hand it was possible to live off the enemy's land. But if one had to march 200 miles through lands of allies food had to be procured from somewhere. This was as true in Ireland as it was for Edward I's invasions of Scotland when supplies had to be shipped from Ireland. From the 12th century onwards all chiefs and lords preferred to depend on mercenaries. A few highly trained soldiers were better fighters and easier to arm, feed and shelter than a large number of conscripts. In Anglo-Norman areas, especially in England, cash was preferred to military service so that mercenaries could be employed. The Gaelic lords drew heavily on the Scottish Highlands whose troops were hard fighters, fast-moving, and could be fed on oaten meal which they could carry with them. They could cover perhaps 100 miles in 3 days carrying all their food with them. It is doubtful if Anglo-Norman armies, as distinct from small groups of horsemen, could travel more rapidly than 10 miles a day.

There was no particular organisation for battle. Groups were formed up under their chiefs or lords in an extended mass with archers and cavalry on either side. The only permanent formation was a 'company' of 50 to 200 mercenaries under a 'captain'. Only in 1505 did the Spanish king introduce the rank of *'colones'* in charge of several companies, each 'column' having about 1,000 men. These columns were later called regiments (Barnett, 17). Barnett also notes the tremendous waste of life in medieval armies, largely from diseases, poor diet and poor hygiene (*op. cit.*, 9). Fevers and dysentery could ravage an army, so fresh men were constantly needed. Medical treatment was primitive.

Cash to pay armies was always in short supply. In 1361, a royal clerk (cleric?) was appointed clerk of wages in Ireland to pay wages to sailors, county levies, indentured retinues, masons and carpenters and to any Irishman who might be retained (Connolly, 106). The office of paymaster to an army was traditionally an office of great profit, but often in Ireland Lord Deputies had to pay considerable sums from their own revenues. A particular annoyance was purveyance, the right of the Crown to requisition goods and services for royal use. The system was wide open to abuse because the purchasing officers set the price so those who had to supply the goods were regularly cheated.

The ability of the Gaelic lord to demand tribute from subordinate clans came from military strength, and the military strength depended from two sources. The first was the power to enforce military service from the territories under his control. The second was the ability to enforce the provision of food, lodging, and clothing for his mercenaries who formed the core of the Irish military strength. The tribute took the form of military service, food for the overlord and his retinue, agricultural labourers for his land and to build his castles, lodging for the chief and his followers, and animals to carry his belongings. The exactions of labour increased in the 15th cent as the population declined; this explains why so many lords were able to construct tower houses in the later Middle Ages (O'Dowd, 'Gaelic Economy', 123).

Effects of War

It is difficult to determine the effects of war on the largely rural population. Armies were small and raids were likely to be short and swift. The raid would advance along predictable lines and the rural workers would have traditional knowledge how to deal with them. At the first signs of the approach of an army, smoke for example on the horizon, all livestock would be driven into hiding. The women and girls too would rush to the traditional hiding places. There were few sieges, so armies were constantly on the move. Any army, whether invading or defensive, was likely to strip a place of anything that could be eaten or drunk. The path of the army might be little more than half a mile wide, but like locusts would clear everything the raiders found. Those places close to frontiers, like along The Pale, or at the boundaries of great lordships, might be frequently attacked while other more remote areas seldom or ever attacked. A greater problem was the woodkerne who followed the flanks of the army and could find people emerging from hiding. Their bands would have been small. A great wasting campaign like that of Edward the Bruce was probably rare, and recovery from that might take ten or more years.

The common farming people were not the only people to suffer. The big houses of the local lords appear to have been undefended, or defended with only a wooden palisade. If it could hold out for a few days, the attacking army which had to scour the countryside for food might move on. Did they too gather their belongings and their households and retreat out of harm's way? Very little records are kept with local detail. (There was a similar problem in the 18th and 19th centuries in determining the extent and effects of agrarian crimes and combinations (Ó Gráda, 331-7)) In the Anglo-Norman areas, even small towns surrounded themselves with expensive walls, but obviously the targets for looters were greater there. These walls however seem to have been badly maintained.

Chapter 5

The Economy

General Observations

As has been observed earlier it is difficult to get an overall view of the economy as it is for society as a whole. The Middle Ages was a period of great economic development, so we will expect the economy to be much better at the end of the period than at the beginning despite the fall in population and output following the Black Death. On the other hand, the economy and production did not develop evenly over the whole of Ireland. As usual were can draw up the parameters from the better documented and studied English economy and try to work out how much applied to Ireland and what differences there were between regions. Gaelic areas are commonly almost without relevant documentation. There are no trade figures for Gaelic areas. We may suspect that trade from those areas rose towards the end of the Middle Ages as Gaelic chiefs increased their revenues. The need to import guns, powder and shot did not arise until Tudor times.

In the United Kingdom throughout the 19th century national income and population grew. More importantly, as steam and horse power were used in numerous ways income per capita grew at an estimated 1%

per annum. In the fields horse-drawn machinery replaced hand labour. In factories steam machinery often replaced hand-operated machines. Steamships and railways lowered the cost of transporting goods. By 1914 absolute poverty as measured by mid-century reformers had virtually disappeared and was replaced by relative poverty. In Ireland in the Middle Ages obviously there could not be such a development nor were there any significant changes to technology or agriculture. Nevertheless, in eastern Ireland when new markets were opened up and the best practice in agriculture introduced from England there can be little doubt that not only did population and national output increase but that there was a per capita improvement. This per capita improvement probably continued after the Black Death because of the fall in population. The improvement in living standards would have been seen in slightly better and larger houses, warmer and finer clothes and boots, more and better furniture, and a greater abundance and variety of food. In the Gaelic areas it is more likely that the standard of living for the working classes declined all through the Middle Ages. Firstly there was a great growth in the numbers of the non-productive classes as the warrior, clerical and learned families grabbed more and more land. Secondly, exports in the later Middle Ages were composed largely of animal products like hides, and most of the cattle were owned by the chiefly families. Thirdly there were no towns so market opportunities to sell produce would have been limited. In Tudor times the betagh class were usually described as impoverished. As such they would have borne the brunt of local famines which regularly followed crop failures and invasions.

There is little doubt that the general improvement in the economy of Europe which commenced after the year 1000 also affected Ireland. The economy was dominated by agriculture, along with the other aspects which flowed from it: local food and textile processing, building, and crafts. Foreign trade became associated with coastal towns which were also sheltered ports with port facilities, or from open beaches and sheltered harbours. Skills in the use of stone were imported and developed. Roads and bridges as they were built facilitated trade as well as military movements. Money, at least in English-speaking areas, became increasingly important not only for the renting of property but for the exchange of goods.

The Irish economy was under-developed in the 12th century in comparison with feudal Britain, but it is not always obvious to what degree. A large immigration of skilled workers from Britain helped areas in eastern Ireland at least to catch up. The differences between Ireland and the western districts of Britain were not great. The economies in both English and Gaelic Ireland grew throughout the Middles Ages, but the English-speaking areas always remained the more advanced and productive. The Normans in the eastern parts of Ireland increased trade, more helped by the availability of markets in Britain than by improvement in agricultural techniques. The only major basis for the economy was agriculture. Products of mining, of hunting and trapping, of forestry, and fishing were of little importance except locally and at certain times.

There were differences between land holding and management in Norman districts and in Gaelic districts, but they should not be exaggerated. In the Norman districts wealth was measured by holdings of land, and in Gaelic districts by holdings of cattle. In Norman areas, the feudal system applied. All the land was owned by the king. He let out great tracts of land to his major tenants in return for military service. These lords sub-let to cultivators in return for goods and services, and increasingly for cash (socage). Gaelic lords did not, originally at least own much land, but owned most of the cattle which they then rented out to the husbandmen in return for a share of the produce of the herd. These differences of themselves did not affect agricultural techniques.

The Norman system was based primarily on tillage, and on production for the market. It was often based on a three field system of manorial but not rigidly so. When well-managed, the three-field system produced a safe and regular return for market, and even in the worst years normally produced enough to ensure survival until the following year's crops were harvested. It was not originally designed for producing a surplus for market though when markets developed villages managed to produce a marketable surplus. But its chief aim was to avoid crop failures leading to famines by concentrating on several reliable crops and animals as it was unlikely they would all fail simultaneously. (Those parts of Ireland badly affected by the Great Famine were those where little but the potato was planted. The unwisdom of this had been known for thirty years but no diversification of crops had been attempted.) The tillage was part of a system which included towns, markets, systems of transport, and systems of exchange, normally cash. It also ensured a considerably denser population.

To achieve this in Ireland colonisation was necessary. This in turn required a steady flow of cash from other sources, normally from estates in England. It required the importation of workers, skilled in the various trades and especially the numerous aspects of agriculture. There was not, contrary to common belief, any notable improvement in agriculture in the manorial system, but there was a great fund of common knowledge to be drawn on, for example the best breeds of animals to survive harsh winters, and the most reliable varieties of cereals and other crops. This importation of workers, commonly called colonisation, doubtless caused considerable local disruption in the individual manors to which it was introduced. It depended too on the willingness of workers from England and elsewhere to settle in Ireland, and in the earldom of Ulster these proved to be in short supply. It would seem that in most of the manors in Ireland the open field agriculture characteristic of eastern England was not adopted, but a similar system based on Welsh cantreds. There was no connection between the great plough and great fields and the manorial system; they could be found equally in Gaelic areas.

The expense, the lack of colonists, and possibly the nature of Brehon Law may explain why Gaelic chiefs did not undertake the same schemes to develop their wealth and power. By the 12th century the old system of free farmers and of chiefs making their profits by leasing cattle to clients for a specified return had disappeared. Chiefs had achieved virtual ownership of the farmsteads and installed their relatives in them. But these did not do the farming themselves which was left to the betaghs and hired men. The practice of agriculture in itself was not altered. Even before 1170 it is safe to assume that the best agricultural practice in eastern Ireland was as good as that in the western parts of England. The skills in the other crafts, now including stonemasonry would have been comparable. In either country master craftsmen would have been rare. Skills in woodworking, metalworking, spinning, weaving, dyeing, shoemaking, tailoring, building, and so on at local level were not likely to be high.

Weights and Measures

Weights and measures were not standardised until the 19th century when 'Imperial' weights and measure were standardised and imposed on the whole of the United Kingdom. Despite the promise of uniform measures given in the Magna Charta there were no uniform standards in Britain. Travellers had to find for themselves the local terms and measures in each town. The apothecary, the silversmith and the wool merchants had different words and measures. Hampshire alone had three different acres, and the bushel was different in each market town. The weight of a standard loaf varied from week to week and from town to town as the local mayor fixed the price through the assize of bread, a practice which continued until the 19th century. In other places the weight of the loaf was fixed and the price varied from week to week. The Irish Government had officials called the clerk of the markets and the keeper of weights, jobs often combined with that of the king's escheator. Allegations of fraud were frequently made (Otway-Ruthven, 162). Everywhere there were local weights and measures.

All weights, measures, and coins used in the Anglo-Norman parts of Ireland in the Middle Ages were roughly equivalent to their English counterparts except in the later period Irish silver coins had less silver than English ones to prevent the export of Irish coinage from the country as happened earlier. Standardisation commenced in England about the beginning of the 13th century when by royal edict certain measures were approved, though these did not exclude other measures which continued in used.

The basic unit of weight in the British system is the grain—originally based on the weight of a grain of barley. Money however was based on the grain of wheat, and three grains of barley weigh the same as four of wheat. This grain is the troy grain. The *avoirdupois* pound became the pound in general use today. As its name implies, it was intended to be used for weighing heavy goods. This pound is of 7,000 grains of barley from the middle of an ear of barley, allowing standard checks on local weights. The pound avoirdupois was standardised by London merchants in 1303 because of local variations. It was divided into 16 ounces. A stone was 14 pounds for most things but could be 14, 15, or 24 pounds for wool. The hundredweight consisted of 112 pounds, and the ton of 20 hundred weights. Workers in coins and precious metals preferred a pound troy of 7,000 grains of the lighter wheat (*Wikipedia* passim). Wool was exported in sacks of 42 stones.

Liquids were measured in pints, quarts, and gallons, and also similar things like cereals, peas, or meal and flour. A quart was approximately one litre. Two pints made a quart, and four quarts a gallon. For dry measure there was the bushel equal to 8 gallons. The bushel seems to have been the first to be standardised as the contents of a cylindrical vessel 18½ inches in diameter and 8 inches high. A bushel of barley would have weighed 48 pounds. Another dry measure was the peck. Two pecks make a kenning (obsolete), and four pecks make a bushel. A peck could be a different size for each kind of grain, peas or beans. One crannock was considered sufficient capacity to hold the wheat from 17 sheaves. A peck is an imperial and U.S. customary unit of dry volume, equivalent in each of these systems to 2 gallons, 8 dry quarts, or 16 dry pints. In Ireland, the crannock or crannoc of wheat ranged from 8 pecks to 8 bushels; of oats 7 to 14 bushels. The original Winchester measures were made from wood, so doubtless standard measures in other places were also made of wood. It was a long time before they were standardized nationally. (Even in the 19th century, the Irish exported wheat in 'barrels' of 280 pounds and the English imported them in 'quarters' of 480 pounds), Keenan, *Pre-Famine Ireland*, 170).

The yard was first defined legally by Edward I, but there were local standards before that. Such measures might be enforced by the local mayor who would set up an iron bar of the appropriate length on a wall. An inch was the length of three grains of barley. Four grains of wheat were regarded as the equivalent of three of barley. There could be no great exactness as the wheat or barley were themselves the unit of measurement. There were twelve inches to the foot and three feet to the yard. The rod is a historical unit of length equal to 5.5 yards. It may have originated from the typical length of a mediaeval ox-goad. A chain was 4 rods or 22 yards (66 feet) or 44 furrows (up and down twice). The furlong (meaning furrow length) was the distance a team of oxen could plough without resting. This was standardized to be exactly 40 rods or 220 yards. One furlong by one chain equalled an acre so we may suspect that many intermediate measures were derived from the use of the great plough. The mile was introduced after 1066, originally the Roman mile at 5000 feet; in 1592 it was extended to 5280 feet (1760 yards) to make it an even number (8) of furlongs. A league was usually three miles or about an hour's distance on foot.

In England a hide was estimated at 120 acres with considerable variation. These *measures of land* were defined as 1 hide = 100 lands or selions; a half hide = 50 lands; a yard land (alternatively a virgate) = a quarter hide or 25 lands; a land or selion = 3 roods or three quarters of an acre (i.e. a hide of about 75 acres). The selions were strips of land in the open fields. Originally, an acre was a selion of land one furlong (220 yards) long and one chain (22 yards) wide; the measure appears to have begun as an approximation of the amount of land an ox could plough in one day. Traditional acres were long and narrow due to the difficulty in turning the plough. For the same reason they were not straight but slightly S-shaped to facilitate the entry and exit of the plough. However a hide was a unit of value and not necessarily of size. A carucate was an area equal to that which can be ploughed by one eight-ox team in a single year; approximately 120 acres. A bovate was the amount of land one ox can plough in a single year (also called an oxgate); approximately 15 acres or one eighth of a carucate. A virgate was the amount of land a pair of oxen could plough in a single year; approximately 30 acres (also called yard land). A hide was four to eight bovates. A unit of yield, rather than area, it measured the amount of land able to support a household for agricultural and taxation purposes. A hundred or wapentake was 100 hides grouped for administrative purposes (*Wikipedia*, 'English unit'). These measures were not exact, but rough and ready and what the ordinary farmer could visualize. They no doubt took into account the different characteristics of the local land.

As we would also expect the names used were not necessarily the same over the entire British Isles. In Ireland the carucate, ploughland or hide seems to be the equivalent of the townland. A tate was a townland in Monaghan and Fermanagh. A ballybetagh could have 12 or 16 tates. By the end of the 15th century the fiscal unit was the carucate or ploughland of 120 acres of arable land, not counting rivers, meadows, moors, pastures, hills and woods, and giving allowance for pasturage at the rate of grazing at a rate of 300 cows for every town of eight ploughlands (MacCurtain, 95). The nineteenth-century surveyor Thomas Larcom, who was the first Director of the Irish Ordnance Survey, gave his summary of traditional measurements as follows: 10 acres = 1 Gneeve; 2 Gneeves = 1 Sessiagh; 3 Sessiaghs = 1 Tate or Ballyboe; 2 Ballyboes = 1 Ploughland, Seisreagh or Carrow; 4 Ploughlands = 1 Ballybetagh, or Townland; 30 Ballybetaghs = *Triocha Céad* or Barony (Wikipedia, 'Townland'). It is clear that what Larcom calls a ploughland was a carrucate, hide or townland of 120 acres and the ballybetagh was four of these. But terminology was not necessarily the same all over Ireland, and the ballybetagh may have been more common in Gaelic areas) Assessment of value did not necessarily correspond with the ploughing capacity of oxen. More to the point the assessment was a measure of what a chief or lord might expect from a given division of his territory. (After all the Domesday Book was an assessment of revenue, actual and potential, from the whole of England. William cannot have been the only ruler to get the idea.) Also, 120 is a useful size as it is divisible 2, 3, 4, 6 and 12. Assessments and valuations by townland continued into the 19th century. The parish tithe was assessed on the townland, and every tenant or small-holder had to pay their proportionate share.

These measures are evidently derived from places where the great plough and open fields were in operation. They were in constant use in the records of manors. The lands or selions were very important to the individual tenant for they measured his share of the common fields.

We can guess that similar standard measures were to be found in the Gaelic parts and that milk, ale, and grain would have been measured in standard wooden containers within a *tuath*. Things like butter could have been measured with standard stone or metal weights. The hand, the foot, the yard or stride, are natural units. Considerable effort was evidently made under the Brehon Laws to standardize measurement. The length of three barley grains was an inch or finger breadth. Four inches or finger breadths were a hand or fist, and three hands or fists a foot. As hands, fists, and feet would admit of considerable variations, depending on the individual, the legitimate hand which is used for estimating and measuring is prescribed and the term lawful measure is emphasized. (O'Loan, 68, the whole article is recommended.). A sack of wheat was another measure of compensation. Any rents or dues to be paid in kind would have required a standard measure at least for that landowner. As so many containers were made of wood or leather or basketwork they were of their nature perishable. Trade in wine and oil came in pottery jars which then could be used locally as a standard measure.

Primary Sector

The Structure of Agriculture

The basic structures of society closely resembled each other in both Gaelic and Norman areas. Both depended largely on agriculture, both depended on exports for imports, towns facilitated trade for both sectors and both depended on foreign merchants. Techniques were more or less the same. Ireland, like the rest of Europe was overwhelmingly rural, and the urban population was tiny. Life revolved around the local chiefs or lords Gaelic and Norman, and their 'big houses'. Three inter-tangled aspects of agriculture have to be distinguished, the structure of society as a whole, systems of tenure, and systems of agriculture. They were not necessarily the same in any given district. Some attempt must be made to examine developments in each of these over the period though sufficient evidence is usually lacking.

Medieval Tenures of Land

This section is concerned with the holding of land by the cultivators, not with tenure by military service of the great lords. The great plough was introduced into many parts of the British Isles in the post-Roman period and resulted in hides or townlands or ploughlands in many places of about 100 acres which was the most convenient size for a team of eight oxen. The fields could be owned by a single individual or shared in common by several individuals. The hide or townland became the unit of assessment or taxation whether held by one or many. The townland/hundred/ hide/carucate was an easily understood and widely used measure of value like the knight's fee and apparently also of the knight's Gaelic equivalent, the *ógláech*. Like the knight's fee it was divisible, holders of a portion paying a proportionate amount of any tithe or assessment.

Medieval tenures are more easily studied in England because of the wealth of documentary evidence surviving. In Gaelic areas of Ireland little was recorded at local levels. In England the hides were grouped into manors and varied enormously in size from 2 to a 100 hides. The English manor has been described in an earlier chapter. (See above, The English Manor.)

Norman tenures and Management in Ireland

There were two classes of tenants in Normanized areas, free tenants who held by military service of 40 days a year or by socage (i.e. with financial or non-military obligations), and the unfree tenants. A knight's fee was about 3,000 acres and was known as a manor and the tenant owed military service to the king. The manor was made up of townlands or carucates. In feudal theory all the land was owned by the king, so there was no allodial land. The first Norman knights who came with Strongbow endeavoured to acquire lands from the local chiefs in return for services. These were not originally feudal holdings, but the king on his arrival made them so.

Free tenants in socage who held from the tenant-in-chief or the mesne lord were free to attend his honour court on paying the prescribed annual sum. The principle cultivators were the unfree tenants with leases from the local lord (copyholders) but who differed from those who held by socage in that they attended the manor court not the lord's court. All tenants who held only from the lord of the manor would have had the status of villeins who were free only of the court of the manor. Any Irish farmer who still remained on his farm in these areas automatically lost his free status in Norman law. He was no longer a freeholder and so had no right to appear in the local lord's court, the shire court, or any of the king's courts but only the manor court. Native Irish tenants who were already called betaghs would have had the same status.

There were five kinds of unfree tenants, copyholders inaccurately called farmers, gavillers, cottagers, betaghs, and burgesses (Otway-Ruthven, 109). Apart from the burgesses they correspond to the classes on an English manor. Gavillers seem originally to have been tenants-at-will but did in fact pass on holdings from father to son and came to be regarded as copyholders. Cottiers or cottagers held small properties. There were probably large numbers of these living in hamlets as everyone who had a principal occupation like woodman, boatman, and ploughman and so on would try to get a small patch of land from the lord of the manor or the *ógláech* to cultivate some food. Betaghs were to be found on some manors but not others. As their name implies they were native Irishmen, who had the status of villeins and were ***adscripti glebae,*** attached to the soil. The word 'betagh' is derived from the Irish word for food *bia*. It means 'food provider' and in Ireland, it was the common name for a vassal. They were not necessarily poor or have small holdings, but their rents were always in the form of labour services or food renders. A betagh with 30 acres had to find three men to carry out his duties to his lord. This implies that a betagh with 10 acres carried out his own duties. This group were serf-like, tied to the soil and personally unfree in the courts of his Norman lordship. Burgesses had a peculiarly Irish tenure. They attended their own court not the court of the manor. They may have originated in proposed towns which were never built. A burgess court would have developed into a town court (Otway-Ruthven 110-113). Some of these centrally managed English-type manors probably existed in South East Ireland (McNeill, 83). At the beginning rents were paid by labour services or by food renders in kind but later by cash, though as McNeil notes in Ulster nominal cash rent was often paid in kind. This was normally in flour ground in the lord's mill which was easier to transport (***op cit,*** 88). It is estimated that the entire population of an average sized manor was 4 to 5 hundred people (Barry, 'Manorialism').

The full open-field system may have been introduced in places but it was not essential. The tenants of the manors did not hold in common, (as in rundale tenancies) but each held individual amounts of land for which they paid a money rent and other renders. These were acreages in the open fields not defined pieces of ground. Where the great plough was used each tenant was assigned a proportionate number of strips (selions, runrigs) and a number of animals for grazing. Enclosures, increasingly common in England in the later Middle Ages, may not have taken place in Ireland until much later. But it is likely that practice in eastern Ireland closely followed that in England. In some cases small holdings were consolidated and given to a single tenant or leaseholder. Leases or tenancies for rent could be given for quite long periods. The lot of the English tenants improved later when the kings took powers to transfer cases from all courts to the king's courts. Though aimed at curtailing the powers of the barons it eventually benefited the common man. There is no indication of any use of a smaller plough or smaller fields so enclosures would imply fewer tenant farmers, who as their name implies paid a fixed rent, and more agricultural labourers. (In medieval times a farmer was a person or body that paid a fixed annual sum in place of annual assessment. The fact that betaghs in Tudor times had to seek different masters would seem to imply that they had become sharecroppers and agricultural labourers (Ellis, *Tudor Ireland*, 44).

The structure was similar in the earldom of Ulster though no gavillers were recorded. At the top were the big land-holders who were free of the county or honour court and the manor court. Then came the farmers (copyholders) who paid a fixed rent, and the burgesses who also paid a fixed rent. At the bottom were the betaghs and cottiers though few of these were named (McNeill, 79). The basic agricultural unit was the manor with perhaps 3,000 acres, not necessarily with open fields. Large farms from this were given to rent paying farmers who also owed feudal allegiance and service. The manor house was surrounded by a fence and motte and contained the house and farm buildings. The strong farmers were, when possible, drawn from abroad; many Irish were retained but as villeins. The tenants also had to plough the demesne lands of the lord, harrow, sow, weed, scare birds, reap, tie, stook, cart, stack, and thresh. Some of the tenants probably held land in common and tilled it by the openfield system with strips. Haymaking was introduced. The rights of grazing, pannage, hunting, cutting timber etc were closely controlled. The lord of the manor had the only mill; wool and hides were exported on a considerable scale (Mitchell, 173).

In the earldom of Ulster the manors were dispersed settlements or vills. Manors were fiscal centres where tenants went to pay their rent or deal with minor crime or local administration. These centres were not villages in the accepted sense but houses where a seneschal or steward could deal with administration. They were placed on mottes and were reasonably secure (McNeill, 87-8). The system seems to have been taken over from the Gaelic lords who preceded them. The demesne lands were usually also parcelled up and assigned to rent-paying tenants (copyholders), not cultivated by the villeins. Many of the vills can be identified with modern townlands. They probably correspond with pre-Norman farming units owned by one family or several. It is however difficult to disentangle the administration of the earldom as a whole which was as large as a county from the 'manorial' control of rents and profits of farms. The vills seem to have corresponded to manors and would have had a permanent resident bailiff appointed by the lord to collect profits and rents, to assign duties like harvesting, and resolve disputes on his patch. Almost certainly, those who formed the manor court would have elected a headman or reeve to speak for them and perhaps other parish officers like aletasters or jurymen, but we do not know how much of English practice was brought to Ireland.

Elsewhere labour services were normally required on the manors though they were less onerous than in England or in the Gaelic-speaking areas. Normally the tenant was required to work six days a year for the lord, but at Kells 15 days were required. The demesne lands in English speaking areas were often put out to rent (Ellis, *Tudor Ireland* 36). Norman intensive settlement was largely confined to areas where there was good land suitable for tillage to produce a surplus for markets. In many parts of Connaught, especially in the lands of the de Burghs (Clanrickard) this may not have been the case. Patrick Duffy describes the penetration of English placenames into the grants of lands in north Louth. There were more English placenames in the fertile areas along the coast and in the river valleys. Of interest is the long narrow parish of Ballymascanlon on the southern side of the Cooley peninsula. This grange was granted to the abbey of Mellifont by Hugh de Lacy between 1230 and 1240. Duffy notes that the placenames close to the coast are English, while those further from the coast are Irish. It amounted to 6,000 acres divided into 24 townlands.

In Ireland the Norman knights preferred the cantred which they were used to in Wales to the manor. The organisation was similar. The frequent use of the term cantred is especially significant; it was the most appropriate term available to the Anglo-Normans to describe a type of large non-manorial domain common in Wales. It is noticeable that not only did John's enfeoffments recognise the existing cantred structure, but that this continued to survive under the new lords, and that subinfeudations were commonly made in terms of commotes, vills, or packages of services dispersed through the cantred (Warren, 'King John and Ireland' 36.) (It is another reminder that the structures of Gaelic and Norman societies closely resembled each other.)

Gaelic Tenures and Management

When Henry II arrived he obtained the right to the whole of Ireland from the feudal submission of the chiefs. Henceforth, any chief who rebelled was liable in theory to have his lands escheated to the crown (confiscated by the crown). In most parts of Ireland no attempt was made for centuries to change the lands of the greater Gaelic lords into feudal holdings.

Gaelic society had a pyramidal structure similar to the feudal one with its local lords (knights or squires), chiefs of *tuatha*, mesne chiefs, and provincial chiefs. The tenure of land applied only within the *tuath*. It is clear that at local level there were 'lords' (*ógláech*) corresponding in rank with the Norman knight and supported by the renders of a part of the *tuath* corresponding to the manor or parish. On the other hand, in places like Monaghan, the *tuath* seems to have remained the unit and these developed into the great medieval parishes. Free farmers had virtually disappeared, and the land was held, in fact if not in law, by the chief families, or by the clergy or professional men like brehons or physicians. Much of the land was held within the *tuath* as commonage where the cattle were grazed as in the Welsh cantred. The arable and meadow lands were rented out to the farmers who did the actual cultivation and paid in kind. Cattle were the chief source of wealth, and were used like a currency to pay tributes, fines, rents, dowries, and so on (Roche, 21). Unlike in the Norman areas where wealth was measured in acres, in Gaelic areas it was measured in numbers of cattle.

This does not mean that tillage was neglected nor does it imply that the great plough was not used. On the contrary, the holding of a *boaire* or free farmer described in the law code corresponded to a townland, ploughland or carrucate (Keenan, *True Origins*, 190). These probably remained intact after the *boaire* lost his free status and had to pay rent in kind or cash. It is clear that townlands would only have been established and marked out in areas where the great plough was used. (In other areas townlands were introduced much later, perhaps as late as the 19th century when the system of land description was harmonised. In less favoured lands, the use of the light plough would have continued, and the use of the spade. In areas of shifting agriculture a family would have had the right to specific acreages, but the origins of these rights are lost in the mists of time. The local *ógláech* would have had a right to specific returns and would have enforced that right. The townland was of course, as in England, subject to division and parts could be rented out to individuals or to groups in a common or rundale tenancy. Tenancies of halves and quarters of townlands seem to have been common.

It had proved easy for an unscrupulous and land-grabbing lord with the assistance of venal judges to reduce the free farmer (*boaire*) to unfree status (*biatach*). Within each lordship the ruling families grabbed land at the expense of the other landowning families; the process is also found in South Africa. Lax traditions of marriage meant that more children had to be provided with land. The original free farmer (*boaire*) was reduced to the rank of the landless (*biatach*) when the land went to the relatives of the chiefs. The chief might have custody of the lands of an absentee; or clans might occupy lands lying waste or made waste. In theory allodial land might be alienated only with the consent of other members of the *derb fine*, but in practice it was achieved by a kind of mortgage with no real intention of redeeming it. This resulted in a confusion of titles between the possessors and the new owners, members of the chiefly families who were intruded (Ellis, *Tudor Ireland,* 42). Other beneficiaries could be skilled tradesmen, or the Church. Scholars, churchmen, and poets ranked with the lowest degree of nobles. Immediately below these were skilled craftsmen including smiths of all kinds, house builders and shipwrights.

By the twelfth century society closely resembled that of contemporary England. Some free farmers (*saertach*) still existed, if only because the chiefs had not been able to reduce them all to clientship, or because a relative of the chief had taken the farm. Most of the original class of *boaire* or free farmer seem to have been reduced to the unfree ranks of *biatach*. The client farmer or *biatach* was much more profitable to the lord for he had to pay higher dues. The *biatach* or betagh was gradually being reduced to penury by the exactions of the lords.

As Ó Corráin remarks, rack-renting was common among the Gaelic landowners at least from the thirteenth century. There is no indication that the conditions of the working classes improved in Gaelic areas in the period after the Black Death as they did in England. The third category was the *dimain* who had no land of his own, and who may have been a sharecropper, or perhaps a cottar who was given a small patch of land in return for cultivating the lord's lands. The other smaller people, keeping alive by one means or another, doubtless still survived. There were probably as many people with tiny holdings like the cottagers of the English manor. These would have had other occupations like labourers, woodmen, boatmen, fishermen, and so on. These were very vulnerable to famines as they were in the Great Irish Famine. (See The English Manor above.)

By the end of the Middle Ages land holding in Gaelic areas closely resembled that in Norman areas. But the farming unit and the farmer would have been unchanged, the only difference being the imposition of a useless family belonging to the overchief's sept who would be disgraced if they ever did any work. 'Farmers' at the end of the Middle Ages were the lowest grade of nobility, the knight or *óglaech* who held land equivalent to a knight's fee. He cultivated his lands either directly with paid labourers of by means of sharecropping with betaghs (Nichols, 135). He was the equivalent of the minor lord commonly in England called the squire, and his holding of land was equivalent to a parish. In rural Ireland, the parish not the village, was and remains the most significant local social unit.

The chief duty of the betagh was to supply the food and all the needs of his chief's family. The rent of the lands was in services and food renders to the Gaelic chiefs. They were tenants at will and had no legal rights in land. The great export was hides and the chief would take half, a common system called *metayage*. Later in the Middle Ages, exports of linen grew requiring considerable labour services. Food renders were often discharged by the practice of coyne, namely installing a mercenary soldier on the farm to be fed. It was to develop into the notorious coyne and livery of the later Middle Ages (Ó Corráin, 44, Ellis, *Tudor Ireland*, 41). More and more land passed into the hands of the chief. By Tudor times MacCarthy of Muskerry held half the land in his chiefdom as demesne or mensal land (MacCurtain, 39f).

If the betagh had stock of his own he might prosper in clientship to his lord who would allocate grazing rights to him. But if he was dependent on the lord for stock he was only a sharecropper. The Brehon system of gavelkind which forced the owners of property to divide their property equally among their sons resulted in successive generations possessing ever smaller portions of property and they had little opportunity to increase their holdings (Nicholls, 78). (It should be noted that the land actually belonged to the *derb fine* and was not itself actually divided, all sons and grandsons however numerous had equal rights. Also the reproduction of the ordinary family may not usually have exceeded replacement except temporarily.) However with poverty and famine regularly thinning the ranks of the betagh's family the holdings may not have been reduced to the extent they were in pre-Famine Ireland. The betagh in theory was *adscriptus glebae* and so had no rights of tenure of any kind. It would seem however that the betagh, at least by the end of the Middle Ages, was not bound to the service of any one lord but at the end of a term he could always seek another one if he could find one as a tenant-at-will or a farm labourer. The betaghs by the end of the Middle Ages were in a far worse position than their opposite numbers in England having virtually no legally enforceable rights or protection of the law. They attached themselves to a lord promising labour service which meant in practice that the lord took half the produce. Towards the end of the Middle Ages local lords, like their counterparts in England were trying to tie their tenants to the land (Ellis, *Tudor Ireland*, 44). The conditions of the betaghs by the end of the Middle Ages can be compared with the condition of the peasants in France before the Revolution. The only court from which he could hope for redress for actions of the lord or any member of his family, his relations or friends was the lord's own court.

Drainage and Land Reclamation

In the early Christian period there seems to have been extensive colonisation and occupation of waste land. By the end of the eighth century it would seem that all land of economic value was appropriated (Ó Corráin, 49). This would only have been true with regard to the technological and economic possibilities of the time.

It may very well be that in 1169 less than half of the surface of Ireland was occupied in any real sense, though herds of cattle and sheep may have been kept in the forests and on bogs and wastelands in the summertime. It is a curious fact that the distribution of monasteries over Ireland scarcely varied from 800 A.D. to 1500 A.D. Over large parts of Ireland there were no monasteries at all. Not all of these blank areas would have been devoid of population and presumably in much of it there were small patches of tillable soil which were refuges for broken clans who never had enough surplus land to endow a monastery. Many perhaps had no more than a few hundred tillable acres in the woods, bogs, and mountains. As in England at the same period, large parts of the country were still primeval forest or wasteland and boglands. The great forests did not disappear until much later. In the settled parts timber suitable for building disappeared, but the absence of proper roads and wagons made timber-felling in the deep and mountainous forests uneconomic. This would have been especially true where the woods were intersected with streams with boggy verges. (See above, The Land: Geographical Aspects.)

Local drainage and land reclamation was probably attempted at parish level as occurred in England. Drainage of water-logged soils was the easiest way to improve productivity. This of its nature was a communal effort and much easier to be undertaken by a controlled manor, and was probably practised in the colonized areas of eastern Ireland. Ploughing with the great plough formed drainage channels between the ridges with the run-off into a stream. Whether a cantred was able or willing to reclaim land is not obvious. But if it just required digging drains to the nearest river it was probably done locally, and agreed at the court of the *ógláech*. There was no organisation of farmers apart from the local lord's court. Large scale drainage did not occur before the 17th century. Large areas too could not be drained before the passage of Drainage Acts in the 19th century and the use of gunpowder to lower cills in the rock.

The plantation of western Ulster early in the 17th century showed how quickly a backward area could be modernised after the land was acquired by rich companies in London. It was estimated that a million acres of wastes were reclaimed between 1670 and 1840. Much of this was probably rough scrubland and peat bogs on which potatoes, the new wonder crop from South America, and flax could be grown as in Monaghan and South Armagh. Other parts like the *Ard Cianacht* around Collon in Co. Louth with its wet heavy clay soil had probably been reclaimed by the Cistercians in the Middle Ages but through neglect reverted to waste land. Anthony Foster, in the 18th century, put in great surface drains and limed the soil heavily. Reclaimed land was notorious for reverting to rushes (*juncus effusus*).

The Systems of Farming

General Aspects

As has been pointed out before in this book, much of the island was not cultivated. Much of this land was marginal to tillage. Ireland, like the rest of the British Isles was affected by the deterioration in climate in the later part of the Middle Ages.

Agriculture was static in this period with little change between 1170 and 1500. This contrasts sharply with the enormous development in livestock, seeds, crops and techniques between 1600 and 2000. There were some changes; horse shoes and harness allowed a greater use of horses, windmills were added to watermills, there was an increasing use of money and so of money crops; markets and market towns facilitated exchange. Many of these improvements were probably only marked in regions of intensive cultivation like Flanders. Agriculture was mostly defensive: warding off famine was more important than earning more money. Iron tools were introduced. Good quality iron tools were superior to those of stone or bronze, but much of the iron available to the poorer classes was probably of low grade. The most important tool was the plough. All the other tools would have survived from Neolithic times. The spade was now given an iron tip, and this was probably true of many tools. It had long been obvious that any tool for cutting or thrusting was best shod with iron even when made largely with wood.

Agriculture can be divided into subsistence and commercial. By subsistence is meant that all necessary food is grown in a given area, but not necessarily on every plot or farm. The large hundred-acre farm might produce nearly all its own needs but still barter locally for things like fish, wool, vegetable dyes, forest fruits and furs, and such things. The absence of roads or suitable communication meant that there were few imports from outside the districts. Local chiefs might exchange furs for wine, but not lesser people. Commercial agriculture implied markets and reasonable communication at least by packhorse. A fertile region might specialise in tillage and rougher regions in producing wool. Districts around towns would find a market for all kinds of produce, eggs, butter, wool, firewood, grain and so on in the town.

Real commercial agriculture arose when there was a demand for a product outside the area. The prosperity of England was based on the export of fine wools to weavers in Flanders. This produced a demand for wool of rougher quality for the clothing of the poorer sorts. Ireland, especially in the earlier part of the Middles Ages, was able to supply grain and wool to England, and the prosperity and stability of the eastern parts of Ireland was based on this. Irish agriculture was based, most of the time, on cattle rearing. But in the Normanized parts tillage was more important. Towards the end of the Middle Ages, as in England sheep rearing for the export of wool gained in importance in some areas. In general the Irish economy during this period was gradually moving from subsistence agriculture to a system geared at least partly to production for a market. There were exchanges between town and the surrounding countryside. A true commercial agriculture cannot be said to have existed.

The co-operative system where several farmers banded together for mutual assistance and protection was widespread in Western Europe and was the practice in much of southern England. Their open field system, though often associated with manorial tenure was adopted in large parts of England before the arrival of the Normans. The aim of the manor (as it was called in French) was to be self-sufficient in food even in the bad years, not to produce a surplus for the market (Pretty). Whether this great change in agricultural practice was an initiative of the peasants or the local lords is not known. The adoption too was antecedent to the widespread use of money. Dyer notes the transformation of agricultural practice and rural settlement in South East England between 900 AD and 1200 AD but there is no record of it (Dyer, 'Economy and Society', 144). In Gaelic areas, tillage by the 'rundale' system later became common where a group of small farmers took a large field to be worked in common. It is not clear when the rundale system of holding in common commenced. As the name implies the fields were large ones worked with the great plough, as the plough cast the soil into long ridges, runrigs, with shallow drainage valleys between them, rundales. Flat fields and undersoil drainage became common only in the 19th century, as also did single or two-horse ploughs.

Sowing was normally done in the spring. Cattle were small and their yield of milk was small. Cattle and sheep produced the two great exports, hides and wool (Nicholls, 137). Cattle were occasionally subject to a murrain of cattle plague, and this inevitably resulted in famine. With cattle being clearly the most important element in their economy and milk products being basic in their diet, they also grew a number of crops such as wheat, oats, rye, barley, beans and flax. The principal variety of wheat grown in the ancient world was *einkorn*, which had twice the protein value of modern grains. *Melde*, later called **Fat Hen**, today regarded as a weed, yielded edible seeds and leaves with a higher food value than modern cabbage and spinach. A boaire would have tilled about eight acres a year (out of his hundred) for cereals and planted two varieties of wheat, with barley, rye, oats, beans, peas, and flax (Mitchell, 165 ff). Even on a 15 acre or 30 acre holding considerable diversification was necessary and possible. The most common cereal was oats, wheaten bread being regarded as a delicacy. Later root crops became more common (Ó Corráin). Many of the fields identified in the in-field were quite small, scarcely more than an acre. But many smallholders probably still used the spade and hoe. The poorer people would have used a wooden spade tipped with metal as they did up to the nineteenth century. There was no haymaking.

It is not clear why the village system, so prevalent in north western Europe was not adopted more widely. But the dispersed settlement pattern even with the open-field system had its own advantages. In places like Ireland, Scotland and Wales where cattle-raiding was endemic it was better to keep the stock dispersed as the raiders would have to split up into small groups to locate them. The same was true of small tilled fields hidden in the scrub. There would be the same number of cultivators but the raiders would have to split up to find them and their equipment could rapidly be hidden in the local bushes or ponds. A wooden village can swiftly be fired but dispersed houses take longer. Almost certainly though, when a minor lord occupied the local *lios* and farmhouse the workers would have gathered nearby into collections of huts called clachans in Scotland. The craftsmen, smiths and woodworkers, would have their holdings of land close to the lords who gave them most of their work.

In the absence of markets trade was limited and it was difficult to transport significant quantities of cereal on horseback. Later in the Middle Ages relatively higher priced exports like wool, blankets, and hides could more profitably be transported to seaports. Eastern counties had a great advantage in this and were seized by the Normans. Roads suitable for wheeled traffic and commerce were often not built in western areas until the 19th century. (As late as the 19th century butter from Kerry for export had to be taken on horseback to Cork city.)

Gaelic

Nor is it clear why in Gaelic areas such a priority was given to cattle-raising when tillage would have supported a larger population. It would appear that certain aspects of Gaelic society are to blame. The code of laws allowed and promoted the transfer of land and wealth to the richer classes. Wealth, prestige, and status in the courts were measured largely in the number of cattle a lord possessed. Agriculture was used to promote the interests of the ruling classes not to increase the number of farmworkers. Cattle were more easily dispersed and saved in a time of raiding whereas standing crops could be easily destroyed. Shrubs and undergrowth provided food for cattle and could be used as places for concealment and ambush. It was easier to block paths through woodland.

It makes sense to describe the basic production unit, what might be called the family farm or townland, while recognising that much sustenance came from the flocks and herds in the forests, and to some extent from the hunting of wildlife. Other sources of goods whether from warfare or from trade from outside the tuath passed directly through the hands of the chiefs or the markets and fairs they permitted. The organisation of the farm tells us nothing about the quality of the farming, nor with the type of government, Gaelic or Norman. There had been farming in Ireland for thousands of years and much thought given to what worked best. Attempts may have been made in many areas to adopt the great plough but were discontinued as unsatisfactory. Descriptions of the farm of a *boaire* in the Brehon Code would appear to place the formation of the ploughlands/townlands earlier in Ireland.

The introduction of the great plough to northern Europe in the post-Roman period apparently led to a division of land into roughly 100 acre units, which came to be called ploughlands/hides/carrucates in England and townlands (*baile*) in Ireland. It is also reasonable to assume that the parts of Ireland which adopted the great plough roughly corresponded with the land held by Anglo-Normans in the later Middle Ages, though of course the Gaelic farmers were using the great plough and the townland long before the arrival of the Normans. (The present system of townlands over the whole of Ireland now numbering 64,000 was commenced in the Tudor period and finalized in the 19th century.) We can be sure that Mellifont Abbey had a fully organised manorial system of agriculture on the Burgundian model before 1150 for they made a point of standardising everything. Outside this area of townlands and the great plough we can assume that smaller square fields and the light plough continued.

Prominent in the Brehon Code (c 800 A.D.) was the typical economic unit, the family farm of about 70 to 100 acres, the basic unit of production. The boaire (bo aire cattle-minder, perhaps cattle boss) was the typical free farmer who had an allodial right to his family farm. This was still apparently the basic four-generation family. As the holding was allodial, it was presumable marked out by the original settlers when a decision was made to adopt the great plough. It was obviously based on the use of the great plough. The townland remained even after the land was divided amongst rent-payers and tithe-payers. Every noble, free man, important craftsman, and learned person would have possessed one or more farms/townlands. This remained so even when the land was farmed out to rent-payers. There were also numerous specialist producers, house-builders, smiths, and so on that would have their skills in addition to the family farms. Though spinning and dyeing would have been done by all women, weaving that required a loom, was probably mostly done by specialist weavers. Cattle-raising on the open ranch was by far the dominant economic activity, and wealth was counted by the number of cattle possessed. We have no idea what proportion of a *tuath* was thus held as open range, and how much was unclaimed forest, bog and mountain. There would have been no hedges or fences; indeed it was in the 18th century that these became common. Hedges and fences where used were to keep animals out not fence them in. Tilled land may have been surrounded by temporary fences, but children may have been used to keep out animals. A stockade probably surrounded the farm buildings for the protection of some animals at night. The farmer's hall where he, with his family and domestic servants lived, was a simple wooden rectangular structure like those in England. The hall of a chief was somewhat larger in size, but not essentially different.

Conditions on the farmstead would have been much like they were a thousand years earlier and a thousand years later. There would have been a large hall, and several other smaller buildings all surrounded by a circular enclosure called a rath or lios. The farmstead would also have had a fold for sheep, a pen for calves, a sty for pigs, a barn, a kiln for drying the grain, all within the circular fence or rath, Traces of at least 30,000 raths are known to survive. The outer fence was normally banked with earth at this period that explains why so many from this period survive. The boaire would have had a share in the watermill if such existed but betaghs had to use their lord's mill. They were becoming more common towards the end of the period (Ó Corráin.) During this period water-driven corn grinding mills were being introduced, a horizontal watermill being known from the seventh century. This was not a very efficient mill. Corn-drying kilns became equally widespread. Damp corn quickly rots. All cereal crops were subject to great fluctuations in yield, whether from poor sprouting lack of rain, too much rain, and numerous diseases. It is likely that this kind of 100 acre or townland farm with its associated rights of pasture, turbary, piscary, pannage, etc. persisted throughout the Middle Ages though largely sub-divided among betaghs who were in effect tenant farmers who paid in labour services and food dues instead of cash. One lord could have several of these farms and appoint bailiffs to see he got his dues.

The family farm produced almost all the daily essentials in the line of shelter, food, and clothing, and so could have had many kinds of servants like herdsmen or milkmaids. It was a subsistence economy, with no production for markets. Presumably much of the work was done by family labour except in the case of the noble families. A hired labourer at least in the eleventh century was paid one cow and one cloak for a year's labour, and this may have been the practice too at an earlier date. Slaves were kept for the heaviest work. The number of slaves kept probably varied as the supply. Slaves at the time of St Patrick would have been abundant, and also again in Viking times. The slave would have been given his daily food and a garment, probably a cast-off. Actual slavery with the buying and selling of slaves seems to have ended in the 13th century. In the Middle Ages slaves seem to have been less numerous than formerly, and paid labour more frequent. The conditions of serfs, descendants of slaves, was not much better however being much the same as betaghs.

Associated with the family farm or townland were smaller specialist producers, apparently all belonging to the unfree classes, like fishermen, fowlers, fur trappers, or woodsmen who presumably had a cottage and a small patch of ground on which to live. There also categories of labourers or herdsmen, employed on the farms, who probably also had small pieces of ground and a cottage or hut, and who were used as hired labour. The laws mention the categories of bothach, fuider, and sen-cleithe but it is unclear how many of these classes survived into the Middle Ages. Whatever they were then called their occupations would have remained. Bothach (bodach) is translated as cottier. His name (from bo a cow) would seem to imply that he was a herdsman. Fuiders were similar, and may originally have been mercenaries whom a lord settled on his land. Sen-cleithes seem to have been serfs bound to the soil, perhaps originally bothachs and fuidirs who had not kept up their payments. Bothachs (bodachs) did not own land but could be given land by the chief to work in return for services or on the share-cropping principle and no doubt the cows with which their name seems connected. It is likely that associated with every farm or group of farms, there was a village or clachan composed of little wattle-and-daub huts, each with a patch of land. Most of the cattle they herded would have belonged to others, the clients of the lords. In the English Doomsday Book in the eleventh century, numerous villani (villagers) bordarii (smallholders) and cotarii (cottagers) were mentioned which obviously correspond to the Gaelic categories as their situations were alike. The term *bodach* came to mean oaf.

There was a fear in the upper classes, both Norman and Gaelic, both men and women, of losing their status in society and being forced to descend to the indignity of doing manual labour. The day was to come, far in the future, when O'Neills and O'Briens, Butlers and Fitzgeralds, would follow the plough and dig potatoes. But they did not know that.

It is obvious that in areas unsuitable for the great plough different systems would have been in force. These is a good deal of guesswork and comparison with other areas involved in this as contemporary records either do not exist or have not been studied (Nichols p. x; Mary O'Dowd, 120). Though the name townlands was applied to them only much later, it would seem that areas were designated by the chiefs for their own purposes from an early period giving a return equivalent to a townland (Nichols, 138). Wasteland, woodland, marshes, bogs and often mountains with land unsuitable for tillage would have covered many areas so pastoralism would have been more prominent. Because the amount of food produced from an acre of good land from grazing is much lower than from tillage all tillable patches would have been used. Cattle are less vulnerable to destruction in warfare than crops so it is likely that pastoralism kept growing in the later Middle Ages. Cattle are more easily hidden (Nichols, 133). This may have led observers in Tudor times to have concluded that there was little tillage in Gaelic areas. The tilled areas would have been smaller and possibly more numerous where only the old light plough or spade tillage could be used. Life support was not merely a matter of pastoralism or tillage but of using all local sources, fruit, nuts, and berries in the woods, fish in the rivers, lakes, and the sea, and wild animals that could be caught or trapped.

Where there was limited good-quality tillable land with much rougher grazing and large expanses of wooded or heather-covered mountains, as in many parts of Scotland, Wales, and Ireland, the infield-outfield system probably prevailed. There were probably small settlements of clustered insubstantial houses, with no church and usually, considerable ties of kinship between the families in the clachan. It is now generally agreed that a clachan has the following characteristics: small settlements of clustered houses, no church, no shop or school. Usually, there were considerable ties of kinship between the families in the clachan. Most of the houses would have been of wattle and daub roofed with thatch, and easy to move about when the land was exhausted. The little houses of wattle, clay and branches could be easily disassembled and reassembled. The land around the clachan was held under a system of land tenure whereby farmers within the clachan had scattered plots or strips of good, medium and poorer quality land as in the open-field system. But the cantred, not the manor, would have been the area within which such rights were assigned. And having being once assigned they became hereditary and customary.

The better land was usually found close to the cluster of houses and was known as the infield; poorer quality land was found in what was often referred to as the outfield, since it was further away from the cluster. The pastures were held 'in common' e.g. the land around the houses and the mountain land. The mountain land was allocated in soums—e.g. one soum entitled a farmer to graze a cow or so many sheep. The number of soums that a farmer held was related to how much land he held in the infield/outfield area. (www.antrimhistory. net 'The clachan'). Small fields close to the rath or farmstead could have been ploughed with a light plough drawn by oxen. The small square fields were about 70 yards square. Heavy manuring would have maintained fertility but would not have prevented a build up of weeds and pests. In the fallow year, the land was ploughed two or three times at intervals of a few weeks and constantly harrowed. Agricultural techniques and skills would have been the same as in the openfield areas. The outfield would naturally not be manured as heavily as the infield because of the difficulty in transporting heavy wet manure. The entire group of insubstantial farm buildings could have been shifted periodically round the townland. This would have been a substitute for fallowing. But the outfield would have to be tilled from time to time to gain the benefit of naturally accumulating nitrogen. As it would have been covered in weeds and scrub one assumes that it would first have been burned.

Modern landscapes like the glens of Antrim with small holdings reaching far up the sides of the glens are not a suitable model. It was just too dangerous to move far into the woods. Robbers, wild animals and bands from a hostile *tuath* were too common. Herdsmen and woodmen would have kept in groups. So too would women and children if they had occasion to go milking or gathering nuts and berries. Sheep and cattle would not have been just turned out on the mountain.

In more remote and less fertile areas slash-and-burn agriculture may still have been practised. There would not have been the infield and outfield, nor any permanent settlements. Each family or group of related families would have had their rights from the local lord in a particular district. Most of the land would have been covered with scrub and their collection of huts moved round their district every few years. A certain patch of scrub would have been cleared and the scrub burned on it. The ash contained all the fertiliser a crop needed resulting in good cropping for a year or two. Then the next patch was cleared and the scrub allowed to regenerate. The scrub would be used as pasture for cattle and goats and they too would contribute to manuring the soil. Indeed the nutrition from the scrublands was probably as good as from grass if not better. There is no reason why all three systems could not have been in use in the same district, as well as the great plough, the light plough and the spade.

Manorial

As said earlier, Norman areas were associated with the open field system and the great plough which was already in use in Ireland. What the Normans brought was a much greater emphasis on tillage and production of a surplus for export. Outlets for export normally improve productivity for farmers find that if they work more or work better they can improve their standard of living. The construction of roads, bridges, market towns and ports were more important than the actual method of agriculture.

But it does not follow that there were no improvements before their coming. Heavier horses were being imported from Britain, but whether this was primarily for farm work or military purposes is unclear (Ó Corráin 58). There was also a great importation of wine in the twelfth century that surprised Giraldus and obviously corresponding exports to pay for it. Wine was for the richer people alone, so we have an indication of the concentration of wealth. The exports continued to be hides for leather and the 'forest products' of all northern countries, though Ireland was not as well endowed with these as the Baltic countries and Russia, and later America. Timber was an export until the seventeenth century, but when the export commenced is difficult to say.

In a manor, farming like all aspects of life, was strictly controlled. The principal duty of the officers and the bailiff was to ensure that the standards of farming were maintained in accordance with decisions made at the assembly; all tenants contributed, therefore, to the choice of crop rotations, the setting of dates for ploughing, sowing, reaping and the post-harvest release of livestock onto the arable fields (Pretty). The bailiff was there to see that his master got the best dates. This system, as Pretty observes did not of itself lead to higher productivity and was aimed rather at security as all crops were liable to fail at one time or another and all animals liable to mortality. The allocation of the number of animals or fowl each villein was allowed in woods or on commons would also be decided by the jury and punishments imposed on transgressors for breaches of the manor's rules. This was the only court that villeins had access to.

It is not obvious to what extent the full manorial system was introduced, and evidence from the earldom of Ulster indicates that in many cases current Gaelic practice was followed where there were insufficient English colonists induced to settle.

Food

Quite a lot has been written about food in the Middle Ages but almost all of what has been written concerns the food of the upper classes. The food of the working classes would have been very simple and very restricted. For thousands of years men lived as hunter-gatherers, and often the emphasis was on the gathering which was done by women. Things that could be gathered were nuts, berries, seeds, roots, mushrooms, eggs of wildfowl, seaweeds, and shellfish. Things that could be hunted were game and fish and perhaps larger animals like deer and wild boar. Then came the Neolithic Revolution with the domestication of animals and the domestication of crops about 7,000 BC. The most important crops to be farmed were cereals which had large seeds which were easily stored. Animals domesticated were cattle, sheep, goats, asses, and horses. These could be milked and gave a supply of dairy products. Agriculture developed over the next two or three millennia and by the time it reached Ireland by 4500 BC it had largely been worked out what was successful and what not. In the ensuing millennia new developments on the Continent found their way to Ireland. Some use was made of salt to preserve food, but it is not clear to what extent. The warrior ruling classes decreed that hunting of the large animals was restricted to themselves, and likewise the larger fish.

In the ancient world the basic monotonous food of the poor was some form of cereal, wheat, barley, oats, rye, rice, or maize. Efforts were always made to vary the diet, perhaps with a bit of meat or vegetable, spice or sauce. Butter and cheese were also useful in this respect. In the Roman army the basic foods for the common soldier were corn, beans, wine, vinegar, and salt. Eggs and vegetables could be added if they were available and meat was issued on festive days which were numerous. The cereal could be eaten as bread or porridge (Rodgers, 134). The higher ranks dined much better. Some kind of vegetable could be used, and St Benedict prescribed that two kinds of dishes be cooked for the main meal of the day, one probably of cereal and the other of a vegetable or pulse, along with a pound of bread, and some fruit or young vegetables if they were available (*Rule*, Chap. 39). This would have been followed to the letter by the Cistercians, and taken as a norm by the other religious orders.

These examples show the limits of food available to ordinary people. In Ireland the basic bread or porridge would be supplemented with dairy products, especially skim milk, whey, and buttermilk. It is not clear how long a working man could survive on milk products alone. It would have been impossible in the winter when the cows were dry. The basic food of the poor must have been a cereal whose seeds could be stored through the winter. By the same token the summer and autumn diet must have had a large component of milk products, fruit, berries, eggs, and early-maturing crops like fat hen. Poultry were unlikely to be eaten until their laying days were over except by the rich who would demand tender fowl. The hens would have been small, the eggs small, and relatively few in number. They were fed largely on what they could scratch for themselves. It should be noted that as cooking pots were rarely available ducks and geese with abundant layers of fat would have been better for roasting. If a suitable clay was to be found locally small birds could be covered in clay and cooked on embers. Fish too could be wrapped in wet moss, placed on hot stones and steamed. We have no idea how resourceful the ordinary people were in gathering the fruits of nature. In the sub-culture based on the potato which had burgeoned in Gaelic-speaking parts of Ireland before the Great Famine basic foraging and cooking skills were apparently lost. People died in sight of the sea which teemed with fish. Corpses had green mouths from eating grass and leaves as none knew what plants were edible. This was not necessarily the case in the Middle Ages, but a long harsh winter would mean that all seasonal fruits were consumed as well as the stored cereals which ought to tide them over the winter.

In some ways Ireland was at the limit for the successful cultivation of cereals, especially wheat, but it is possible that in the warmer climate of the Middle Ages it was possible to grow wheat at lower levels everywhere in Ireland. Oats and barley could be grown in most places, especially oats in the more northerly parts. Oats was the most common and was eaten in the form of porridge or oatcakes, but barley, wheat and rye were also grown. Nichols mentions that due to a shortage of cooking pots it was more usual to bake oaten bread (133). Wheaten bread was a delicacy and doubtless left to the upper classes. The other main component of the diet was the pulses like peas, beans, and vetches. Like cereals their seeds can be stored. There were root crops like onions, celery and a vegetable like a carrot or parsnip and a leafy one like kale, and perhaps fat hen (goosefoot) and apples (Ó Corráin 52 ff; Columcille xxviii). The storage period for vegetables and roots was limited. (The later potato could be stored for several months but would rot by the following summer, and could not, like cereals be stored from year to year.) The woods, at the proper times, would have been scoured for nuts and berries and no doubt the very poorest were assiduous in this.

With regard to animal food cattle sheep and goats were kept. Milk products of all kinds were regarded as very important, and the boy herders had to keep the calves away from the cows. Milk can be used to drink, to make butter and buttermilk, cheese and whey. Cheese was important because it could be stored. Butter seems to have been preserved in places by burying firkins in bogs. It could also be salted. Sheep and pigs were eaten, and at times salted. Every part of the carcase would have been used, the poorer people no doubt getting the worst bits. But food was too precious to throw any bits away, and pigs' feet and offal were popular with the poor until recent times. Sheep and goats were also milked. There is no doubt that the common practice of culling the older animals was practised in the autumn. A calculation had to be made with regard to how many animals could be kept alive during the winter, and certain pastures had to be set aside for this. Because cattle was a store of wealth there seems to have been a reluctance to slaughter more than the minimum. Cattle were not expected to thrive during the winter, merely to survive. There seems to be fewer references to salting than one might expect so probably early winter was a period of feasting. Corn was fermented to make ale. As the ale did not keep brewing was probably a weekly task from the stored grain.

With regard to the richer classes the fare was much better for those who could afford it or could afford gardeners. They could have fine wheaten bread, oat bread, barley bread, peas, beans, onions, cabbage, carrots, watercress, honey, beer, and the flesh of cattle, sheep, and pigs, deer and wild boar and other game from the forests, poultry and other fowl, the newly introduced rabbits, doves, eggs, fish of all kinds especially salmon, newly caught and salted, and all kinds of the products of milk, besides enormous amounts of imported wine. A host of by-products like sausages and black puddings could be made from livestock, nuts and fruits both wild and cultivated. Apples were cultivated in orchards. Mitchell mentioned the fruits sold in the Dublin markets, apples, pears, plums, damsons, and sloes, cherries, raspberries, and strawberries; blackberries and bilberries, even figs, raisins, and walnuts (Mitchell, 171). The tables for the guests at rich abbeys like Mellifont would have been equal to those of the greater lords. But many abbeys were impoverished and convents of nuns more so.

Forest and Wastes: Foraging

Gathering the fruits of nature always remained an important part of the economy. Though obviously not usually as productive as tillage the natural value of forests and wastes was not negligible. Nobody would bother tilling the soil if an equivalent amount of nourishment grew naturally. Woods were used extensively to feed animals. Pigs were fed on oak and beech mast. Cattle, sheep, and goats browsed on the grass and low shrubs. Furze was a cultivated crop, used for feeding animals. Large timbers and small timbers were used in building and as firewood. By the end of the Middle Ages trees had virtually disappeared from within The Pale. There must therefore have been systematic trading with the local Gaelic chiefs to get wood. This would largely have been small wood capable of being carried on horseback or in ox-carts. Large-scale coppicing, such as was to be found in South East England seems to have been unknown. Nuts, berries and fruits could be gathered in the woods. Bogs, marshes and fens could supply ferns, bracken, sedges, reeds and rushes for roofing, bedding and litter. Nearly all houses even in towns were thatched. Osiers, reeds and rushes could be used for making baskets and fish traps. Heather could be grazed by sheep. Bogs supplied peat for fuel. Uncultivated grassy places were grazed by animals. In the absence of a pottery industry and the expense of metal, wooden vessels and baskets were widely used and making them was a local industry. Shellfish collecting and sea bird egg collecting could be done along the coasts. Marshes abounded in wildfowl and provided a living for fowlers. Rivers and lakes provided fish. Hares could be caught for fur and flesh. Heather and birch could be used to make brooms. Herbs could be collected for medicines. Not all of these were available in every place, but could provide a basis for local trading. Wild birds were an important part of the diet: those consumed at medieval feasts might include species of bustard, crane, curlew, finch, gull, heron, lark, mallard, partridge, pheasant, pigeon, plover, quail, snipe, swan, teal, thrush, and woodcock (Pretty 4). Forest fruits like crab apples, hazelnuts, sloes, elderberries, cherries and plums could be collected.

Both in Gaelic and Norman societies access to the woods and wastes was strictly controlled at least in the neighbourhood of each settlement. Pasture, the most widespread right, was the right to pasture cattle, horses, sheep, geese, or other animals on the common land. Piscary was the right to fish. Turbary was the right to take sods of turf for fuel. Common in the soil was the right to take sand and gravel. Mast or pannage was the right to turn out pigs for a period in autumn to eat mast (acorns and other nuts). Estovers was the right to take sufficient wood for the commoner's house or holding; usually limited to smaller trees, bushes (such as gorse) and fallen branches. On most commons, rights of pasture and pannage for each commoner were tightly defined by number and type of animal. For example the occupier of a particular cottage might be allowed to graze fifteen cattle, four horses, ponies or donkeys, and fifty geese—the numbers allowed for their neighbours would probably be different (*Wikipedia* 'Common land'). In the manorial system these allocations and rights were closely watched by the villeins to ensure that nobody cheated. Thirdly, communal decisions were taken against individuals who had attempted to overconsume or underinvest in the communal resources—in particular those who had encroached onto the common wastes, had over-used the commons, over-gleaned the fields, or had neglected their obligations to maintain roads, ditches, hedges and gates (Pretty). It is not clear how fair shares were enforced in Gaelic and Norman Ireland between the villeins and betaghs themselves.

We can infer that a similar system was in force in Gaelic areas, for though the allodial farmer, when they still existed, had complete rights over his own farm he did not have such rights over common lands. Also rights were enforceable within the cantred or commote. But there must have been some mechanism of control. But it was of the nature of holding in common that there had to be local control enforced by the community. The commote however seems too large for such local control so it must have been done in each vill or division of the commote, or in the court of the *ógláech* in charge of a parish-sized unit. Though in disturbed times at the end of the Middle Ages such local controls may have become ineffective.

Wood was the material most used in Ireland to make things. Metal objects apart from weapons were rare. A pottery industry scarcely existed. Stone was little used except for prestigious buildings. Almost everything had to be made from wood, houses, containers, baskets, fortifications, hurdles. Many boats were made by stretching hides over a wooden frame. Fish weirs and devices for catching fish were made of wood. Most weapons, tools and implements were made of wood tipped with iron, for example spears, arrows, ploughs and spades. Mills and bridges were made of wood. In much of Ireland too wood was used for fuel.

The area of woodland gradually decreased in eastern Ireland though by Tudor times extensive woodlands were still to be found in Gaelic Ireland. Much of this was likely to be scrub which was useful to lords for military purposes, and which could still be used for grazing cattle, and for wattle-and-daub housing. With a decline in population and tillage in the later Middle Ages many woods may have regenerated giving to Tudor observers the impression of a well-wooded country. There probably always some kind of tree preservation for various reasons, hunting, timber for construction, and obstacles to invaders. How widely or effectively it was employed we do not know. Large stands of timber remained in inaccessible areas until Tudor and Stuart times. In the south of England extensive woods of mature timber survived until Napoleonic times and were used for the building of battleships. It is agreed that Ireland was effectively deforested in Tudor and Stuart times, but we do not know how much mature timber survived until then.

Farming: General Observations

Agriculture was largely subsistence, but growing a surplus for sale became increasingly common. Climate was improving as was technology. Horseshoes and stirrups were invented as was horse harness in particular the padded horse collar. This allowed horses to pull carts, ploughs, heavy objects etc. without a yoke pressing on its windpipe. The great plough was introduced giving a boost to tillage, and organising cultivation in the now standard townland or hundred where feasible. Watermills became common and were generally the property of the lord or chief. Windmills appeared in the West useful where there was no falling water. Specialist traders arose who built small defended towns and ports, but the import and export trade in other areas could continue over open beaches in sheltered harbours protected by the local chief. The size of ships increased allowing the export of cereals from eastern Ireland to England. They could easily carry horses.

Tillage

Three systems of tillage maintain the fertility of the soil. The chief factor limiting food production was the fact that nitrogen in the soil through tillage was used up faster than it could be replaced by the natural process of washing it from the air through rainfall. Another factor limiting output was the concurrent growth of inedible weeds. The third chief factor was excessive wetness of the soil. All these factors were known at the time and steps within the known technology of the time were always taken to counteract them. Which techniques were used depended on local factors and conditions.

The aims of tillage were to produce a well-drained area free from weeds, and with the soil reduced to a texture best suited for seed to sprout and grow, and with sufficient nutrients for plant growth. The implements for this were the plough, the spade and the harrow. Cultivation was done in such a way as to allow channels at intervals for drainage. To increase yield nutrients were added, often animal manure, and seed grain was sieved to remove weed seed. It was not an age of agricultural improvement, and the Normans brought no new techniques. Yields could be increased by close attention to the relatively simple skills. It has been shown more than once that crop yields can be increased fourfold by ploughing at the proper time, producing a fine seed bed, selecting and cleaning the seed, applying fertiliser, careful weeding, and again harvesting at the proper time. When villeins/betaghs owed labour services to their lords it was difficult for them to do the various works on their own lands at the proper times. Pretty considered that the productivity of the villeins own strips was 50% that of the demesne and this was probably true also in Ireland.

To maintain the fertility of the soil four systems of tillage were devised. The first was called 'slash and burn' or 'long fallow' system. A stretch of scrubland was cleared with axes, and the scrub burned on the spot. This released nitrogen and other elements sufficient to produce good crops for a few years. Then it was abandoned and a new stretch cleared while natural growth of weeds and shrubs resumed on the abandoned patch. A cycle of several years could be maintained. But no attempt was made to control the growth of weeds. The second system was the 'infield-outfield' system. In this system, the part nearest the farmstead was heavily manured, while parts further away were grazed, or cropped only rarely. It was often used when fertile patches were small. Manure had to be carried on human backs or in drugs or sleds. The third system was the 'open field' system usually in conjunction with the great plough. This allowed for a fallow year when every effort was made to root out weeds. It fitted in particularly well with the manorial system and the close management of the manorial court, but originally had no connection with it. The hundred acre farm was not tilled as a single unit. Towards the end of the Middle Ages enclosures of open fields became common, and the individual tenants paid rents, but the use of the great plough and the fallow year continued, The fourth one, which was post-medieval was the rotation, especially the Norfolk rotation which dispensed with the need for a fallow year. At the height of the open field system a third of all agricultural land was out of cultivation in a given year due to fallowing. There is little doubt that all three systems were used in the British Isles though details are lacking about local practices.

Yields could be sparse because of lack of fertilizer, lack of crop rotation, heavy soils, a high water table, a cold climate, inefficient harvesting, and ploughs which could not cut deep enough to kill weeds. The farmer grew his own seed, so that from each unit sown, and from a three to five fold yield, one part must be kept for the next year's crop. Therefore, the amounts of land and labour required to produce an adequate harvest were considerable. In any case the chief aim of agriculture was to avoid crop failure. Five bushels of seed yielded 2½ crannocks at harvest at Cloncurry Co. Kildare (Lydon *Ireland in the Later Middle Ages* 9). (This would seem to indicate a ratio of 5 to 1 but if the following year's seed is removed 4 to 1. This corresponds with the figures for southern England given by Pretty. The number of cultivated crops was very limited, wheat, oats, rye, barley, beans and flax.

Horses replaced oxen in the course of the Middle Ages but to a lesser extent than might have been expected. As late as 1781 the argument for the superiority of oxen was still being made. Oxen are cheaper than horses, their food, harness, shoes, and attendance on them much cheaper, and their dung better for the land. They were also less susceptible to disease. Horses when old have no further use whereas oxen can be fattened and sold. Horses use a vast amount of oats which oxen do not need. Oxen can be trained to plough as fast as horses, and the Dutch in the Cape use nothing else either in wagons or for ploughing. Finally the more oxen the cheaper are leather and food (*Saunders' Newsletter* 20 June 1781). Thus horses were more costly to keep and required between six and twenty times more oats than oxen, which could be maintained mostly on straw and hay. In addition, though oxen had a shorter lifespan and worked more slowly, they were more reliable and less liable to fall sick. Even so, on English manors the use of horses rose to 30% by the 14th century (Pretty). Ploughing, with 4-horse teams and the old plough was adopted in Gaelic areas from the end of the 13th century. It must be presumed that this was a requirement of their lord who required a stock of horses for military purposes and for prestige. Heavier horses, as elsewhere in Europe were introduced later in the Middle Ages. It should be noted that as cavalry horses became more and more used by the fighting classes more and more land and labour had to be devoted to feeding them.

Where the great plough was used, a two field system of rotation was probably used, alternately ploughed and fallow. The larger, heavier plough required a larger oxteam that in turn required larger fields. When first introduced the great plough, which ploughed deeper, brought an increase in output by bringing up minerals, but this effect was soon exhausted. Associated with it was the 'field' or 'open field'. The word field meant open unfenced land as opposed to dense woodland or lightly wooded areas suitable for hunting which were called forests. The word field is cognate with the Dutch *veldt* and corresponds to the Latin word *campus*. Fields, by their nature were treeless and unfenced. (It is interesting to note that the surveyors for the Domesday Book had to enquire how many ploughs a manor had or could have.)

The heavy plough suited to the heavier wetter soils of northern Europe was drawn by a team of eight oxen, and it shaped the division of the land, and the landscape. It furrow was deeper and it could be used on heavy clay soils. It had a vertical blade or coulter in front of the horizontal ploughshare and a rudimentary mouldboard which stood the ploughed sod on its end burying most of the grass or stubble and weeds. Bearing in mind the contours of the land, the need for surface drainage, and the difficulty of turning an ox-team, the furrow was made as long as possible, about 220 yards. The system of ploughing with the great plough naturally threw up ridges. A straight furrow was ploughed for 220 yards casting up a sod about 18 inches wide and up to 9 inches deep. The return sod was turned up against the first and so up and down until a ridge or strip about 66 feet measuring an acre resulted. Then the next strip was commenced 66 feet from the centre of the first and another ridge formed allowing drainage in the valley or 'dale' between the ridges. (These strips were the unit of cultivation, and strips in each field were assigned to each tenant.) In turn the ploughland or townland was established at from 60 to 100 acres, and each free farmer was expected to have his own team. By the 12th century sharing a team was the common practice, for the free farmers were now serfs or villeins with much smaller holdings. There were no fixed boundaries to ploughed areas. At first there was a stimulus to crop yields as the great plough brought up nutrients from a greater depth, but after a few years these were exhausted and the crop yields fell back.

When the ploughing was completed the ground was harrowed to make a fine seed bed and to remove weeds. Bush harrows could be used which consisted of branches and twigs fastened to a wooden from. Bigger farmers could use iron or wooden spikes attacked to a rectangular wooden frame, but as the spikes were set square to each other they tended to follow each others tracks. A triangular or hexagonal harrow with staggered tines did not appear before the 16th century. The cereals were cut with a sickle, only the heads being removed, bound and carried home at the end of the day. Animals could then graze the stubble. Threshing was done with wooden flails. By modern standards yields per acre were very low, and crop failure not infrequent. Often two crops (maslin) were sown together to minimise failure. In Gaelic times ploughing and sowing was done only in spring but autumn sowing following a fallow was probably adopted in the Middle Ages. Grain could be stored in baskets and the possession of a cat was recommended to lessen the destruction by rats and mice, a plague in all primitive economies. All agricultural implements were made largely of wood. In a plough, only the ploughshare and the coulter would have been made of iron. Production of iron was limited and most of it would have been used by the military.

It had long been recognised that after cultivation for two or three years a field had to be 'rested' as pasture for several years. This was not intensive cultivation and allowed weeds and shrubs to re-colonise the land (Nichols, 132). To restore nitrogen to the soil different systems were used. The easiest and perhaps the most ancient was to move the cultivated area around and let scrub and grasses recolonize the exhausted ground, the slash-and-burn system. Animals could graze the wild grasses and shrubs, and their dung returned some nitrogen to the soil. After several years the scrub could be burned and the ashes returned nitrogen to the soil. This was known in places as long fallow. In the infield-outfield system the land nearest to the farmstead was intensively cultivated in successive years, and manure from around the farmstead was spread on it. The outfield was not manured, but benefited from the droppings of grazing cattle. It could be ploughed occasionally. In the open-field system, land was tilled and rested in alternate years, the till-and-fallow system.

Alternate crops of wheat and oats could be used, though peas and beans were probably not grown on a sufficient scale to be part of the rotation. Towards the end of the Middle Ages, the three year rotation became common in many places with the third as a fallow year. This meant that 66% of tillable land was ploughed each year. The fallow year when correctly used allowed the removal of most weeds, and the accumulation of nitrogen from the air. In the fallow year, the field was ploughed and harrowed several times to kill as many of the weeds as possible. As hay was not made there would have been time for this. As with haymaking a hot dry summer which killed off the weeds was better than a wet one. The ground was then sown in the autumn with winter wheat or barley. In the long fallow system animal manure allowed a certain amount of fertilizing while the animals grazed the growth. But it did nothing to kill the weeds.

Agriculture was very labour intensive especially on a well-run manor, and most of the villeins/betaghs owed labour services. These were ploughing, sowing, weeding, bird-scaring, mowing, tying, stooking, carting and stacking in the haggard, threshing, winnowing (Lydon, *Ireland in the Later Middle Ages* 5f). The grain then had to be ground and sieved before baking. Women worked in the fields along with the men, except that they did not do ploughing. Much of women's work was concerned with dairying (Power, 71). Increasingly paid farm labour was used. In England the traditional wage was a penny a day for an unskilled labourer though this increased after the Black Death. Lydon quotes a penny a day and board for a man thatching ricks, and 1½ pennies a day for a roofer. In Gaelic Ireland two sheaves were given at the end of each day to each reaper. Every third sheaf was paid as rent (Nicholls, 134).

As in England several types of cereal were grown but not necessarily all of them in all areas. The further north one went the greatest was the concentration on oats which was easy to grow, could be grown on poorer land, was less liable to disease, and useful for human and horse food and for brewing. Nevertheless the chiefs were liable to demand wheaten bread when they came round with their retinues (Nicholls, 133, Ó Corráin, 52). When markets began to develop, even local ones, production could be raised to a limited extent by a more careful application of the rules. When the owner of the manor or local lord was prepared to accept cash in place of labour services the villeins could concentrate on their own patches. The owners of demesnes, where they existed, were then able to cultivate them with hired labour which was becoming the norm in English-speaking areas. Nevertheless hunger and scarcity were never far away.

In poorer areas unsuited for large fields the amount of tilled land was relatively small, and a light plough drawn by a single ox would have sufficed. The infield-outfield system was probably used. This was used in ancient times and also widely used in Scotland where there were small areas of fertile soil and large areas of 'rough grazing'. What was called the infield, the fertile land close to the settlement or clachan was ploughed intensively, and the animals folded on it during winter to provide manure. The animals grazed the outfield, and manured it, and it was cultivated occasionally. The plough had no mould board to invert the sod, so the ploughing was done twice at right angles to each other. In Mediterranean lands with dry hot summers, by ploughing in summer it was possible to eradicate most of the weeds by this method, but in more northerly climes weed extirpation was poor. In more fertile areas, the clachan could be moved around and the area tilled would have been changed from time to time. Small ploughs were much cheaper than the great ploughs and could be drawn by one or two oxen. But there can be little doubt that these three systems were used both in the Gaelic and Norman lordships.

Almost certainly there were tiny fugitive families clinging to isolated patches in forests, scrublands, and bogs who practised slash-and burn tillage, burning an area of bog, heather or scrub, tilling it for one year either with spade or light plough, and then allowing it to regenerate for several years. Unfortunately such people keep no records. Cottagers probably always used the spade which remained in common use in Ireland until displaced by the light iron plough in the late nineteenth century. The spade was tipped with iron. Almost certainly an implement like a mattock was used also tipped with iron. It was shaped like a broad pickaxe and would have been far better at breaking the sod, while the spade or shovel would have made the ridges. Their harrows could have been thorn bushes cut from the woodland. Where medieval hedges were found they were probably the result of assarting, usually illegal clearances in woods or forests and resulted in 'hedges' up to 20 feet wide. (Oddly the remains of some of these can be traced in London to the present day.)

It should be remembered that there were no hard-and-fast rules with regard to land-holding and tillage. There could be a mix-and-match where bits of one system were combined with bits of another. What was important was that all on the same manor or commote used the same system, and this became the custom of the manor.

Gardening and Orchards

In pre-Norman times onions, chives or leeks, and either parsnips or carrots, peas, and also a variety of the cabbage family, perhaps kale, were grown in ridges. Apple trees were cultivated, but whether these were in special gardens on in a strip in an open field is not clear. The Benedictine Rule prescribed fruit and green vegetables when available and doubtless these were provided in gardens. Herbs for medicines and to flavour foods would also have been cultivated in a place protected by a fence or hedge. Fr Columcille noted that the Cistercians grew beans, peas, parsley, lettuce and onions though the first two would have been field crops. Gardens and orchards were included in those things to be tithed (Columcille, xxix, xxxi). Mitchell mentions the fruit and vegetables on sale in the markets of Dublin: peas and beans, cabbages and onions, seasonally. Fruits were apples, pears, plums, damsons, sloes, cherries, raspberries, strawberries, blackberries and bilberries, even figs, raisins, and walnuts. Some of these obviously were imported, and others gathered from the hedges and woods (Mitchell, 171).

In the Middle Ages the great Norman lords introduced gardens, orchards, dovecotes, peacocks, and even vineyards. The gardens produced apples and pears. Monastic gardens even grew flowers and roses for sacred decorations. Towards the end of the period the manors of the Gaelic lords were emulating the lifestyle (Bowe, 110). An inquisition regarding the lands attached to Mellifont Abbey in 1628 recorded 100 gardens. The great gardens in England could be very diverse, and by the thirteenth and fourteenth centuries royal and monastery gardens were known to cultivate up to 250 species of food, herb, and ornamental plants (Pretty). It is likely that cottagers on their small holdings grew the higher value vegetables and fruits which then could be exchanged or bartered or used to pay rent.

Livestock

In most places there was probably as much waste land of bog, forest, and swamp as there was tillable land. When not overgrazed the productivity of wastes and forests is quite high. Cattle and goats are natural browsers eating leafy bushes instead of grass. Though cattle-rearing was fundamental to the way of life, especially of the lords and chieftains, little enough is known about it. Cattle were used to display wealth, as a unit of exchange, and as payments. They were used as sources of power, whether drawing ploughs or oxcarts, as a source of meat for eating, as a source of dairy products, and as a source of leather. There seems to have been a reluctance to slaughter cattle for food, though in the Middle Ages it was common to reduce stock in the autumn and to salt the meat. Pigs were eaten in large numbers. While some livestock like prize horses and cattle of unusual size may have been kept by lords and chiefs for prestige purposes the over-all quality ordinary people desired of their livestock was that the should survive the winters in the open. Only chiefs could afford a stall-fed ox. In general all animals were smaller, leaner, and tougher than most seen nowadays. Some attempts were made in England to develop more specialised breeds like Gloucestershire cattle (Henson, 19ff)

In the Gaelic societies initially hay was not made so cattle rearing depended on having as many cows ready to calve in the springtime that could be driven into the woods and rough pastures as far as possible from the homestead to browse and graze on the leafy shrubs, weeds, wildflowers and grasses throughout the summer. In places where the terrain was suitable and safe cattle with the milking cows would be driven to summer pastures on the hills and a temporary camp would be established where the women could perform their duties as milkmaids and dairy maids. This practice was called booleying (Ó Corráin 53). Calves were removed from their mothers as soon as possible and children were given the task of keeping them away. It was not the practice to eat meat during the summer months, though if bull calves were not castrated to make oxen there was no point in keeping them. The herd had to be culled in the autumn and the older cows and oxen would be killed. Some of this was probably salted and kept in wooden casks. Rich people were likely to have a metal pot for cooking. Lesser people could only cook meat by roasting or by putting heated stones into a bucket of water. Some pastures and woods near the homestead were reserved for winter grazing with the aim of keeping as many as possible of the cattle alive through the winter. They would be very thin when spring arrived and there could be a heavy mortality in a bad year.

O'Loan analysed texts referring to cattle in the Brehon Code and concluded that Irish cattle were large and comparable in size to modern Friesians. It was more likely that they were small black cattle like the Kerry or Welsh cattle with a height of 100 to 110 cm or 42-43 inches at the shoulder and up to 800 lbs weight. It is difficult to get a comparison of milk yield. But O'Loan makes a rough calculation of 800 gallons per lactation. This is comparable to the best herds in the year 1900 though the worst milkers might give only 400 gallons and the average for Ireland in 1901 was estimated as 450 gallons (*Farmer's Journal* 16 Feb 1901;

This after more than a century of improvement!). In both cases we may assume that the 800 gallon milker was the best of her class and where possible a chief might demand. As a warning we should however note the averages of 150 gallons quoted by Pretty for English manors and the equivalent of 140 gallons given by Nichols in the Middle Ages so the 800 gallon lactation should be treated with some caution. The Brehon Law also required that the flesh should be one third fat which was very necessary when roasting over a fire. O'Loan notes the close attention given to stock which is comparable to that at an Irish fair or mart today. The Brehon Code applied to the rich and was concerned with compensations among themselves. Calves were priced in sacks of wheat (obviously a standard amount). Some bull calves were roasted in summer as veal. An older castrated bull calf was boiled the following summer between 15 and 18 months old. Clearly the richer lords had meat in their diet summer and winter. Obviously careful attention in some herds was given to breeding good dairy cattle and good beef cattle (O'Loan passim). The chief quality required of cattle was an ability to survive in the open in winter with little grazing. Larger cattle may have been kept for prestige purposes by chiefs. Haymaking was introduced into Norman areas.

The native Irish sheep, now extinct, resembled the Shetland or Soay. For sheep too the desirable attribute was ability to survive. It had a long hairy fleece which was plucked not shorn. Wool was used for weaving. Sheep and goats were milked. Skins could be used to make vellum or fine leather. The milk could be used to make cheese. Sheep could be killed for their mutton. Bellamy noted that sheep, if not overstocked, could graze bogs without adversely affecting either the sheep or the habitat (Bellamy, 22). The exact variety is hard to establish for the Vikings probably introduced Scottish and Norse breeds. They may have been kept on hills and mountains in summer or during the day, and always with shepherds, but wolves and thieves were too numerous to leave them alone. As in England the importance of sheep increased as the ability to export woollen goods increased. As English weavers began to specialise on the finer, more finished, and more expensive cloth for export, Irish weavers were able to export rougher and thicker cloths. These were valued also as far away as Italy for use in cold weather. The yield of wool per sheep might have been less than a pound. Even in the 20th century the unimproved Irish sheep might give only 2 pounds (*Farmer's Gazette* 31.5.1924, Pretty for England gives about 1 pound). This is common for sheep in northern Europe.

Pigs were different from cattle and sheep in that they were foragers who could eat almost anything. In particular they could eat oak and beech mast (beech nuts and acorns) which grew in tremendous quantities in beech and oak forests and were toxic to grazing animals. The right to keep pigs in a forest was valued though the great fluctuations in the crop of mast made it difficult to keep the size of the herds constant. Pigs were useful as a source of meat, of pigskin leather, and of bristles for making brushes. In English manors with great beech and oak forests nearby, the manor could have over 1,000 pigs, but this was rare (Hinde, *passim*). The same is probably true in Ireland. At the beginning of the 19th century the native Irish pig was described as big bony animal which fattened well, though what relationship it had with the medieval Irish pig it had we do not know. In the 19th century they were replaced with English breeds with more lean meat which were the result of crossbreeding with pigs from south east Asia.

Horses were increasingly important in Ireland as elsewhere in Europe in the Middle Ages. Though they could be used as pack animals and farm animals, the chief impetus to keeping and developing horses was probably warfare. From the time of Charlemagne, the horsed knight provided the capable and necessary defence against armed raiders. All of feudal society was organised around the need to have horsed knights. The knight needed to have one or more horses for battle, but also horses to ride towards battle or on other journeys. He had to be accompanied by squires who required less valuable horses and they had to have pack horses to carry their equipment. These would just have been bred by eye.

Apart from war, however central it was to aristocratic life, horses had other uses. Three inventions in the Middle Ages widened the scope for using the horse, the horseshoe which allowed the use of the horse on stony ground, the stirrup which gave a more secure seat to the rider and the padded horse collar which allowed the use of horses for draught, whether pulling the plough or carts and wagons. Carts and wagons led to the development of roads and bridges.

A lot of travel was done on horseback and riding horses were also common. The best known is the palfrey. This used the gait known as the amble which was almost as fast as the trot (8 m.p.h.) but smoother and easier on the rider. The trot and the amble were used for long distances. Faster gaits like the canter and the gallop, up to 30 m.p.h.) were used for short distances. For carrying goods, the pack horse was usually used. Carthorses or draught horses were rare because of the poor state of the roads and the absence of bridges. Even when Roman roads survived, the wooden bridges had long since decayed. Still they were increasingly used on farms, in drawing carts between towns, and in warfare.

When Henry II transported 1,000 horses to Ireland in 1171 he was bringing a force to overawe all opposition and it did. No armour was used by the Irish, and their cavalry seem to have been used to carry men using a short spear or throwing javelin. They seem to have used a hackamore rather than a bit for control. There was no way they could withstand a charge by the armoured knights. The armoured knights seem rarely thereafter to have been used in Ireland for they were easily avoided and a lighter horse especially for carrying archers used. In the later Middle Ages the Irish hobby was esteemed. It was a small or middle sized horse with an ambling or pacing gait. The men-at-arms who used it were called hobelars. The hobby had various military uses but not in battle. As riding a horse was associated with aristocracy more and more of the petty chiefs and their followers preferred going into battle mounted though this was no longer the best option as the used of gunpowder spread. (Ireland was not unique in this and cavalry regiments in every European army preserved a social cachet up to the First World War.) The prestige of the horse and aristocratic nature of Irish society probably meant that far more resources were used to breed the delicate horse than was economically necessary. Though this in turn led to an export of horses. For villeins and betaghs the ox was a far better bet, less delicate, much cheaper to fed and maintain, and with more uses.

The day was to come when the small tenant farmer with about 20 acres would keep a horse for ploughing, drawing a cart, and riding at the back of the hunt and developed the versatile Irish Draught in the 19th century. But that was far in the future.

The horse native to Ireland (as in the rest of the British Isles) was a pony. (A pony is not a distinct species from a horse, but has some particular characteristics the most obvious of which is that the length of the legs in proportion to the body remains constant throughout life.) Ponies could survive in the wild on poor forage in places like Exmoor, Dartmoor, and Connemara. A pony was sufficiently strong to carry a grown man on his back though medieval men were smaller than today. The fact that they could survive on poor forage probably meant that most horses, even those used for warfare down to Tudor and Stuart times were ponies or crossed with ponies. Such a pony could be used for tillage, as pack animals, and as riding animals for the landowning classes. Though from an early date bigger stronger horses were being introduced from England. Doubtless donkeys and mules were also used, the donkey later being known as the poor man's horse.

Poultry, geese, hens, pea fowl, doves, and ducks, were usually kept in the Middle Ages. Geese were grazed in common on the common and presumably also the others. Ducks and geese needed access to ponds. Ducks were domesticated at the beginning of the Middle Ages, though wild duck was caught and eaten before that. It is not clear when domestic ducks were introduced to Ireland, but presumably they came with the Normans. Ducks and geese have large amounts of body fat and goose grease was a valued commodity in its own right. The feathers of all poultry could be used in quilts and other bed coverings. The eggs of domestic poultry like those of wildfowl could be eaten. As usual it is difficult to establish how often poultry products featured in the diet of ordinary people. We can assume that most villeins and betaghs would have tried to keep some fowl and bees around their cottages. But grazing rights for geese might have been limited. Like all dearer products the richer people would have consumed most of them. Rabbits were probably introduced by the Normans and kept in warrens. When they escaped into the wild to be snared by poachers is not clear. Fishponds, a feature of manors and monasteries in England, also came in with the Normans, and by the end of the Middle Ages we can expect that the Gaelic lords who began to live in castles also adopted sources of food like fishponds, rabbit warrens and deerparks. Bees were kept for honey but it is not clear how common this was. The straw beeskep was easy to make but had to be destroyed each autumn to get the honey. Poultry, eggs and honey would have been valuable for food renders and for exchange. Poor people have to make the best of what they have. It should be noted that great numbers of animals, great and small, were kept in towns.

Fisheries

Fish was very important in the Irish diet. The rich could have an abundance of every kind of fish. How often poorer people were able to eat fish is not clear. Fish could be caught in the sea, in rivers and in the innumerable lakes. Fishing weirs abounded, and many were not removed until the 19th century in the interests of drainage and navigation. Almost certainly, by the Middle Ages, all fishing weirs were in the hands of the lords, Gaelic, Norman, and ecclesiastical. Fr Columcille, in his book on Mellifont Abbey lists the various weirs, sometimes called salmon weirs and 16 (one-man?) fishing boats called currachs on the Boyne (253-9; see also river fisheries in the earldom of Ulster, McNeill, *Anglo-Norman Ulster*, 137, 139). The appropriation of fishing rights by the local lords seems to have occurred before the coming of the Normans. Fishing weirs were numerous in tidal waters and estuaries as well as along rivers. The fact that Giraldus could comment on the abundance of fish in Irish waters indicates that fishing rights were closely controlled and poaching severely punished. Unrestricted fishing in inland rivers and lakes would soon remove all fish.

Shellfish were abundant and we can again assume that gathering was also strictly controlled. Sea fishing seems to have been carried on in small leather boats (currachs) close inshore, and deep-sea fisheries never developed in the way they were in Spain, Portugal and Norway (Ó Corráin 59-60). When offshore fisheries were developed later in the Middle Ages off the southern and western coasts it was carried out by foreign vessels. This was very profitable for the local lords who could charge for the use of harbours and drying grounds for fish and nets. The markets for these fish were on the Continent, not in Ireland itself. There may have been such a trade for in the 19th century it was possible to carry fresh fish in panniers on horseback up to 40 miles inland. But on the other hand there may have been no markets for fish in rural areas in the Middle Ages, the local lords having enough of their own fish and the others unable to afford them. In the 19th century efforts to promote local fishing on the west coast was hampered by the difficulty of getting good salt.

The Normans took care to develop fisheries on the east coast in conjunction with the Italian merchants (Burke, 18). A prise or presage on fishing often provided a local income for port towns. Local mayors of seaside ports would have taken care that their fishmarkets were always supplied with fish, but would also have taken care that they were not over-supplied. (If the over-supply of fish caused the price of fish to halve, fishmongers and fishermen would have to work twice as long to make the same profit!). Lydon notes that in 1394 Richard II instructed his officers to bring fishermen with their boats and tackle to Ireland to feed the court (Lydon, *Ireland in the Later Middle Ages* 113). Yet later in the Middle Ages the east coast fishing ports were exporting fish, fresh, salted and smoked, though the Irish fishermen were being swamped by English and Welsh fishermen on their own coasts (O'Sullivan 'Fishing' in *Medieval Ireland*). Whatever the reason, Ireland, unlike other countries on the Atlantic seaboard never developed a major deep-sea fishing industry.

Hunting and trapping

There are various kinds of woodland, dense woodlands with the tree canopy unbroken, open woodlands with considerable amounts of grass and shrub, and scrub which is woods that have been cleared and are regenerating. This latter is almost as good as grassland for feeding browsing animals. Deep forests are only useful for their timber, but this timber is very useful for construction, whether the building of houses or ships or the making of wooden objects. Trees in deep forests are tall and straight and the timber lacks knots which weaken it, but the amount of wildlife tends to be low. Open woodlands, or forests as they were called, gave good grazing and browsing and were by far the best for hunting. Kings and lords tended to restrict hunting to themselves and the 'Forest Laws' of the Norman kings of England were notorious for their ferocity. Deer and wild boar were the animals the lords pursued. Nevertheless, commoners often obtained rights of commonage for their cattle in forests which endure to this day.

Woodlands were also the habitat of small furry animals which were pursued for their furs. The fur of the pinemarten was valued for export as also those of foxes and wolves. The export of furs and skins continued throughout the Middle Ages. Hares and rabbits also provided fur for local use. Wildfowling was widely practised in the Middle Ages, chiefly with nets.

Extractive Industries

The introduction of stone churches, and later stone castles led to a development of local quarrying. In the Middle Ages no attempt was made to cut or handle large blocks of stone. As water communication was poorly developed inland local sources of stone had to be found. Though vast deposits of minerals were not found, small amounts of gold, silver, lead, copper, and iron were to be found. Most of the iron worked in Ireland was probably bog iron which develops in bogs and swamps. It is a renewable source and was probably sufficient to supply Ireland's limited demand for iron until iron could be imported from abroad later in the Middle Ages. Copper mining continued in some areas, but tin and lead was probably imported. Gold seem not to have been mined in this period. The extraction of silver in the Silvermines district in Tipperary commenced in the late Middle Ages. Metal objects of art are rare from this period and may have used recycled objects or coins. Some salt was produced along the coasts but not on a large scale

The building industry would have used large amounts of timber and stone. This would have to be quarried or felled and then transported to where it was needed. Teams of horses can drag large trees out of woods, but then, in the absence of water transport, some kind of wheeled vehicle would be required to transport it further. This is true even if the timber is sawn into baulks on the spot. The same can be said with regard to stone.

Other Aspects

When the Normans came to Ireland in the late 12th century they realised that the lands they had been given could be made vastly more profitable. Some introduced wholesale colonisation with organisation into manors with villages, towns, roads, bridges and ports and an effective defence. In most places they contented themselves with a more efficient organisation. McNeill shows from the valuation of parishes in 1306 how much richer were the parishes in the earldom of Ulster than in the contiguous areas outside its borders. The values of parishes in east county Down (diocese of Down) with those in the west of the county (Dromore) were remarkable. The values of an Anglo-Norman parish could be as high as those of a Gaelic diocese. The value of the parish of Billy was £36 while that of the diocese of Clogher was £32 (McNeill, 33, 40-41). As he points out the farmers in the earldom had access to external markets through the ports of Coleraine, Carrickfergus, Strangford, Carlingford and Dundalk. Some exports were of cereals, but most were the traditional hides, wool and sheepskins. Fisheries too provided a source of income, while payments at the lord's mill added to his revenue.

Most of the customs revenue came from ports in south Leinster and north Munster. Later in Tudor times as the Gaelic chiefs had to export in order to import large quantities of guns, gunpowder, musket shot and cannon balls besides the latest in fashionable clothes, exports grew from their areas as well.

The Secondary Sector

Industry

Towns and the Economy

This section deals only with towns as part of the pattern of production and trade. A town was a place where merchants and craftsmen gathered for the purpose of manufacture and trade. They also had 'fields' outside the town on which to grow basic foodstuffs, and keep cattle and sheep, but usually depended on their market to purchase the products of the surrounding countryside either for consumption or sale. Villages where the farmers built all their houses in one place, but still depended solely on their own agriculture, were not towns.

There had been quite large settlements around the larger monasteries, but as their function was to serve the monastery they were not regarded as towns. These would have housed all the people necessary for the functioning of a large monastery. All the trades would have been there, including women's trades like baking, brewing, milking and preparing milk products. Fr Columcille notes the trades practiced in a monastery: there were shoemakers, cobblers, saddlers and harness-makers, tanners, fullers, weavers, clothmakers and tailors, masons, bricklayers, carpenters, plasterers, thatchers, blacksmiths, brewers, millers, bakers, dairymen, and cooks; many also were engaged in tilling the soil, and herding cattle and sheep and swine (Columcille, xxivff). The same gathering of houses and trades would have been found beside or within the *lios* of the local lords.

Viking towns existed in Ireland. Viking Dublin was the great centre of trade through which even silk was imported. There can be little doubt however that the Norse trading centres could not have prospered without the slave trade. The greater Irish chiefs had an inexhaustible supply of useful prisoners with which to pay for their imports of luxuries. Ó Corráin however considers that most slaves were imported not exported. But if this was the case, what was being exported? With the Viking towns came the use of coinage, though much, and indeed probably most, Irish business was conducted without cash at least until well on in the eighteenth century. The old trade over the beaches controlled by the local chiefs continued in places until the end of the Middle Ages. There were no Viking towns in western Connaught anymore than there were in the lands of the *Ui Neill*, while there were many towns along the east coast. Nor were there any in the interior of Ireland. The O'Briens controlled Norse Limerick, the MacCarthys controlled Norse Cork. Control of the largest Viking port was claimed by the kings of Leinster, and by the would-be high king. Rory O'Connor was inaugurated as high king in Dublin in 1166. The town of Bristol handled a considerable part of the Irish trade. The men of Bristol were not strangers to the chiefs of Leinster. Two towns were built near the mouth of the Boyne on opposite banks to handle the trade on the best waterway into the interior. They were later joined in 1412.

The Normans took over the Viking towns and the king reserved the principal ones into his own hand. As in England the great Norman lords established towns and markets, and the king or lord gave them charters. The early ones were all ports on the east coast, and presumably these were already the trading centres on the coasts. These stretched from Coleraine on the north coast to Kerry in the south west. At least 50 of these towns were built in the eastern and southern parts of Ireland and served the same purposes as Brecon, to hold the area for the lord and to increase his revenue. Local lords manipulated trade to benefit themselves (The lordship of Brecon originally belonged to William de Braose who was also lord of Limerick.) The markets and fairs which the town was allowed to have were for the benefit of the whole lordship of Brecon. (Thomas, 29). Inland towns were also founded invariably on inland waterways. The de Lacy stronghold was at Trim on the river Boyne.

The nature of their trades is indicated by the market tolls they were allowed to collect: wine, salt, foodstuffs, horses, cattle, hides, wool, woolfells, cloths of all kinds, iron, lead, tin, dyestuffs, timber, fuel, millstones, nails, cordwain (Spanish leather) and wax (Otway-Ruthven, 124). These towns specialised in providing local services to the local population, the overwhelming majority of whom lived outside towns. In Brecon in Wales in the 15th century there were bakers, butchers, brewers, tailors, shoemakers, weavers, glovers, tanners, blacksmiths, carpenters, masons and thatchers. Some of these enjoyed a monopoly of their trade within the lordship (Thomas, 29).

Trade and manufactures in the towns were controlled by the trade guilds of which the guild of merchants was the most important. They established the rules for their members, the price of labour, the number of apprentices and journeymen, and the quality of the work. Guilds usually obtained the exclusive right to trade within the lordship, an extension of a monopoly of ownership of watermills. Often originally there was a single guild embracing the merchants and all crafts, but later in places separate craft guilds were established. (By the 19th century Dublin had 25 craft guilds with representation on the Common Council but this number was rare, Keenan, *Pre-Famine Ireland*, 223-4.)

It was in the interest of each town and its lord to maintain roads to the next towns. This might mean filling up ruts, building bridges and fords which wagons could cross during most of the year. Most important was that scrub should be cut away from along the road. This had two advantages. It allowed the surface of the road to dry after rain thus lessening ruts and gave no place of concealment to robbers. (Modern construction of road surfaces dates from the 18th century and was introduced in to England by Thomas Telford and John Loudon McAdam on the great Holyhead Road after 1815.)

On the whole it may be said that towns did not play a great role in Irish life in the Middle Ages. The importance of towns was in the exact proportion to Ireland's foreign trade. This seems to have sharply declined after the Black Death. As the revenue of the Irish Government was largely derived from customs this proved serious for defence. Otherwise towns played the same role in local markets as monasteries and the houses of local lords. We have no idea what proportion of foreign trade passed through ports with customs. Towns were too small to be major centres of manufactures. Nor is there an indication that the products of towns were superior, for the most part, to those of rural manufacture. Even so there was by the standards of the time a considerable concentration of wealth in the towns and many of them could afford to build walls as much for status as defence. They also attracted numerous beggars. They were small by contemporary English standards, had fewer trades, and rarely traded with each other. Yet their role was not negligible. Around them was built the road network which carried the trade of Ireland to and from the ports until the present day. Even in the Middle Ages much of the imports and exports of the Gaelic areas seems to have passed through the towns.

Building and Construction

As elsewhere in Northern Europe the onset of the High Middle Ages was marked by a return in building in stone. This was very costly, and was largely confined to ecclesiastical and military buildings. Besides the fact that wooden churches with thatched roofs were liable to be burned to the ground, there was a question of prestige, of having splendid public buildings. Even austere orders like the Cistercians, and Franciscans built in stone. Stone vaulting was in most cases too expensive, but it was possible to have an excellent roof resting on oak beams. Naturally the stone vaulting survived better. The cost, relatively speaking, might not have been as high as we might expect. Even journeymen stone carvers probably did not earn more than a penny or two pence a day. Shaping stones was a mechanical skill. The master builder would of course be highly paid

With regard to building in wood there is no reason to believe that craftsmen in wood were any inferior to those elsewhere in the British Isles. The felling of trees and the splitting of logs and the transport of the split timber from the forest were all within their capabilities. At some point the skill to saw timber along its length became necessary. While smaller dwellings could be built out of poles, the roofs covered in thatch and the walls made of wattle, larger halls would have been made with a timber frame and infilling with wattle and plaster. Unfortunately we have no examples of what the hall of a chief in the 12th century looked like, though later in the Middle Ages they were described as poor-looking dwellings. In the earldom of Ulster houses with timber and sod walls were built. The skills for building wooden houses were the same as for building ships and the Vikings were highly skilled in this. There is evidence of oak-framed churches with rafters, which were to be replaced by churches with masonry walls and rafters. The art of joinery (joining two pieces of wood without nails or screws) was very well developed, but we do not know what the normal standard in Ireland was. As usual, we can suppose that later wooden dwellings in the towns matched those in Chester and Bristol. Irish wooden churches were small, but so too were many English parish churches of the period. The rural population was quite thin by later standards.

Building in stone involves three different skills, the use of lime mortar masonry, stone carving, and engineering in the use of vaults. Lime mortar is made by burning limestone in kilns to produce quicklime to which water is added to produce slaked lime. This is then mixed thoroughly with sand and it sets to form a hard bonding material. A wall is built with small pieces of broken stone set in the mortar. (If the wall is not too high it is possible to build 'drystone' walls without mortar.) The skills required are simple and easily learned. The surface of the wall is rough but it can be covered with a lime mortar plaster or render. Alternatively, stone carving can be done on larger pieces of stone to provide smooth faces on either side, the inside of the wall being filled up with smaller stones and mortar. This kind of wall is much more expensive. Openings in walls like doors and windows can be headed with a long block of stone if such can be obtained locally. It is easy to construct an arch by building a removable wooden frame on which the stone and mortar arch can be built. When the mortar has hardened the wooden support is removed. Again, stone carving can be used on the outer faces of the arch. When the walls were finished, roofs with wooden rafters were added. High buildings required other skills of the mason's craft, how to make scaffolding and how to raise weights. Most of the churches and cathedrals were of quite modest height and not requiring the same degree of skill needed for the great English or French cathedrals which were wonders of the world.

There are two surviving buildings in Ireland which can stand comparison with the great English cathedrals and monasteries, Christ Church and Saint Patrick's in Dublin. These were undoubtedly built by English masons and their successors. More typical was St Canice's cathedral in Kilkenny with simple, though well-executed arcading in the nave with a wooden roof. Even simpler is Boyle Abbey. The stone carving is however excellent (Harbison *Irish Art and Architecture*, 90, 93). Relative poverty rather then lack of skills was the reason for the lack of ambition of Irish builders. Fashions in architecture followed those in England. It is not clear who these masons and craftsmen in stone were, whether they were native Irish or foreigners, or whether they had stable homes or moved around to where builders were required. The level of under-development of the Irish countryside at the end of the 12th century is underlined by the fact that a parish church in New Ross was larger than many existing Romanesque cathedrals in Irish dioceses.

The other use of stone was for military purposes. Stone walls for towns were often constructed with nothing remarkable about them. Castles too were built for defence, and required little more than thick sturdy walls. Little was needed for their construction than an elementary knowledge of masonry. The Normans built stone castles after their arrival. Not until the 14th century, and not in every part of the country, did Gaelic chiefs build castles as their residences. These were normally tower houses. Stonework was always painted in bright colours if possible. The binding agent was likely to be the slow-drying linseed oil or similar resins and the colouring matter crushed and powdered rocks. Where these came from is not clear.

Processes and Manufactures

It is important to note that the most superb craftsmanship can be carried on in the most primitive surroundings. Most work was carried on out of doors. The great illuminated manuscripts were probably written at the door of a hut, moving a stool and table outside the door or just inside depending on the rain. The same was probably true of gold and silverwork. Agricultural work was done in the open as was building work. The various crafts, spinning, weaving, washing, dyeing, house painting etc. and even cooking were probably done outside. Monks lived in an open cloister and did all their reading there, going in to particular buildings to pray, eat and sleep. A monastery was a collection of buildings connected by an open arcade called the cloister. It was not necessary to have a great building to make something or to produce a work of art. Even in towns the work was done and the goods sold in open-fronted 'shops' if it was not done in a backyard. There is no indication that these were larger or very different from those in rural areas or around castles or monasteries. Where towns had an advantage was that they were more likely to attract foreign craftsmen who were aware of the latest skills. In Gaelic areas the skills were handed on within a family where outsiders might not have been welcome.

Though manufactures in general tended to be conducted on a larger scale as the Middle Ages advanced this did not affect the individual workshop. The number of apprenticeships and journeymen each master craftsman might employ was allowed by the guild. The size of shops was only likely to increase where it was possible to use water power and later wind power. There was a limited use for powered equipment. The earliest was the water mill which local lords used to grind the cereals in their lordship and forcing all their tenants to use them. (The quern probably remained for domestic use while the mill would grind the rents and renders for the lord.)

The more important towns had the richer crafts. Dublin, from an early date had silversmiths and goldsmiths. Metalwork in the precious metals continued but almost no example of their output survives. The potter's wheel was introduced by the Normans, and pottery was made in Dublin and other towns. The rough pottery in the earldom of Ulster may have been a rural craft. Leather was manufactured and used for a wide variety of objects. Like other crafts it was very complicated and various kinds of leather could be produced. Parchment (vellum) was made from the skins of calves, sheep and goats and was used for writing on.

The textile industry was very important in medieval Europe and was the first in which power-driven machinery was used. The first industrial use of water power was for the fulling of cloth an extremely labour-intensive job. In Leinster, in the disturbed conditions of the later Middle Ages, the woollen industry tended to concentrate close to Dublin where there were streams running off the mountains. Spinning by women was so common that unmarried women were called spinsters, the feminine of spinner. The spinning wheel gradually replaced the hand spindle. Looms were improved. Though weaving for local use was a rural craft it was also carried on in urban centres and finer cloth produced. The looms were probably simple warp-weighted looms with threads from a beam kept taut by means of weights. The manufacture of woollen cloth is a very complicated process from the original selection of the wool to the fulling, dyeing and finishing of the cloth. The finishers of woollen cloth were often more important than the weavers. By the 19th century up to 40 different crafts were involved in producing finished cloth. Some of these were obvious, sorters, carders, spinners, sheermen, dyers, and would certainly have been present in the Middle Ages (Keenan, *Pre-Famine Ireland*, 193). Dyeing was a very important industry. Richer people favoured brightly coloured fabrics. Vegetable dyes were used which tended to fade rapidly and would probably have to be re-dyed frequently. The Flemings led Europe in cloth finishing. There was an export market for the older heavier woollen cloths and cloaks which were prized in cold weather. It may be that the natural grease was not fully removed from the cloth making garments which were naturally waterproof. (They were probably also smelly but few complained about that.) Little is known of the linen trade, but by Tudor times it was very well developed, and linen was in common use. The centre of the industry seems to have been the earldom of Ulster where it was to remain. It was exported to the cloth fairs in the Middle Ages (Burke, *Irish Industrial History*, 23).

The Middle Ages in Europe saw a move from ships powered by muscle and wind to larger ships powered by sail alone that could also move against the wind with the help of a lateen sail. The sternpost rudder was invented and a magnetic compass. The astrolabe which could accurately measure the angle of the sun to tell latitude and marine charts also appeared. The clinker built boats of the Vikings with overlapping planking were replaced by carvel built ships with the planks set edge to edge. In the latter method a frame is built for the ship, and the planks fastened to it. Clinker building was retained for rowing boats as it gives a very strong hull with no interior obstructions. The workhorse was the single-masted cog larger, higher and stronger than the Norse merchant ship the knarr. Fore and after 'castles' could be built on to them in wartime or for defence to provide fighting platforms against pirates. It could carry 30 horses. Later two-masted and even three masted vessels were being built. The Portuguese began building caravels and the huge carracks which showed the way the shape of ships were going. The smaller caravels of up to 150 tons had two or three masts with lateen or square sails and were very handy. The three or four-masted carrack of up to 200 tons was the model for the typical Tudor ship. Carracks and caravels could trade from southern Europe to Ireland.

Shipbuilding and boatbuilding continued along the Irish coasts. It is fair to assume that the shipbuilders in the east coast ports kept up with the steady improvement of ships at least in England throughout the Middle Ages. John Cabot in the *Matthew* of Bristol of 50 tons reached Newfoundland in 1497. There is no reason to believe that shipbuilders in Dublin or Waterford were not capable of building similar ships. On the western coasts and inland waters like Lough Erne and Lough Neagh boats, generally of Norse design, suitable for local traffic would have sufficed. Log boats continued to be made and were probably used extensively on inland waters. Currachs too survived being made of skins stretched over a wooden frame. They could be quite large and able to reach as far as Iceland (Severin)

Evidently some craftsmen in some places reached the highest standards, but it is difficult to determine where individual works of art were produced or whether the craftsmen were Gaelic or Norman. Equally it is impossible to determine what the general level of craftsmanship was. In the textile industry standards were always rising. Weavers in parts of England began to specialise in broadcloth (1.75 yards or 63 inches wide) which was to be a great English export for centuries. It required two weavers sitting side-by-side. The quality of weaving in Ireland doubtless ranged from the excellent to the bad, the best cloth going to the richest customers. Some craftsmen had a high status in Gaelic society, probably gold and silver smiths and perhaps stone carvers. Most craftsmen had a much lower status. Brewing was a domestic industry. In England it was often done by women. As it contained no preservative like hops it had a very short life and so was brewed every few days in small vessels. Brewing was essentially a simple process. Crushed barley was added to hot water, left for a while and cooled down. Then herbs and a proper yeast was added and fermentation allow to proceed producing a small beer with perhaps 1% of alcohol. If the yeast was poor the flavour might be foul. (An interesting experiment was carried on the production of beer in Gaelic societies which did not have pottery or metal pots, for example in most Gaelic parts of Ireland. http://mooregroup.wordpress.com/2007/10/08/ the-archaeology-ireland-article.) As we know little of the barter and exchange mechanisms we have no idea how much was made for sale or exchange. Almost certainly bakers and pie makers in the towns exchanged their products for rural products on market days.

There were two aspects to the iron industry. Iron ore had to be located and there were sufficient deposits of bog iron for local needs. The oxides of iron in the iron ore were reduced to fairly pure metal in small bloomeries where charcoal and iron ore were burned in equal quantities, carbon monoxide reacting with the oxides to release pure metal. The temperature in the bloomery was below the melting point of iron. The resulting iron had to be hammered to remove impurities. The smith then made objects from the iron. Highly skilled smiths could produce weapons like swords, and spears and arrow tips, and also body armour in the form of chain mail. Iron could also be used in limited amounts by lesser people to make ploughshares and spades tipped with iron. As the use of horses grew a local smith who could make horseshoes and pieces of harness like bits became important. The knowledge of iron-working dated from 1000 B.C. and was handed down in families as closely guarded secrets in Gaelic Ireland. In Norman Ireland masters of the smith's craft or mystery took apprentices who could be members of the smith's own family

As noted above wood was the most important material used to make most things. Specialist craftsmen were skilled in making wooden boxes and containers. Some vessels to contain liquids could be made from staves bound with hoops, or they could be carved from blocks of wood. It is not clear when metal hoops replaced wooden ones or if they ever did. Pottery and metal vessels were almost completely absent except in the dwellings of the rich, so almost all domestic tools and equipment would have been made or carved from wood. The lathe was introduced in Norman times.

Though there is abundant evidence of local crafts there is little indication that they served more than local markets, except in the textile industries. Even towns did not trade with each other as they did in England.

Trade and Transport

From the point of view of the foreign trader or his Irish agent it made little difference whether he traded in a town or in a chief's rath as their wares were purchased by the rich only. But local Irish traders in towns were likely to hold stocks of foreign goods which could be sold in tiny quantities to lesser folk after the merchants had left. There were also likely to attend the various gatherings of the various local chiefs.

Markets, Fairs and Ports

The principal point in having markets was to provide income for the local lord. He, whether Gaelic or Norman, retained control over all commercial activity in his own territory and promoted it primarily for his own benefit. It was later realised that profit was better and more certain if left in the hands of the merchants who paid him an annual sum. But he would often retain responsibility for roads and bridges usually exacting a toll from them too. Markets are usually associated with towns, and one of the points in establishing a town was that it should there conduct a market and attract merchants (*mercatores* professional traders) to the lord's manor, both to buy and to sell, often of a weekly basis. There would also be inns where they could stay. Fairs were originally feast days, where merchants might assemble in greater numbers often on the feast of a patron saint (for example, St. Bartholomew's fair in London). Fairs tended to be larger and rarer. In Gaelic Ireland when chiefs proclaimed assemblies, those with horses, cattle etc. would also come to buy or exchange. Though there were markets in Anglo-Norman towns dedicated to visits by foreign merchants, these merchants did not cease to visit to the other semi-urban groupings around monasteries, cathedrals, and the raths of the Gaelic lords. We can assume that local exchange between the residents in these places and the local countryside continued.

The lord who established the market established tolls on merchants travelling to his market and also on merchants travelling through his lands to other markets. This toll was nominally for the merchant's own protection and to pay the costs of the market. In time the merchant guild or the corporation gained or bought the right to pay a fixed annual sum or farm to the lord in lieu of the market tolls and other revenues from the town.

Fr. Columcille quotes a charter of Mellifont Abbey which throws an interesting light on trading conditions. The monks of the abbey and their successors while carrying their own goods whether bought for their own use or to be sold were to be free of toll, passage, pontage, geldage, lastage, and stallage and of all other customs (Columcille, 79). [toll, a tax or charge; passage, a charge on travellers; pontage, a bridge toll; geldage, a local tax payable to the king; lastage, a toll payable by merchants attending markets and fairs; stallage, a toll for permission to erect a stall in a market *Oxford English Dictionary*.] The main taxes or customs were taken at the ports, like the prisage of wines. Particular industries might have their own charges. Weavers had to pay alnage to get an official seal on their cloth. Wool fairs had their own special charges of 'treat' and 'cast' which survived in places until the 19th century.

Though inland towns were not large, and their trade mostly local, they were doubtless lively places where people from the surrounding countryside came on market days. These were not necessarily all farmers but all kinds of craftsmen. Towns might have their fields in which to grow things, but liked products of the countryside, milk products, ale, nuts and berries, pieces of cloth woven at home and so on. The merchants would keep a stock of imported goods for lesser people to buy. The chiefs, lords, higher clergy, abbots and so on would import their own. But the chiefs themselves liked to come to the towns. The O'Neills of Ulster were particularly fond of Dundalk, which apart from Carrickfergus was their nearest town, and indeed had a residence there (Gillespie, 'Transformation of the Borderlands', 77). There would naturally be greater crowds on fair days when livestock was being bought and sold, and in places like Mullingar where there were wool fairs.

The chief Irish towns were the chief Irish ports and were the major centres of trade. Of its nature foreign trade had to pass through some kind of port. Towns which were ports provided protection for boats and shipping both from storms and from enemies, places where ships could get supplies and get repairs done, take on or discharge ballast usually in the form of stones. It was necessary too to have warehouses of some kind where goods for export (wool, hides) could be accumulated and stored, and likewise imported goods like wine which were to be forwarded to the lords and chiefs. Foreign fishing boats liked to have a local safe harbour where they could obtain supplies or put in to make repairs or to dry their nets and fish, bringing income to the local town or chief.

The Norse, where they were allowed to settle, had usually identified the best places on the coasts for such purposes, though Norse towns were tiny and primitive compared to what the Anglo-Norman ports were to become. Some like Dublin and Drogheda were some distance from the sea at a fordable point on a river, and this was to cause increasing problems as ships grew larger. Steam dredgers did not come before the 19th century. There was no prohibition on trading with the Gaelic lords except of course in times of war. The Anglo Norman ports routinely traded with the Gaelic lords.

Roads, Land and Water Transport

One might say that there were no roads in Ireland only passage ways which were passable in summer and impassable for wheeled traffic in winter. This remained true of much of rural England up to the eighteenth century. But then there was little wheeled traffic in Ireland. People went on foot, on horseback or used pack horses. Routes, some long distance and stretching back to pre-historic times, existed which joined up dryer parts on raised ground to fordable places on rivers. To keep a road open it was more important to have the scrub cut back from the road, because of ambushes, than to have an all-weather surface. The situation regarding roads was commonplace all over Europe except where there were Roman roads. But even on Roman roads the wooden bridges had long since disappeared.

Bridge-building commenced in Ireland before the coming of the Normans. They were wooden structures and easily destroyed in warfare. They were probably very narrow, just allowing two packhorses to pass each other. In the Middle Ages, towns were allowed a pontage tax to build and maintain bridges and roads adjusted themselves to take advantage. Some of these bridges were built from stone. An important bridge was built over the River Barrow close by a Norman castle by a canon of Kildare cathedral in 1320 for local use. In the later Middle Ages it provided the safest route from Dublin into Munster and linking the capital with Kilkenny and Waterford. There were stone bridges at Trim, Slane, and Ardee. A fortified bridge was built over the Bann at Coleraine an important port in the earldom of Ulster of which nothing remains (McNeill, 92). The bridge of Athlone was the gateway to Connaught and was defended by a castle.

Much travel was done by water. As late as 1800, before the development of the mail coach road the easiest way for a woman to get from Cork to Dublin was by sea. The east coast was studded with small Norman ports, but the absence of ports and harbour facilities did not mean that there was no seaborne traffic elsewhere. Sea travel was far from easy. It was unwise for any seafarer to venture into any part controlled by any local chief. Piracy was endemic so protection would have to be bought from the local chief. Merchant ships at that time were armed and the crews were prepared to defend them. Merchant vessels could be changed to war vessels overnight. An unusual feature was the lighthouse at Hook Head on the eastern side of Waterford harbour first erected by the Normans in 1172. William Marshal charged the local monastery with its maintenance. It was an open fire burning turf.

There were few long-distance water routes in Ireland but numerous shorter ones. Lough Neagh and Lough Erne with the rivers flowing into them provided passage for travellers and war bands. Despite its size and length the Shannon was a difficult river to traverse. Falls close to the sea prevented ships sailing further than Limerick. In winter it might be too swollen and its lakes too stormy, while in summer it might get too shallow. Nevertheless for small local boats, the Shannon and its tributaries connect a large area in central Ireland. The difficulty of connecting with the sea made it useless for trade. It should be noted that the long water communication afforded by the two Lough Ernes enabled the O'Donnells of Donegal to control the area surrounding them, the present county Fermanagh.

Who were the travellers on these roads and waterways? Few people travelled away from their own neighbourhood, however defined, in those days. In other words, he did not leave the territory of his lord. In Brehon Law a man had no rights outside his own *tuath*. Most of those later to be called peasants had no rights outside their own manor or lordship. Minor lords were probably able to travel through the jurisdiction of their overlord. In the Anglo-Norman areas it is likely that any man free in his own lordship could travel anywhere in the king's dominions in Ireland.

It is likely that the clergy could travel anywhere in Ireland, whether in the domains of the Anglo-Irish lords or of the Gaelic lords. It is likely too that those of the learned professions and members of the families of noted craftsmen were free to travel. They might be of some benefit to the local lord and were no military threat. Merchants too would be afforded the same facility. It is likely that entertainers, harpers, singers, tumblers, etc. of all kinds were allowed passage. Many or most of these would have had to pay the local tolls and tributes ostensibly for their own protection. The privilege of the monks of Mellifont to carry goods for their own use everywhere in the Lordship free of local charges has been mentioned. It is likely that all travellers went in groups, as was almost universal in the Middle Ages, and would seek refuge in a town or monastery at nightfall. Like elsewhere in Europe, the land and seas abounded with robbers and pirates. Noblemen and bishops would provide their own armed escort.

Imports and Exports

The very expenses of trade meant that imports could only be products for the rich. In under-developed countries most wealth is concentrated in the hands of a few landowners or lords who have control of extensive lands (and nowadays oil wells) from which they can derive rents and taxes. As an economy develops middle classes tend to increase, the manufacturers, merchants, minor clergy and other professionals, and yeoman farmers. Exports tend to be primary products like metals, wool, hides or wheat and gradually simple manufactures like cloths or dried fish.

We are very ignorant about the exports from Gaelic areas. Luxury goods like wine and probably fine cloths continued to be imported. Almost certainly too iron in the form of scrap iron, for it was essential for making arms and armour. Silver too was imported perhaps mostly in the form of silver coins for making silver objects. If there are imports there must be corresponding exports. The former great export namely slaves seems to have come to an end, undoubtedly from lack of demand in England and France where slavery was going out of fashion. Forest products like furs could not be large. Ireland lacked the enormous northern forests which provided most furs. It may be that there was a demand for thick, rough, and largely waterproof woollens. There was probably, even in the 12th century a market for hides, though this would depend on the needs of the English and continental leather workers. Foreign trade was still in Norse hands and they must have found some items they could export.

After the arrival of the Normans markets opened up in England whose economy was rapidly expanding for a wide range of products. Exports were helped by the fact that the kings often needed food to feed their armies though this could not be guaranteed annually. Fr Columcille lists farming exports in the heyday of the 13th century as wheat, barley, oats, malt of wheat, malt of oats, flour, oatmeal, peas, beans, onions, honey, hay, beer, cows, pigs, sheep, and salt beef, dried fish, and oddly enough, lime (Columcille, xxvii). The Cistercians of Mellifont in Co. Louth were well placed to profit from this export trade as much of their land was close to the Boyne, at whose mouth was Drogheda. Much more exports went through the south eastern ports of Waterford, New Ross in Co. Wexford, and Cork. South Leinster and parts of North Munster were the great exporting areas (McNeill, 42). These figures from customs records are quite inaccurate for a great deal of unrecorded smuggling went on. Though exports from the earldom of Ulster were not as great, yet the assessments of parishes in Ulster indicated just how comparatively rich the Anglo-Norman parishes were compared with those in the Gaelic parts of Ulster (McNeill, 35).

The industrialisation of Europe may be said to have commenced with the wool trade. The great exports were raw wool and hides of animals but gradually linen and woollen cloth began to be exported even as far as Italy. Particularly popular were thick Irish cloaks. But volumes were quite small. For exports there had to be a market abroad which was often a niche market. For example if English or Italian weavers could get better prices for weaving finer cloths for export their merchants might be willing to import rougher and cheaper cloth. Similarly, if the English farmers could not produce a sufficient surplus of cereals it might be necessary to procure it from Ireland. Until that is better and cheaper sources were found on the southern Baltic coasts. Raw wool and hides were in great demand to supply the burgeoning requirements of English manufacturers. At times too it might be possible to supply linen or woollen yarns if English spinners could not keep up the supply. Fish was hard to export because Continental ports could more easily and profitably send their own ships to fish off Irish coasts than to allow Irish boats to land their catches in Continental ports. If the Irish threatened local producers in those countries the local rulers would exclude them. This remained a problem for Irish producers up until the Act of Union (1800). Fish could be dried and exported, and this was done at times but one expects that the drying was only practicable in summer time. (Salt was too expensive to make salting profitable.)

At the beginning of the Middle Ages almost all foreign trade was in the hands of the Italians who displaced the Vikings, and their merchants made great investments in the Irish woollen industry. This would seem to indicate that the Irish sheep of the period was producing wool of a desirable quality. A fine wool would have been produced by sheep of the Shetland type. Some sheep have fine wool and coarse wool on different parts of their bodies so wool-sorting was always an important part of the woollen industry. But Irish coarse wool was also being exported

The export of hides became increasingly important, with exports to the Continent more important than to England. Other skins and furs continued to be exported. The income from the tax on the export of wool and hides gradually declined in the 14th century, though some of the money collected may have been spent locally, and there may have been increased exports through non-customs ports. Hides was a commodity Gaelic chiefs could export for they owned most of the cattle.

The great import was wine, but salt and iron were other items besides various manufactured items including broadcloth, spices, silks and satins, figs and raisins, all luxury goods for the rich (Lydon, *Ireland in the Later Middle Ages*, 11-13). With the invention of gunpowder, guns and powder rapidly became prime requirements for the lords.

The Tertiary Sector

Financial Systems

Coinage

Viking coinage was used less and less, and the Normans introduced their own coinage from England. Local mints were established in the old Viking towns making silver half pennies and quarter pennies (farthings) for local use. Henry II did not introduce English money, but allowed separate currencies for Ireland and Brittany (Warren, *Henry II*, 561). John, as Lord of Ireland introduced the English silver penny which was interchangeable with the English one. John de Grey (d 1214) organised the Irish currency on the English model. It was always open to the Justiciar, Lord Lieutenant, or Lord Deputy to authorise a new minting of coins.

Minting was done by private moneyers who struck the coins in authorised mints. A silver penny was a weight of silver approximately 1.5 grams. The silver was melted; when cooled circular discs of the proper size were cut from it, and the images guaranteeing the proper weight was struck on either side with a hammer from dies. Mints were authorised in various towns at various times. Under John there were mints in Dublin, Waterford, Limerick, Kilkenny, Carrickfergus and Downpatrick. In 1251, following a reform of the English coinage, a similar reform was carried out in Ireland, and a royal mint was established in Dublin. All payments to the crown had to be made in the new coinage, while the old coinage was devalued. Most of the coins were in fact transmitted to the king in England (Dolley, 145). (There were always complaints in the Middle Ages about draining gold and silver from the kingdom, whether to the king or the pope. Only much later was it recognised that an inflow of gold and silver causes far more harm.) Under Edward I there were mints in Dublin, Waterford and Cork. Later mints were established in Drogheda and Trim. In 1474 there were mints also in Carlingford and Limerick. It is not obvious where the silver to make these coins came from. Silver was not otherwise used except for some ecclesiastical objects. Around 1295 Edward I reformed the coinages of both England and Ireland. The Irish coins were minted in Ireland by authorised mints. Minting fell off during the 14th century and old, foreign, debased and forged coins circulated. Minting was resumed by the Lord Deputy, Thomas Fitzgerald, in 1460 with less silver in the coins, and with brass farthings and half farthings (Halpin 'Coinage';

DNB, 'Thomas Fitzgerald'; Burke, *Industrial History*, 29). From this date it can be considered that there was a separate Irish coinage. (This separate coinage was discontinued in 1826.)

Coinage was based on the silver penny (plural pennies or pence) supposed to be equivalent to the Roman *denarius denier* and so represented by the letter d in £, s. d. The shilling of 12 pennies was not minted until Tudor times. It was regarded as corresponding to the *solidus* or *sou* and written as s. In 1344 the gold noble worth a third of a pound, or 6 shillings and eight pence was introduced. The mark worth 2 nobles or 13 shillings and four pence was introduced as a unit of account, but not as a coin. An English groat worth four pence or a third of a shilling was first minted under King Edward I. Scots groats were not issued until the reign of David II. Scots groats were originally also worth four pence, but later issues were valued at eight pence and a shilling. Irish groats were minted first in 1425. The pound (pound sterling) *(librum, livre* or L/£) was a pound weight of silver, 240 of silver pence. The more commonly useful half penny coins date from the reign of Edward I. It was worth half a silver penny. It was a small coin exactly half the weight of the silver penny. Silver farthings were commonly minted from the reign of Edward I. Before that it was more common to cut the silver penny into two pieces or four. The coins in use in Ireland eventually were the farthing, the half penny, the penny, the groat (4 silver pennies), and the noble (80 pence), with the mark as a unit of account. The gold noble was the largest coin. A gold pound coin was introduced in 1813, though earlier a gold coin called a guinea worth 21 shillings was introduced in 1663. The pound or pound sterling (240 pennies) and the shilling (12 pence) were units of account without a corresponding coin. (Foreign coins circulated freely in Ireland until the 19th century.)

In the 16th century the annual cash rent on a carucate was 10 shillings or one penny an acre (MacCurtain, 41) Mowing cost 5 pence an acre. The cost of ploughing an acre with the ox team and great plough was 8 pence, while harrowing with a one-horse harrow cost 3 pence. Cheese was sold at 8 pennies a stone. (Lydon, *Later Middle Ages,* 9) Skilled workers like thatchers or ploughmen were paid more. Small farmers paid a rent of 10 pence per half acre (Lydon, *Later Middle Ages,* 5). Wages rose sharply after the Black Death. (It is assumed that wages and prices in eastern Ireland and western England were broadly comparable.) The discovery of a hoard of pewter tokens cast some light on the retailing of beverages as a pint of ale or a dozen eggs probably cost less than a farthing. McNeill warns that in the earldom of Ulster where coinage was used nominal money rents may have, in fact, been paid in the traditional days of labour. Payments to men harvesting cereals would be more gratefully received as cut and tied sheaves than as coins. This was probably true over large parts of Ireland. Otherwise many more farthings and half pence should have been found (McNeill, 106).

Banking and Money lending

There was no such a thing as a bank in the British Isles before 1694 when the Bank of England got its charter. The supply of currency depended either on the Government, or importations of coins by merchants. In the early part of the Middle Ages there was a nett loss of coins which was regarded as a disaster because of the export of silver it implied. However there can be little doubt that the shortage of coins inhibited internal trade.

Money lending would have been essential for anyone who wished to travel abroad, to go to Rome for example, to go on a crusade, or to appeal to the peripatetic king who might be in the south of France. We can presume that when clerics like Saint Malachi wished to travel to Rome they had to borrow money.

Up to the expulsion of the Jews in 1290 money lending was in the hands of the Jews. Thereafter financial affairs with foreign countries were handled by the merchants of Northern Italy commonly called the Lombards after the old Lombard kingdom. After the expulsion of the Jews, the Lombards (or merchants of Genoa, Lucca, Florence, and Venice) succeeded them as the money-lenders and bankers of England. About the middle of the thirteenth century these Italians established themselves in Lombard Street, London remitting money to Italy by bills of exchange, and transmitting to the pope and Italian prelates their fees, and the incomes of their English benefices. In Ireland between 1278 and 1284 the tax revenue varied between £5,600 and £6,600, and the Italian tax farmers paid £1,000 p. a. for the privilege (Burke, *Industrial History*, 31).

In 1283 the Dublin mint was in charge of an Italian merchant from Lucca. During the 13th and first half of the 14th century Italian traders were the controlling influence in Irish as well as English trading. Not only were many of the mints in their hands but they also undertook the business of money lending and tax collecting. The Italians were noted as money lenders all over the south of Ireland. They were principally wool merchants exporting to England and the Continent. A large part of the Irish Government's revenue came for customs duties. Medieval trade fairs, such as the one in Hamburg, contributed to the growth of banking in a curious way: moneychangers issued documents redeemable at other fairs, in exchange for hard currency. These documents could be cashed at another fair in a different country or at a future fair in the same location. If redeemable at a future date, they would often be discounted by an amount comparable to a rate of interest. This banking service was probably used only by the Italian merchants. It was very useful for a small and easily concealed piece of parchment obviated the need to transport silver.

The Non-Monetary Economy

In England money played little part in the rural economy until the middle of the 14th century when, for various reasons, silver became more common (Briggs and Jordan, 32). The same was true in Ireland. In pre-Norman Ireland a man could be hired for a year for a cow and a cloak. In the Gaelic part of the earldom of Ulster a garrison of soldiers were paid in cows. The unit of value was the *sét* which was the equivalent of a heifer or half a milch cow. The highest unit of value was the *cumal* or slave woman which was the equivalent of six *sets*. Gradually the ounce of silver came to be used as a basic unit of account. The ounce of silver was divided into 24 scruples, and a scruple was valued at three silver pennies (Ó Corráin 47, 73; McNeill, *Anglo-Norman Ulster* 12). (This was derived from a Roman system of weights, and survives in the troy and apothecaries' systems of measurement. Presumably the system was introduced by merchants.)

The Vikings adopted coinage and began minting coins some time after their arrival in Dublin. Viking coins were used in the parts of county Meath under the rule of *Clan Cholmain*. Chiefs and lords were the only people liable to have any use for coins. Few could see a need to provide small coins for rural workers. When parishes were instituted in the 12th century payment from the parishioners was demanded in kind, namely every tenth sheaf or sheep. (The idea of contributing a tenth to God was derived from the Old Testament.) The exactions of the chiefs too were in kind in 1607 but some were prepared to receive cash instead (Nicholls, 35).

Remuneration in Middle Ages

Though money was widely available in the Roman Empire it never came into use in Ireland. We are not speaking here of rich farmers or merchants whose efforts rewarded themselves. It concerns those in affairs of religion, warfare, or public administration who had to be provided with an income commensurate with the dignity of their office. As is common in underdeveloped societies income distribution was very unequal. Most surpluses went to the rich while the poor were extremely badly paid.

It was the duty of the head of a household to distribute wealth equitably among his household. Even the eldest son and his wife depended on his father until an independent farm was secured for him and he could head his own household. This arrangement persisted into the 20th century. It was the duty of the chief to arrange an equitable distribution of spoils of war. But the equity was in accord with the ideas of the time. If this was done fairly it was called distributive justice in the Middle Ages, whereby a ruler or a steward gives to each what his rank deserves.

As almost everything necessary for the support of human life came from the land support for any institution had to come from endowments of land. Monarchs and chiefs normally had the greatest endowments. But churches and monasteries were also recipients of grants of land. As with gift exchange these grants were rarely absolute or complete. Though gifts to churches or monasteries might be difficult to revoke the church or monastery would find it difficult to resist the demands of their patron. Unwanted sons or daughters could be shunted into monasteries. Lords could demand hospitality or grazing for their animals. Even friars whose gifts from the lord amounted only to their convent were still under pressure to oblige the lord.

Endowments of lands were made by feudal and other monarchs to various warriors to provide cavalry for mobile local defence to combat Vikings and other raiders. Usually a large territory about the size of a county was granted to a chief warrior who then assigned parts of it to local warriors who came to be called knights. Their holdings were often called manors. The grant was intended to provide support for the knight, his horses, and his household. The same system was used by Gaelic chiefs as they came to depend on foreign mercenaries, the gallowglasses.

A further development was the assignation of the surplus revenues by the pope of king *in commendam* to someone else for a particular purpose. For example, if a bishop or cardinal was sent as a legate by the pope the latter would assign the surplus revenues of a well-endowed monastery to him to cover his expenses. The principle came to be widely abused and the future Abbot de Rancé got ecclesiastical revenues from several sources. The king too claimed the revenues of bishoprics *sede vacante*, i.e. between the death of one bishop and the confirmation of his successor.

Another means of remuneration was the right to charge fees for the discharge of particular duties. This applied to both secular and clerical offices. A cleric could charge a fee for writing out a particular document, or applying a seal. Though all the sacraments had to be celebrated gratis it was allowable to charge some extra fees for attendant circumstances, for example registering marriages and baptisms, or attending funerals. Fees became the great support for numerous lawyers who could lawfully charge for all kinds of things. Official appointments were offices of profit. Sheriffs were paid through fees and not through a tax on the county as is done nowadays. All the sheriff's officers were remunerated in the same manner. The gaoler had the right to make as much money as he could from his prisoners. It was an office of profit. The gaoler was obliged to keep the prisoner secure. He was not obliged to supply food, firewood or bedding. The system was ripe for extortion.

Cathedrals were quite expensive to run. Costs were incurred not for maintaining the fabric of the church which was often neglected but for the support of the cathedral clergy, especially the senior priests called canons. The endowment of the diocese went to the support of the bishop and his household including his chaplains. In the cathedral each individual canon, or as it was put 'his stall' in the church, had to be endowed separately. The revenues from these lands in various parts of the diocese supported the canon who had to appoint a local vicar to discharge the local duties. Individual parishes had three sources of revenue, a glebe, a townland or ploughland, the right to the tithe of the parish and offerings or altarages.

Ordinary soldiers had to have their daily expenses paid. For the rest they were paid when they were discharged from service, being given a cow or a cloak. They had their own means of increasing their reward so that the distinction between soldier and robber was not clear to most people. The occupations were interchangeable. More permanent mercenaries were just billeted on farmers or merchants who had to provide them with food, drink, and firewood.

Salaries were not unknown but the sums paid were intended to cover all the expenses of the office. The same applied to money paid out to raise and equip a regiment, as Falstaff noted when he clothed his regiment from the hedges as they marched along (Henry IV, Pt 1, Act 4 Scene 2).

Chapter 6

The Church in Ireland

Organisation

The general organisation of the Church was dealt with in Chapter 1. Irish dioceses corresponded closely with the territories of around 30 principal Gaelic chiefs or lords. The clergy were closely interwoven with the ruling families in each territory or diocese, and the clergy and learned families formed the privileged classes. In the Middle Ages few laymen could read or write so clerics, who became known as clerks in English, were normally used by kings and lords to keep records and to conduct their correspondence, and draw up charters and treaties.

The Influence of Monastic Reforms

The general desire for ecclesiastical reform shared by many religious and secular rulers had spread to Ireland at the beginning of the 12th century but progress was slow for the next quarter of a century. Then St Malachi introduced two reformed religious orders from the Continent, the Arrouaisian Canons, an Augustinian order, and the Cistercians. The life of the canons was suitable for those reforming priests and bishops who wanted a modern religious form of life suitable for their ministry, and these canons had a profound influence on clerical life in Medieval Ireland. Their influence was overshadowed in the 12th century by the Cistercians whose sole aim was to lead a life of prayer in solitude. A Cistercian monastery had to have at least 12 monks, and they had no pastoral ministry. All over Europe they struck numerous people as an ideal of Christian life. In Ireland, as elsewhere in Europe, many men asked to join them, and rulers were anxious to donate tracts of waste lands to them, and support them in their difficult early years when wooden monasteries had to be hastily built and waste lands recovered for cultivation. Every monastery had to be provided with a complete set of liturgical books, and have a cantor who knew over a thousand liturgical chants by heart. The first Cistercians got the best manuscripts they could of the books of the Bible and the lectionary containing the services for the Sundays and feast days. So if any priest or bishop wanted to find what were the appropriate rites for Sunday services or Holy Week ceremonies he could go along to the nearest Cistercian monastery to find out. Similarly if any bishop or abbot wanted the true version of the chants he did likewise. Everywhere there was dignity and restraint. Church and cathedrals were now being built of stone, and the monastic church at Mellifont with its simple form of Burgundian Transitional Gothic provided a model. It was a model affordable in most dioceses. Though the Cistercian had the greatest influence at the beginning of the period, the Augustinians came to dominate Medieval Ireland, most reverting to the normal Augustinian Rule (Gwynn and Handcock, passim).

The Synod of Cashel (1171)

There can be little doubt that the reforming Irish clergy welcomed the coming of Henry II. If anyone could restore order to the country it was he. The idea was that the decrees of the Synod would be backed by the royal authority in both parts of Ireland, the parts confirmed by feudal grants, and the parts under Rory O'Connor. It was agreed that every church in Ireland would for the future adopt the usages, practices, and rites of the Church in England. This was taken to mean the Sarum rite, though it is likely that many were already following either Cistercian or Arrouaisian forms. Uniformity was necessary, while drawing together a rite based on 'Celtic' tradition would have been beyond the skills of the reformers and against the current of reform which tended to adopt Roman practice. Readymade and acceptable canons were already in existence on the other side of the Irish Sea. As a start for making provision for parish priests tithes were introduced in principle though it was probably a long time before they were adopted in Gaelic parts of Ireland. Its other decrees were much the same as in other Irish synods of the time, and indeed any synod at the time of the Hildebrandine reform.

Ecclesiastical Boundaries and Political Power

The Irish Church was not modelled on the present-day counties and provinces. It might even be said that the reverse is true. The dioceses, deaneries and parishes were based on the existing secular divisions. The dioceses indicate to us the important chiefdoms around 1170. When Ireland was being organised into ecclesiastical provinces at the synod of Kells/Mellifont in 1152 only 4 were formed as the territories of the *Ui Neill* in Ulster and Meath were considered one province. The ecclesiastical boundaries of the provinces and dioceses provide us with a snapshot of the realities of the distribution of political power in Ireland from the 12 to the 16th centuries. There were about 37 dioceses, to which Dromore was added and Glendalough subtracted, compared with 31 nowadays. (It is difficult to state an exact number. Some existing bishoprics were allowed to continue until the see became vacant. Duleek in Meath in the territory of the formerly powerful

Sil nAedo Slaine seems to have persisted for a while. Four of the non-viable sees, Mayo, Annaghdown, Kilmacduagh and Kilfenora were west of the Shannon (Dolley, 39-40; Watt, *The Church in Medieval Ireland*, 24-26). Dromore was separated from Down around 1197 and undoubtedly other centres like the monasteries of Ardmore, Cong, and Mungret (or their local rulers) were still hoping for recognition. A local diocese was always very useful for providing 'livings' for sons.

Ecclesiastical reformers had to keep several things in mind: recognising tribal boundaries; recognising the relative importance of the clans; providing a focal point for the diocesan cathedral; and weighing up the ancient claims of existing dioceses which probably then numbered about fifty, based on fifty monasteries. It goes without saying that the cathedral should be in a centre of population, but as the great monasteries were already there it was a question of picking one of them. Large parts of any diocese were probably scarcely inhabited.

The Shannon was a great barrier even in the post-Viking age when river boats were commonly used in warfare. Fords at a few places like Athlone were passable in summer time. There was a formidable and long contested barrier of woods and bogs between Meath and (South) Leinster. There was a similar barrier of low hills and woods separating Leinster from Munster reaching from the sea to close to the Shannon. A difficult belt of woods, bogs, marshes and lakes extending across Ireland from Dundalk Bay to Donegal Bay formed a barrier between Ulster and the rest of Ireland. The border between Northern Ireland and the Irish republic runs through it to this day.

These relatively difficult barriers resulted in five regions or 'fifths' (*cuige* from *cuig* five) to which the ecclesiastical division of province (*provincia*) was applied though in this division Ulster and Meath, for historical reasons were formed into a single province. They were five areas with a relatively high density of population and cultivation and relatively fertile soils, separated from each other by belts of bogs, forests, forested hills, swampy riverbeds, and areas of poor drainage.

The ecclesiastical provinces were Armagh (Ulster and Meath); Dublin which included the lands of the Vikings and Leinster including Ossory (Kilkenny); Cashel which included all the territories in the South and county Clare on the other side of the Shannon; while Tuam covered all the rest of Connaught. The various provinces were also subdivided into defensible sub-regions and these formed the dioceses.

The Province of Armagh

In Ulster the diocese of **Raphoe** (Donegal) represents O'Donnell (*Cenel Conaill*) territory. The O'Donnells remained powerful local lords until the 17th century. **Clogher** (Monaghan and Fermanagh) represents O'Carroll/MacMahon territory. Several small clans of the *Oirgialla* along the southern borders of Ulster were forcibly united by Donough O'Carroll who also claimed to rule over similar groups in County Louth. The original monastery and local diocese of Clogher may date back to Patrician times. The territory of Clogher divided into three in the Middle Ages, the part in county Louth going to the Anglo-Normans, the part in Monaghan going to the MacMahons, and the part in Fermanagh going to the Maguires. **Derry,** originally Ardstraw, was partly O'Neill (*Cenel Eogain*) territory and the territory of the *Ui Fiachrach Arda sratha* (Ardstraw) which had been over-run by the O'Neills and their offshoots the O'Cahans (*Clan Connor*, O'Cahans) and O'Gormleys (*Cenel Moen*). The site of the diocese was moved to the great Columban monastery of Derry in 1254. It was regarded as the diocese of the *Cenel Eogain*. The territory was ruled by the O'Cahans throughout the Middle Ages.

Though it was not strictly in their territory, the dominant O'Neills had backed the claims of **Armagh** to be the primatial diocese of Ireland with the right of tribute from all other dioceses. The nominal boundary of the *Cenel Eogain* in the Later Middle Ages was the river Blackwater between Tyrone (*Tir Eogain*) and Armagh but the O'Neills never respected that. They at least got metropolitan status for it. The monastery and local bishopric of Armagh was situated among a group of minor families belonging to the *Oirgialla*. The church at Armagh had claimed to be the first Christian church founded by St Patrick who allegedly became its first bishop and so had claimed the right of primacy with its attendant dues. A Patrician mythology was built up. The minor family of O'Rogain was sited here, but more locally important were the O'Hanlons of *Oirthir* (Orior) who survived until Cromwellian times. The small clans of County Louth were counted with the *Oirgialla* and were incorporated into Armagh diocese, though the O'Carrolls of Clogher incorporated them into Clogher diocese for a while. **Connor** originally the diocese of the *Condaire,* was the territory of the *Dal nAraide,* to which was added the territories of the *Dal Riada*; it originally comprised most of the present county Antrim. Counties Antrim and Down by the 12th century were the territory of the *Ulaid* from whom Ulster takes its name. **Down** was the territory of the *Dal Fiatach* into whose affairs John de Courci was invited to intervene. Their land extended further north into present day south Antrim and included the present diocese of Dromore. The cathedral was at Bangor in the north of county Down but was transferred by John de Courci to Downpatrick, reputedly the burial place of St Patrick. (The story that the saints Patrick, Brigid, and Columcille were buried in the same grave takes some believing. Apparently it was an idea of John de Courci) **Dromore** was the small territory of the *Ui Eachach Coba* (Iveagh) whom the Normans failed to subjugate. It was later formed into a tiny diocese of 19 parishes with its own cathedral in Dromore. It remained in Gaelic hands under the rulership of the MacGuinness family.

Meath, and its principal monastery Clonard, was the territory of the Southern *Ui Neill* (ee nale). The leading family *Clan Cholmain* (O'Mellaghlin), like other clans wracked with fratricidal struggles, was beginning to disintegrate. The territory was initially split into three dioceses based on three great monasteries of Kells, Duleek, and Clonard. The Anglo-Norman bishop made them into the diocese of Meath in 1216 with the cathedral at Trim. Meath was to become one of the richest and most prestigious dioceses which politically corresponded with the great Liberty of Trim. **Ardagh** was the diocese of Annally or Teffia whose leading family the O'Farrells maintained their independence up to Tudor times. It was to become County Longford. **Kilmore** was the territory of the *Ui Briuin Breifne* as it was extended in the 12th century by Tiernan O'Rourke who expanded his territory at the same time as Donough O'Carroll was doing in Oriel just north of him.

The Province of Dublin

This province was the easiest to divide up. Glendalough was in the north east, Kildare in the north west, Ferns in the south east, Ossory in the south west, and Leighlin in the centre corresponding with the five centres of power. To Leinster was added the Norse diocese of Dublin, which was not an older Irish diocese. The tiny and lately founded Norse diocese of **Dublin,** which claimed in any case to be subject to Canterbury, was an odd choice for a metropolitan see. By ordinary rules of antiquity the monastery and see of Kildare in north Leinster should have had the honour. But Dermot MacMurrough would never allow the honour to go to a rival family, and probably failing to get the honour for his own Ferns, could have put forward Dublin, whose legitimate ruler he claimed to be, as a compromise. Dublin cathedral was built by the Norse. At an early stage it took over the diocese of Glendalough.

At a slightly earlier period the archbishopric would have gone to **Kildare.** Its territory was based on the largest stretch of arable soil in Leinster and Kildare was arguably the most ancient church in Ireland still at the centre of an important political grouping. It was the territory of the *Ui Dunlainge*, until recently the provincial chiefs of Leinster and less important families, the *Ui Muredaig, Ui*

Dunchada, Ui Faelain, Ui Failge, and *Loigse.* It was centred on the great monastery of Kildare allegedly founded by St Brigid and St Conleth. It was the *Ui Dunlainge* lands that Dermot MacMurrough assigned to Strongbow.

Glendalough, a monastic church in a deep valley in the Wicklow Mountains was made the centre of a diocese which corresponds closely with County Wicklow, but with an extension westward to reach the Barrow at Athy lands of *Ui Muredaig.* Among the displaced *Ui Dunlainge* were the O'Byrnes and the O'Tooles who decamped into the Wicklow Mountains. The Norman archbishop of Dublin united the two sees in 1216. The centre of population was in the valley of the Barrow touching on Kildare (and Leighlin) but there were also tiny settlements all along the Wicklow coast. The diocese and the county were hollow with no roads crossing the centre of the county until 1798.

The need for a separate diocese of **Leighlin** is not obvious. It was united to Ferns in 1597 while the Catholic diocese was united to Kildare. It may have been intended as a see for the *Ui Muredaig.* Most of the population seems to have been in the valley of the Barrow and the cathedral was at Old Leighlin near Leighlinbridge on the Barrow. The monastery there of St Laserian was one of the most important in Leinster. The diocese of **Ferns** corresponded with the home territory of the *Ui Chennselaig* (O'Kinsella) whose ruler in the 12th century was Dermot MacMurrough. There were minor families like the *Fotharta* and *Ui Bairche* (Forth and Bargy) whose *tuatha* MacMurrough granted to his Norman followers. The Normans became heavily involved in Dermot MacMurrough's own *tuath* and strongly developed it commercially. **Ossory** was the final diocese in Leinster and was the territory of the *Osraige* who had managed to install themselves in the broken country along the Nore. The chief church and monastery was at Aghaboe but this was later replaced by Kilkenny. The most important parts were assigned by Dermot MacMurrough to Normans and it became a Norman stronghold.

The Province of Cashel

The province of Munster was not so easy to divide up geographically as the province of Ulster. In Munster the *Eoganacht* families had carved out lordships in separate places all over Munster, from the south of Cork and Kerry as far as the north of Tipperary. Furthermore the expanding *Deisi* carved out a lordship from Waterford to Clare, apparently at one stage extending the whole way across the province with the *Eoganacht Caisil* to their north. The whole of Munster appears to have been underpopulated and with large parts of it with no population at all.

There was an ancient diocese of **Cashel** stretching allegedly back to the time of Saint Patrick. It was in the territory of the *Eoganacht Caisil* the most powerful of the widespread *Eoganacht* group of families until the rise of the O'Briens under Brian *Boru* around the year 1000. The O'Briens retained their capital near Limerick and designated the *Eoganacht* lands around Cashel for the support of a modern archbishopric. The diocese today covers most of County Tipperary. *Emly* was a diocese which had no obvious focus and for which there was no obvious need except perhaps to keep Cashel for getting too strong. The territory came under lesser *Eoganacht* families, the *Eoganacht Aine* and *Eoganacht Airthir Cliath* with remnants of the *Deisi* and *Muscraige*. As usual these had grabbed the best lands, and in turn had them grabbed from them by the Normans. Emly was enlarged and made into a county in itself by King John, but gradually the civil county was absorbed by Tipperary and Limerick. Emly was united to Cashel by the Protestants in 1562 and by the Catholics in 1718.

Lismore was the territory of the *Deisi*. It corresponds roughly with the present County Waterford. Being the territory of an important secondary family it was always going to be a diocese the only question being whether the cathedral should be at the monastery of Ardmore or that of Lismore. It became part of the vast earldom of Desmond in the later Middle Ages. One of the local *Eoganacht* families, the O'Sullivans, were expelled and carved out another domain for themselves in Cork. **Waterford** was a Viking town nominally under the overlordship of the MacCarthy lord of Munster but seized by Dermot MacMurrough. The lands necessary for its survival measured about 15 miles by 7. The Viking town sought its own bishop from Saint Anselm of Canterbury in 1096. Henry II reserved it to the crown. It was joined to Lismore in 1358 by which time it was one of the richest towns in Ireland. The chief Norman lords were called le Paor or Power. **Cloyne** was centred on the monastery of Cloyne and corresponds roughly with the northern half of the present County Cork. In the south east was the territory of the *Ui Liathain*, a branch of the *Corcu Loegde*; in north around Fermoy and Glenworth, the *Eoganacht Glendamnach*. Further north were the *Fir Maigh Fene* (Fermoy) and in the south the *Muscraige Mittine* (Muskerry) along the Lee. The *Ui Liathain* seem to have been the dominant family at this period. The boundary with Cork dioceses for a considerable way followed the River Lee and was to mark the boundary between Norman Munster and Gaelic Munster throughout the Middle Ages. **Cork** throughout the Middle Ages came under the dominion of the MacCarthys, the disposed *Eoganacht* of Cashel, but they were not so dominant in this area in the 12th century. Its territory was Cork south of Lee plus a section north of Cork city; lands of the *Eoganacht Raithlind* in the east and *Corcu Loegde* in west and possibly *Muscraige Mittine* on the Lee. At Rathbreasail and Kells/ Mellifont it was recognised as a see for the *Eoganacht Raithlind* based on St Finbarr's monastery near Cork City. Later in the Middle Ages a branch of the *Eoganacht Caisil*, the MacCarthys of Muskerry took over the region, and built Blarney castle as their stronghold. The small Viking town on an island in the River Lee was surrounded as usual by its own cantred to supply their agricultural needs. It was made into their city by the deposed *Eoganacht Caisil*. It was captured by the first Normans but taken into royal hands by Henry II. The base of the chief of the

Eoganacht, known later as MacCarthy *Mór* was in south west Cork into which they were driven by the expanding Normans. There was no Norse bishopric in Cork.

Ross was the territory of the *Corcu Loegde* and it is not obvious why it was given the status of a separate diocese. The name of the ruling family in the Middle Ages was O'Driscoll. The region was also called Carbery. The diocese, strangely, kept its separate existence until 1958. It was centred on the famous monastery and school of Rossaliter.

Ardfert (Kerry) was originally in the fertile lands of central and north Kerry, in the valleys of the Laune and the Main controlled by the *Eoganacht Loca Lein.* Other local families were the *Ciarraige* (Kerry who later gave their name to the diocese and the *Corcu Duibne* (Corkaguiny). The centre of the see was placed at Ardfert and that was the official name until it was officially changed in 1952 to the diocese of Kerry. The northern and more fertile part was granted to various Norman lords. Tralee in County Kerry was the chief seat of the earls of Desmond whose lands at the height of their powers were spread across the whole of Munster.

Limerick was originally a tiny Norse see, but the town was adopted by the O'Briens as their own. It occupied the middle section of the stretch of fertile land which stretched from north Kerry into south Tipperary. Lands south of the Shannon estuary in the basins of the Maigue and the Deel, were the territory of the *Ui Fidgente,* but there were also many small clans in the outlying areas. The claims of Mungret to be a separate see were again passed over. In the Middle Ages it swallowed up most of Emly to its east, but lost a small bit north of the river at Limerick. **Killaloe** and Limerick remind us that the grip overlords had on their subject chiefs was often precarious. Killaloe represented the O'Brien overlordship of Thomond (North Munster). But North Munster geographically and politically was split into two, Thomond west of the Shannon and Ormond east of the Shannon. The latter was an extension of the Great Central Plain over which *Clan Cholmain* of Meath tried to wrest overlordship from the *Eoganacht Caisil*. The O'Briens then succeeded in getting control of Ormond from the *Eoganacht* but could not hold it. King John granted it to the Normans who held it for quite a while, but the region was gradually encroached on by the expanding *Loigse*, *Ui Failge*, O'Carrolls, and sub-families of the O'Briens, the O'Mulryans and O'Kennedys. Kells/Mellifont assigned this area to the diocese of Roscrea for the *Eli* whose leading family was the O'Carrolls but it was taken over by Killaloe. In the Middle Ages this eastern half of Killaloe was in the Norman palatine county of Tipperary. Thus in the Middle Ages Killaloe like Armagh was half in the Anglo-Norman area and half in the Gaelic area. At the same time, Kilfenora was assigned to the *Corcu Modruad*, and **Scattery Island** to the *Corcu Baiscind* in west Clare and Mungret to the *Ui Fidgente* in Limerick. Of these three only Kilfenora survived the revival of O'Brien power under Dónal *Mór* O'Brien. **Kilfenora** was the diocese of the *Corcu Modruad* in north Clare. At Rathbreasail it was included in Killaloe but at Kells/Mellifont it was given separate status. In the Catholic Church it remained a separate diocese until 1749. It was first joined to Kilmacduagh and both were joined to the Wardenship of Galway to form the present diocese of Galway.

The Province of Tuam

Kilmacduagh was a small territory at the head of Galway Bay of the *Ui Fiachrach Aidne*. It was made a separate diocese at Kells/Mellifont but proved scarcely viable. The *Ui Fiachrach* were formerly dominant in Connaught but were now subject to the O'Connors. Their other branch, the *Ui Fiachrach Muaide* was in north Mayo. The area was lightly settled by the Normans who established three towns or manors at Kilcolgan, Ardrahan and Kiltartan. The important Norman centres of Galway and Athenry were to the north of it on the road leading to Athlone, Meath and Dublin. It was ruled by the O'Shaughnessys. It never formed a county on its own. It survived as a separate diocese until 1883. **Clonfert** was simple. It lay inland between Kilmacduagh and the Shannon, the territory of the *Ui Maine* (O'Kellys and O'Maddens) who were mesne lords of minor *tuatha*. The Normans establish several towns and manors chiefly along the Shannon, but also at Loughrea on the road from Ballinasloe to Galway. The Burkes (de Burgo) of Clanrickard became strong in the area. **Elphin** (Roscommon) was also simple; it was the territory of the *Ui Briuin Ai* (O'Connor, MacDermott, MacDonough). The O'Connors were the overlords of Connaught in the 12th century and their principal territory was in Roscommon. They were displaced from the overlordship by the de Burghs and split into branches, the O'Connor Roe, O'Connor Don, etc. It was made a county as Roscommon. It was not however made the archdiocese, that honour going to the O'Connors' other territory around Tuam. **Achonry** corresponds roughly with county Sligo. It was centred on the monastery of Achonry though it is not clear who in 1150 was the local overlord. Local lords in the Middle Ages were O'Haras and O'Garas, MacDermotts, de Burghs and O'Connors. Its northern tip was just a few miles from the southern tip of Raphoe and the O'Donnells had great ambitions in this direction. **Killala** was in northwest corner of Mayo, *Tir Amalgada* (Tirawley), *Iorras* (Erris), and *Tir Fiachrach* (Tireragh) in Sligo whose overlords were the *Ui Fiachrach Muaide* (O'Dowds) who probably ruled as far south as Killary harbour. After this matters get complicated for three other dioceses besides Tuam were recognised at various times in western Connaught, Cong, Mayo, and Annaghdown. **Cong** was recognised at Rathbreasail but not at Kells/Mellifont. **Mayo** was recognised at Kells/Mellifont, while **Annaghdown** was recognised later as the diocese of the *Ui Briuin Seola* (O'Flahertys). It was based on the monastery of Annaghdown on Lough Cong. Cong and Annaghdown were in west Galway and presumably covered much the same area. The chief lords in Mayo were the *Ui Mail* (O'Malley). All were absorbed into Tuam. Though Mayo diocese was absorbed by Tuam as early as 1220, when

Connaught was shired it was not included in Galway, but grouped with Killala and western Achonry to form County Mayo.

The 'Wardenship of Galway' was carved out of Tuam in 1485 to serve the interests of the town of Galway surrounded as it was by the fierce O'Flahertys. The church of St Nicholas was made a collegiate church with a warden as their head. The arrangement, sanctioned by a bull of Innocent VIII, was to have the church of St. Nicholas, at Galway, a collegiate church governed by a warden and eight vicars; these having jurisdiction over the whole town, as well as over a few parishes in the neighbourhood. And warden and vicars " were to be presented and solely elected by the inhabitants of the town". It was a peculiar arrangement. Though, like a diocese, it was a separate ecclesiastical jurisdiction. The warden exercised episcopal jurisdiction, appointed to parishes, visited the religious institutions, but did not, of course, confer orders. The warden, like mitred abbots, was allowed to wear a mitre and carry a crosier, but depended on neighbouring bishops for ordinations. The eight vicars resembled somewhat the canons of a cathedral church. It survived, with its unique position until incorporated into the diocese of Galway in 1831. Kilmacduagh was added in 1883.

The diocese

In a previous book I described the origins and growth of the Christian Church in Ireland up to the adoption of the decrees of the synod in 1152 (Keenan, *The True Origins of Irish Society*). The 'Hildebrandine' reform of the Irish Church had been advancing slowly since the beginning of the 12th century. The definitive decisions regarding the structures of the Irish Church were taken in principle at the Synod of Kells/Mellifont in 1152 but that was only the start of the reforms, structural and religious. In the first place in Ireland a proper hierarchical structure with dioceses and provinces was to be established. Within each diocese a proper modern structure was to be established with a bishop, a chapter, parish clergy, and diocesan officers to supervise the parish clergy. Cathedrals and parish churches, preferably built of stone, had to be constructed. Lands to maintain all of these had to be provided. All this was intended to bring the Irish Church up to contemporary standards. It may be said at the outset that providing for the training of the parish clergy was not a priority. As Corish points out this was not seriously tackled until after the Reformation, though the friars, in Ireland as elsewhere, tried to supply for the deficiencies of the parish clergy (Corish, 68).

In beliefs, language, rites, moral practice, and canon law the Irish Church was more-or-less the same as the Roman Church. Its defects, the ignorance of the lower clergy, the interference of laymen with Church affairs, the neglect of Christian values, were the same as those in other parts of Western Europe. The Hildebrandine reform in Ireland was essentially the same as elsewhere. The great problem lay in the organisation of the Church where for local reasons it had developed somewhat differently from that of the rest of the Latin Church. Part of the reason seems to have been that the local rulers preferred to endow monasteries rather than diocesan churches with lands. The principal towns in a chiefdom were those which grew up around monasteries. There was a widespread tradition that a bishop should live in a monastery so that the cathedral clergy should benefit from monastic life and chant the offices along with the monks. (This idea was taken up again in places in the Middle Ages, notably in Christ Church cathedral in Dublin with a prior in charge.) The result in Ireland in many cases seems to have been that the abbot was regarded as a person of greater consequence than the bishop and the abbot's court as more important than the bishop's. There were no defined territorial boundaries to a diocese, subjection to a bishop or abbot being personal. This was in tune with secular dependence on chief whose territories might or might not be contiguous.

The old structures and the old problems remained largely in place. The secular rulers still maintained close control over what went on in their territories. They had given the lands to the diocese or to the monastery in the first place and felt they had first rights regarding what went on there, especially the appointment of abbots and abbesses. Besides these were the bishops and their families, the monks of the monasteries and their families who all had expectations. Besides the clergy, there were in each diocese and attached to each monastery coarbs and erenaghs and they had their families to provide for. The coarbs claimed to be the lineal descendants of the founders of monasteries and claimed the right to have each abbot drawn from their family. The erenaghs were the hereditary stewards of the lands of the monasteries. Despite the exotic terminology the practise was not greatly different from elsewhere in Europe. The rights claimed by the family of the coarb resembled those of the family of the lay lord or patron who had originally founded a monastery. Erenaghs were stewards or seneschals and as elsewhere the office was transmitted in families. They could be tonsured clerics or in minor orders and the tendency in the Middle Ages seems to have been to make them so.

Under the new dispensation the diocese was to be divided systematically into parishes to provide everyone with the opportunity to attend divine service and to receive the ministrations of a priest. The provision of this had been very haphazard in the past. If the diocese was large or there were difficulties, linguistic or other in travelling, the bishop could divide it into deaneries.

By far the most important source of income at the time came from revenues from land. So land had to be obtained for the support of the bishop, and also for the support of each member of the chapter and the diocesan officers. This was done in the time-honoured fashion by the Gaelic chiefs who simply dispossessed their enemies and gave the land to the Church. (After 1171, in Anglo-Norman lands where the king had taken feudal possession of the lands and assigned them to various tenants-in-chief there was no difficulty in assigning lands to bishops as tenants-in-chief or in socage.) In either case the actual owner was often just reduced in status and the revenues and dues in cattle, cereals, and other renders just transferred to the bishop who was usually non-resident. As Otway-Ruthven notes the transfer of lands met with considerable resistance from the coarbs and erenaghs. There seems to have been numerous endowed monasteries with no monks but with coarbs and erenaghs still in place. The solution seems to have been to make the erenaghs head tenants and to subject them to food dues (Otway-Ruthven, 39). This included coshering where the bishop and his household which might number 100 descended on his lands distant from his cathedral and stay for some time (Keenan, *True Origins*, 472). This was in line with the practice of the secular lords. In time many of these services were commuted into cash, though in Clogher the bishop and his seneschal retained a right to 8 gallons of ale out of every brewing (M'Kenna, 144).

The first task each bishop had was to build a cathedral of suitable style for the new diocese if this had not already been done. The new stone-built monastery church or first church of Mellifont, built in a restrained Transitional Burgundian style, and consecrated in 1157 provided a model. He then had to appoint a chapter and acquire sufficient prebends or sources of revenue for each member of the chapter. This of course meant more grants of land.

As in England the kings took a particular interest in appointments to sees but there not great evidence to show that they imposed unworthy men. Rather, as in the appointment of judges, they were more concerned about appointing capable administrators. Very often, too, sees were left vacant for years during which time the king's officials or the Irish princes, as the case might be, wasted the property of the diocese either with the connivance of, or against the wishes of the diocesan chapters. A greater much greater evil was the ready recourse which the Popes allowed for appeals for offices to be made directly to themselves. This was of great financial benefit to the clerics of the papal courts who were able to charge appropriate fees. To become an abbot all that was required was to denounce the incumbent as unworthy and to recommend one's self as an appropriate replacement. The problem was compounded during the Great Western Schism when there were rival Popes at Rome and Avignon.

The Parishes

There was a problem regarding parishes for it is difficult to decide what the exact state of canon law was at any given date. Some writers, as in the *Catholic Encyclopaedia* tend to look at the legislation of the Council of Trent (1545-63) and project it backwards. There seems however not to have been any general law regarding the provision of parishes and of parish priests, and consequently no particular obligation on the bishop or dean to provide such parishes. In the Anglo-Saxon Church, if a local lord wanted a parish church of his own he just built one, and presented a nominee of his own to the bishop for ordination. This practice survived in places in Ireland until the 19th century (Keenan, *The Catholic Church*, 56).

The Synod of Cashel decreed that the practice of tithing should be introduced to Ireland to provide for the support of parish priests. This represented an enormous jump in taxation: a 10% tax on all produce. Often in practice the tithe did not go to the intended recipient, the parish priest, but to an abbey or a Church dignitary. Abbeys which had received great tracts of land could split them into parishes. The parochial vicar had to be content with the altarages but he might not get even those and might have to be content with a small stipend. But as parish priests were regarded as having the same income as a ploughman and being just as ignorant the recipient was probably grateful for what he got. Irish rural churches were tiny, and considerably smaller than their English equivalents. Members of the families of the coarbs no doubt regularly presented themselves whenever there was a vacancy in their parish, but we have no idea of the conditions on which the erenaghs and coarbs of monastic lands were bought out. But nobody in the Middle Ages threw away a possible source of income no matter how tiny. It was often a matter of life and death.

In the Anglo-Norman parts of Ireland the practice in England of making the manor and the parish the same was continued. It was not necessary to have the full manorial system with common fields. Such parishes were usually smaller than in Gaelic areas, where usually the *tuath* was taken as the unit. In much of Ireland a *tuath* would have at least one small monastery which had supplied local needs even if it was deserted by the 12th century. Usually too the original ruling family from which the *tuath* took its name had been displaced by members of the now dominant local family which might complicate rights of patronage and rights of coarbs. The practice of monks and friars ministering to spiritual needs continued even after the formal erection of parishes. Parish sizes in Co. Louth was in the range of three to five thousand acres, while in the neighbouring counties of Monaghan and south Armagh they were in the range of seventeen to twenty five thousand acres (Duffy, 'Geographical perspectives', 12-13). There were only 13 parishes in the present county Monaghan, clearly formed from old *tuatha* (M'Kenna, 16-17.) The parishes in the earldom of Ulster were significantly richer than Gaelic parishes in Ulster, or even Irish dioceses. This indicates the effectiveness of the commercial development of the earldom (McNeill, 35, 39f).

In England, and in Anglo-Norman Ireland, the right of nomination to a parish (advowson) seems to have belonged to the lay patron, who presented him to the bishop for installation, and ordination if he was not already a priest. The lay patron was the descendant of the landowner who originally built the church, or his successor in those rights. It is not clear at what stage the Cistercians made their large extents of mostly reclaimed land into parishes. The Cistercians avoided any connection with a pastoral ministry and the vicars they appointed to parishes were not monks. At the dissolution of the monasteries in 1539 several monks of Mellifont were appointed parish priests on the monastery's estates with stipends of £2 or £3 per annum plus the altarages, this being considered a generous settlement (Columcille, 172-3). In Gaelic areas the nomination seems to have resided either with the family of the coarb, the descendant of the original abbot, or with the family of the erenagh, the hereditary stewards of church lands.

The Church in the Late Middle Ages

Much attention has been paid in the past to the shortcomings of the Church in the later Middle Ages. But this was not the whole story. A vibrant religious life flourished as described above in Chapter I. Parishes were established even in Gaelic areas, and churches, mostly wooden, were built which formed the centre of life for the ordinary people of the parish. In theory all laymen were equal in the church. In theory the local lord might build it and have special pews or seats for services on Sundays and holy days but the church was the church of the whole parish. On week days, the building, usually the only large one apart from the hall of the lord, could be used for many things.

As often we have to deduce what was done at local level from descriptions of parish life in England or France, but there is no indication that Ireland was any different from those places. Surviving sources show that there was little difference between practice in Ireland and elsewhere. The various orders of friars who were spread all over Europe brought the latest trends. Each parish as it was formed seems to have been given a local saint with some connection to it as a patron saint. The patron saint's day was then celebrated annually. This annual celebration was called the 'pattern'. This was the common European practice. Many patterns survived until the 19th century when they were suppressed by the local bishops because they had become occasions of drunkenness and disorder. The patron of the parish of Killeavy in south Armagh, for example, was St. Moninna who was alleged to be a contemporary of St. Patrick and St Brigid and to have founded a convent in the parish. Her feast day was on 6 July. Some patterns are still being celebrated especially if there is a holy well involved, for example at St Brigid's Well, Faughart, Co. Louth.

Public worship in Ireland was the same as elsewhere, as were private devotions as described in an earlier chapter. It was still firmly centred on the public worship of the Church. Devotion could be expressed by pilgrimages or attending sermons of a friar. Relics continued to be highly valued. Trade guilds were formed and they were anxious to display their religious devotion. The Guild of St Anne, founded in Dublin in 1430, maintained six priests and two clerks to maintain religious services in its chapel and to pray for the living and the dead. Many guilds presented pageants at the great Eucharistic procession on the feast of Corpus Christ (Corish, 53f). As elsewhere devotional literature began to be found in lay hands, in rich families of course. Two lists of books belonging to the earls of Kildare survive, but as Corish notes, the richer merchants would have had similar collections *(loc. it.)* Saint's *Lives* were always a great staple. They were devotional not historical and could be composed by anyone given the minimum details, man or woman, priest or layman, martyr or confessor. The religious books were in Gaelic and seem to have been derived from Continental sources. The pilgrimage to the supposed relic of the True Cross at Holy Cross monastery in Tipperary was famous. The other great place of pilgrimage was Lough Derg, in County Donegal. The carving of religious scenes especially on tombstones continued.

Unlike in England, France and Italy there were no widespread heresies in Ireland in the Middle Ages. Nor as noted earlier was there any tradition of writing on mystical prayer.

"The reforming zeal harnessed at Kells/Mellifont continued for some centuries but gradually waned. Some bishops, abbots and religious superiors maintained high ideals and did their best. But, even though the bishops as a body had been as zealous as individuals amongst them undoubtedly were, they often had no power to put down abuses. The patronage of Church livings, including rectories, vicarages, and chaplaincies enjoyed by laymen, as well as by chapters, monasteries, convents, hospitals, etc., made it impossible for a bishop to exercise control over the clergy of his diocese. Both Norman and Irish nobles were generous in their gifts to the Church, but whenever they granted endowments to a parish they insisted on getting in return the full rights of patronage. The lay patrons nominated their own dependents and favourites, while both ecclesiastical and lay patrons were more anxious about securing the revenues than about the zeal and activity of the pastors and vicars. Some of them were openly immoral, and many of them had not sufficient learning to enable them to preach or to instruct their flocks. It ought to be remembered also that in these days there were no special seminaries for the education of the clergy. Candidates for the priesthood received whatever training they got from some member of the cathedral chapter, or in the schools of the Mendicant Friars, or possibly from some learned ecclesiastics" (McCaffrey, *History of the Catholic Church, passim.* His style is characteristic of his period; Watt, *The Church in Medieval Ireland*, 183-92). It was probably true, as Corish observed about the Dark Ages, and other writers indicated about Tudor times, that the Ten Commandments were not observed outside monasteries. It may be added that at times not even there.

A good deal has been written about the linguistic dispute in the monasteries regarding what language should be spoken and who should be admitted to various monasteries (Columcille, 102-4). Though Fr. Columcille appears to interpret the word race in its modern sense a better translation would be root or stock, i.e. the local Gaelic families who still claimed nomination rights. But the problem ante-dated the Normans. Dermot MacMurrough excluded women of the local stock, the *Ui Faelain* in favour of his own stock, the *Ui Chennselaig* (Furlong,

37-8). The problem was less in the diocese because it was usually possible geographically to split the diocese into a Gaelic deanery and an English-speaking one. But there was some trouble among the friars especially the Franciscans. (Friars supported Edward the Bruce and were suspect afterwards. In the post-Reformation period they were active in politics (Watt, *Church in Medieval Ireland*, 80)

Yet the whole picture was not bleak. As usual, records from the Middle Ages are scarce but some survive. The ecclesiastical courts in Armagh were busy, usually with matrimonial cases and the forbidden degrees of matrimony (Watt, *op.cit*, 203-8). Reforms were attempted in the religious Orders which paved the way for the great reforms which followed the Council of Trent (1545-63). The 14th century was a bleak century characterised by the Hundred Years War, the Black Death and successive plagues, the Peasants' Revolt against conditions on the land, the decline in the English population and economy which hit Irish exports, and the growing power of the Gaelic chiefs and their habits of wasting the lands of weaker neighbours (The English were doing precisely the same in France, Dyer, 160). In the 15th century reform movements grew up among the mendicant friars, and there was a revival in church-building.

Religious Orders

Monasticism had come early to Ireland and for a while flourished. There is no need to suppose that it was any better than in 6th century Italy where there were sarabaites and gyrovagues (Keenan, *True Origins*, passim). In the 12th century the Augustinians and the Cistercians were widely introduced. With the Normans came the military orders, the Knights Templars and the Knights Hospitallers. These needed considerable extents of land to provide for the maintenance of their defense of the Holy Land and to patrol the routes thither. This had become necessary after groups of Turks from central Asia who had adopted Islam and seized parts of the Byzantine Empire began robbing and murdering pilgrims. Some other minor foundations were made by orders like the Crutched friars, a branch of the Augustinian friars, and the Trinitarians who collected funds for the redemption of Christian captives from the Muslim states.

Much more important in the 13th century were the mendicant friars, the Dominicans, the Franciscans, the Carmelites and the Augustinian friars. Their distinguishing characteristics were that they were preachers devoted to the pastoral ministry, that they had no landed property or any sources of income except gifts, and that they could go about preaching. As preachers they valued learning and they filled the new universities as students and professors. They attracted large numbers, and landowners liked them for they required little land beyond what was required for a church and a monastery. Because they depended entirely on gifts it was essential that they should be sited in towns, and soon almost every town in Ireland had one or more friaries. These towns were exclusively in the Anglo-Norman part of Ireland until late in the Middle Ages (Watt, *Church in Medieval Ireland* 60-86).

There seems to have been little attempt by the native Irish rulers in the Middle Ages after the 12th century to establish more religious houses until the 15th cent and then only reluctantly in Ulster. Between 1420 and 1530 there were founded numerous small friaries of the Franciscans Third Order Regular mainly in the Gaelic areas of the west and north. This may be because they had small Latin schools. The various orders of friars continued to expand into the Gaelic areas from which they had been absent before, which would seem to argue an increasing density of population. Lists of the houses of the principal orders ware given in Moody, Martin, and Byrne (*New History of Ireland*, vol. IX).

Lessons had been learned from the past regarding the decline of monasteries and regarding the steps taken by the Cistercians and other orders to maintain disciple. Strict constitutions and customaries *(consuetudines)* were drawn up for each Order. The widespread mendicant orders found it more convenient to divide the whole Order into provinces, and to place each province under a superior called a provincial. Delegates from the provinces attended the general chapter. A superior general presided over the whole Order. This remains the basis for the government and maintenance of discipline to this day. The Holy See was very strict about this and the Franciscan Order founded by the free-spirited St Francis of Assisi was compelled to follow the same discipline as the others. Approval from the Holy See was sought, and exemption from episcopal jurisdiction granted. This latter was necessary to prevent any local bishop interfering, and to allow friars to be moved by their superiors from diocese to diocese. The friars did not seem to attract the same type of recruit as the richly-endowed earlier abbeys. Undoubtedly people desirous of devoting their lives to God began to be more attracted by the mendicant ideal than by that in richly endowed monasteries. The various bishops seem to have been content to allow the friars to preach to the poor while they themselves looked for advancement and good livings. This was cost free for the friars educated their own members.

The decline of the great monastic houses, particularly of the Cistercians is well documented. The evils of the Dark Ages where the rich families claimed the right to impose abbots from their own families returned. The friars were not so badly affected yet even here there was a lessening of discipline. The Franciscan friars in the Gaelic areas managed to reform themselves in the 15th cent; there were 40 Observant houses in the province of Tuam, 28 in Armagh, 18 in Cashel, and 4 in Dublin, either new foundations or Conventual houses who adopted the stricter interpretation of the Rule. There were also 40 houses of the Franciscan Third Order Regular who seem to have been concerned with education to the benefit of parish priests (Corish 57).

Neither in pre-Norman nor post-Norman Ireland was there any great enthusiasm for founding houses for women religious. There were some of course some. The vast majority of the relatively few women religious were Augustinian canonesses, mostly Arrouaisian (Corish, 34). None of the Orders of mendicant friars introduced the female branch though they were common elsewhere. The situation was much the same in England where nunneries were few and poor (Power, 89f).

Chapter 7

Other Aspects

Education and Skills

By education we normally mean book education, and this was rare in the Middle Ages. This does not mean that skills were not taught. Young men of noble family had to be exercised in horsemanship and the arts of war. The children of craftsmen were instructed and trained in the skills of their craft at times to a very high order. Husbandmen and tillers of the soil were instructed almost as soon as they could walk. The level of skill varied. We know from 19th century Ireland that the poorest were the least skilled. Men knew enough about tillage to plant potatoes by the lazybed method, and to construct a tiny mudwalled cottage roughly thatched, and to boil potatoes. At the other end of the scales culinary skills would have been high in monasteries and in the houses of lords. There was everything in between.

Originally, instruction would have been given by a parent or close relative, but in the Middle Ages in the towns, apprenticeships were introduced by which master craftsmen instructed others. At the end of his apprenticeship the tradesman became a journeyman paid by the day as his name implies. Spinning and weaving can be done crudely, but techniques were always improving up to the 19th century. The guild system which could set minimum standards for journeymen was useful for maintaining or raising standards. Standards in weaving and finishing cloth were constantly rising, and the pace was set by the Flemish towns.

Primary Education

By primary education is here meant instruction in the vernacular. Those who wished to be educated began by studying Latin. In England we know that a surprising number of women of good families were taught to read and write English (Jarman 120-122). There is some evidence that teaching, probably in English was done by anchoresses, chaplains, holy water carriers and such kind, for the archbishop of York forbade them. It is fair to assume that what was done in England would very shortly be done in Anglo-Norman parts of Ireland, and very shortly after that in the Gaelic parts of Ireland, each following their own class. So aristocrats in Anglo-Norman Ireland would soon follow aristocratic trends in England. Fairly soon they would be copied by upper class women in the Gaelic areas. Townspeople in Ireland would quickly follow English fashions. Though there were no proper towns in Gaelic areas there were still craftsmen and traders.

Eileen Power examines the scanty evidence from England and concludes that a fair number of women could read and write English. It is not obvious how boys of the same class was taught English when most of those who were educated were taught Latin. She concludes that aristocratic women and the better off bourgeoisie learned to read and write English (Power, 76-86). Leyser notes that mothers taught their daughters to read and write. The Statute of Artificers (1406) explicitly allowed the education of girls in schools (Leyser, 138). It would seem however that by Chaucer's time (d. 1400) boys who were taught Latin were also given some instruction in reading and writing English though the principal language of education was Latin. John Wycliffe (1382) certainly considered that there was need for an English translation of the Vulgate.

Knowledge of reading and writing Gaelic seems to have been widespread in Gaelic areas among the upper classes. The clergy conducted their schools in Latin for all the theological and liturgical works they needed to read were in Latin. But there was also a great learned class, who along with the clergy and the nobility formed the privileged castes. An ability to read and write Gaelic was a requirement for entry into the bardic schools (Dowling, 10).

Grammar Schools

Throughout the whole Middle Ages Latin was the language of the learned and upper classes. It was the language of diplomacy, of law, and of learning. As late as the 17th century Isaac Newton was writing his chief scientific work in Latin. Latin, or as they were called, grammar schools, appeared before vernacular schools. In the Dark Ages, the cathedral and monasteries kept the Latin language alive. St Benedict in his *Rule* presupposes that monks will be able to read spiritual books. A young boy would be started with Psalm 1, v.1 *Beatus vir qui non abiit in consilio impiorum,* (Blessed is the man that walks not in the counsel of the wicked), to memorise by heart and then write it. In Ireland, up until the end of the Middle Ages, this was the normal way to learn to speak and write Latin. The standard textbook was the *Ars Grammatica* of Aelius Donatus, the teacher of St Jerome. This was probably in use in Ireland as well. All the religious houses would have taught their members in this way.

It is known that in this period some medieval monasteries maintained schools; a report in 1539 mentioned six which taught English including the Cistercian houses in Dublin, Great Connell (Kildare) and Jerpoint and the nunnery of Grace Dieu for girls; there was also a school in

Christ Church, Dublin. Outside The Pale schools were attached to monasteries of Third Order Regular Franciscans whose system in Ireland was preferred to the cathedral and chantry schools in England. There were other collegiate churches [with schools] founded in the later Middle Ages (de Breffney, *A Cultural Encyclopaedia*, 'Education'). With regard to England Bolton notes that though the purpose of grammar schools was to teach Latin, the full curriculum of the *trivium* and *quadrivium* was probably taught only in monastery schools. The study of Latin grammar included rhetoric and poetry (Bolton, xxi). It is not clear however where the bulk of the clergy acquired the Latin that was essential for any office above the humble rural parish priest.

Higher Education

No university was founded in Ireland in the Middle Ages, so Irishmen wishing to proceed further had to go abroad. Oxford was the favourite university and the Inns of Court in London for those studying Common Law. The secular clergy preferred the study of civil and canon law leaving theology and scripture to the religious Orders. In the 14th century medical students began to go to the Continent for further study (Nichols, 113). A papal bull was obtained in 1312 to establish a *studium generale* or university in Dublin and Archbishop Bicknor put the plan into effect but it was not successful. In 1467 Parliament was held by the Earl of Desmond who backed a plan for a University in Drogheda. Accused of being a traitor by consorting and supporting the Irish he was found guilty and beheaded, which probably explains why the plan was not proceeded with. Walter Fitzsimon, archbishop of Dublin tried to get a university erected in St Patrick's Cathedral in the 1490s but was unsuccessful. In 1518 a college established by the Earl of Kildare at Maynooth was approved by the then archbishop of Dublin, William Rokeby. The Irish universities were not supported with ambitious clerics seemingly preferring to study in England.

Gaelic Schools

The learned classes were very important in ancient Ireland and were still very well endowed with land. They were the traditional purveyors of legal, historical, poetical, and medical lore. Such lore was handed down in families and it is not clear if they began to conduct schools. If they did they would be open only to members of the same class of scholar. It is quite possible that a leading brehon could take as scholars brehons from other parts of Ireland. Dowling quotes Richard Stanyhurst that schools of medicine and law were maintained where several young men lay on straw and committed Hippocrates and the Civil Law to heart, but cast some doubt as to whether they were studying Latin texts. They could have been translations of the Latin texts. He also quotes a description of a bardic school, where again the students lay on their beds. These were presumably in the wooden thatched hall of the master (Dowling, 9, 15). There is some evidence that some efforts were being made to incorporate more recent scholarship from the Continent. It is clear that quite a high standard of scholarship could be maintained by memory alone even in the least prepossessing huts. All received a basic training in spelling, grammar and metrics (Simms, 'Bardic Schools').

Art and Architecture

Some stone churches had been built in Ireland before 1100, but they seem to have been plain affairs following a simple plan common on the Continent in Merovingian times. (Harbison, Potter, Sheehy, p. 80) Architecture revived at the same time as Church reform, and the first essay in the Romanesque style was probably in Lismore about 1110 (*op. cit.* p. 81). The Cistercians who came to Mellifont in 1140 introduced the Burgundian Transitional style. Boyle abbey in Roscommon built at the end of the century is regarded as a better example of the early Cistercian churches. At Inch Abbey (c. 1190) lancet Gothic was introduced. From 1150 to 1250 was one of the most important periods of Irish architecture. Like in the nineteenth century almost every church was rebuilt, or if none existed one was provided. The relative poverty of Ireland meant that architecture had to be kept as simple as possible. The results were competent rather than outstanding. The two great cathedrals in wealthy Dublin were the exception. The coming of Norman knights and noblemen as local lords in Ireland was to provide a fresh stimulus. But they introduced nothing radically different. Metalwork of a high standard was still being produced. Noteworthy are the shrine made for St Patrick's bell and the Cross of Cong. The powerful Viking influence on local art reached its peak in the first half of the century. The Irish craftsmen preferred to develop the Hiberno-Norse style rather than adopt the contemporary Romanesque style. There are however few surviving example of medieval artwork.

Health and Medicine

Diseases

Little study has been done on the health of the population. In many cases, especially among the poor, the greatest cause of death was probably starvation, not all caused by crop failure. The Four Horsemen of the Apocalypse, War, Famine, Plague, and Death (*Revelation*, 6) were linked and commonplace. The first to die in famines were those at the bottom of the social heap. Their land would be taken by relatives of chiefs. Over the centuries chiefly families always had a better chance of survival which explains why so many people in Ireland bear the surnames of medieval chiefs.

The plague would have been what was later called famine fever or typhus. Ague, a form of malaria, was common in Ireland in Tudor times, but as in England, natives of marshy areas may have been largely immune to it. Dysentery was common in later armies and may have been present. But it is largely a problem for stationary forces. Leprosy and smallpox were common in the Middle Ages. There were occasional visitations of foreign plagues, the Black Death being the most notorious. (See also the next section.) Wounds from battle or hunting among the privileged classes would have received the first attention of the physicians.

Remedies

In Gaelic Ireland healers were among the privileged classes. Healing ran in families, with traditional lore handed down in the family. There is some evidence that efforts were made in the Middle Ages to incorporate the ancient treatises like those of Galen. The **Rosa Anglica**, the mediaeval medical text-book of John of Gaddesden dealt with Tertian Fever, Sanguine Fever, Ephemera, Hectica, Cardiaca, Apostema, Lethargo, Hernia, Paralysis, Dropsy, Smallpox, Arthritica. It was translated from Latin into Irish. To the end of the Middle Ages, however, and far into the Renaissance the three factors, ancient folk elements, degraded classical material, and Arabian contributions, can all be discerned. They are discernible in the work which we have before us (Irish Texts Society, **Cumann Na Sgribheann Gaedhilge**, vol. xxv, [1923] 1929).

Irish medicine was obviously no better and no worse than English medicine at the time. For sprains: Get cow dung and boil it with milk. Make a plaster of this mixture, and apply. For stings: Mix horse dung with blue clay, and apply to part stung. The fact that the experts attributed diseases to an imbalance of the four humours, blood, yellow bile, black bile, and phlegm did not help. In the universities the teachers were clerics, and as clerics were forbidden to shed blood surgery was excluded from the curriculum. Still more dissection. Regular blood-letting was left to the barber surgeons. The barbers of former times were also surgeons and dentists. In addition to haircutting, hairdressing, and shaving, barbers performed surgery, bloodletting and leeching, fire cupping, enemas, and the extraction of teeth. Thus they were called barber surgeons, and they formed their first organization in 1094 (*Wikipedia*, 'Barber'). They also tended the wounded after a battle. In Gaelic areas the distinction did not apply.

It was recognized that much could be done by good nursing, and hospices were often attached to monasteries. They at least provided a bed to lie on, warmth, food, and religious consolation. Women were accepted as healers (Malcolm). In the home it was the duty of women to look after the sick (Power, 85).

Science and Knowledge and Learning

The period was not distinguished by works of literature, law, or science, though the usual copying and redacting of older manuscripts continued. The *Book of Leinster* was compiled in Leinster in Dermot MacMurrough's time. There seems little doubt however that greater attention was being paid to the study of the Bible, of Canon Law, and theological works in general. This was particularly so in the school of Armagh. The study of medicine continued, as it was to continue until the seventeenth century, by students who learned traditional texts by heart. On the standard of medical lore see the preceding section.

The Bible was the great encyclopaedia of the age. Most of the cathedrals and larger monasteries probably had a full copy of it. The version used was the Latin version of St Jerome known as the Vulgate or common version. The liturgy prescribed it to be read in order throughout the year, beginning on Septuagesima Sunday. In the course of a lifetime a monk or priest would acquire a great deal of heterogeneous information. History-writing commenced in Palestine at the time of the Davidic monarchy about 1,000 B.C. and there are quite detailed accounts of the Israelite kingdoms and their neighbours, and of the Egyptian, Assyrian, Babylonian, Greek, and Roman Empires.

Warfare was endemic and the hearers and readers of the Bible in the Middle Ages could picture exactly what was involved. The revolts of the petty kingdoms at the death of an emperor mirrored what happened in Ireland. Towns might not exist in many parts of Ireland so people could derive their ideas of town life from the Bible. Genealogies, which established a man's place in society, abounded in the Bible and in Irish traditional lore. The legal code in the Book of Exodus chapters 21-23; Deuteronomy 21-23 has close resemblances to the Brehon Code. Both give examples of judgments given in a rural but rather violent society.

With regard to law, the Code of Justinian was unknown though some ecclesiastical writers in the late Roman period had probably been familiar with it. With regard to Canon Law, some cathedrals and monasteries may have had a copy of the *Collectio Canonum Hibernensis* (English: Irish Collection of Canon law) (or CCH), an Irish ecclesiastical work written in Latin before 725. It is the work of two Irish scholars working in 8th century Europe, Cú Chuimne of Iona (died 747) and Ruben of Dairinis (d.725). Its title reflects its origin as a compilation of over two hundred years worth of Canon Law and synodal decrees.

Almost every great monastery and cathedral would have a member sufficiently versed in mathematics to compute the date of Easter. This was by this date a mechanical process; if you followed the procedures you got the right answer (See *Wikipedia,* 'Computus'). We must bear in mind that the Julian calendar was in use and Roman numerals. The Jewish seven day week was imposed on the Roman months and divisions of months.

There was a large body of other writings in Ireland none of which can be considered scientific. The compiling of Annals continued: The Annals of Boyle, of Clonmacnoise, of Connacht, of Innisfallen, of Loch Cé and of Ulster. Books were scarce as they all had to be copied individually by hand. Copying though was a great industry in its own right. The library of a monastery or cathedral was a book box (*bibliotheca*). In general the learned classes enjoyed their privileged status up to the 16th century and continued handing on their bodies of traditional lore, their genealogies, and their mythological tales and so on. The clergy kept abreast of what was being taught in Oxford and other universities. There was no outstanding figure unless one counts Duns Scotus.

Lifestyle

General

General behaviour was less formal. At the time of the Renaissance both the Spanish Court and the Papal Courts vied with each other and borrowed from each other with regard to formality. We can see the culmination of this trend on state occasions and especially in England when the queen attends a state function in a cathedral. This formality is matched by that of the clergy. All rise or sit in unison. Even in ordinary Sunday services the rites are now carried out exactly in the prescribed forms; all members of the congregation, rise, sing, pray, sit or kneel at the same time.

In the Middle Ages there was less emphasis on exactness. Soldiers walked rather than marched. They streamed along as the wideness of the path allowed. They formed themselves for battle in groups. Strict lines were not required. Soldiers arranged themselves in such a way that they had the greatest freedom to swing their weapons. In Roman times strict drill required that the soldiers stand close together and so only the points of the swords could be used to thrust. A battleaxe or claymore required room to swing and slash. A movement was commenced among the armoured knights to keep their horses closely bunched and to rely on the thrust of the lance and this proved highly effective.

Life was hard for most people. But this does not mean that they were mournful or sad. Still less that they were oppressed by an oppressive religion. It was noted in pre-Famine Ireland that the very poor who scarcely had enough to eat or cover themselves were happy and carefree, given to singing, dancing, and listening to music. The numerous Church festivals gave everyone time to rest, take part in games, or singing, or simply to talk.

Church festivals would have seemed haphazard, but everyone knew the rules and what had to be done, but there was no need for everyone to do everything at the same time. One could hear a mass, listen to a preacher, venerate the relics, take part in a procession, watch a procession, join in a litany, visit the ale shop or pie stall, give alms, do all of these or some of them as one fancied. Some order was kept by the tolling of the church bells every three hours. The sacristans could measure the hours by hourglasses or by watching the sun, but ceremonies were not strictly timed. Nobody had a watch.

Whoever could afford it used colour. Monasteries and cathedrals were painted in colours that later generations associated with travelling circuses. The rich wore the most colourful garments. The horses of the wealthy were richly caparisoned. Likewise their ships. Secular and religious occasions vied in the use of colour. It was an age of pageantry.

In general life was lived outdoors. This was particularly true of men and boys. But even for women much work was done outdoors. Houses were for shelter at night and when it was raining. In monasteries monks lived outside in the open cloisters and went into special buildings for special purposes, the church, the refectory, the dormitory, etc. which were linked by the cloisters. The buildings at first had no glass in the windows, though glass was becoming important for buildings like churches. That did not mean that buildings like dormitories had glass in their windows. The old Gaelic or Anglo-Saxon hall had a fire inside which probably provided the only light. As monasteries were founded further and further north in Europe the monks added layer upon layer of clothes or wore furs. This last option was denied to the Cistercians.

They were allowed a small room with a fire called a calefactory into which monks could enter for brief periods.

Brehon Law had a relaxed attitude towards sexual relations which was totally at variance with Canon Law. One of the objectives of the Hildebrandine reformers was the enforcement of its laws with regard to marriage, for marriage was a sacrament and thus a major concern of the Church. It did not succeed then or indeed until long after the Reformation. Chiefs were notorious for divorcing wives as local policy prompted them. They often had numerous illegitimate children, which was socially very important for they all had to be provided with at least a farm of land, and that had to be taken from somebody. In the course of the Middle Ages the Church became more and more strict with regard to the forbidden degrees of marriage, but the prohibition was relaxed by the Fourth Vatican Council in 1215 to the prohibition of the marriage of third cousins or closer. Brehon Law allowed the marriage of first cousins. Most Irish marriages were invalid in Canon Law and remained so.

Wealth

The Lorenz curve of income distribution displays the inequalities in the distribution of wealth. It is well-known that the more primitive and warlike the society the more likely it is the curve is highly kinked, for the warriors and nobles grab as much of the wealth they can. Where there is allodial possession of land, or where there are numerous manufacturers and traders wealth is better distributed and the curve is less kinked. There is a wealthy middle class. It is quite possible to have a situation where 10% of the population has 90% of the wealth and the income which flows from it. This explains the enormous wealth of the pharaohs of Egypt and the riches buried in some royal graves. The wealth-owning classes were the warrior chiefs and their families, the higher clergy who usually belonged to those families, and the skilled craftsmen, especially those making weapons or ornaments of silver or gold.

In Gaelic areas, where the bulk of the land had passed into the hands of the chiefs by the end of the Middle Ages, and the cultivators were subjected to numerous exactions, the disposable income of the cultivators was not likely to be far above starvation level. The curve would be correspondingly highly kinked. Problems of measuring this are acute but the notion of the Lorenz curve should always be kept in mind. The lives of the poor could be made miserable by excessive exactions by the rich, and these became increasingly common. But judging by primitive societies nowadays where exactions were less they were probably both happy and happy-go-lucky. Every so often, perhaps at intervals of several years there might be great mortality caused by plagues or crop failures. But the other years would be good and the population would grow again. The worst place to be was in an area targeted for acquisition and so having annual wasting raids.

Wealth in Gaelic society was measured and displayed in the number of cattle a chief possessed; in Anglo-Norman societies in the number of acres he owned. The Gaelic chief farmed out cattle from which he expected an annual return; the feudal lord farmed out portions of land. Expensive or precious objects might be used to be worn, but also they had their uses as presents to subordinates, or to members of the chief's family. For some people like robbers, the only value of precious objects was the weight of gold, silver or precious stones they contained and were likely to be chopped up for sale.

A totally flat Lorenz curve is not necessarily a good thing. A certain accumulation of wealth enables the construction of large buildings for example, the employment of quarrymen, carters, stone carvers and stone masons, woodsmen, carpenters, metalworkers, tile and glass makers, merchants, shipbuilders and sailors, and so on who would not otherwise been employed. The building of churches and the commissioning of works of art creates wealth. But the employment of this surplus to hire foreign mercenaries could only be destructive.

The number of stone tower houses built and the increasing use of mercenaries at the end of the Middle Ages would seem to indicate a concentration of wealth in the hands of the lesser lords. In Tudor times money was needed by these lords for the purchase of firearms and gunpowder, though the making of a musket was not beyond the skill of a local metalworker.

It is generally agreed that the 14th century was a disastrous one both in England and in Ireland for the unending series of plagues and famines of which the Black Death was only the most famous. But the problem started earlier in Ireland with the invasions of the Bruces from Scotland (1313-18). Unable to capture most of the important towns they contented themselves with wasting the countryside. Many local Irish chiefs took advantage of the troubles of the Government to go wasting and spoiling on their own account. The revenues of the Government fell off sharply. But there is an interesting discussion in Barry's work with regard to whether the decline was reversed in the 15th century (Barry, 168-98). The customs receipts of the central government had certainly fallen. Large parts of march lands were certainly waste, and many of the resurgent Gaelic families like the O'Mores and O'Tooles were frankly parasitic, neither producing much themselves not allowing others to do so. A growing demand for labour in England after the Black Death resulted in emigration from Anglo-Norman areas. But the heartlands of the Anglo-Norman settlers were in good condition. The pattern of trade altered from the export of cereals to the export of animals, hides, and wool. Not only were tower houses being widely built but there was also a resurgence in church-building. There was a shift in power away from central Government to the provincial power bases of the Anglo-Irish lords and Gaelic chiefs. It is fair to conclude that in Ireland as in England there was an economic revival in the 15th century. Then, as for many centuries into the future, an economic surplus in Ireland depended almost exclusively on access to English markets.

Housing, Clothing and Diet

Housing, like elsewhere in Europe was made of wood. Stone was very expensive and rarely used except by the great builders, the barons and the ecclesiastics. Towards the end of the Middle Ages, some Gaelic lords began constructing tower houses like those on the Scottish borders. As in England, and unlike in Norway, it is unlikely that tall timber was available. Gaelic chiefs did not build great wooden palaces, but contented themselves with the old fashioned hall or *aula* until the end of the Middle Ages. The shape of the hall changed from round to rectangular, and was probably about 30 feet long. When Henry II was expected to arrive in Ireland, Strongbow had a palace hastily constructed of wattle erected for him just outside the walls (Roche, 101).

For the Norman lords, their first motte-and-bailey castles introduced no new principles except the building of a defensible mound, fenced about on top, which was easy to defend. The hall in the bailey was traditional. Gradually however the living quarters were built into the defensive structure, which was now made of stone masonry. This was the castle proper. King John in particular was responsible for building castles at strategic points. The de Lacy castle at their 'capital' at Trim, Co. Meath appears in all the textbooks. Most of the stone buildings in the Medieval period were monasteries. Towards the end of the Middle Ages a fashion for building tower houses grew, perhaps more for ostentation than necessity (de Breffney and ffolliott, Harbison, and de Breffney, B.).

Many of the houses were constructed of wattle covered with mud or clay and whitewashed. Inside there would have been a fireplace, not necessarily for cooking, and perhaps a few chairs and beds. But most people would have sat down or slept on straw or rushes. There would have been no tables for dining. As late as the end of the 19th century some of the people on remote islands were sleeping of beds of straw or ferns and had no furniture in their huts and no knowledge of carpentry (*Irish Industrial Journal* 26 June 1920). By the ninth or tenth century, a few farmhouses may have built of stone. There would be other buildings, some of them lean-tos inside the rath or lios. Almost all work was done outdoors, and these works would have included spinning, weaving, cooking, metalwork, copying manuscripts, and so on.

The cottages of the ordinary people were probable small and flimsy and constructed of wattle and daub with light poles covered with branches and rushes for a roof. Hazel woods would have been common in Ireland and the trees easily coppiced to produce numerous strong thin rods. The colonists doubtless used the same wattle and daub or post and wattle techniques they were used to in England. The lesser farm houses usually had two rooms, one for people and the other for animals, which were liable to be stolen at night by the numerous outlaws and cattle rustlers. (In cases of a cattle raid the houses would have been abandoned and the livestock scattered into hiding places in the woods.) Town houses with a timber frame with infills of wattle and daub as in English towns would have been built in the towns until the end of the Middle Ages. If a fire started it could easily consume an entire town. The town houses would have resembled those still seen in English towns like Chester. Though still built in wood and thatched later town houses would have been larger and better built than the flimsy Viking houses (O'Sullivan).

It is difficult to get representative picture of Irish **clothing** in this period. It is fair to assume that the style of dress did not differ significantly from that in England, though perhaps in places up to a hundred years out of date. The form of the dress was common to all classes, only the materials and dyes differing.

As with most things, with wealth so unevenly distributed, the rich would have had splendid garments of both wool and linen, and often brightly dyed. As all the dyes were vegetable dyes, they would have to re-dyed frequently. The dress of the poor (and the Franciscans and

Cistercians) was of undyed wool. Black and purple were the most expensive dyes and favoured by the clergy. The ancient 'Celtic' dress resembled the Roman, and consisted of a long tunic, and a blanket which the Romans called a *toga* and in Ireland a *brat*. There is no indication that it resembled the belted plaid of the Highlands of Scotland at a later date. Breeches were used by horsemen both in Rome and Ireland. St Benedict in his *Rule* prescribed that each monk be given two sets of garments, a tunic and a cowl, stockings and sandals. A cowl was a hooded garment, and the hood was to become universal in the Middle Ages. He also prescribed that in winter the cowl should be warm and shaggy, but lighter in summer. (The Benedictine *cuculla* or cowl was a long sleeved garment with a hood. The term cowl was also used to describe a much smaller garment covering only the head and shoulders.) This was doubtless the attire of working people in the late Roman Empire. The tunic was knee length. This remained the custom for warriors going into battle and for workmen. For the nobility, men and women, the clergy and the learned classes the tunic gradually got longer to reach the ankles. Shoes were moccasin-like one-piece construction without separate or additional soles and heels. For harder outdoor wear a thicker leather was used. Armies marching may have preferred to go bare foot. As the roads were just of beaten earth the wear on the sole may not have been as great as one might expect. The thick-soled Roman open sandal seems to have disappeared from Northern Europe.

All classes wore garments of essentially the same type, distinction in rank being indicated by the costliness of the material and its ornamentation. Ladies in high position spent much time carding, spinning and needlework. Then as now the rich used the finest wool (Brooke, *English Costume, (1)* p 10). Women's costumes were much the same only longer. Ecclesiastics too tended to favour long sleeved garments, which remain official to this day. It is interesting to note that Cistercian rules in the Middle Ages when the monks lived in open unglazed cloisters they were, in northern latitudes, allowed to wear three tunics and three cucullas simultaneously as they were not allowed to use fur. Doubtless all classes wore as many garments as they could afford in harsh weather. Doubtless too threadbare or lighter forms were used in summer. Thickly woven woollen *brats* or cloaks were highly esteemed. As with the Romans a form of trousers was worn on horseback and for some outdoor activities (Fitzgerald, 'Clothing' in Duffy, *Medieval Ireland*). As they were not mentioned in the Rule the Cistercians disallowed coats, fur garments, linen shirts, hoods too and drawers (http://www.scourmont.be/exordium/exdtext1.pdf). These therefore were probably common at least among the clergy.

The differences in attire between English-speaking and Gaelic-speaking areas were not great, but it was obviously noticeable. If a Gaelic-speaking countryman came to a town fair he was distinguishable by his dress, and some of the Statutes of Kilkenny were directed against such attire. In Tudor times the different attires were distinguished as 'civil' (from the towns) Irish and 'wilde' (from uncultivated lands) Irish. The later medieval and Renaissance periods were times of rapidly changing forms of dress as the modern style of men's dress is evolving and began to give way to the doublet and hose. From illustrations it is often difficult to know how much of the lower part of the legs was being covered, the lower parts like stockings, leggings, or gaiters, the upper part like drawers, *femoralia* or *brachae,* or both.

Like elsewhere in north western Europe **diet** was conditioned by what could be grown or gathered in the neighbourhood. It was possible to transport cereals up to 20 miles from an outlying farm or grange in oxcarts on the rough country tracks. That was about the limit, though the English colonists improved the roads in the eastern part of Ireland. Transport by boat or ship was easier, but nearly all the Irish rivers had shallow fast-flowing stretches near the coast. The climate was warmer in the early part of the Middle Ages and most crops then known could be grown in most parts of Ireland. As in other matters it can be assumed that knowledge of farming spread easily enough. The economy everywhere was based on mixed farming. The precise method of tillage, open field, great plough, light plough, or spade cultivation would not affect the nature of the seeds planted. It was noted that cattle were kept primarily for milk though obviously bull calves would have to be killed, probably in the autumn. Similarly with pigs, sheep and goats. Diet varied between the classes, the great lords getting everything the country could produce, and the cottagers getting little more than oaten bread and porridge. At a great banquet, whether of spiritual or temporal lords there would have been several courses of beef, pork, mutton, and fish. Most ordinary families lacked a metal or pottery cooking pot, so food had to be baked or roasted.

As was common in the Middle Ages every local source of food was exploited. The countryside was combed for fruits, nuts and berries. Fish were caught in the rivers usually at weirs which would have been carefully controlled by the local lords. Seashores searched for shellfish, and it can be presumed that these were controlled also by the local lords. Sea-fishing seems to have been confined to small boats. Marshes would have provided a constant supply of wildfowl. Specialist cottagers like wildfowlers would have to exchange most of their catch for oatmeal and whey. Some root crops like an early variety of carrots may have been grown in gardens to add to soups. As usual in primitive society quite a large part of the cereal crop was reserved for making ale. No hops were added as a preservative so ale had to be constantly brewed for it went off very quickly. Pretty notes that a manor in southern England had about 35 different kinds of food from the fields, gardens and woodlands. Irish manors may have been more restricted, and the farms of the Gaelic lords even more restricted but still with quite a variety. The diet of the poor, as in pre-Famine Ireland, would have been limited and monotonous and very likely to become inadequate if there was any failure in an important crop.

Popular Beliefs and Superstitions

Beliefs and superstitions in Ireland were little different from those in Britain and the rest of Europe as mentioned earlier. The four principal pagan festivals, like those elsewhere in Europe, survived in a Christian guise. The old year ended and began in November with the feast of *Samhain* which became All Saints' Day (All Hallows) and All Souls' Day. The rites still survive as Halloween. It was a commemoration and propitiation of the dead. The next feast was *Imbolc*, at the beginning of February. In Ireland it became the Feast of St. Brigid (February 1) and like the rest of Europe, the Feast of the Purification of Our Lady (February 2) Candlemas Day. Next came *Bealtine* (Beltane (the Feast of fire) which became May Day which did not attract a Christian feast. It was celebrated with bonfires as was also Midsummer's Day which became the Feast of St John the Baptist. Finally, came *Lughnasa*, the harvest festival which became Lady Day the feast of the Assumption on 15th August. The Church everywhere made great efforts to 'Christianize' these feasts with lights, processions, and ceremonies, knowing that if they did not the people would celebrate them anyway.

Languages

Towards the end of the twelfth century there were two major languages written and spoken in Ireland. One was Gaelic, spoken only in Ireland and parts of the Highlands of Scotland. The other was the universal language of Europe, Latin. Clerics in all west European countries learned to write and speak Latin as a matter of course. They had no difficulty in communicating with clergy in other countries. Some amount of Norse, Norman French (the dialect of Normandy) and English may have been spoken in the various ports. The Normans then brought in French which became the language of the upper classes, and their colonists brought in English. The latter replaced Gaelic as the working class language in areas of Norman occupation. It suited the purpose of the Gaelic and Norman lords to marry into each other's families. Women were married off to suit policy. We can be sure that many people on either side spoke both French and Gaelic at least in the earlier part of the Middle Ages. Only later did Ireland split into Gaelic and English-speaking areas. By the time of the Statutes of Kilkenny (1367) there were probably many in eastern Ireland who spoke only English and in western areas who spoke only Gaelic. But great chiefs like the O'Neills were probably always bi-lingual, and likewise the great earls.

As the Middle Ages advanced so too did the speaking of English and Norman French. Royal commissions were issued in Latin in 1361, the language of (clerical) administration (Connolly, 106). French, as in England, would have been spoken by the nobility and gentry, while the common colonists would mostly have spoken English. Protests to Edward III in 1341 were still being written in French (Frame 'English Policies', 97). Over most of Leinster and all of north Munster French would have been the official language and the language of the ruling classes and even of the manor courts. From Carrickfergus in Antrim to Tralee in Kerry French was spoken. Towards the end of the Middle Ages, as in Britain, the upper classes abandoned Norman French. By that time its pronunciation would have been very different from that of Paris. Some of the upper classes began to speak English and others Gaelic. There are no obvious reasons why a language survives in one place and dies in another. Why for example did French die out in Munster instead of becoming the dominant language?

As in England, and about the same time, French disappeared, as the upper classes began to use the local vernacular. In those areas where colonists were numerous this became English. In others the Gaelic language was adopted or the people became bi-lingual. The households of the lords of Clanrickard in Connaught were probably completely Gaelic-speaking.

Women

As usual there are excellent studies from the better documented regions in England which give us a good idea of conditions in England which also apply to the colonised areas of Ireland, and also partly to Gaelic-speaking areas of Ireland. Such is the study by Simon Penn on female wage-earners in 14th century England. Eileen Power noted that there was a considerable excess of females in many European countries. We can assume however, that class for class, there was very little difference in the position and duties of women in Gaelic or Norman areas. A woman's work in the fields or in the house were very likely to be the same.

The ideal of what a woman's life should be, can, as so often the case in the Middle Ages, be found in that universally read book, the Bible. Two ideals were set out. One was for dedicated virgins or widows, and this usually meant retirement to a convent. The other was for married women.

Mulierem fortem quis inveniet procul et de ultimis finibus pretium eius

Confidit in ea cor viri sui et spoliis non indigebit.

10 The truly capable woman—who can find her? She is far beyond the price of pearls.

11 Her husband's heart has confidence in her; from her he will derive no little profit.

12 Advantage and not hurt she brings him all the days of her life.

13 She selects wool and flax, she does her work with eager hands.

14 She is like those merchant vessels, bringing her food from far away.

15 She gets up while it is still dark giving her household their food, giving orders to her serving girls.

16 She sets her mind on a field, then she buys it; with what her hands have earned she plants a vineyard.

17 She puts her back into her work and shows how strong her arms can be.

18 She knows that her affairs are going well; her lamp does not go out at night.

19 She sets her hands to the distaff, her fingers grasp the spindle.

20 She holds out her hands to the poor, she opens her arms to the needy.

21 Snow may come, she has no fears for her household, with all her servants warmly clothed.

22 She makes her own quilts, she is dressed in fine linen and purple.

23 Her husband is respected at the city gates, taking his seat among the elders of the land.

24 She weaves materials and sells them, she supplies the merchant with sashes.

25 She is clothed in strength and dignity, she can laugh at the day to come.

26 When she opens her mouth, she does so wisely; on her tongue is kindly instruction.

27 She keeps good watch on the conduct of her household, no bread of idleness for her.

28 Her children stand up and proclaim her blessed, her husband, too, sings her praises:

29 'Many women have done admirable things, but you surpass them all!'

30 Charm is deceitful, and beauty empty; the woman who fears Yahweh is the one to praise

31 Give her a share in what her hands have worked for, and let her works tell her praises at the city gates (Proverbs 31.10-31 *New Jerusalem Bible; Vulgate*).

The Proverbs were obviously written for wealthy families and it was precisely this kind of family which would read them in the Middle Ages. It is noteworthy that it has no specifically religious element, but deals with the ordinary duties of the wife of a fairly rich man, a man who sat on the town's or clan's council. Such a woman was never idle; she kept control of her tongue and was wise in counsel for young people whether her inferiors or equals.

Many women would have had to support themselves. But even married women (and daughters) worked at their husband's trade, and this was provided for in guild regulations which otherwise excluded women. Widows carried on their husband's trade (Power, 55). Working women were heavily involved in the spinning and weaving industries. They were also involved in retailing or huckstering in shops, and also involved in the preparation of food like pies for sale, and in the brewing of ale. Brewing was largely in the hands of women and carried out in small batches in their homes. Women were also involved on farms especially in gathering and binding sheaves at harvest time, planting beans, binding and stacking the sheaves, gleaning the stubble after the corn had been cut or tedding and cocking the hay following mowing. Women were also employed cleaning wheat for seed, hoeing, weeding, threshing, winnowing. Women were often employed in these jobs up to the 20th century. The wife of a cottager would have helped with all jobs. He would wield the sickle while she bound the sheaves and helped to carry them home in the evening. In the manufacture of cloth most work seems to have been done by women (Penn).

All the domestic work was done by women. This involved not only cooking, but gathering firewood, maintaining the fire, looking after the children and tending to the sick of the family. This would have included gathering the herbal remedies, or bartering for them (Power 86; Leyser 142). Teaching of girls to read and write English was left to women of the better classes in towns. Early in the Middle Ages some upper class women were taught Latin, but the study of Latin declined even in convents (Power, 86). Peasant girls like Joan of Arc were illiterate.

The legal position of women in the records normally refers to aristocratic women especially heiresses. The Church, since the days of the Apostles had reserved all offices in the Church to men, so in that sense, women were second class citizens. They were always welcomed as lay assistants. A lady of noble family might outrank the cleric and if she was abbess of an important abbey might be a very powerful person in her own right. At all levels status counted for much. Ladies of rank who entered a convent were automatically made abbesses or prioresses as it was inconceivable that she could be commanded by a person of lesser rank. Women often played a more important role than their legal status might imply. This was particularly true of the highest ranks. An example was the Empress Matilda (1102-67), mother of Henry II who became the first queen of England in her own right. Another prominent lady was Lady Margaret Beaufort (1443-1509), the mother of Henry VII.

With regard to property, and for the aristocratic classes that was the first consideration, the land was more important than the heiress. By feudal law women could inherit both property and titles in default of direct male heirs. The daughter of an earl became a countess *suo jure* while her husband became earl *iure uxoris*. Her inherited property passed from her father to her husband on the former's death. This remained the law until the end of the 19th century. Legally these applied to married women (*feme covert*) but not to unmarried women (*feme sole*). (*Feme = femme*). In practice ladies married to men of property had to be prepared to manage that property, which might be for years if her husband went on the crusades (Power, 42). Joan de Geneville, 2nd Baroness Geneville and Countess of March managed the estates of her executed husband, Roger Mortimer. Her grandmother Maud de Lacy was equally famous for managing her estates at Trim and Ludlow. A *femme sole* had the right to own property and make contracts in her own name. A woman in a town could become a *femme sole*, and her husband would then be her guardian, and she would be able to trade as if she were single, and allowed to make contracts and was responsible for her own debts.

There is this difficulty with regard to the situation of Irish women under Brehon Law and that was the brehon courts mostly did not keep records and the Brehon Code was obsolete almost as soon as it was compiled (before 900 AD). A wife's honour price was half that of her husband, so an officially married wife had the same status as an adult son still living at home. Status depended on property which could only be transmitted through male heirs. Women could get moveable goods from their father, but could only act in the courts through a male relative. Secondary wives or concubines had lesser rights. (In Common Law, primogeniture and the exclusion of bastards from succession ended plurality of wives.) Divorce remained common usually on the grounds of the nullity of the earlier marriage. The marriage dowry was regarded as important especially if it was a regiment of soldiers. But if it was in cash the money could be used to pay ransoms. Though Brehon Law moved more slowly than Common Law to harmonise with Canon Law, and may have met with greater resistance, the difference between the codes was not great. The wives of chiefs played much the same role as the wives of lords did in England (Simms, 'Women' in Duffy, *Medieval Ireland*). However, as the lands of a chief reverted to his *derb fine* on his death or expulsion, they were not inherited by his daughters.

The absence of towns in the Gaelic areas meant that the opportunities of markets and trades open to townswomen were not available to them. But it should be remembered that there was always a traditional equivalent in rural areas. Trades were handed down in families and presumably the women in those families were instructed in the trades. In place of regular markets there were occasional fairs where the exchange of common produce like butter, eggs, fish, wildfowl, nuts and fruit, etc could take place. Much trade was doubtless carried on at the back door of the 'big house' or its medieval equivalent. Prostitutes were often sole traders, who in the absence of urban centres travelled from place to place like other entertainers. Illiteracy among women was probably higher than in the towns, but like everything else, the better off families would have tried as best they could to keep up with the women in the towns. It must have been frustrating for the women in Ulster that the only shops even in Tudor times were in Dundalk and Carrickfergus and they could only go shopping when their husbands or fathers wanted to go shopping there. Otherwise they had to depend on the occasional merchant's ship to come to their shores.

One may perhaps judge the status of working women in Ireland with that of the women in the cattle-rearing cultures of east Africa. There, the bulk of agricultural work is done by women. The men undertook to look after the bulls and provide defence against animals and raiders. The women were responsible for putting the cattle into the fields, finding those that strayed, bringing them home in the evening, doing all the milking and food preparation, feeding the calves, and so on. If a cow escaped the women were collectively beaten and sent out to find it. When slaves were common, much of the tillage was done by them. Later it is likely that much of the ploughing, sowing, harvesting, threshing, storing and grinding was done by women. The betaghs however would have had to do their work on the lord's land personally. They probably also held and guided the great plough though a wife or child could carry the goad. All of these would have been illiterate. Unlike in the Anglo-Norman districts there would have been no escape into the towns. Brehon Law was not concerned with these. Women in such cultures are an economic asset so a bride price must be paid for them. Women in the upper classes are an economic liability so a dowry must be given.

Part 4

History of Ireland
1170 to 1509

Chapter 8

1170-1215

Writing the history of these centuries is somewhat easier than writing the history for the preceding centuries. Now at last Ireland had a central Government and a capital to form the basis of a central administration. Though often ignored it was always there. In the preceding centuries there was only a mythical centre of government. Tara was an abandoned but symbolic site. The kingship of Tara or high kingship merely meant a right to tribute and an obligation to follow the high kings hosting, both of which were often disregarded.

The period can easily be divided into 4 phases, the 12th century until the death of John in 1216, the 13th century, the Age of Prosperity until the Bruce invasion in 1315, the 14th century, the Age of Disasters until the death of Richard II in 1399, and the 15th century, the Age of Recovery. These four phases were not peculiar to Ireland but were applicable to the whole of Western Europe.

The first phase is concerned with how the kings of England tried to deal with the rather unwanted situation which arose in Ireland when a potential powerful marcher earl, Strongbow, established himself in a major sub-kingdom in Ireland. Their main preoccupation was to prevent any chief or lord, Gaelic or Norman, from becoming too powerful. Attempts too were made to establish an administration based on counties as increasingly it was in England, rather than on feudal lordships. The two middle phases lay between the last visit of John in 1210 and the second visit of Richard II in 1399. In this long period of nearly 200 years no English king felt it necessary to visit Ireland. The 13th and 14th centuries were however very different. In the first Anglo-Norman power, customs, language, laws and commerce were expanding in a century of prosperity. In the second, all these were in retreat though not to the extent that they were at times portrayed. The 15th century saw an economic recovery and the increase in power and influence of the three great earldoms. It also saw the increase in direct involvement of the great Irish lords in English affairs. This latter was settled up to a point by Poyning's Law but could only remain stable if the great earls were willing to abide by that law. Precisely that situation that Henry II and John had tried to prevent had arisen when the English monarchy was involved in the Wars of the Roses. Henry VII tolerated it but Henry VIII did not.

The apparent Gaelic revival in the 14th century was caused chiefly by the fragmentation and incessant squabbling among the Anglo-Norman lords which prevented them from forming a rich and powerful centre to dominate the whole island. Yet by the 15th century wealth and power was concentrated in only three earldoms, and in the counties of The Pale. No Gaelic chiefdom could have stood up against the Great Earl of Kildare or his son. There is little doubt that the weakness of the power of the Government in the 14th century was caused partially by deteriorating climatic conditions and numerous epidemics. Yet this would not have mattered had the earls been able to work together and control parliament between themselves.

England and Wales 1066-1170

In 1066, William of Falaise, Duke of Normandy, won the battle of Hastings. Some of the English noblemen submitted to him and retained their property. Those who did not submit had their property seized and given to William's followers who had accompanied him in the expectation of receiving such feudal fiefs from him. Also, when an English noble died without issue, William I took the property into his own hands and gave the fiefs to his followers. He was careful, in giving fiefs to ensure that they consisted of several properties in different parts of England to prevent a grantee from easily building up a local force against himself. He was well aware of what had happened in France. As bishoprics became vacant he secured the appointment of French clerics to them. For the next few centuries French became the language of administration. When Northumbrian nobles resisted him he carried out what was called the Harrying of the North in which all property was systematically ravaged and burnt, reducing the lords to poverty. He came to an agreement with the kings of the Scots who recognised his suzerainty over Scotland and were left unmolested.

In the early Middle Ages those who held land *in capite* from the king were called his barons, meaning that they owed him feudal service. The land they received was called a barony. An earl had originally been an Anglo-Saxon rank, but the Norman kings began to bestow the title of earl on barons as a mark of honour but with no increase in powers. (Nominally the title earl should have indicated powers over a county while a baron had only a barony.) By the end of the Middle Ages the most powerful noblemen were earls. In Parliament, after the introduction of commoners, knights and burgesses, earls and barons sat in the 'House' of Lords.

With regard to Wales William made no attempt to conquer it. To provide for the defence of England from raids by the Welsh he departed from his own rule and erected three powerful fiefdoms along the Welsh border, the Welsh marches. Towards the south, facing the southern Welsh chiefdom of Deheubarth, he placed the William FitzOsbern as 1st Earl of Hereford, whose followers began pushing into south Wales. Towards the north, Hugh of Avranches was created Earl of Chester and he began pushing into north Wales. In between them Roger *de* Montgomery was made Earl of Shrewsbury who pushed into Montgomeryshire. The town of Shrewsbury had been earlier seized from the Welsh chiefs of Powys, and they wanted it back. The king gave extensive powers to these marcher lords, what was later called palatine jurisdiction. Of chief interest to Ireland was the fact that some Norman lords like Hugh *de* Lacy and Philip *de* Worcester had extensive estates in the marches.

In the south of Wales the Normans made good progress taking advantage of the incessant warfare among the Welsh chiefs. Deheubart was under a strong king, Rhys *ap* Tewdwr who however faced strong opposition. Twice he was restored to his position by military help from Ireland (Evans, 161-166). In 1088 Bernard of Newmarch advanced from Hereford into Deheubart in the valley of the Usk, seized the cantref of Brycheiniog and established the lordship of Brecknock which he proceeded to subinfeudate to his knights. Its main castle was at Brecon (Aberhonddu). He founded the town of Brecon under the walls. Typically he married a Welsh lady called Nest. After his death the lordship passed to William *de* Braose (Thomas, 3-12). Bernard signally defeated Rhys *ap* Tewdwr in 1093, Rhys being killed in the battle. The whole of Deheubart in south Wales was now open to the Normans (Evans, 167). A string of manors was placed along the coast as far as Pembroke where a castle was built.

Henry I appointed Gerald of Windsor as the castellan of Pembroke Castle, from whom descended one of the most famous Irish names in the Middle Ages, the Fitzgeralds or Geraldines. Henry, it seems, had a relationship with Nest (Nesta) a daughter of Rhys *ap* Tewdwr of Deheubart and she bore him a son. He then married her to Gerald of Windsor to whom she bore several children. The boys were brought up as Norman knights and became lords of cantreds.

Her immediate descendants who came with Strongbow to Ireland were later named 'the brood of Nesta'. Her son by Henry I of England was called Henry *fitz Roy*; his sons were Meiler and Robert *fitz* Henry.

Married off to Gerald of Windsor, her children by him were William, Maurice who joined Strongbow, and David, bishop of St David's. Her daughter Angarad *de* Windsor married William *de* Barry and her sons were Robert, Philip, Walter, and Gerald *de* Barry, *Giraldus Cambrensis*. Philip and Robert went with Strongbow. Another daughter was the mother of Miles *de* Cogan. By Stephen, Constable of Cardigan, she had Robert *fitz* Stephen. A grand-daughter also called Nest married Harvey *de* Montmarisco who was Strongbow's uncle. A grandson, William Fitzgerald married Strongbow's daughter Aline; another grandson was Raymond *fitz* William *fitz* Gerald *le Gros* (the fat or the big) commonly called Raymond *le Gros*.

Strongbow was Richard *de* Clare, Earl of Striguil, who was ruined in fortune because he had backed an opponent of Henry of Anjou when the latter was claiming the succession to the throne of England from Stephen. *De* Clare inherited the title of Earl of Pembroke from his father but the title was not confirmed by Henry. He inherited the title of Earl of Striguil from an uncle (Warren, *Henry II*, 193.)

Following a civil war between the followers of the Empress Matilda, daughter of Henry I and Stephen of Blois his nephew which was won by Stephen it was agreed that Matilda's son Henry Plantagenet of Anjou (or Henry *fitz* Empress) should succeed the childless Stephen. When Stephen died in 1154 his successor was known as Henry II. (Angevin is the adjectival form of Anjou.) Matilda had been married to Henry V, the Holy Roman Emperor, hence the title fitzempress.

Ireland to 1170

I have dealt with the history of Ireland to 1170 comprehensively in an earlier book *The True Origins of Irish Society*. A brief introductory summary of historical events leading up to 1170 is all that is required. Between 500 A.D. and 1500 A.D. the political scene changed with glacial slowness. There were five basic regions, later called provinces, each with its own provincial ruling family. From about 800 A.D. attempts were made by various provincial overlords to gain control of the whole island, the so-called highkingship. None succeeded for very long. Much depended on the military skill of the individual rulers.

There was an extraordinary stability in the ruling families. In many cases families who provided local or provincial chiefs in 500 A.D. were still providing chiefs in 1500 A.D. Some families however split, were conquered, or died out and were no longer recorded. They were usually replaced by other families who profited by their decline. In Ulster there were four major families or groups of families. These were the *Cenel Connaill* (O'Donnells) in Donegal, the *Cenel Eogain* (the O'Neills) in mid-Ulster, the *Ulaid* (earldom of Ulster) in east Ulster, and the *Oirgialla* (MacMahons, Maguires) in south Ulster. (The names in the later Middle Ages are given in brackets. These were ruling families not hereditary chiefs.) I have described at some length in an earlier part of this book the ruling families in each province (See above 'Leading Gaelic Families'). These are briefly recalled here because the feudal grants of Henry II and John were not indiscriminate but carefully targeted to maintain peace in the country. Contrary to the impression fostered by the Romantic Nationalists Gaelic society was not devoted to the arts of peace and religion. It was a dog-eat-dog society where the only crime was to be weak. If you could not defend your land it was taken from you.

In Meath were the dominant *Ui Neill* families, the *Sil nAedo Slaine* around Slane in east Meath, and *Clan Cholmain* (O'Mellaghlin) further west who were replaced by the Liberty of Meath. These were riven by internecine disputes and much of their land was given to Hugh *de* Lacy who divided it among his followers. The *Sil nAedo Slaine* disappeared from history but the O'Mellaghlins as a much reduced family survived. North of these were the *Ui Briuin Breifne,* in Cavan and Leitrim (O'Rourke, O'Reilly). Along the Shannon in Co. Longford were smaller clans of which the *Conmaicne* (O'Farrell) became dominant, and their territory was called Annaly.

In Leinster (south Leinster) were two dominant families. Around Kildare were the *Ui Dunlainge* (O'Byrne, O'Toole) and in Wexford were the *Ui Chennselaig* (MacMurrough). Lesser families were the *Loigse* (O'More) in Laois and the *Ui Failge* (O'Connor *Faly*) in Offaly, and the *Osraige* (Fitzpatrick) in Kilkenny. All survived throughout the Middle Ages.

In Munster the original dominant family was the *Eoganacht* (MacCarthy) who once challenged for the high kingship. Around the year 1000 they were challenged by the *Deisi,* originally from Waterford who established an overlordship in north Munster driving the *Eoganacht* into the south of Munster. A branch of the *Deisi,* the *Dal Cais* (O'Brien) under Brian *Boru* successfully conquered all the other chiefs in Ireland and held the highkingship effectively until his death in 1014. His successors failed to form a ruling dynasty so successive provincial warlords contended for the highkingship and the tribute from the whole of Ireland. The O'Briens and MacCarthys were fairly evenly matched throughout the Middle Ages, and the Government in Dublin took care that they remained that way. Other clans were the *Ciaraige* in Kerry and the *Ui Fidgente* in Limerick who were breaking up and their lands were given to the Normans to prevent the other two getting their hands on them. These lands formed the basis of the earldom of Desmond. In south east Cork, the *Corcu Loegde* (O'Driscoll) managed to hold out against the ever-spreading MacCarthys.

In Connaught, the dominant families were the branches of the *Ui Briuin*: the *Ui Briuin Seola* (O'Flaherty) and the *Ui Briuin Ai* (O'Connor) in Roscommon. A lesser family was the *Ui Maine* (O'Kelly) along the Shannon. The *Ui Fiachrach Muaide* (O'Dowd) survived in Sligo and the *Ui Fiachrach Aidne* (O'Heyn) survived in Galway but with ever decreasing influence as the power of the O'Connors and later the de Burghs (Burkes) grew.

As every ruling four-generation family had to shed a generation at the death of each chief the discarded families had to take a new name.

They did this by prefixing *Mac* (son) or *Ó* (grandson) to the given name of the new head of the family. The new clans were liable to be called to the hosting of the provincial chief, O'Neill, O'Brien or MacCarthy, for example, so the military power of the great chiefs was not diminished. That is, if the new families heeded the call to the hosting.

By the middle of the 12th century there were three major contenders for the highkingship, the O'Briens of Munster, the O'Neills of Ulster, and the O'Connors of Connaught. Watching their chances of making a bid were the MacMurroughs of Leinster and the MacCarthys of Munster. The O'Mellaghlin family of Meath was riven by internecine disputes so Dermot MacMurrough on one side and Tiernan O'Rourke on the other were anxious to grab bits of the O'Mellaghlin land, or the whole if they could. It was however the century of the O'Connors of Connaught. Though weak in the early part of the century, by 1150 under Turlough O'Connor the O'Connors imposed their authority over the whole of Ireland. On his death in 1156 a resurgent O'Neill family under Murtagh MacLoughlin for ten years ruled Ireland until the O'Neills on his death commenced a half century of internal feuding and never afterwards contended for power outside their province. O'Connor power was restored under Rory O'Connor (1166-72). After his death the O'Connors too started feuding, leading to the resurgence of the O'Briens under Dónal *Mór* O'Brien. None of these leading families were ever after able to contend for the highkingship, and so had to concede the overlordship to the king of England, while largely ignoring his authority in their own lands. They were largely occupied in the Middle Ages in consolidating their own provincial power bases.

The immediate cause for the intervention of the Normans in Ireland was a complicated dispute between Dermot MacMurrough, the provincial overlord of Leinster and Rory O'Connor. O'Connor was victorious, so MacMurrough fled to England and sought the advice of a friend, Robert Fitzharding, the portreeve or port warden of Bristol. Fitzharding advised him to get clearance from the king, Henry II.

After prolonged negotiations the king allowed him to recruit knights in Wales. He contacted the elderly Earl of Striguil, Richard *de* Clare, known as Strongbow, and promised him his daughter's hand in marriage. Dermot then recruited a group of knights in south Wales who were largely related to each other, the so-called Brood of Nesta. Dermot's attempt was successful, perhaps too successful for the king's liking. He summoned Strongbow to England where Strongbow surrendered all his lands in Normandy, England, and Wales which Henry had seized into the king's hand and received them back as a feudal fief for the service of 100 knights. He was allowed to keep his Irish lands which were regarded as his new wife's dowry, the king retaining only the Irish towns. This charter has not survived but presumably it was of the kind current in the Welsh marches, palatine jurisdiction. The archbishop of Canterbury, St Thomas *à* Becket was murdered on 29 December 1170. On 1 May 1171 Dermot MacMurrough died.

(Presumably the 100 knight's service was due from all his lands including those in England which were restored to him. His Irish mensal lands were largely in Kildare but he apparently retained the title of Lord of Leinster and so was tenant-in-chief with regard to the other lands in Leinster which he and Dermot MacMurrough had granted to Strongbow's followers. He would thus have parity with Hugh de Lacy who held Meath for 50 knights. Furlong denies that Strongbow was ever Lord of Leinster, Furlong, 173, 198-9. The Lordship of Leinster, if it existed presumably ended with the death of the childless Anselm Marshal in 1245 and the lands were divided among his four sisters and their husbands. Otway-Ruthven has no doubt that there was a liberty of Leinster, though it was temporarily divided after the death of Strongbow in 1176, and apparently restored in its entirety to William Marshal on his marriage to Strongbow's daughter in 1189, Otway-Ruthven, 61, 77. In the absence of the court of a liberty control of the province would revert by default to the MacMurrough Kavanaghs. The O'Kinsella lands of the MacMurrough Kavanaghs were not touched until the 16th century. The title 'king of Leinster was not claimed by the MacMurrough Kavanaghs until the end of the 14th century.)

Meanwhile, the Church reform, called the Gregorian or Hildebrandine reform was proceeding slowly. A synod was called to discuss the matter at Rathbreasail in Co. Tipperary but little came of it until 1139 until Archbishop St Malachi O'Morgair was sent to Rome to get confirmation of its decrees. He was advised to return to Ireland and again convoke a synod to make a formal application to the Holy See for the erection of four archbishoprics. This he did at Inishpatrick off the coast of Dublin in 1148. The synod did as required and when a reply was received from Rome another synod was convoked at the monasteries of Kells and Mellifont in 1152 and a new hierarchy was decided on. This was just a start, for much work remained to be done.

Ireland 1170-1199

Dermot's death was as usual followed by a revolt of the subordinate chiefs against Strongbow and the MacMurrough family. Only an illegitimate son of Dermot, Dónal *Caomhanach* or *Cavanagh* MacMurrough, supported Strongbow. (*Caomhanach* is obscure but may be connected with a monastery of St Kevin where he was fostered.) But Strongbow with the Norman knights put down all opposition. The MacMurrough Kavanaghs got their reward in lands as did Strongbow's other supporters. Strongbow had to eject opponents from their lands to provide knight's fees for the hundred knights, or at least those due from his Irish lands.

Whether Henry was particularly worried about Strongbow's powers and the possibility he could emulate the Normans in Sicily by setting up his own kingdom, or whether he just wanted to avoid the papal legates dealing with his excommunication following Becket's murder, we will never know. He came to Ireland with a huge feudal army, arriving at the Viking town of Waterford on 17 October 1171 and received submissions from the various Gaelic lords. This was not a feudal submission for the king did not own their lands but an oath of loyalty to his person (Warren, *Henry II*, 201). He reached Dublin on the 11 November and was received in a palace newly constructed out of wattle and spent the winter there (Roche, 101). He decided to taken into his own hands all the lands in Meath owned or controlled by the O'Mellaghlin chiefs. This would prevent other chiefs seizing them and also would provide a counterweight to Strongbow. He gave Meath as a feudal fief with a service of 50 knights to a Norman baron, Hugh *de* Lacy, the 5th Baron *de* Lacy who had extensive lands in the Welsh marches and elsewhere.

At this stage he considered Strongbow a greater threat than *de* Lacy and took steps to limit his powers. He placed many of the Brood of Nesta in the garrison of Dublin under Hugh *de* Lacy. He took the Viking towns into his own hands. Wexford and Waterford he garrisoned with his own men, while nominal troops were placed in Cork and Limerick, the first being controlled by the MacCarthys and the other by the O'Briens. The greatest warrior among the brood, Raymond *le Gros* (the fat), and Milo *de* Cogan he placed in his own retinue. He took care of the trade of Dublin, now vacated by the Hiberno-Norse leaders and gave a charter to the merchants of Bristol many of whom were probably on the spot. (When the Hiberno-Norse returned they had to settle outside the walls.)

Henry then summoned, as expected, a reforming synod at Cashel which met during the winter 1171-72 and which was presided over by a former papal legate and former Cistercian abbot of Mellifont, by then bishop of Lismore, Gillachriost O'Conarchy. Henry was represented at the synod by the Cistercian abbot of Buildwas in Shropshire and the archdeacon of the diocese of Llandaff in south Wales. There seems to have been great unanimity about what had to be accomplished and the synod was not prolonged. Decrees were passed ordering tithes to be collected for the parochial clergy, for collecting Peter's Pence for the pope, for the regulation of marriage and baptism, and the freeing of churches from lay exactions. The various local rites in the various dioceses were to be discontinued, and one of the Anglo-Norman rites was to be adopted (Curtis, 54). These were the standard Hildebrandine reforms. It would seem that the Anglo-Norman rite of Sarum was adopted in general form at least in most dioceses. (The Roman rite and Roman missal were not fully standardised until the Council of Trent.) The claim of the Archbishop of Canterbury to jurisdiction in Ireland was not mentioned. Nor was the wish of the Irish bishops to have the judgments in the Brehon Law replaced with English law expressed. This was particularly the case with regard to the very lax provisions of the Brehon Code regarding marriage. Gaelic chiefs were to cling to the freedoms of the Brehon Code in spite of Canon Law until the Reformation. The chief problem which the Irish bishops faced at this time was to get some means of supporting parish clergy in the parishes which were now being formed, and in particular to get church lands out of the hands of the erenaghs who held on to the properties of monasteries even when there were no monks in them.

Strangely the king did not publish the Bull *Laudabiliter,* of Pope Adrian IV, and apparently it was not published until a synod at Waterford in 1175. It was issued by Pope Adrian IV (Nicholas Breakspeare, the only English pope) around 1155 giving the papal blessing and authority for Henry to enter Ireland for the reformation of religion. It was not regarded as of great significance at the time. The Irish bishops may have known of it and approved of it. But it became a point of acute embarrassment in the heyday of Irish nationalism, and the dispute over its authenticity still rages. Warren considers its authenticity beyond doubt. The approbation of Henry's actions in Ireland by Pope Alexander III is beyond distrust. Also the authenticity of the bull was never questioned in the Middle Ages (Warren *Henry II,* 196-7).

Henry came to Ireland to deal with the immediate problem of one of his earls establishing himself in an Irish principality over which Henry had no feudal authority. He did not come to conquer Ireland though he was prepared to do so if he was resisted. He knew that he could spend very little time in Ireland for if he did not immediately make peace with the pope his kingdom might be placed under interdict and he himself excommunicated. Henry had discussions with the various Gaelic lords that were to bear fruit in 1175 with the Treaty of Windsor which set out his programme for Ireland. He solved his immediate problems and got a nominal submission from the Irish chiefs which he took at face value. To continue his work in his absence he left Dublin in the hands of Hugh *de* Lacy who apparently was not officially appointed justiciar or royal representative. This may have been an oversight or the official document may have been lost, for *de* Lacy is commonly regarded as the first justiciar. The justiciar's court was tiny to start with and moved around with him.

Norse Dublin was probably already the largest port in Ireland, though it was to be rivalled by Waterford. It was already surrounded by a wall, which the Normans repaired and strengthened. Land was gradually reclaimed from the river, so that a new northern wall had to be built further north (Barry, *Archaeology*, 31). At the beginning of the 14th century a wall was built round the suburbs on the north side of the river and included the Norse settlement. Parishes, churches, monasteries and St Patrick's cathedral were built outside the walls. The archbishop of Dublin, an Irishman called St Lawrence O'Toole, introduced the Arrouaisian canons to his cathedral, Christ Church. About 1173 he came to an agreement with the Normans that a new larger and more splendid cathedral should be built. The old Norse cathedral was demolished and work on the new one commenced. The construction of Dublin Castle did not commence until the reign of John. Walled Dublin was a tiny area around the cathedral and the castle.

It was not until 1175 that Henry made what he hoped would be the definitive settlement in Ireland based on an existing agreement with the Welsh chiefs in central and north Wales. By the Treaty of

Windsor Henry was to have Meath and Leinster and the ports as feudal dependencies. Rory O'Connor was to recognise Henry as overlord, but not feudal overlord, was to pay him a tribute, and was to be recognised as the lawful overking *(ri na hEireann,* king of Ireland) by the other Irish chiefs. In the other provinces he would keep order and collect a tribute for Henry. A curious result of this arrangement was that when some local families in County Down intrigued with John *de* Courci in a dispute about the local chieftainship it was O'Connor's duty to settle the matter. He could call on the help of the justiciar if he needed it and did so on occasion (Warren, *Henry II,* 201-4). The chief problem was wholesale collusion between Gaelic families and Norman knights. Landless Norman knights wanted land while Gaelic chiefs wanted skilled warriors. Another problem was that Rory was past his best days as a fighter and was no longer able to enforce respect. Respect which could not be enforced was no respect.

Hugh *de* Lacy had received the overlordship of the O'Mellaghlin lands in Meath with the obligation to provide the king with the services of 50 knights armed for war. This territory largely corresponds with the Protestant diocese of Meath and includes Meath, Westmeath, and parts of Offaly (Freeman, 112). But it included parts of the present County Dublin and it was in this section the de Lacy installed his first knights. At its southern end there is a common frontier with the diocese of Killaloe in Munster. The O'Mellaghlins and O'Briens were expanding towards each other, but the land was assigned at the Synod of Kells/ Mellifont in 1152 to the O'Brien diocese of Killaloe. This effectively recognised it as legally part of Munster with tribute and service due to the O'Briens. The part of Killaloe east of the Shannon, now north Tipperary around Nenagh, was and is poor marginal land (Freeman, 387). It was not until the 17th century securely held by anyone for long. (On land grants in Thomond Empey prefers the boundaries of medieval deaneries to modern baronies. The process is too complex to be summarised here but his monograph 'The Settlement of Limerick' illuminates the course of action.)

The O'Mellaghlin overlordship was a pyramid of chiefs (urraghs) with obligations of tribute and military service. When it came under Norman control every knight had to be provided with a knight's fee in land, i.e. sufficient to sustain himself, his horses and retainers. This was roughly 10 farms or townlands amounting to around 1,000 acres (See above 'The Norman Lordships'.) We have no idea how this was gone about. In England after 1066 most of the nobles resisted William I and their lands were declared forfeit. There was no similar opposition to Henry II in Ireland. There was doubtless considerable negotiations on all sides about how *de* Lacy could fulfil his obligations, namely which of the lesser lords would have to lose their lands. It was not royal policy or *de* Lacy's policy to evict the higher Irish chiefs and he proceeded with the subinfeudation chiefly around Dublin in lands probably taken from the Norse. The policy was to safeguard the ancestral lands of the provincial chiefs but to deprive them of the overlordship of the province. (The failure of the O'Mellaghlins in Westmeath left a power vacuum where none was intended.) However if a local petty chief stepped out of line and attacked somebody his lands could be declared forfeit.

Though the expansionist days of the O'Rourkes of Breffney came more or less to an end with the death of Tiernan O'Rourke in 1172, *de* Lacy placed along the frontier with Breffney strong baronies, which with the lordships of Pippard, de Verdon, and Mellifont and the towns of Dundalk, Ardee, Collon and Kells, provided a strong barrier down to Elizabethan times. These baronial families were the Dillons, Daltons, Delamers, Nugents, Plunkets (Plunketts), and Flemings. On the southern side of Meath were the Tyrells and Berminghams while Strongbow's successors were on the Leinster side. It is clear too from later events that the Norman knights pressed the extent of their entitlement to the utmost. Land was not mapped in those days and the local overlord made arbitrary decisions based on political considerations or indeed on pique. The poets, the genealogists, the clergy and other learned families then provided the rationale.

Hugh followed the pattern of marrying into the local nobility, this time getting the hand of Rory O'Connor's daughter without first getting Henry's permission thus earning Henry's disfavour. (One would have expected an alliance with the O'Mellaghlins, but perhaps they were unwilling or just too weak.) Henry came to prefer Strongbow. *De* Lacy was called to assist the king in France. Much has been made of the fact that Irish chiefs were excluded from the royal and liberty courts. The heads of the 'Five Bloods', the ruling families in the five provinces always had access to the justiciar's court. There seems no doubt that it was intended that English law should become the general usage of the septs of the submitters, and thus gradually be introduced throughout the whole country, but this was resisted in Gaelic areas. In Norman areas, Gaelic chiefs who did not hold their lands through subinfeudation had no right to attend the court of the liberty or honour but had to attend their own courts. It seems however that if they sought to hold their lands by subinfeudation and recognised the lord of the liberty as their feudal overlord they could attend. Otherwise they had to ask someone free of the court to represent them. Throughout the Middle Ages many Gaelic gentlemen did seek access to the Common Law courts, though it was not in the interest of local Anglo-Norman lords to allow them as explained earlier. (See above 'Laws'.) Nor was it in the interests of the greater Gaelic chiefs to allow them to seek the protection of the king's courts.

In 1176 Strongbow died and as his heiress was still a minor, the grant of Leinster was taken into the king's hands. William *fitz* Aldhelm was sent to Ireland. He was accompanied to Ireland by a newcomer John *de* Courci, and by Robert *fitz* Stephen and Miles *de* Cogan. We know little or nothing about the intrigues between the various branches of the Gaelic chiefs and the various Norman knights. However this period was marked by civil wars in all the provinces except Thomond where Dónal *Mór* O'Brien was secure. John *de* Courci was invited to assist a faction of the *Dal Fiatach*, the over-chiefs of the *Ulaid* (McNeill, *Anglo-Norman Ulster,* 5). He quickly established himself in the cantreds of the *Dal Fiatach* in east Down and south Antrim, and swiftly constructed motte-and-bailey castles at Carrickfergus and Dundrum to secure the northern and southern ends of the *Dal Fiatach* lands. It was several years before *de* Courci and the *Dal Fiatach* could restore hegemony over the rest of the *Ulaid* and the invading *Ui Tuirtre*. These original conquests formed the core of the earldom of Ulster and were the only parts properly colonised and commercially developed. The authority of the earldom was to spread gradually over Ulster and much later a castle was built on the shores of Lough Foyle in Co. Donegal. When the earldom declined these eastern cantreds were all that survived at the end of the Middle Ages. All attempts to dislodge *de* Courci were unsuccessful. Miles *de* Cogan led a similar expedition to Connaught to assist Rory O'Connor's son Muirchertach's (Murtagh's) revolt against his father, but this was unsuccessful. Raymond *le Gros* was authorised to assist Dermot MacCarthy against his son's revolt. It would seem that the very presence of available Norman knights was provoking rebellions and it was not in the Government's interest that they should succeed. Among the O'Neills, two branches, the O'Neills and MacLoughlins fought each other until Brian O'Neill (of the Battle of Down) eliminated his rivals in 1241.

Henry decided that as Rory O'Connor was powerless a stronger position should be taken. Ireland would be made over to his youngest son John (Lackland) who would thus be provided with a suitable piece of his father's possessions to support himself. (The attitude of a medieval monarch with regard to his dominions was not nationalistic, but rather like a modern business tycoon owning an international business assigning divisions to his sons.) Henry also made grants of land in obscure circumstances around the towns of Cork and Limerick presumably with a view to protecting royal rights and preventing anyone else seizing them. Robert *fitz* Stephen and Miles *de* Cogan occupied the little Norse town of Cork which the MacCarthys had captured. As the Normans were assisted by Murtagh O'Brien the MacCarthys let them occupy seven cantreds. A similar grant to Philip *de* Braose was not followed up presumably because no suitable opportunity presented itself. No grant was effective until the lord turned up with an armed force.

The archbishop of Dublin, Lawrence O'Toole with five other bishops attended the Third Council of the Lateran in Rome in 1179 apparently the first ecumenical council attended by Irish bishops. The Council is chiefly famous for the canon restricting the election of the pope to the College of Cardinals. He died on the 14 November 1180. The king then used his influence to have one of his chief clerical administrators, John Cumin, a Benedictine monk of Evesham, elected as archbishop of Dublin. This was not part of a royal policy to Normanize the Irish Church. Cumin, a monk but not yet a priest had served as an itinerant judge, and was one of the circuit judges appointed when the four circuits were established in 1179. Recommendation to a bishopric was a common reward for good administrators.

Neither he nor Henry was in any haste for him to take up his duties in Ireland. A large part of these duties would have been to serve on the justiciar's council. In the event, some years later he was sent to Dublin to prepare for the arrival of Prince John. If there was no royal policy to impose Norman bishops on Ireland in the way they had been imposed on England it was usually left to the local diocesan chapters to elect a bishop. (See above 'The Chapter'.) The king might give a *Congé d'Elire* accompanied by a recommendation, yet there always powerful local forces brought to bear on the canons as well. If the local lords were Norman the likelihood was that a French-speaking cleric would be elected; otherwise not. Cumin introduced Norman law and practice into the church lands in Dublin and enforced the latest Anglican practice.

As a feudal noble he constructed a castle at Swords, Co. Dublin to the north of the city. He continued with the re-building of Christ Church within the walls of Dublin and erected a collegiate church of St Patrick in swampy land to the south of the walls of Dublin. His aim seems to have been to promote study. There were 13 prebendaries who had to be provided with lands for their support. These were allowed to retain their emoluments and commons if studying overseas. This was the first of several attempts to form a college later called a university.

Henry had made Prince John Lord of Ireland in 1177, and in 1185, at the age of 19 he was sent to Ireland for his first visit. It was not a success, at least if the account of Gerald of Wales is to be believed. But Gerald judged people according to the way they treated his relatives, the Brood of Nesta. Henry would not have allowed his inexperienced son to do anything without the consent of experienced councillors. These were Ranulf *de* Glanville, justiciar of England, Theobald Walter the king's butler, Bertram *de* Verdun (or *de* Verdon) his steward or seneschal, and William *de* Burgh (*de Burgo* in Latin) who were to found great houses in Ireland. Hugh *de* Lacy had been removed from the justiciarship which was given to Philip of Worcester and was uncooperative. Civil wars and disturbances continued among the Gaelic lords. It may be that John spent the money intended for troops on entertainments and had no intention of intervening militarily.

Feudal grants of marginal lands were given in MacCarthy lands in north Cork and Tipperary and O'Brien lands along the Shannon, and to Bertram *de* Verdon and Peter Pippard in County Louth from the O'Carroll lands (Otway-Ruthven, 70-1). Recent historians are inclined to believe that these grants were made in collusion with the respective Gaelic lords for they were recent conquests in difficult lands. Such lands were liable to be held either by chiefs of recalcitrant *tuatha*, or by robber bands, kernes. The grants in MacCarthy and O'Carroll lands proved largely successful, but the Fitzwalter (Butler) lands in north Tipperary had to be abandoned in the later Middle Ages. Some token motte-and-bailey castles were built but little was done until John's next visit as king. He agreed with Archbishop Cumin's request that the sees of Dublin and Glendalough be joined on the death of the existing bishop of Glendalough. The union of the sees did not in fact occur until 1214. On John's departure for England, the justiciarship was given to John *de Courci*, now back in royal favour.

The grants of lands around Maynooth and Naas to William *fitz* Maurice *fitz* Gerald were confirmed. He was the eldest son of the Maurice *fitz* Gerald who came over with Dermot MacMurrough and who died in 1176. From these came two of the most powerful families in the late Middle Ages, the earls of Kildare and of Desmond but they were small fry at first. They came to prominence during the invasions of the Bruces. His younger brother Gerald *fitz* Maurice *fitz* Gerald, 1st Baron of Offaly, from whom the earls of Kildare, received half of William's lands from him. From the third son, Thomas *fitz* Maurice *fitz* Gerald came the Fitzgeralds earls of Desmond, the Knights of Kerry, the Knights of Glin, the White Knights, and the Fitzmaurices, Lords of Kerry. From Theobald *fitz* Walter (Theobald *le Botiller*, *Theobaldus Pincerna*) the king's butler came the Butlers, earls of Ormond (or Ormonde) and Chief Butlers of Ireland, the great rivals of the earls of Desmond, and the Fitzwalters.

These early grants in the future counties of Louth, Meath, Dublin, and Kildare, accompanied with extensive colonisation were to form the solid and irreducible core of English law and practice and collectively came to be known as The Pale. From them modern Ireland developed. They were connected by a narrow strip of land with the other great area of early colonisation in south Leinster and north Munster in the future counties of Wexford, Waterford, and Kilkenny. Most of north Munster eventually came under the great earldoms of Desmond and Ormond. Historians now agree that Ireland was seriously underpopulated and that the influx of working class colonists did not displace the local population. Those who lost lands were the minor lords and they had the choice of accepting reduced status or fleeing to the neighbouring hills or bogs and displacing somebody else. The O'Tooles and O'Byrnes fled into the Wicklow Mountains and the O'Carrolls of *Eile* fled into the Slieve Bloom Mountains.

Miles *de* Cogan was killed in 1182 and Raymond *le Gros* died in the same year. Robert *fitz* Stephen died in 1183. In 1185 Dermot MacCarthy died and was succeeded by his son Dónal Mór *na Corra* MacCarthy (1185-1206). Hugh *de* Lacy was murdered in 1186 and the liberty of Meath, like that of Leinster reverted to the king, his sons apparently being minors. His eldest son, Walter *de* Lacy had his father's Irish lands restored to him in 1194. In 1186 Rory O'Connor was deposed by his sons and retired to a monastery. He was succeeded by Connor *Maenmaige* O'Connor who was widely accepted by the great Gaelic chiefs as successor to Rory's rights. In 1189 William the Marshal who had been married by the king to Strongbow's daughter received his father-in-law's lands. Art O'Mellaghlin died in 1184 and thereafter *Clann Cholmain* declined still further. In 1189 Connor O'Connor was murdered and was succeeded by Cathal *Carragh* (Scabby) O'Connor. The succession was disputed by his uncle Cathal *Crovderg* (the red-handed, presumably a birthmark) O'Connor with the inevitable civil war that lasted until 1202. Both sides sought the assistance of William *de* Burgh.

Dónal *Mór* O'Brien, the most effective of the Irish provincial chiefs died in 1194 resulting in the by now inevitable internal disputes regarding the succession. (*Mór*, the great, can refer to height but more usually refers to power as a chief.) The original home of the *Dal Cais* (O'Briens) was at Bruree in Limerick. They were driven from there by the *Ui Fidgente*. In 1178 the O'Briens returned and drove out the *Ui Fidgente* now fighting among themselves. But after the death of Dónal *Mór* the O'Briens seem to have had difficulty in holding on to their gains, which provided an opportunity for King John to intervene. Again John was able to take control of the Norse city of Limerick and its lands. Limerick city became and remained a possession of the crown. William *de* Burgh, a brother of Hubert *de* Burgh, later justiciar of England, who came to Ireland with John and had received grants of land on the Waterford/Tipperary border married, in the customary manner, a daughter of Dónal *Mór* O'Brien. He was therefore in an excellent position to interfere in the struggle for succession. Finally in 1210 Donnchad *Cairprech* (Donough of Carbery?) *mac* Dónail *Mór* O'Brien (1210-1242) stabilized Thomond. Connaught was stabilised when Cathal *Crovderg* O'Connor (1202-24) regained the throne. Ulster was not stabilized until 1241 when the O'Neills eliminated the MacLoughlins. The MacCarthys of Desmond remained fairly stable except for a brief episode in 1206.

Henry II died in 1189 before he could get John recognised as king of Ireland. His son, Richard I, the famous Lionheart, was determined to go on a crusade. Ireland's participation in the crusades came exclusively from the Anglo-Norman area and was largely confined to providing estates of land to provide support for the warriors abroad. The effect of the Third Crusade (1189-92) on Ireland was slight. More important was the imprisonment of Richard by Duke Leopold of Austria while he was returning through Germany. Factions grew which supported either Richard or John. Some of the Irish barons supported Richard, which John did not forget when he suddenly became king in 1199.

Ireland 1199-1215 The Reign of John

Henry II had little interest in Ireland apart from ensuring that the Norman barons would not establish an independent kingdom as had been done in Sicily. Richard I had no interest at all in Ireland. Prince John had only a sporadic interest in his Lordship of Ireland, and it was left largely to under-funded justiciars to cope with local circumstances as best they could. (This was probably the same in most parts of the great Angevin dominions.) Norman and Gaelic lords intrigued with each other and against each other. The justiciars could interfere on one side or the other in the succession disputes in the four great provincial lordships but did not attempt to take them over. Such an attempt would have been beyond their military capabilities. They could and did give grants of marginal lands which were not core lands of the great chiefs. They could, for example, give grants of the *Ui Fidgente* lands in Limerick creating a buffer between the O'Briens and MacCarthys which both accepted.

Those appointed by John (and later kings) to senior administrative posts in Church and state were usually men of great administrative ability and experience. John appointed an old warrior, Meiler *fitz* Henry, who had come to Ireland first with Dermot MacMurrough as justiciar. The great lords, John *de* Courci, William the Marshal, Walter and Hugh *de* Lacy, Richard *de* Burgo, and William *de* Braose either sided with the justiciar or opposed him as suited themselves. *Fitz* Henry was told to build a proper castle in Dublin as a secure place of defence for the royal treasury and as a court for the justiciar, and the people of Dublin were ordered to build proper town walls. He brought into Ireland his father's reforms with regard to the baronage. In 1204 he ordered that all royal writs should run everywhere in Ireland, in particular the writs of *Mort de ancestre, Breve de recto*, and *Novel disseisin* (see above, 'The Government of Henry II'). In 1205 he laid down that it was no defence in law that the victim was Irish. He revised the charters of Meath and Leinster taking back the pleas of the crown, appeals of felony, appeals of default of justice in the courts, and complaints of injury by themselves or their courts (Dolly, 106-7; 109). He reformed the Irish coinage making it the same weight and fineness as English coins. He wished to see Common Law applied to the whole of Ireland, and the Catholic bishops would have liked this for Brehon Law was extremely lax with regard to marriage and divorce. Jury trial was brought to Ireland. Charters were granted to towns which gradually gave liberty to the merchants to manage their own affairs. An attempt was made to introduce the county system, with counties around Dublin, Waterford, and Cork, and one in Munster which seems to have occupied the whole of Norman-occupied Munster not in either Cork or Waterford. These were ruled by sheriffs directly appointed by the crown, non-hereditary, and whose first duty was to pay the profits of the crown into the Exchequer in Dublin. (County and honorial jurisdictions could overlap though it is not clear if this was the case in Ireland.)

A feudal monarch could not rule without the acquiescence, however unenthusiastic of his barons. The marcher lords, besides their lands in Ireland had often greater estates in England, and also in Normandy. John wished to keep any of the barons from getting too strong, and seems to have used *de* Burgh as a check on *de* Braose. In 1206 *de* Braose was at the height of his power with 352 knights' fees, probably the strongest baron in England. The *de* Lacys coveted the lands of *de* Courci, and in 1204 John summoned *de* Courci to England; he preferred to stay in Ireland to defend his lands, but was defeated by the *de* Lacys, and in 1205 Hugh was given *de* Courci's lands and was made Earl of Ulster. This was the beginning of the earldom of Ulster which extended over the present counties Antrim and Down and corresponded with the former territory of the *Ulaid*.

Warren gives an excellent summary of policy of King John with regard to land grants and castle building (Warren, 'King John and Ireland'). His chief aim was to provide buffer zones between the Norman and Gaelic lords. The first stage was to establish a line of baronies under new men along the border between Munster and Leinster (and between the O'Briens and MacCarthys). The second stage was to make grants in the border area north of Drogheda (chiefly in County Louth) between Ulster and Meath (and between *de* Courci and *de* Lacy). The third stage was to establish a major royal base in the centre of Ireland at Athlone to be a buffer between Meath and Connaught. Finally a major royal base was to be established at Clones in County Monaghan to be the centre of a strip of royal fiefdoms along the whole border between

Ulster on one side and Meath and Connaught on the other. In fact with a string of strong castles in Louth, at Clones in Co. Monaghan, and at *Caol Uisge* on Lough Erne, the Government would have a strong band of manors with castles across south Ulster. John intended to control the marches of Ireland.

We can safely assume that suitable Irish people like bishops and abbots were consulted who knew which the hereditary lands were and which were recent acquisitions of the great chiefs. Every effort was made to reach an accommodation with the provincial Gaelic chiefs even to assisting them with troops and arranging matrimonial alliances. Donough *Cairprech* O'Brien was knighted by John and given a feudal lordship in socage for 60 marks a year. Cathal *Crovderg* O'Connor was accepted as a feudal tenant-in-chief *per baroniam* or knight service for one third of his lands. His object was to get succession to his eldest son under feudal law. *Crovderg* assisted the feudal army in 1213 against Cormac *mac* Art O'Mellaghlin who was not giving up his chiefdom without a fierce struggle. (An O'Mellaghlin chief surrendered to the queen in 1600 desiring to hold his land from the queen.) It is clear that though Gaelic chiefs could seek the status of feudal lords there would be great opposition to this among the leading members of the ruling family. The inheritance would go to the eldest son or into the king's hand if there were only daughters thereby excluding the chances of succession of other leading members. This remained a problem even after the Tudor policy of Surrender and Re-grant. The exclusion of Gaelic chiefs from feudal and royal courts was the result of their own decisions.

John also tried to reduce the powers of the great liberties of Leinster and Meath but was frustrated when his brother Richard I confirmed Walter *de* Lacy and William the Marshal in their inheritances. This was part and parcel of his attempts to restrict the rights of the baronage which led to his confrontation with them in 1215. In Ireland it was meeting as much objection from the barons as it was in England. It was a long-time concern of the kings of England to get a single system of justice with the right of appeal from every court to a royal court. This was eventually achieved, but often a king was not in a position to enforce his will against a recalcitrant baron. (This was as true in England as it was in Ireland.) It should be noted that John proposed setting the new feudal baronies in regions of poor but improvable agricultural land. (The Cistercians had shown how waste lands could be made profitable.) After his death the barons had no scruple about seizing the best lands when they could. As Warren points out there was an economic reason for this. The Irish economy was always highly dependent on exports to England, and the early Middle Ages were a particularly favourable period. There were great opportunities for exporting agricultural produce to England, and good land properly managed could produce a satisfactory surplus. This did not necessarily mean introducing the manorial system. It did mean an ability to collect a surplus (McNeill, 84; Warren, *loc.cit.*).

John *de* Courci was in and out of royal favour, as most Norman lords were from time to time. All lords and chiefs were constantly testing the willingness of their overlord to enforce his authority. John *de* Courci had slowly but successfully extended his little barony in east Ulster and indeed became the most powerful lord in Ulster during the reign of Richard I. In England John got into a dispute with the pope over the election of an archbishop of Canterbury. The pope, Innocent III, placed England under an interdict in March 1208. One of the bishops reading out the interdict was Giles *de* Braose, son of William *de* Braose. William was backward in paying the money he had promised John for the 'honour of Limerick'. (The honour of Limerick was an honorial court with palatine status but not palatine powers (see above 'Local Government'). John ordered him to be taken prisoner, but he fled to Ireland where William the Marshal was a feudal tenant of his, and Walter *de* Lacy was a son-in-law, and got protection there. John could not ignore the challenge of the three most powerful feudal barons in Ireland. He had first to deal with problems in Wales and in Scotland but by 1210 he was ready to lead an army into Ireland. William the Marshal accompanied him having sent *de* Braose to Walter *de* Lacy. Walter's own knights were unwilling to oppose the king. Hugh *de* Lacy still resisted though *de* Braose fled to Wales. John captured Carrickfergus castle and *de* Lacy escaped by sea. John took the lordships of Meath and Ulster and the honour of Limerick into his own hands, leaving Marshal in Leinster.

John favoured the Gaelic princes and was eager to protect them from the depredations of the Normans. Twenty of the great Irish chiefs did homage to John in Dublin. Among these was O'Mellaghlin of Meath, O'Rourke of Breffney, and Aedh *Meth* (the fat) O'Neill who paid a tribute of 321 cows (Warren, 'King John and Ireland', 39; Otway-Ruthven, 81). Aedh *Meth* O'Neill was chief of the O'Neills from 1196 to 1230 and undisputed after Connor MacLoughlin was killed by the O'Donnells in 1201. He was a formidable warrior. John ordered the strengthening of castles now in his hands. Those in Limerick and Carlingford are still referred to as King John's castle; though in both cases they seem to have been commenced before his arrival. He had commenced the castle in Dublin.

Great early medieval stone castles are rather rare in Ireland. In the Norman areas there were numerous motte-and-bailey castles. The motte was a mound with a usually wooden defensive enclosure on top of it, and a hall and other buildings at its foot surrounded by a fence. It was usually all that was needed. In Ulster many mottes did not have baileys, with the hall placed on the motte and they seem to have been sufficient for local defence. Those with baileys were placed along the borders. Motte-and-bailey castles are only found in the eastern parts of Ireland and date from the period 1170 to 1230 (McNeill, 65-9, 84-9; Barry, 36-43). It is thus unclear what the defensive arrangements were as the Normans advanced into Cork, Limerick, and Tipperary, for they must have had some form of defence not involving a mound. (See above 'Defensive Measures'.)

Ireland, as an island off the shores of the Continent, was always in danger of closing in on itself and becoming xenophobic and backward-looking. (Portugal was the reverse.) It received three salutary shocks, the coming of Christianity and the Viking and the Norse invasions. Religion apart, Christianity brought reading, writing, and the Latin language. The Vikings revolutionised ship-building, markets and trade, and rejuvenated art. The most powerful influence was that of the Normans who developed towns, trade, roads, bridges, ports and ships. Agriculture was reorganised to produce a marketable surplus. Standards of building and masonry soared. The great developments in government administration, in laws and law-making, in a court system where judgments could be reviewed poured into Ireland through the Norman ports. There was not, though there could have been, a corresponding development in Gaelic areas.

Some older historians in the Romantic tradition tried to make out that the Normans engaged in racial conquest. But that was utterly foreign to the ideas of the time. The Norman knights were just trying to get land for themselves. To help to achieve this they had no hesitation in marrying the daughters of local Gaelic chiefs. The Gaelic chiefs welcomed them as warriors as they too were looking for land. There were no permanent friends or enemies, just constantly shifting alliances. It was inadvisable to be too greedy for someone else's land, unless that person was unimportant, for you might need his help next year.

The Norman knights like the Gaelic lords were illiterate but skilled in practical matters. They appreciated far more than the Gaelic lords the benefits of towns for the purposes of trade and manufacture. They appreciated the need for the production of a regular agricultural surplus both for the benefit of the towns and for the benefit of exports. All lords at the time (and also sheriffs, mayors, and justiciars) had to be military captains, property administrators, and judges. The Norman lords usually entrusted seneschals with taking care of the latter two.

The seneschals would try to attract settlers, and especially townspeople or merchants to build and form towns to develop trade. Some were very successful in attracting those with the required skills from their lord's lands in England and these could establish the full manorial system. Most however seem to have worked on a hybrid system based on existing land management, intensifying the productivity but not the existing structure. The existing Gaelic cultivators were just left in place (McNeill, 89). These matters took time but after 40 years, by 1210 the new economic system was in place along the east coast.

The crown wanted to keep the peace and to get some profit, whether in fighting men or in cash out of the land. The attempt by Henry II to get the O'Connors to rule the Gaelic chiefs and to get them to pay the annual tribute in cows failed, largely it would seem because of civil war in Connaught. The strategy of John was to prevent any chief, Gael or Norman from getting too strong, and to interpose buffer states between the great magnates. This, any king in any part of Europe, would try to do. Henry II did not provide sufficient lands to give the justiciar an adequate local powerbase. Though John added to royal lands it was inadequate. Had he taken the O'Mellaghlin lands into the royal demesne it would have provided the monarchy with a powerful base. But either he did not see the need for it or lacked the time and means to occupy a royal demesne. Nevertheless, after John's measures, no English king had to intervene in Ireland for two centuries (Empey, 'Settlement of Limerick', 1).

In 1211 Aedh *Meth* O'Neill burned de Grey's new castle at Clones, in Co. Monaghan and the following year burned Carlingford. The advance into Oriel was effectively stalled (Smith, 'The Medieval Border', 41). Significantly, the castle at Clones was not destroyed by the MacMahons who probably regarded it as a defence against the O'Neills, but by the O'Neills themselves. For the same reason Cathal *Crovderg* O'Connor attacked the castle at Athlone. The O'Connors had no intention of allowing the king to set limits to their own expansion.

John had to go to France to fight Philip II and was heavily defeated at Bouvines in 1214. He was accompanied to this war by Walter *de* Lacy. The following year, in 1215, the English barons forced him to sign the Magna Charta. The Magna Charta was not about the rights of Englishmen but about preserving the power of the barons from royal encroachment. Among the barons who supported John were William Marshal and Hubert *de* Burgh. (William Marshal brought 500 lances from Ireland in 1213 to support John in his quarrel with the pope (Curtis, 74)). The Magna Charta was extended to Ireland in 1217. On 19 October 1216 John died suddenly aged 48. He was succeeded by his 9 year old son with William the Marshal as regent. He was to reign for 56 years. As Warren noted King John was the most successful high king Ireland had ever seen. He was also, in a very real sense, the last (Warren, 'King John', 39). And no English king had to intervene in Ireland for nearly 200 years and that was at the end of the disastrous 14th century.

The Church 1170-1215

As in most fields change and development characterised the Church in the Middle Ages. Even in outward appearance the Church in 1500 looked very different from in 1100. Change was much slower then than now but still was very perceptible in the 45 years between 1170 and 1215. The Burgundian Transitional church at Mellifont astonished people in 1157. By 1180 John *de* Courci introduced Lancet Gothic to the Cistercian abbey near Downpatrick. Mellifont church itself was remodelled in the 13th century in the Gothic style. More remarkable were the two great cathedrals in Dublin which were commenced at this period.

Nobody in the Middle Ages believed in the separation of church and state. Rather they believed in Christendom's religious arm and secular arm. The archbishop or primate was always a member of the king's Council and entrusted with many administrative duties. The king therefore took care that the canons would elect a cleric suitable for such a position. King John's attempt to get the monks of Canterbury cathedral to accept John *de* Gray as archbishop led to a clash with the pope. In 1209 he was made Justiciar of Ireland. John Cumin was elected archbishop of Dublin in 1181. The next archbishop was Henry of London *(Henri de Loundres)* who was elected in 1212 and consecrated in 1213. In 1214 Glendalough was finally united with Dublin. A report to the pope said that at that time the valley of Glendalough was deserted except by bands or robbers. (These could have been either displaced chiefs or woodkerne.) Glendalough became an archdeaconry *inter Hibernicos* meaning that the inhabitants were Gaelic speaking. In 1213 he replaced Bishop *de* Gray as justiciar.

Contact with the papacy was close at this time. Cardinal Vivian was sent as a papal legate in 1177-8 and Cardinal John of Salerno in 1202-3. Henry of London acted as papal legate in 1216. St Lawrence O'Toole had been a papal legate as had been the Cistercian archbishop of Cashel Matthew O'Heney in 1192-98 (Watt, *Church in Medieval Ireland,* 132, 150). The Fourth Council of the Lateran convened in November 1215. It was attended by 4 Irish archbishops, 14 bishops and 2 bishops elect. 14 were Gaelic-speakers. The Council promulgated 79 canons on a wide variety of topics (*Catholic Encyclopaedia,* 'Fourth Lateran Council').

The archdiocese of Dublin was becoming what it was to remain, the largest, richest and most powerful diocese in Ireland, though Armagh clung to its primacy. In 1216 Bishop Simon Rocheford amalgamated the three sees in Meath, Clonard, Kells and Duleek into a single diocese of Meath with its cathedral at Trim. Dromore did not receive recognition at Kells/Mellifont but obtained it subsequently possibly in 1192. In Dublin, the Benedictine monk, John Cumin was elected archbishop in succession to Lawrence O'Toole and he continued the work of reform and reorganisation. For some reason he decided to remodel the little church of St Patrick in swampy land outside the walls of Dublin into a collegiate church where the priests would study and instruct the local people. It may be that he intended making a college such as that at Oxford (not yet called a university). Endowments were found for 13 clerics. The principal preceptory of the Knights Hospitallers was at Kilmainham, outside Dublin. The Cistercian abbey of St. Mary's Dublin was over the river on the north side. (The oddity of a Cistercian monastery close to a town is explained by the fact that it was originally Benedictine.)

The work of transforming the structure of the Church where most of the original endowments of land had been given to monasteries into the more modern structure of dioceses, chapters, and parishes continued. Every single bishop, canon, dean, archdeacon, and priest had to be provided with an endowment of land for his support. This often meant transferring the use of the land from often vacant monasteries to the new institutions. The presence of a cardinal legate to confirm the transfers would have been useful. The consent of the king and the local lord, Gaelic or Norman, would also have been required for land was never fully transferred away from the ruling family of a district. The consent of the erenaghs, who actually occupied the land, and coarbs who had rights of nomination would also have to be obtained.

The world was changing. In 1215 the Cistercians and the Arrouaisians were still providing the models for Church reform. In 1209 St Francis of Assisi got recognition for his little group of brothers. In 1215 Saint Dominic got recognition for his group of preachers at the Council of the Lateran. The form of life of 'friars' (*fraters, frères,* brothers) who were not 'monks' was approved, and the Franciscans and Dominicans were joined by Augustinian and Carmelite friars. They rejected endowments of land and subsisted on gifts from those they preached to. Besides preaching they devoted themselves to study. They flocked to the universities. The various schools in Paris came together in a 'university' around 1208. At the same time the Cistercians were falling off from their first fervour. The abbot of Mellifont was expelled by his own monks around 1206. Many complaints were made to the general chapter about his successor, and a visitation of Mellifont and some at least of its daughter houses was made in 1216 which the new abbot resisted with armed force. He was deposed the following year (Columcille, 54-5; Dolley, 119).

Chapter 9

Henry III 1216-1272

Reign of Henry

The 13th century was one of great prosperity in Europe. The climate had reached its medieval optimum. Agriculture, trade and all the arts flourished. It was the age of the great cathedrals of Paris, Bourges, and Chartres in France, of Westminster Abbey and Salisbury cathedral in England, and Christ Church and St. Patrick's in Ireland. In Ireland it was the century when the reorganisation of the land in eastern Ireland with an influx of colonists made agriculture prosperous, and all incomes in eastern Ireland depending on the land increased greatly. It was the age of the great universities and of great scholars, St Thomas Aquinas, St. Bonaventure, John Duns Scotus, and Roger Bacon. It was the heyday of the mendicant friars like the Dominicans and Franciscans. Colleges were founded and endowed at Oxford, University College (1249), Balliol (1263) and Merton (1264). Cambridge was formed by an exodus of scholars from Oxford in 1209 and it first college was endowed in 1284.

Henry *fitz* John was born 1 Oct. 1207 and died 16 Nov. 1272, and was King of England (1216-72). He was the son of King John and Isabella of Angoulême. When John died unexpectedly leaving a

9-year old son, Henry, the barons, led by Richard de Burgh, decided on a regency. John on his deathbed got those around him to swear loyalty to his infant son against Louis of France whom many of the barons had invited to be king. The pope, Honorius III, accepted the guardianship of the young prince, and the kingdom as placed under William Marshall, Earl of Pembroke and Striguil, Lord of Leinster, the 'good knight'. (He had married Strongbow's daughter.) He defeated Louis while Hubert de Burgh, a brother of William de Burgh who possessed the honour of Limerick, defeated the French fleet. A council agreed to compensate Louis for his trouble and he left the country. But when Philip II of France died Louis captured most of the remaining English possessions on the continent. Henry's reign was full of wastefulness and bad government, and the border counties continually ravaged by the Welsh. He was regarded as rather feeble-minded and was usually controlled by those around him. He was extremely religious and was a patron of the arts and he rebuilt Westminster Abbey.

The aged William Marshal was regent until his death in 1219. Marshal re-issued the Magna Charta in Henry's name, on 12 November 1216, omitting some clauses and again in 1217. When he turned eighteen in 1225, Henry III himself reissued Magna Charta again, this time in a shorter version with only 37 articles. From 1219 to 1227 when the king came of age, Hubert de Burgh was regent. He acted as justiciar of England from 1215 to 1232. In January 1227 Henry declared himself of full age and commenced to attempt to regain the overseas French possessions that had been lost. In the preceding years he had lost most of his French possessions but by 1225 he had recovered Gascony, and in 1228, for baronial support, he agreed to restore the forest liberties. By 1230 he was invading Poitou and Gascony, and the following year to obtain scutage (a form of revenue) he reaffirmed the liberties of the Church.

His policy was weak and vacillating, and was influenced first by the foreign favourites and relations introduced by his mother, and then by those introduced by his wife. In 1235 to gain foreign support he married his sister Isabella to the emperor Frederick II, and on January 20 the following year he married Eleanor of Provence. This marriage caused England to be flooded with his wife's relations, and the barons again saw the government passing into the control of foreigners. His attempted extortions of money, the undue influence of the papacy over the kingdom, and his numerous grants to his favourites, made him generally unpopular with the barons. To the Poitevans and Savoyards were now added the Lusignans. William de Valence, Earl of Pembroke of the third creation, was the fourth son of Isabella of Angoulême, widow of king John of England, and her second husband, Hugh X of Lusignan, and was thus a half-brother to Henry III of England, and uncle to Edward I. Henry III invited him to England and he soon married a granddaughter and heiress to the great William Marshal, 1st Earl of Pembroke, and so the heiress of Strongbow's title and lands. He became Earl of Pembroke and Earl of Wexford in Ireland. Things might have remained as they were but for Henry III's disastrous foreign policy. Henry accepted the invitation from Pope Innocent IV that Henry's son Edward become King of Sicily. In exchange for the kingship, Henry promised to support the papacy in its struggle against the Hohenstaufen dynasty. That support came in the form of huge grants of money, which strained the English treasury to the breaking point.

By 1239 Henry's behaviour was such that even his brother-in-law Simon de Montfort, 6th Earl of Leicester, who was married to the king's sister (Costain, 239), and his brother Richard, Earl of Cornwall, joined the opposition. Simon was a capable soldier and administrator and was chosen by the discontented barons as their leader. At the 'Mad Parliament' of Oxford (1258) de Montfort appeared side by side with the Earl of Gloucester at the head of the opposition. The barons forced Henry to accept the Provisions of Oxford (1258). The provisions forced Henry to accept a new form of government in which power was placed in the hands of a council of twenty four members, 12 selected by the crown, 12 by the barons. The twelve selected from each side, were to pick two more men to oversee all decisions. The selected men were to supervise ministerial appointments, local administration and the custody of royal castles. Parliament, meanwhile, which was to meet three times a year, would monitor the performance of this council.

The king assented to the controls imposed on his personal administration but had no intention of observing them. He renounced the agreement in 1261. This led to the Second Baron's War. Of note is 'The Great Parliament' which de Montfort made the king convoke. The sheriffs of the counties were to send to Parliament two knights from each shire and two burgesses from each borough. The knights were to be elected by those free of the county court, socmen, franklins, merchants and aldermen worth 40 shillings per annum, the Forty Shilling freehold. As the principal purpose of the parliament was to vote a subsidy for the king from the shires and boroughs their assent was being sought. It was a new concept for the sheriffs and it was to be centuries before it was properly and systematically implemented. But it was a start. (A franklin was a freeman who owned land, but was not of noble birth; a socman was one who held lands or tenements by socage.) This became the basis of parliamentary democracy as it evolved in England and was transferred to Ireland.

The members of the committee soon disagreed among themselves, and in 1263 the Provisions of Oxford were placed under the arbitration of Louis of France, who decided in favour of Henry (1264) and war immediately broke out. Simon de Montfort defeated and captured the king. But only fifteen months later, Prince Edward had escaped captivity (having been freed by his cousin, Roger Mortimer) to lead the royalists into battle again and he turned the tables on de Montfort at the Battle of Evesham in 1265. Henry, weak and senile, allowed Edward to take charge of the government and concentrated on the great work of his life, the building of Westminster Abbey. The troubles of the reign ceased, so much so that Edward was able to depart on crusade, and

Henry died peacefully at Westminster. Soon after Edward's marriage in 1254, Henry III gave him Gascony, Ireland, Bristol, and the march between the Dee and the Conway rivers. In the latter area, as the Earl of Chester, he gained experience in warfare with the Welsh. His attempt to introduce the English system of counties and hundreds provoked Llewellyn *ap* Gruffydd, Prince of Wales. He left for the Crusades in 1271 and fought bravely at Acre and Haifa. While Edward was on the way home, his father died, and he succeeded to the crown on Nov. 20, 1272.

Ireland in the Thirteenth Century

The people of Ireland experienced unprecedented prosperity in the 13th century and it was to be many centuries before the same standards of wealth were attained. The institutions of central government increased and matured as the justiciar's court was split into various specialised courts and offices. The various Norman knights developed their estates, founded and built towns, improved roads and ports and built up. Greater production allowed an increase in population and the recovery of marginal lands. Furthermore, those in the Norman areas enjoyed great peace and stability. This does not mean that everyone was rich. The wealth of the great lords, both Norman and Gaelic probably increased. The very poor remained miserably poor. But for those in between, craftsmen, farmers, labourers, villeins, and betaghs and so on, there was a greater output of agricultural produce and of the products of craftsmen than ever before. The ordinary people had their local courts where they had some control over local affairs. The general improvement in Common Law and its extension to cover all courts, even if only by appeal to the royal courts, were yet to feed through to ordinary people. But they were there in principle.

Ireland was affected to a limited extent by the disturbances in England which led to the two Barons' Wars. Nor had the grants to the various favourites and the resentment it caused much impact in Ireland but there were some repercussions. The surprise appointment of Maurice Fitzgerald of Offaly as justiciar gave a great boost to the fortunes of that branch of the family. The greatest effect passed almost unnoticed namely the calling of the representatives of the 'commons' to Parliament. Nor was the Magna Charta an issue; the leading Irish barons supported John.

By the end of the century Anglo-Norman influence had spread to cover most of the country. By 1297 Anglo-Norman lords controlled up to two thirds of the country including almost all of the good land. They controlled the entire east coast from Lough Foyle in the north down to the Kenmare River between Cork and Kerry. On the west coast the coast of Kerry and Limerick as far as Limerick city was in their hands, as was much of the coast of Connaught. Most of the rest of the coast was in the hands of four Gaelic lords, the MacCarthys, the O'Briens, the O'Flahertys, and the O'Donnells.

Only one substantial stretch of land, 'the Great Irishry' was controlled by Gaelic lords. This comprised the lands of the O'Neills, O'Donnells, various chiefdoms of Oriel in south Ulster, the lands of the O'Rourkes, of O'Farrell of Annaly, and the remnants of the O'Connors. Isolated on the west coast were the O'Flahertys in west Galway, the O'Briens in Clare, and the MacCarthys in south-west Cork. In the midlands there were remnants of the O'Molloys, O'Mores and O'Connors *Faly*. In Wicklow were the O'Byrnes and O'Tooles (Maps, Nichols, *Gaelic and Gaelicized Ireland*, 217-8). This was not the whole picture. Many local Gaelic lords survived even after their best lands were taken and were probably tolerated. The O'Carrolls of *Eile* moved themselves into the nearby Slieve Bloom hills or mountains. They could then purchase freedom of the Norman Lordship court, establish their own Gaelic court, or do both. Such, when Anglo-Norman influence waned, might recover their lands or find them occupied by more powerful Gaelic lords.

The Gaelic chiefs had an ambivalent attitude towards the newcomers and the Government. Mostly they wanted to intermarry with the local Anglo-Norman families. They were useful as allies and had very good fighting men. They also wanted to get the best they could from the justiciar's Government but conceding as little as possible with regard to their own freedom of action. Even within a ruling family there were differences of opinion with regard to engagement with the Government. The advantages to the family of the incumbent chief of holding a feudal fief governed by feudal law was great, especially the adoption of primogeniture, full possession of all the land in their fiefs, and the right to attend the justiciar's council and to be consulted. This would mean excluding perpetually the rest of the *derb fine* from the chieftainship, the supersession of the Brehon Law with Common Law making the brehon families redundant, perhaps the allowing in of justices in assize, and giving up the right to make war and peace. For the senior clergy their position was enhanced, they received adequate endowments of property, and they got Brehon Law abolished, the provisions of Common Law and statute law being more aligned with Canon Law. These of course were theoretical arguments for everyone knew the Norman lords ignored the justiciar if they could get away with it, which was most of the time.

The advance, planned by John into the south Ulster lands of the *Oirghialla* had ended in 1212 when Aedh *Meth* O'Neill burned the preliminary castle at Clones in County Monaghan. On the northern side the advance from the earldom of Ulster reached Greencastle in Co. Donegal in 1305 which proved a high watermark of expansion in that direction. Godfrey O'Donnell destroyed the fort on Lough Erne in 1257 preventing any advance against him from Connaught. The advance against the MacCarthys was stopped by Fineen MacCarthy in 1261 and there were no further advances into their territories. The O'Connors defeated the de Burghs at Athenkip in 1270. The advance into Clare against the O'Briens came to an end at the battle of Dysert O'Dea in

1318. In many ways the Bruce invasions (1315 to 1318) marked the end of the expansion if not actually indicating a retraction.

Henry's long reign can be conveniently divided into four periods. From 1216 to 1231, during the king's minority, the kingdom was ruled by regents, barons faithful to John, who were not inclined to depart from his policies. The 2nd period can be taken as that of Henry's personal rule up the Provisions of Oxford, 1231 to 1258. The 3rd period can be taken as that of the disputes with the barons and the Baron's War i.e. from 1258 to 1267. The 4th phase can be taken as the governing by Prince Edward Longshanks, 1267 to 1272. The Marshals were the dominant family in the early part of the century, the Fitzgeralds of Offaly and Connaught in the middle part and the de Burghs of Connaught in the last part.

Ireland 1216-1231

This was the period of the king's minority when England was governed according to the ideas of those barons who had supported John in 1215. John appointed Geoffrey de Marisco justiciar in 1215. Geoffrey de Marisco was justiciar of Ireland 1215-21, 1226-8, and 1230-2. A member of a Somerset family and nephew of Archbishop Cumin, he held Adare in Limerick and Killorglin in Kerry. In 1210 he accompanied King John against Hugh de Lacy. He was appointed justiciar in the summer of 1215 but was accused of financial irregularities and resigned in October 1221. In 1224 he fought against Hugh de Lacy and in June 1226 was reappointed justiciar and built castles at Ringdown and Ballyleague (Roscommon) on the Shannon. He had received grants of land in Limerick from John. He was also sheriff of John's county of Munster, and was responsible for large renders to the crown including £400 from Donough O'Brien (Empey, 'Settlement of Limerick', 13-16). The office of sheriff was one of profit, which meant that the office-holder paid himself first and it was easy to make accusations of malfeasance.

The racial prejudices of nationalist historians often appear when describing the alleged illegal grabbing of 'Irish' lands. This view misunderstands the character of the period. Lords, Gaelic or Norman, had to justify to their consciences that the war was just. The Gaelic lords maintained poets, lawyers, genealogists, and such like to make out a case for an attack. The Normans relied on legal right no matter how tenuous. There was always a grant given to some ancestor, or else a marriage into a targeted family. The king, of course, in feudal theory could dispose of his own land, remove a lord who was disruptive of the peace of the realm, and give it to someone else. These grants had to be carefully considered for there was no point in antagonising a lord that the king was powerless to subdue. Grants were often given with the consent of local lords, or when authority broke down within an Irish chiefdom as it frequently did. The idea was to gain the maximum benefit for the minimum of expense. Returns to the crown from Ireland rarely justified great expense.

When giving grants the feudal kings designated the lands of specified Irish chiefs. This was not a definite patch of earth but the area from which the chief could collect tribute. It was liable to extend or contract in accordance with the fortunes of the ruling family. A territory could be split between two members of the family. The ancient chiefdom of the *Eile* became split into ElyoCarroll and Elyogarty (Ely of the O'Fogartys). These 'cantreds' were sometimes made into manors with the returns of every vill accounted for. The Normans were very conscious of the cash return and would always interpret their grant in the widest possible terms. When Walter de Lacy (the loyal one) got his lands in Meath restored in 1219 he attacked an O'Reilly crannog in Lough Oughter, Co. Cavan. This was presumably a border dispute, for the O'Rourkes and O'Reillys had been nibbling away at the O'Mellaghlin lands for a century, and de Lacy grant was the O'Mellaghlin lands. The de Lacy town of Drogheda on the southern bank of the Boyne was ceded to the crown.

When Meiler *fitz* Henry finally died childless in 1220, his lands passed to one of the heirs of his half-brother Maurice *fitz* Gerald whose third son, was Thomas *fitz* Maurice *fitz* Gerald of Shanid in Limerick. Thomas had two sons, John and Maurice *fitz* Thomas *fitz* Gerald. These quickly made Kerry a Geraldine (belonging to the family of Gerald) stronghold. In 1220 the archbishop of Dublin, Henry of London, replaced de Marisco as justiciar. In 1224 he was replaced as justiciar by William Marshal the younger, the 2nd Earl of Pembroke of the second creation. Geoffrey de Marisco acted as his deputy. De Marisco was re-appointed justiciar in 1226 and in 1230. Richard de Burgh was justiciar from 1228 to 1230. Gaelic Ireland was in turmoil as each lord tried to take advantage of his neighbour's difficulties. The Norman lords were either invited to assist one side or the other or invited themselves, often accompanied by Gaelic allies.

Aedh *Meth* O'Neill (d 1230) was still the undisputed chief of the O'Neills though the MacLoughlins were menacing in the background. Donnchad *Cairprech* (Donough of Carbery?) *mac* Dónail *Mór* O'Brien (1210-1242) had stabilised the O'Brien chiefdom. Cathal *Crovderg* O'Connor still ruled Connaught. The MacMurroughs and O'Mellaghlins were largely powerless. The MacCarthys had lost much of their lands in the more fertile areas of Munster and were consolidating themselves in south west Cork. Their lands were not safe from encroachment until the victory of Fineen MacCarthy over the Fitzgeralds of Desmond in 1261.

The year 1224 was a momentous one. Cathal *Crovderg* O'Connor died in 1224 and again civil war broke out in Connaught between Cathal's son Aedh and his uncles. Aedh *Meth* O'Neill of course had to intervene. It seems that King John had made a grant of the O'Connor lands to William de Burgh, changed his mind, and decided on an agreement with Cathal *Crovderg* O'Connor in 1210. Hubert de Burgh the Regent decided to revert to John's original policy and give the lordship of Connaught to William de Burgh's son, Richard *Mór* de Burgh. He received a grant of the O'Connor lands in Connaught in 1226, thus originating another great Irish family, the Burkes of Clanrickard (or Clanrickarde, the family of Richard, the c still pronounced hard). Richard was to hold Connaught *in capite* and apparently in socage not knight service at an annual rent of 300 (later 500) marks a year, and the service of 10 knights, reserving Cathal *Crovderg*'s five cantreds to the crown. (These cantreds were the lands of the *Sil Muredaig* (O'Connor) branch of the *Ui Briuin Ai,* which was Anglicized as Shilmorthy. They were returned to the O'Connors.) It seems that it was expected that some deal could be done with the O'Connors for little was prepared for some years apart from building some castles like one at Meelick on the Shannon where his father had built a motte-and-bailey castle in 1203.

Though Walter de Lacy had received back his Irish lands in 1214, Hugh de Lacy, who had fled from de Courci's castle at Carrickfergus in 1210 when John approached with his army, had not got the earldom of Ulster back from either regent, William Marshal or Hubert de Burgh. So in 1223 he returned to Ulster to make trouble in alliance with Aedh *Meth* O'Neill. With Aedh he attacked the lands in the earldom of Ulster, captured Coleraine castle but failed to capture Carrickfergus which had been strengthened by John. He also joined with his half-brother William de Lacy in raiding Walter de Lacy's lands in Meath. (It was not only in Gaelic lands that relatives squabbled over inheritances.) Marshal's son, also called William, 2nd Earl of Pembroke, replaced Archbishop Henry of London as justiciar to deal with de Lacy. Walter de Lacy and Marshal quickly defeated William de Lacy in Meath so he too fled into Ulster. As the Marshal's army approached Ulster and Aedh *Meth* was prepared to defy him, Hugh de Lacy surrendered to the justiciar. McNeill notes that Carrickfergus castle had a garrison of 31 men and Marshal sent an additional 20 knights and 20 men-at-arms to assist in its defence. This indicates the scale of the raiding parties (McNeill, 18). De Lacy's earldom was returned to him under strict conditions. It paid to make trouble.

Aedh *Meth* had obviously become too strong and warlike, but he remained an ally of de Lacy. After his death in 1230 he was succeeded by a member of the rival branch, Dónal MacLoughlin. He was removed by de Lacy in 1237 and Brian O'Neill *Catha an Duin* (of the Battle of Down), son of Niall *Ruadh* (the red) was installed. Dónal returned in 1238 only to be killed along with 10 of the chief MacLoughlins by Brian O'Neill at the battle of Cameirge in 1241. The MacLoughlins were never afterwards a major force in Ulster. The O'Neill succession then passed to the line of Aedh *Meth*'s brother Niall *Ruadh* (the red) O'Neill who had married a daughter of Cathal *Crovderg* O'Connor, and whose son was Brian of the Battle of Down. From Aedh *Meth*'s son Aedh *Buidhe* (the yellow-haired) came the *Clann Aodha Buidhe* or Clandeboy O'Neills. It did not mean of course that the MacLoughlins or Clandeboy ceased their attempts to recover the overlordship of the *Cenel Eogain*. De Lacy strengthened his castles, built others, and occupied north Antrim (McNeill, 21f; Burke, *Peerage*, 'O'Neill'). He was also able to claim de Verdon lands in Co. Louth which he had obtained as his wife, Lecelina de Verdon's dowry (Otway-Ruthven, 75). (This explains how he could grant the lands of Ballymascanlon, north of Dundalk to Mellifont Abbey. It happens to be my mother's parish (Columcille, 77)).

In 1228 Richard de Burgh was made justiciar. The justiciar's salary was fixed at £500 a year. This was deemed adequate but proved hopelessly insufficient (Otway-Ruthven, 147). In Desmond in 1229 Dermot MacCarthy (1207-1229) died, and was succeeded by his brother Cormac *Fionn* MacCarthy (1229-47). In 1251 after the usual civil war, Fineen (*Finghin*) MacCarthy succeeded as chief and was successfully to resist all further Norman incursions into his mountainous territory. In the far North West there was a revival of fortunes too for the *Cenel Conaill* whose ruling family was now the O'Donnells. Under Dónal *Mór* O'Donnell (d. 1241) they attacked the western ends of *Oirgialla* lands of the MacMahons and the *Breifne* lands of the O'Rourkes and

O'Reillys. They installed the Maguires in Fermanagh, reducing the Maguires, O'Reillys and O'Connor Sligo to the status of urraghs or sub-kings. In 1231 William Marshal the 2nd Earl of Pembroke died and was succeeded by his brother, Richard Marshal the 3rd earl.

Ireland 1231 to 1258

The disturbances in England for once had great and immediate consequences in Ireland. It was one of the chief grievances of the English barons (and Irish barons were often English barons as well) that Henry preferred Frenchmen, Poitevans and Savoyards who came to England with his mother Isabella of Angoulême or his wife Eleanor of Provence. The bishop of Winchester, Peter de Roches was from Poitou in France, hence the name Poitevan. He stood by John in the war against the barons, but was very disappointed when William Marshal prevented him from being regent. He had a greedy nephew (or son) called Peter of Rivaux who had a reputation of trying to get as many offices in England as he could to the intense annoyance of the barons (Costain, 47). The bishop was further disappointed in his attempt to get the government of England into his hands when Hubert de Burgh was made regent. But when the king came to his majority he saw his chance. The Marshals had accumulated great lands and he and the king would like to get their hands on him. First however he got the king to dismiss Hubert de Burgh, and then he picked a quarrel with Richard Marshal, the 3rd Earl, and stirred up the de Lacys and Geoffrey de Marisco against him in Ireland. Peter de Roches and Peter de Rivaux were to be in complete control of England for the next two years (Otway-Ruthven, 96).

Richard de Burgh was promptly removed from the justiciarship and Maurice Fitzgerald, 2nd Lord of Offaly, son of Gerald Fitzmaurice, 1st Lord of Offaly and Eve de Bermingham, and grandson of the original Maurice *fitz* Gerald, was appointed. (The cantred or barony of *Ui Failge*, (Offaly in Co. Kildare) had originally been given by Strongbow to Robert de Bermingham. Eve was his sole heiress. Gerald succeeded to the property and title by right of his wife, *iure uxoris*.) For nearly a century the Fitzgeralds and de Burghs would struggle for supremacy in Ireland. (This was then succeeded by the struggle between the Fitzgeralds and the Butlers.) The affairs of Ireland including the royal revenues were placed in the hands of Peter de Rivaux which was to prove his undoing. The release of Felim *mac* Cathal *Crovderg* O'Connor was ordered. He immediately attacked Aedh O'Connor, slew him and many relatives, claimed the overlordship of Connaught for himself, and set about destroying all the Norman castles, which was not wise. The king was advised to recognize Felim and he ordered him to capture de Burgh. He also wanted Cormac MacCarthy installed in Desmond on the grounds that Richard de Burgh objected to him. Richard Marshall sought support in Ireland and was killed.

The downfall of Peter de Rivaux was as sudden as his rise. His enemies approached the king and he was ordered to submit his accounts for all the lands and offices he had grabbed. Following the king's *volte face* everyone had to move quickly to maintain their position. Henry recognised Gilbert Marshal, the 3rd brother, as Earl of Pembroke and restored his lands. Cormac MacCarthy was defeated in Munster and made peace with Fitzgeralds, neither party wishing to get the justiciar involved. Cormac retained the chieftainship. Donough *Cairprech* O'Brien hastily submitted. Felim *mac* Cathal *Crovderg* O'Connor was not expecting the powerful reaction of the Normans, most of whom rallied behind the new justiciar, to show their loyalty.

The grant to de Burgh was now recognised. The new justiciar, Maurice Fitzgerald, baron of Offaly, in 1235 led a large hosting into Connaught including de Burgh and his following and occupied it. Felim *mac* Cathal *Crovderg* O'Connor (1233-1256) was allowed to hold only the O'Connor lands of Shilmorthy at an annual tribute. Connaught was quickly subinfeudated by de Burgh and Fitzgerald but few English colonists were installed. De Burgh's principal estate was in the barony of Loughrea where he built a castle in 1236 and a town was founded. He also founded Galway town and Ballinasloe. The islands on Lough Mask and Lough Orben were also part of his demesne. Rents were paid in cash or kind to the new lords just as they were in Ulster. It was not royal policy to destroy the great Irish chiefs but to reduce their influence. Maurice Fitzgerald got a grant of extensive lands around Sligo and he built a castle there in 1245 as well as rebuilding the fort at *Caol Uisge* near Belleek on Lough Erne. Neither of these land grants were in the core areas of the O'Connors. Maurice Fitzgerald is credited with introducing the Dominican and Franciscan orders to Ireland, and he founded a friary (incorrectly called Sligo abbey) for Dominicans in his new town of Sligo. They were often invited to provide men or cash for the king's wars overseas (McNeill, 69). Felim O'Connor accompanied the justiciar to Wales in 1245. In 1245 he and Felim O'Connor of Connaught were admonished for tardiness in joining the King in an expedition into Wales. After this, among other rights, the Irish Barons claimed exemption from attending the sovereign beyond the realm. But, as Dolley observed, wherever there was a Gaelic chief who wished to co-operate with the king there was always opposition from some members of his own family who urged the contrary. This was not unusual in any part of the world (Dolley, 139).

An important grant was the land around Athenry to Meiler de Birmingham which was to ensure de Birmingham influence and provide a walled town on the road to Galway. Galway was itself founded at this time by de Burgh who built a castle and imported burgesses both Gaelic and English. (It got a royal charter in 1396.) The de Burgh family were now installed as the provincial overlords of Connaught. At the same time a county of Connaught was formed with its own sheriff. It is not clear how this functioned alongside the feudal lordship of Connaught. Later in the Middle Ages the financial returns by the sheriff of Connaught to the Exchequer were virtually nil.

Maurice Fitzgerald's next preoccupation was with Ulster. Hugh de Lacy owed his restoration to Aedh *Meth* O'Neill and so there was friendship between them until Aedh's death in 1230. On Aedh's death the chieftainship reverted to Dónal MacLoughlin as described above. The resurgent O'Donnells raided and wasted as far as Newry in 1236 (Canavan, 28). This resurgence came under Dónal Mór mac Eicnechain, (1207-1241), Máel Sechlainn mac Dónal, 1241-1247 and Godfrey O'Donnell (1247-58) from whome the later medieval O'Donnells took their name.

Then in 1238 Dónal MacLoughlin attacked de Lacy. This caused the justiciar and de Lacy to attack both. In *Cenel Conaill* against O'Donnell they were assisted by the nephew of Aedh *Meth*, Brian O'Neill (of the Battle of Down). It would seem that at this stage the O'Neills acknowledged the overlordship of the justiciar, nominally at least. Brian O'Neill's mother was a daughter of Cathal *Crovderg* O'Connor. The justiciar's aim seems to have been to get the O'Neills to accept the overlordship of the justiciar and at the same time control the lesser chiefs. Meanwhile, Richard de Burgh, with the aid to the O'Connors would reduce the O'Donnells to subordinate status. The strategy worked for a time but was not permanent and the later defeat of Brian O'Neill at the battle of Down in 1260 opened the way for the expansion of the earldom of Ulster until 1330.

The 1240s saw great changes. In 1241 the long-lived but not very effective Walter de Lacy died. The de Lacy grant in Meath, potentially the strongest, began with settlements with numerous colonists in Dublin and east Meath and gradually but more tenuously towards Westmeath and the Shannon. When Walter de Lacy, Lord of Trim and Ludlow, died in 1241 he left two heiresses, Maud and Margery de Lacy, his lands returned to the crown to be married off by the crown. Maud de Lacy married Sir Geoffrey de Geneville, 1st Baron Geneville, and the lordships of Trim and Ludlow passed to her husband by right of his marriage to her. She is sometimes referred to as Matilda de Lacy. Her grand-daughter was to marry Roger Mortimer. Westmeath was allocated to Margery de Lacy who married in May 1244 John de Verdon, Lord of Westmeath. (The de Verdon's apparently had a grant of land in Westmeath from the original Hugh de Lacy by subinfeudation, Otway-Ruthven, 121.) A county of Meath, based on the de Verdon lands was formed in 1297, based on Kells, was formed in Meath, and a liberty remained based on Trim. Looking back this probably weakened the powerful Liberty of Trim in the following century. The county of Meath and the liberty of Trim were technically outside the defence of The Pale. In 1243 his brother Hugh de Lacy in Ulster died without heirs and the earldom also returned to the crown. Under him the earldom had expanded to include north Antrim east of the Bann. It was administered by the crown until 1254 when it was granted to Prince Edward as Lord of Ireland. He granted it to Walter de Burgh in 1264 (McNeill, 29).

The Norman lords still owed their feudal duties to the king and in 1242 Richard de Burgh and other Irish lords were persuaded by the justiciar to join King Henry's expedition to Poitou. Richard de Burgh died there in 1243 and his lands were taken into the custody of the crown, his son Sir Richard de Burgh being a minor. Richard died in 1248 and the lands were restored to his brother Walter. Malcontents among the Gaelic families always liked to see the departure of the Norman lords to the king's wars. The Gaelic chiefs were also summoned to the wars and Felim O'Connor joined Henry against the Welsh. Occasionally they went or paid scutage (McNeill, 69).

When the last of the Marshals died in 1243 the inheritance in Leinster was divided among 5 heiresses all of whose husbands were English. Seneschals were appointed to manage the estates until the crown made other provisions. (Presumable the office and title of Lord of Leinster now ceased.) A descendant of the Brood of Nesta, Maurice Fitzgerald, lord of Naas and Offaly (baronies in Kildare), 2nd Lord Offaly, and justiciar of Ireland, seized his chance to advance his family. He had two sons, Maurice *fitz* Maurice Fitzgerald 3rd Lord Offaly, and Thomas *fitz* Maurice Fitzgerald whose son Thomas *fitz* Thomas Fitzgerald became 4th Lord Offaly and 1st Earl of Kildare. (The 1st Lord Offaly had obtained the lands and title by marriage as noted earlier.) The Earls of Kildare (the Northern Geraldines) were to become the most powerful family in Ireland. Kildare and Carlow became counties, while Kilkenny and Wexford remained liberties. (Carlow, then larger than today, and extending to and including coastal *Arklow*, probably dates from around 1306.) Sir Roger Mortimer, a new name in Ireland, became lord of *Laois*, having married Maud de Braose the daughter of William de Braose and Eve Marshall. The splitting of the great fiefdoms of Meath and Leinster weakened them both though the effects of this weakening did not appear for nearly a century.

The *Ui Failge* spent centuries try to get back their original fertile lands in Kildare from the Fitzgeralds having been displaced into the wooded and boggy areas of present day Offaly. Donough *Cairprech* O'Brien died and his successor, Connor O'Brien paid the king 2,200 marks for confirmation of his title. In 1248 Walter de Burgh succeeded his brother as Lord of Connaught. Felim *mac* Cathal *Crovderg* O'Connor (1233-1256) and his son Aedh *mac* Felim O'Connor (1256-1274) were the most important of the O'Connors in mid-century.

John *fitz* Geoffrey, son of Geoffrey *fitz* Peter, Earl of Essex, was justiciar from 1245 to 1256 though Maurice Fitzgerald deputised for him. (He was distantly connected by marriage with the Marshals and de Clares. One daughter married Walter de Burgh, Earl of Ulster, and another Theobald Butler of Nenagh.) John *fitz* Geoffrey proved an able and vigorous justiciar, and largely pursued Maurice Fitzgerald's policy of reviving King John's plan for controlling the mearings between the great clans in Ulster. Following the success in Connaught there was every hope that the plan could be achieved. If royal castles could be established at Monaghan, Castleblaney, and at the Narrows of Lough Erne the Gaelic chiefs could be split up and their sub-chiefs kept under control. The Gaelic provincial chiefs were aware of this, and strove to prevent it.

In Munster grants were made to various lords, of whom the Butlers of Ormond and Fitzgeralds of Desmond (the Southern Geraldines) became the most powerful. Later in the Middle Ages, the Butler lands around Nenagh in north Tipperary became untenable, so they acquired other lands in Kilkenny, and Kilkenny castle became the stronghold of the Butlers, earls of Ormond. The Butler family had several offshoots like the Butlers of Dunboyne and the Butlers of Cahir. These local Butler lordships in north Munster formed part of the bulwark on the northern flank of the earldom of Desmond against any revival of Gaelic power.

From Thomas, the 3rd son of the original Maurice Fitzgerald, whose children were called *fitz* Thomas Fitzgerald, came the Barons Desmond, later earls of Desmond. Their original lands were in Limerick and Kerry but they came to control Munster between the MacCarthys to the south, and the Butlers and O'Briens to the north. The southern flank of the earldom of Desmond was guarded by powerful local lords, Roche, Barry, Barrett, and Courcey. The Powers (*le Paor*) were lords in Waterford.

The de Burghs became dominant in Connaught, though they were in the next century to split into the Clanrickard Burkes, the Clanwilliam Burkes, and the MacWilliam Burkes. After the battle of Athenkip (1270) the Burkes and the O'Connors were largely responsible for their own territories, the O'Connors in the east, the Burkes in the middle, and various local and largely independent chiefs in the south and west and north. The O'Connors rapidly subdivided into various branches of the O'Connors and MacDermotts, and unlike the O'Neills, O'Briens and MacCarthys failed to maintain a dominant branch. They all ignored the sheriff and the Lord Deputy.

Ireland 1258 to 1267

The events in England had some repercussions in Ireland but not as great as one might have expected. In 1258 the O'Donnells exploited their connections with the Scottish Highlands to bring in foreign mercenaries, or gallowglasses (*galloglach*: *gall*, foreigner + *ógláech*, soldier). Henceforth, the gallowglasses or mercenary soldiers were to dominate Irish wars. It is not clear how exactly they were paid, but many in Donegal got tracts of land like the Normans. Others may have been paid in cattle. The wealth of the Gaelic lords in the later Middle Ages was increasing. Whether from the development of trade or harsh exactions from ordinary workers or both is not clear. Certainly they began to build proper stone castles for themselves. The gallowglasses put the Gaelic chiefs on an equal footing with the Anglo-Norman men-at-arms and archers. There was a limit to the number of gallowglasses a chief could afford, and lesser chiefs probably never could afford them. The bulk of their forces were lightly armed kerne who also had to be hired and paid and who were notorious for plundering, looting and raping. But most warfare consisted of wasting raids. The O'Donnells, with their aid, established themselves strongly in Donegal and could not be subdued either by the stronger O'Neills or by the justiciar.

The O'Connors of Connaught were quick to take advantage. Aedh *mac* Felim O'Connor (1256-1274) married a daughter of Dougal Mac Sorley, the Lord of the Isles, and his bride brought a dowry of 150 gallowglasses. Aedh defeated the justiciar d'Ufford and Walter de Burgh, 2nd Lord of Connaught and Earl of Ulster at Athenkip in 1270 and preserved the O'Connor inheritance of Shilmorthy. The inheritance remained intact for another century until 1385 when it split into two branches, the O'Connor Don and O'Connor Roe. Later O'Connor Sligo and the various branches of the MacDermotts, all fighting each other, emerged. (The uniting of the Lordship of Connaught with the earldom of Ulster was a mistake for one man had to concentrate on two quite separate fronts.) It was at the height of the benign climatic conditions of the Middle Ages, and sea connections between western Scotland and the north and west of Ireland were close. They shared a common language, the dialects of Donegal and Scotland being particularly close.

As Dolley notes, the sheriff in Connaught, Jordan d'Exeter, was killed in a sea fight off the coast of Connemara with pirates from Scotland. This indicates he had naval forces at his disposal. Galway and Sligo were considerable ports and their commerce worth raiding. The hiring of Scottish mercenaries by Gaelic chiefs continued into Tudor times when they were called 'red shanks' a name probably derived from the distinctive Highland kilt. (The MacCarthys and O'Driscolls fought a sea battle about this time, Dolley, 158.) Brian O'Neill in 1253 made war on the justiciar, Fitzgerald; he demolished castles, burned unfortified 'street-towns' and desolated parts of Co. Down.

In 1257 a battle was fought by Godfrey O'Donnell with Maurice Fitzgerald at Creadran-Cille (Credan) to the north of Sligo. The justiciar's forces were routed with great slaughter. It should be noted that justiciars, sheriffs, and barons as well as Gaelic chiefs were still expected to fight in the heart of the battle though doubtless supported by bodyguards. The two men fought each other in single combat and both were gravely wounded. Maurice died of his injuries at Youghal Monastery, wearing the habit of the Franciscans, on 20 May 1257, aged 63 years. In consequence of the success of this battle, the English and the Geraldines were driven out of much of Lower Connaught (North Connaught), leaving influence there to the de Burghs. The castle of **Caol-uisce** which had been recently strengthened was razed to the ground and its garrison slain. Between 1245 and 1295 Sligo castle was destroyed four times by either the O'Connors or O'Donnells who claimed to be the local overlords. In the 14th century the castle and town passed to the O'Connor Sligo branch of the O'Connors and they recognised the overlordship of the O'Donnells.

The wounded Godfrey was immediately attacked by Brian O'Neill. Though the O'Neills were repulsed Godfrey died of his wounds shortly afterwards. The first recorded spelling of the family name is shown to be that of Godfrey O'Donnell, which was dated 1258. An alternative family name for the O'Donnells was **Clan Dálaigh** or **Síl Dálaigh**. The

Cenel Connaill had at an earlier date been one of the most formidable families in Ireland, being often overlords of the *Ui Neill* and exacting tribute from what is now the ecclesiastical province of Armagh, and from Leinster when they could. Their last over-king was Flaibertach (728-734) after which date the *Cenel Eogain* always managed to exclude them (Keenan, *True Origins*, 312). The O'Donnells were now wracked by infighting and did not become a formidable military power until Tudor times.

Maurice was succeeded in 1257 as 3rd Lord of Offaly by his son, Maurice, rather than the rightful successor, his grandson, Maurice, son of his eldest son, Gerald. The destruction of the fort at *Caol Uisge* finally put an end to the plan of King John and John de Grey to put a *cordon sanitaire* across south Ulster and to prevent the attempt of the justiciar Maurice Fitzgerald to link de Burgh lands in Connaught with those of the earldom of Ulster which would have achieved the same purpose. Brian got at least some agreement from Conor O'Brien and Aedh O'Connor that O'Neill should be high king of Ireland. (There is no agreement about what they agreed or who was to be high king.) Brian O'Neill and Aedh O'Connor decided to make a surprise assault on the earldom of Ulster in 1260. Though it was in the hands of the king it was well prepared to meet such an attack and the mayor of Carrickfergus was able to gather forces. The invaders were signally defeated by local levies near Downpatrick. Brian was killed in the battle from which he derives his name and the usual dispute over succession began which was to last until the end of the century.

Aedh *Buidh*, the yellow-haired, a grandson of Aedh *Meth*, became chief of the O'Neills, The O'Neill country was then promptly ravaged by the O'Donnells which gave the faction supporting the younger brother Niall *Culanach* their chance. He was deposed by Niall *Culanach* (from his distinctive hairstyle, with the front of the head shaved) who was in turn deposed two years later (Simms, 'Gaelic Warfare', 101). (Niall was chief of the O'Neills from 1261 to 1263 and from 1286-1291 when he was installed by the Red Earl.) Niall *Culanach* then sought support from the O'Donnells. Aedh *Buidh* repelled an invasion by the seneschal of the earldom, defeated and killed the chief of the O'Donnells, and was himself killed in 1283 by the O'Reillys of *Breifne*. Another dispute broke out between his son and the son of Brian of the Battle of Down. Aedh *Buidhe's* family became known as Clandeboy (*Clann Aodha Buidhe*) and remained a separate sub-group of the O'Neills thereafter. There is no particular significance in this series of disputes except to illustrate conditions in the great lordships when successions were normally settled by battle, and alliances were made as convenient for the moment. Rarely if ever was the chief of the O'Neills able to get the full hosting of the province they claimed a right to.

Dónal O'Neill, son of Brian of the Battle of Down succeeded in 1283 and brought some stability to Ulster. Scarcely had the schism in Ulster which had commenced with Dónal *mac* Ardgal *mac* Lochlainn in 1119 been settled than different schisms sprung up. Dónal was chief from 1283 to 1286 and from 1295 to 1325 and died in 1325. In 1286 he was deposed by the Red Earl of Ulster and was restored in 1295, Neill *Culanach* being temporarily restored until murdered by Dónal's supporters in 1291. (Niall's son Brian succeeded him from 1291 to 1295 until deposed in turn. Brian's son Henry (d.1347) was to be the last chief from the Clandeboy branch.) Dónal O'Neill was the chief of the O'Neills during the invasions of the Bruces. He is chiefly famous for his self-exculpating Remonstrance he sent to Pope John XXII in 1317 to excuse his rebellion against his lawful sovereign. (Burke's *Peerage* does its best to sort out who was who, and who had the right to the chiefdom.)

Walter de Burgh, d.1271, Earl of Ulster, was the 2nd son of Richard *Mór* de Burgh who died on a royal expedition to Poitou in 1243. In 1248 he became Lord of Connaught on the death of his older brother Sir Richard de Burgh. From 1255 onwards he was engaged in constant war in Connaught with Felim O'Connor, the son of Cathal *Crovderg* who had been established on the throne of Connaught by Richard de Burgh. The vulnerability of the earldom of Ulster led to its being granted in 1264 to him. He may have got a right to the title of Earl of Ulster from his mother the daughter of Walter de Lacy but it seems to have been a new creation. With him commenced the great ascendancy of the earldom in Ulster until the male line ended in 1333. In 1269 Aedh *Buidhe* O'Neill acknowledged that he held his authority from Walter de Burgh as Earl of Ulster. Aedh *Buidhe* married the daughter of a cousin of the Earl of Ulster, an Anglo-Norman knight called MacCostello. Once again the Gaelic chiefs were establishing marriage links with the Anglo-Norman lords, a practice which was to be forbidden by the Statutes of Kilkenny. The Irish chiefs also wanted to hold their lands directly from the crown but this was always refused (Lydon, *Ireland and England*, 214). Indeed de Burgh had exactly the same rights over the O'Neills as they claimed over the other chiefs. Later the de Burghs introduced the famous *bonnacht* of Ulster, a standing army of 300 warriors supplied by the Gaelic chiefs. With the decline of the earldom, O'Neill claimed to inherit the *bonnacht*; the chief difference from ordinary billeting or coyne was that it was year round.

In 1254, King Henry made Prince Edward Longshanks (later Edward I) lord of Ireland, and in theory at least had the same position as John had before he became king. He never came to Ireland. In 1264 the first of the new-style parliaments was called to meet at Castledermot. Otway-Ruthven notes that though the baronial war had its repercussions in Ireland and various local chiefs took the opportunity to make local mischief, there was no concerted action against the Government. In Munster a war between the MacCarthys and the Geraldines resulted in a victory for Fineen MacCarthy in the battle of Callan, near Kenmare in 1261. He was killed the following year. However the Geraldines ceased pushing into MacCarthy lands and the border between them stabilised. In 1264 Prince Edward conferred his earldom of Ulster on Walter de Burgh.

1267-1272

In the remaining years of Henry's life his son Prince Edward, Lord of Ireland virtually took over the government of England. He felt so secure at home that he was able to go to the Holy Land on a crusade, the Ninth Crusade 1271-1272, being the last major crusade. He returned when news of his father's death was brought to him. (The capture of Acre in 1291 marked the end of the crusades after nearly 200 years.)

There were the usual minor disturbances in Ireland but nothing of importance. In this period the MacCarthys in south west Cork and the O'Donnells in Donegal established themselves securely so that they were never after threatened. Like other chiefs they extended their powers within their own chiefdoms, and opposed or supported the Government opportunistically. The other major chiefs, whose lands were less defensible, did not achieve this security for nearly another hundred years. It is not surprising then to find them trying to get access to the king's courts as of right. This was conceded only to the 'Five Bloods', the O'Connors, the O'Briens, the O'Neills, the O'Mellaghlins, and the MacMurroughs. The MacMurrough Kavanaghs were secure in their ancestral lands undisturbed by the Government or the Anglo-Norman lords and were strangely quiescent at this period. The O'Mellaghlins, weakened though they were by internal disputes, were still making themselves felt. However, though Edward was willing to agree to this in principle, the Anglo-Norman lords were not. They probably had two reasons. They did not want their disputes with the Gaelic chiefs referred to the king's courts, and secondly, if a Gaelic chief wanted to plead in such a court he had to get an Anglo-Norman to represent him. This representation would not be cheap (Dolley, 160).

The Anglo-Norman barons and knights had been gradually establishing themselves over a century. When a baron or a knight was given a piece of land it was left to himself to occupy it and secure it as best they could. They usually made alliances, often matrimonial, with the local Gaelic chiefs. It was quite strange how often these families left no male heirs so titles to the lands passed to sons-in-law. The lands did not always remain in the hands of the original occupiers. In the earldom of Ulster, de Courci's lands passed to the de Lacy family, and then to the de Burghs of Connaught. From small settlements around Downpatrick and Carrickfergus the earldom gradually spread westward towards the Bann, and then over the Bann far beyond what royal grants had confirmed to them. But they had no choice. If they could not dominate the O'Neills the O'Neills would dominate them.

The Church in the Thirteenth Century

The great failure of the Irish Church and of Ireland in general in this century was with regard to education. There was no university. Universities, when they commenced consisted only of a handful of learned men and perhaps a few score of students in wooden buildings. Its endowment need not have been greater than that of a fairly small monastery. Scotland had 3 universities by 1500. It may be that Irish students mostly preferred the more prestigious institutions in Oxford and London. But even a few score of gentlemen who wanted some higher educations for their sons each year could have kept a college open.

Apart from that the great phenomenon was the coming of the mendicant friars. The first to arrive were the Dominicans whose order had been approved in 1215. They formed friaries in Dublin and Drogheda in 1224, in Kilkenny in 1225, in Waterford in 1226, and in Limerick in 1227. The Franciscans arrived from Tuscany in 1229. The Carmelites came later in 1272, and the Augustinian friars in 1282. Because of their need to survive on alms they had to live in towns and soon every town in Ireland had one or more friaries (Watt, *Church in Medieval Ireland*, 61). The first friaries would have been built of wood like town houses, but they soon followed the monastic orders by building in stone as money came in. The Dominican friary church in

Kilkenny was as good as any other church in an Irish town. A medieval monastery could take up to a century to complete. Their friaries, like the towns, had to be in Anglo-Norman areas. The maps of the distribution of Dominican, Franciscan, and Cistercian houses are curiously alike however (op. cit, 55, 63, and 72). All three are strangely lacking in the more Gaelic parts of Ireland. The Dominicans were called the black friars because of their black cloak, the Carmelites the white friars, and the Franciscans the grey friars for similar reasons.

The Cistercians (the white or grey monks) who had been welcomed as role models in the previous centuries now seem to have been in all sorts of trouble. Brief notes of what was happening were recorded in the decisions of the general chapters held annually in the head monastery of Citeaux in Burgundy. Discounting the fact that words like 'enormity' could often be used to describe quite minor matters, there seems to have been grave irregularities in some monasteries even early in the 13th century. In some monasteries the basics of the Rule seem not to have been observed. This continued gradually to get worse so that by the end of the Middle Ages only two monasteries were said to have been observing the Rule. Many monks had children. One reason for this could have been that the family who founded the monastery claimed the right to present monks to it. If a lad was no good as a warrior put him into the Church and he would be fed and clothed for the rest of his life. The only condition was that he should wear the habit and they did not always do that (Watt, *op. cit.* 54). Though the matter is not clear, it may be that in some of the old 'Celtic' monasteries married couples could live within the monastic enclosure and the man at least chant the offices.

Some disputes may have been caused when an Anglo-Norman took the lands of the original founder and insisted on presenting his own relatives. Visitations by senior abbots were resisted by force. The records of the visitation of Irish monasteries by Abbot of Stephen de Lexington of the monastery of Furness in Lancashire are unusually detailed (Watt *loc. cit.*; Columcille, 50-70). Mellifont received harsh treatment. Those found guilty of conspiracy were banished to other houses of the Order, a new abbot, a Frenchman was elected and new monks, seemingly Norman were brought in from France. As Fr. Columcille comments we would dearly like to know what actually was done wrong (*op. cit.* 69-70). It would seem that some monks, presumably Gaelic-speaking had fled to the protection of the chief of the O'Neills of *Cenel Eogain*, for Abbot Stephen wrote a letter to him. These were allowed to return. The abbots of Mellifont were in good standing with the Order for the rest of the century, though it was not until 1274 that the last of the penalties imposed on the monastery was reversed (Columcille, 85).

There was a problem, which was not unique in Europe, of the use of more than one language in a monastery. Nationalist writers often lamented about the Anglicisation of the episcopate. But it was perfectly normal at the time to try to secure the appointment of members of the ruling families to bishoprics and other senior posts. In addition, the crown had an interest in promoting more highly qualified clergy to senior posts. It seems undeniable that a cleric who had served on the staff of a king of England and large parts of France would be more qualified as a lawyer and administrator than one who had served only a local Gaelic chief. (Training in philosophy, Bible Study, and theology in a university was not highly regarded and was regarded as the province of the religious Orders.) Though the training of the senior Irish clergy in the traditional manner was perhaps adequate for a rural diocese where almost everyone was illiterate, standards of learning and administrative and legal practice were rising rapidly in England and on the Continent. No comparable schools were developed in Gaelic areas. Furthermore, while English clerics often had a good working knowledge of Common Law in the king's courts as well as canon law, the study and practice of Brehon Law was kept firmly in the hands of the lay legal families. Indeed the study of all learning, arts and crafts was kept within families with fathers instructing sons. The practice of the virtually illiterate local parish priest giving a rudimentary training to his sons seems to have persisted at the lowest level until the Reformation. There were still churches and monasteries where Latin was taught and this would, we presume, be normal for sons of richer families aspiring to benefices. The simple ceremonies of the mass and the sacraments, and the offering required for each, would have been known to all. What the priest would have to teach his son (or his nephew) was the Latin words to accompany them. The religious knowledge of the priest was probably no worse than that of his parishioners. The message of Christianity was quite simple. It was Martin Luther and his followers who insisted that everyone should memorise a catechism where the distinct doctrines of Protestantism were set out.

Much of the plans of the 12th century reformers were in fact carried out in the course of the 13th century. The work of transferring old endowments to new dioceses and chapters continued. Where necessary deaneries were formed and endowed, usually based on existing cantreds. Parishes on a geographical basis were formed often designating the lands of small clans as parishes (See above 'The Parishes').

Watt notes that the interest of the papacy in reforming the Irish Church and bringing up to date seems to have come to an end with the appointment of John of Salerno as legate in 1202-3. Afterwards the chief interest of papal legates was to collect money for Rome (Watt, 134-5).

Chapter 10

Edward I 1272-1307 and
Edward II 1307-1327

During this period the Anglo-Norman expansion reached its peak. But already a virtual equilibrium had been achieved. The more important Gaelic chiefs had reached a point where they were confirmed in their ancestral lands, though losing much power over their urraghs, and were beginning to see advantages to themselves from closer co-operation with the crown. Access to crown courts and to the king's council in parliament would put them on an equal footing with the Anglo-Norman lords.

The Reign of Edward I

Edward I (17 June 1239-7 July 1307), also known as Edward Longshanks and the Hammer of the Scots, was King of England from 1272 to 1307. Already, in the last years of his father's reign, he was the virtual regent of England, so there was no change in policy. He continued the policy of earlier kings in trying to establish uniform laws, reduce feudal privileges, and bring the barons to some extent under the control of the royal courts. All kings found this a prickly subject so, although he had beaten the barons in the Second Baron's War, he had to proceed cautiously. In 1295 he summoned what was called the Model Parliament. He accepted the contention of the barons and of Simon de Montfort that knights and burgesses and representatives of the lower clergy should be summoned. Edward proclaimed in his writ of summons, that what touches all, should be approved of all, and it is also clear that common dangers should be met by measures agreed upon in common. He is famous for his expulsion of the Jews whose position as moneylenders was soon taken up by the 'Lombards', merchants from northern Italy, especially Milan. His more immediate problems lay in Wales and Scotland.

The policy in Wales backfired. South Wales was under Norman control. Llywelyn the Great (*Llywelyn Fawr*), full name Llywelyn *ap* Iorwerth, (c. 1173-1240) was a Prince of Gwynedd in north Wales and eventually *de facto* ruler over most of Wales. By a combination of war and diplomacy he dominated Wales for forty years. This was in accord with the policy of Henry II so long as the Welsh chief paid his feudal respect. But when the English overlord was in difficulties with his barons it was easy to ignore feudal dues. It was still more difficult to refrain from interfering or trying to get ancient lands back. Llywelyn *ap* Gruffydd (c. 1223-1282) was the last prince of an independent Wales before its conquest by Edward I of England. He was the second of the four sons of Gruffydd, the eldest son of Llywelyn the Great. He and his grandfather had profited by the barons' wars to establish a powerful chiefdom covering north and central Wales. The Norman marcher lords were reduced to a strip along the south coast of Wales. His support for Simon de Montfort did not please Edward, nor did his marriage to de Montfort's daughter. In 1275 Edward called on Llywelyn to do homage for Wales and he refused. Edward invaded Wales, defeated Llywelyn and built a famous series of strong castles along the coast of north west Wales. Llywelyn was confined to his ancestral lands. Later a rebellion broke out, Edward led in another army and Llywelyn was killed. This time even the ancestral lands were annexed. In 1301 he proclaimed his own son Edward Prince of Wales, a tradition carried on by British monarchs to this day.

Edward, apart from the Welsh castles, is probably best known as the Hammer of the Scots. The issue of paying homage to Edward was not a great issue because the Scottish kings had lands in England. A question arose over the royal succession when the king died leaving the throne to a three-year old girl, Margaret, the Maid of Norway. When she died there were 14 claimants to the throne, only two of whom were important, John Balliol and Robert the Bruce. John Balliol was appointed but refused to do homage for Scotland, and made an alliance with France against Edward. Edward invaded Scotland, deposed Balliol, and imposed English administrators. When Edward died and his son proved incompetent, the Scots of the Lowlands, many Anglo-Norman by origin, largely united behind Robert the Bruce, were to seize their chance.

Edward I and Ireland

The original 'Welsh' policy of Henry II of accepting the feudal subjection of Leinster and Meath, and allowing the Gaelic high king to control the rest of Ireland with a token subordination to himself failed. The policy initiated by John of occupying the lands between the great provincial lords had largely been successful. The Gaelic chiefs were confirmed in their ancestral lands but isolated from each other. They could and did combine, but it was now hazardous for a provincial chief to march an army far from his own province.

Edward took an interest in his Irish Lordship and wished to make the Government efficient and lucrative. In 1275 the customs dues at the Irish ports on wool, hides and leather were granted to Edward by a great council. It became known as the Great Custom, and provided a solid revenue for the crown (Curtis, 90). The Act also allowed the free export of Irish goods.

In 1280 Richard *Óg* de Burgh, the Red Earl, became Lord of Connaught and 2nd Earl of Ulster and was to become the most powerful of the de Burgh earls. He was a strong supporter of King Edward. He began the expansion of the earldom along the coast west of the Bann. He defeated the O'Neills and O'Connors. He exacted the bonnacht, the obligation of the chiefs to send warriors to his hosting. He built a castle at Greencastle, Co. Donegal from where he exerted pressure on both the O'Neills and O'Donnells. At this time some of the Irish chiefs went with the king's forces to Flanders and Scotland along with those of de Burgh (McNeill, 70). In 1295 the effective John de Wogan was made justiciar. A parliament on the model of de Montfort's parliament at Castledermot in 1264 was called with the aim of raising an Irish army for the war in Scotland. Some consider this the first real Irish Parliament. Much of the legislation of Edward I was applied to Ireland, but the application of laws was not systematic, so that in 1494 a general law was passed applying all English laws to Ireland. Royal policy varied with regard to counties and liberties, but at this time Kildare and Meath were made into counties.

In 1301, de Burgh sent an Irish contingent to assist Edward I in Scotland. A larger involvement was organised by de Wogan in 1303 (Lydon, 'Edward I, Ireland, and the War in Scotland, 1303-04', 44). The justiciar had to scour the ports to find shipping to carry the largest army raised in Ireland during these wars. They managed to find 37 ships of suitable size in good state of repair. Peter of Paris was appointed the first Irish admiral (*admirallus flote Hiberniae*) (Lydon, *op. cit.*, 48). The ships had to be of sufficient size to carry horses, but smaller craft from the north of Ireland were also used. De Wogan did not go for unexplained reasons. It may be no coincidence that the O'Connors, 'the robbers of Offaly' were making their presence felt in the Midlands. Or it may be that John *fitz* Thomas Fitzgerald, the arch-rival of de Burgh stayed at home. The total Irish contingent reached a total of 3,457 of who 29 were knights, 503 hobelars, and 2,633 were foot (*op. cit*, 47, 57). The expeditions however nearly bankrupted the Irish Exchequer.

Maurice *fitz* Maurice Fitzgerald died sometime before 10 November 1286 at Ross, County Wexford. He had been justiciar briefly in 1273-3, and in 1276 took part in an attack on Wicklow when the Government forces were defeated. As he did not have any sons, he was succeeded by his nephew John Fitzgerald, 4th Lord Offaly who would be created 1st Earl of Kildare on 14 May 1316. John was the son of his brother Thomas by Rohesia de St. Michael. At this period the de Burghs had the advantage over the Fitzgeralds.

Roger Mortimer, grandson of Roger Mortimer, 1st Baron Mortimer, who fought for Prince Edward at the battles of Lewes and Evesham, was betrothed young, to Joan de Geneville the wealthy daughter of Sir Piers de Geneville, of Trim Castle and Ludlow Castle in England. They were married in 1301 and Mortimer acquired the de Lacy lands, a fact much resented by other de Lacys.

In 1306 in Scotland Robert the Bruce (Robert de Brus, **Robert de Bruys**), Earl of Carrick, murdered his rival John Comyn and had himself crowned king of Scotland. Edward I again gathered an army to defeat him and died on the campaign in 1307.

The Reign of Edward II 1307-27

The 14th century was entirely different from the 13th where favourable climatic conditions prevailed in the British Isles. The weather gradually took a turn for the worst. Crop failures became more common. There were numerous failures of crops followed by local famines. Epidemics regularly ravaged the region. The economy went into decline and population started to fall (Dyer, 160; Bellamy, 127). By 1340, much land in the English midlands was deserted. Trade shrank and there was no longer a demand for Irish products. In England three successive wet summers in 1315, 1316, and 1317 brought famine. The Black Death struck in 1348-9 and killed half the population of England. It was to come again in the 1360s.

Few people have much good to say about Edward II. He was incompetent as a soldier, and governed by giving offices to favourites. He was suspected of having homosexual tendencies, and his chief favourite was Piers Gaveston a young knight from Gascony. He was fond of pleasure, had little interest in warfare, and withdrew from the army. Bruce, a fierce warrior, gradually subdued his Scottish rivals and then turned his attention on the English forces and captured their castles. Not until 1314 was a major English effort made against him, and the English army was decisively defeated at Bannockburn. Then the Bruces turned their attention to Ireland and wasted among other lands those of Roger Mortimer in the Liberty of Trim. Roger Mortimer was appointed Lord Lieutenant of Ireland 1317-18. Piers Gaveston was murdered by the barons so the king increased favour to his nephew-by-marriage (who was also Gaveston's brother-in-law), Hugh Despenser the Younger. But, as with Gaveston, the barons were indignant at the privileges Edward lavished upon the Despensers, father and son, especially when the younger Despenser began in 1318 to strive to procure for himself the earldom of Gloucester and its associated lands. In 1321 the marchers lords in Wales led by the Earl of Hereford and Roger Mortimer invaded and wasted the Dispenser lands and advanced on London. For once Edward II acted like his father and forced the Mortimers to surrender. Mortimer was imprisoned and his lands declared forfeit. A Scottish invasion by Robert the Bruce was beaten off but rather ineffectively and a truce was signed. The Dispensers were left in control of the country. Roger Mortimer escaped from the tower and fled to France. Queen Isabelle was sent to France to deal with her brother, King Charles IV, regarding the homage the French king demanded of Edward concerning his lands in France. Isabelle, aided by Roger Mortimer, rebelled against him (Bryant, 216-25). In 1326 he was induced to resign in favour of his son Edward III who was a minor aged 14, and he was later murdered in 1327.

In 1309 French pope, Clement V who was born in Bordeaux moved the papal residence from Rome to Avignon on the Rhone where it remained until 1377. He was a tool of the French crown and at its behest suppressed the Order of Knights Templars, their lands and houses or preceptories being given to the Knights Hospitallers.

Edward II and Ireland

It was a peculiarity of this century that most of the Governments military expeditions were petty ones, the vast majority of them in Leinster. Indeed if one excludes the antics of the Earl of Desmond there was little Government activity outside Leinster.

The barons in 1308 secured the dispatch of Piers Gaveston to Ireland as the king's Lieutenant, (commonly referred to as the Lord Lieutenant) a title which now replaced that of justiciar. He replaced John de Wogan, (d. 1321), who was justiciar 1295-1308 and 1309-12. Though totally inexperienced in Irish affairs he showed some military competence in Wicklow where the O'Byrnes and O'Tooles were becoming aggressive. Whether he met Sir Roger Mortimer, 1st Earl of March, who was in Ireland at the time is not clear. After a year he was recalled and John de Wogan again was made justiciar. An expedition against the O'Byrnes and O'Tooles led by Sir Edmund Butler, the 6th Chief Butler of Ireland, subdued them temporarily. Butler was then appointed justiciar after de Wogan resigned. Butler hired kernes from the O'Briens and put them at coyne (billets) on Anglo-Norman farmers (Curtis, 119). Using Gaelic troops was common, but not the coyne which was now becoming a frequent practice. To deal with the invasion of Edward Bruce, an English cleric with experience in Ireland, John de Hotham, was sent to Ireland to shake up the administration, and Sir Edmund Butler was made Earl of Carrick (-on-Suir) (Phillips, 63).

In 1315, the year after Bannockburn, Robert the Bruce decided to attack the English in Ireland. Why exactly he did this is not clear. It was probably intended only as a diversion from the main front in the north of England, but may also have been intended to weaken support from Northern Ireland to the Gaelic clans in the Highlands who had close connections with Northern Ireland. A request for assistance from Dónal *mac* Briain O'Neill was granted on the condition that Dónal and his urraghs would recognise Edward as king of Ireland. This was agreed to though it is doubtful if either party treated the promise seriously.

The campaign, which was of the usual kind of burning and wasting, went well at first. The Scots were joined by O'Neill and his urraghs, defeated the local troops in the earldom of Ulster led by Sir Thomas de Mandeville. They captured Carrickfergus town but not the castle. The disturbance of the invasion allowed several local disputes to flare up to take advantage of the Government's difficulties. But there was no rush to join the invaders. In the meantime Edward was recognised as king of Ireland by O'Neill and his urraghs. He advanced into Leinster and destroyed the de Verdon town of Dundalk and massacred all the inhabitants. Two armies combined to meet him at Slieve Breagh, high ground in the south of Co. Louth. One, from Connaught, was led by Richard de Burgh and Felim *mac* Aedh O'Connor, the O'Connor chief from 1310 to 1316. (Felim had become chief following a civil war among the O'Connors.) The other was led by the justiciar, Sir Edmund Butler. Edward and O'Neill withdrew northwards where they sacked Coleraine and destroyed the bridge. De Burgh followed him but both armies suffered from lack of supplies. Edward persuaded Rory *mac* Cathal O'Connor, Felim's predecessor, to proclaim himself chief, so Felim O'Connor had to return to deal with him, taking some of the de Burgh troops. In September Edward attacked de Burgh's forces and routed them. De Burgh escaped to Connaught.

By mid-November 1315 Edward the Bruce was again marching south where he was met by Roger Mortimer, Lord of Trim, and he defeated him at Kells in north Meath. He was joined by de Lacy claimants to the Liberty of Meath who claimed to be the rightful heirs. He could not take Trim castle but proceeded in his wasting raid until met at Ardskull and his advance was blocked by forces under the justiciar Sir Edmund Butler and John Fitzgerald. The barons and knights failed to follow up their advantage. Edward found it difficult to supply his troops from the wasted countryside and withdrew north again. In Connaught Felim O'Connor with the help of Rickard de Bermingham defeated Rory, and then changed sides. At the Second Battle of Athenry on 10 August 1316 Rickard de Bermingham, William *Liath* de Burgh, and Murtagh O'Brien led their forces to victory in a devastating defeat for the O'Connors. Among those killed were Felim O'Connor and Tadhg (Teigh) Ó Kelly, chief of the *Uí Maine*. Civil wars continued among the O'Connors until Turlough *mac* Aedh O'Connor became chief in 1324 and remained chief until 1342. The death of Felim benefited the O'Donnells.

Edward Bruce, though crowned king of Ireland, had not the capacity to be king. In culture he was much closer to the Anglo-Normans than to the Gaelic chiefs, and he failed to co-ordinate the various local conflicts towards a common end. In December 1316 Robert the Bruce himself arrived with fresh troops including gallowglasses. Carrickfergus castle finally surrendered. By February he reached the outskirts of Dublin but did not attack it. He ravaged southwards towards Limerick but did not attack it either. With his army starving and exhausted, and fearing an attack by the justiciar on his rear he too retreated northwards and returned to Scotland. Nothing further happened until October 1318, after a good harvest, Edward and the de Lacy claimants marched south again. The were met at Faughart, north of Dundalk, by the tenants of the de Verdons led by Sir John de Bermingham, 2nd son of Piers, 3rd Lord of Athenry, of Tethmoy in Offaly and was surprisingly defeated and killed when leading an impetuous attack. He may have just been unlucky or may have underestimated the fighting power of what were largely county militias and servants of barons. Had he delayed until reinforcements arrived he might have won. (Theobald de Verdon had gone to his English estate and died suddenly in July 1316, leaving only daughters. The defence of the Irish lands was left to his brothers Milo and Nicholas. The de Verdon lands were wasted by Bruce. Though the de Berminghams are usually associated with Co. Galway and Athenry in particular, their original grant was in Leinster. The family were lords of Birmingham in England, having been granted lands by William the Conqueror in 1066.

Unsurprisingly Edward the Bruce was blamed by Gaels and Normans alike for the destruction he had brought on Ireland. Richard *Óg* de Burgh (the Red Earl) took no part in the campaign in Connaught led by William *Liath* de Burgh, for he was arrested on suspicion of complicity with the Bruces because one of his daughters was married to Robert the Bruce. He cleared himself and quickly recovered his lands in the earldom of Ulster. The devastation of the Bruce invasions and concurrent local wars was magnified by the years of crop failure and famine. In one way Edward could not have picked a worse time if his army was to live off the land through plunder. In the Middle Ages local societies usually recovered pretty rapidly after isolated disasters. It was the repeated, widespread and successive disasters of the 14th century that wore down society.

Richard de Mortimer was made justiciar and he went about Ireland dealing with those who had sided with the Bruce. He was given in 1319 a commission to allow all the Irish gentry who should desire it access to common law. A charter of English law was granted to the O'Maddens of *Ui Maine*. The Earls of Kildare and Louth were empowered to admit to English law any of their own tenants who requested it (Otway-Ruthven, 240). However the Norman advance into O'Brien lands in Clare was halted permanently when Murtagh O'Brien defeated Richard de Clare, a descendant of Strongbow, at Dysert O'Dea in 1318. (His father Thomas de Clare had been made Lord of Thomond by Edward I during a civil war among the O'Briens. He rebuilt Bunratty castle in stone.) Richard de Clare was killed and their stronghold, Bunratty castle was captured after it was abandoned (Hayes-McCoy, 41). The O'Briens were the third Irish family to stabilize their borders and this time occupied the lands from which they had formerly exacted tribute. John Fitzgerald was made Earl of Kildare, the first of the line, to balance the Earldom of Carrick created for Sir Edmund Butler. Butler's son James was later created Earl of Ormond in his own right in 1328 alongside Roger Mortimer, who was created Earl of March. John de Birmingham was created Earl of Louth; partly as a reward and partly to give him status in dealing with the de Verdon brothers (de Bermingham was from Mortimer's part of Meath). The Meath de Lacys who had sided with Bruce fled but were to resume their struggle a few decades later. (The de Lacys and the younger brothers of Theobald de Verdon were claiming the Liberty of Meath which was held by the crown, Theobald's children being daughters.)

One effect of the Bruce invasion was to destabilize Ireland. Everywhere, both among Gaelic and Norman families the opportunity was taken to try to settle old scores and to grab back lands anciently held. The issues were local and Gaelic and Norman lords combined locally to achieve their aims. Settlement in the post-invasion period was not easily achieved when the disputes between the Mortimers and Dispensers spilled over into Ireland. Richard de Burgh recovered his badly-wasted lands and his castles in the earldom and restored his authority there. He died in 1326 leaving as his heir his grandson William, 3rd Earl of Ulster, the 'Brown Earl'. Dónal O'Neill paid heavily for his involvement with Bruce. Dónal O'Neill sent a self-justifying Remonstrance to the pope at Avignon trying to establish that his treason towards Edward II was morally justified. The pope did not concede this but wrote to Edward requesting him to act in the spirit of the bull *Laudabiliter* (Dolley, 186). The Irish and Scottish troops were dispersed by John de Bermingham and many of the Ulster Chiefs were executed, including Dónal O'Neill's son Brian. O'Neill was expelled from his lands in Tyrone and was forced to hide in the mountains for seven years before dying in 1325. He was succeeded by Henry O'Neill of the rival Clandeboy O'Neills. The Clandeboy O'Neills took advantage of the Bruce invasions and later of the murder of the Red Earl to expand their territories east of the Bann. By the end of the century the chiefs of Clandeboy had cut the earldom in half, holding Belfast and Castlereagh. Their territory stretched from the head of Strangford Lough to Lough Neagh. Henry was deposed as chief of *Cenel Eogain* by the justiciar Ralph d'Ufford in 1344 in favour of Aedh *Mór* O'Neill the son of Dónal. Henry repulsed an invasion of Clandeboy territory by Aedh *Mór* and survived as chief of Clandeboy until 1347. Needless to say, these unending succession disputes among the O'Neills in the Medieval period seriously limited their power.

In 1320 Archbishop Bicknor founded a college in St Patrick's cathedral in Dublin with a view to founding a university which struggled along somehow until 1494, probably as a collegiate school.

Despite forfeiting his lands in rebellion against Edward II in 1321-22, Roger Mortimer had his lands restored, and in the minority of Edward III had the de Verdon lands in Meath granted to him and also the Liberty of Louth which had lapsed on the death of John de Bermingham, Earl of Louth in 1328, and got the administration of the lands of the earls of Kildare during the minority of the heir of Thomas *fitz* John. These grants lapsed with his execution in November 1330, though his widow Joan (de Geneville) regained the Liberty of Trim. Most of the family honours were restored to her grandson Roger Mortimer, 2nd Earl of March. He inherited the Liberty of Meath on her death in 1356. In 1326 Richard de Burgh died leaving his son aged 14 a minor so the lands temporarily escheated to the crown. The lands in Connaught were disputed by the sons of William *Liath* de Burgh (Otway-Ruthven, 255). The earls of Desmond at this point come to the fore. Their estates were second only in size to those of the de Burghs and Maurice *fitz* Thomas Fitzgerald, the future Earl of Desmond, married a daughter or Richard *Óg* de Burgh in 1312.

Chapter 11

Edward III 1327-77

There is much discussion regarding the tipping point of the Middle Ages in Ireland, when the expansion of Anglo-Norman influence ceased and was reversed. In 1333 the Brown Earl of Ulster was murdered leaving an infant heiress. The O'Neills were quick to take advantage. The de Burgh estates in Connaught were divided, weakening their lordship in Connaught. In 1337 the Hundred Years War commenced, and the interests of England were diverted from Ireland and Scotland to France until 1453. On the other hand the creation of the earldoms of Desmond and Ormond allowed powerful lordships in central Munster. The three earldoms of Kildare, Ormond, and Desmond were largely to dominate life at the end of the Middle Ages, and the Earl of Kildare was to become the virtual ruler of Ireland at the end of the 15th century. Edward III, though his chief preoccupation was France, made several attempts to improve matters. Much of this may have been due to self-interest, a wish to increase the revenue of Ireland. (S. Harbison considers that a threat from the navy of Castile may have been a reason, 'William of Windsor's Administration', 154. It should be noted that the southern coast of England was subject to French raids at this time. Be that as it may, Edward's attempts to restore order form the one bright spot in the period.) He sent a stream of capable administrators, including his own son, to try to establish peace and order. Often this meant replacing corrupt or inefficient officials with Englishmen which caused great resentment among those who had offices or expectations. These did not believe in the best man for the job but a local man however incompetent with the right connections for the job. It was an age when public offices, secular or religious, were seen largely as a source of income and status. Any duties attached to the offices, apart from taking bribes, could be discharged be a paid official. (This state of affairs largely persisted until the 19th century.)

The Reign of Edward III

Edward was 14 years old when his mother Isabelle of France and Roger Mortimer, now Earl of March, procured the resignation of Edward II in favour of his son, with themselves as regents. Isabelle brought the war with Scotland to an end with the unpopular *turpis pax* (base peace), recognising the independence, temporarily at least, of the Scottish king, Robert the Bruce, who died in 1329. David II was the son of Robert the Bruce and Elizabeth de Burgh. He agreed to marry Joan, the daughter of Edward II and Isabelle but the marriage was childless. The *turpis pax* was repudiated by Edward III when he attained his majority. His mother Isabelle of France was a daughter of Philip IV king of France, and she made Edward pay homage for his lands in Guienne. With the death of Charles IV of France in 1328 without surviving male heirs, the House of Capet which had begun with Hugh Capet in 987 came to an end. The throne passed to the House of Bourbon. Nevertheless Isabelle put in a claim for her son as grandson of a French king, and this led to the Hundred Years War. Edward married Phillipa of Hainault in Flanders and had five sons and four daughters. His sons were Edward of Woodstock, (later called the Black Prince but not in his lifetime), Lionel of Antwerp, John of Gaunt (Ghent in Flanders), Edmund of Langley, and Thomas of Woodstock, named from the places they were born. (Flanders was then a rich, independent, and commercial county, whose Flemish footsoldiers were famous. The woollen trade between England and Flanders was very important. The Flemings had recently defeated a French attempt to take them over.)

In 1330 the seventeen-year old Edward III had Roger Mortimer and his mother Isabelle seized; Mortimer was quickly executed and his mother banished from court. Edward focused largely on military matters in Scotland and in France, where his pursuit of the crown through his mother's line contributed to the start of the Hundred Years' War. He had a very good relationship with the nobility, who profited from his military exploits, and was generally well-liked by the populace. Edward's court was a prime example of the chivalric values of high medieval society, and he created Britain's highest knightly order, the Order of the Garter. Pageantry is a word associated with his reign. His sons, the Black Prince and John of Gaunt, were among the most famous soldiers of the age. He was given an opportunity to intervene in a civil war in Scotland. He defeated David II and put Edward Balliol of the pro-English faction, on the Scottish throne. However the Bruce faction recovered while Edward transferred his attentions to claiming the crown of France.

In 1337, Edward in order to defend his French possessions and to claim the throne of France led an army into France. He campaigned on a vast scale and soon, like his grandfather, Edward I, nearly bankrupted the country. In 1346 he won the great battle of Crécy in 1346 chiefly by adopting the longbow from the Welsh marches. Though ineffective against armour, the arrow was quite heavy and a fire could be sustained causing injury to horses and footsoldiers. In 1347 he captured Calais which the English were to hold until the reign of Mary Tudor. The following year the Black Death swept over Europe and the climate began to deteriorate rapidly.

In 1351 was issued the Statute of Provisors against papal provision, and the Statute of Labourers to control wages. In 1352 the Statute of Treason defined treason. In 1353 the Statute of Praemunire controlled appeals to the pope. In the same year the staple towns for the export of wool were named. These statutes following the Black Death were largely economic in intention, particularly in regard to the pope draining gold from England, and the king's need for great quantities of money for the war in France. They were not anti-papal but were designed to assert the king's rights while not denying those of the pope. Yet the most significant legal reform was probably that concerning the Justices of the Peace. This institution began before the reign of Edward III, but by 1350, the justices had been given the power not only to investigate crimes and make arrests, but also to try cases, including those of felony. With this, an enduring fixture in the administration of local English justice had been created. In 1362, a Statute of Pleading ordered the English language to be used in law courts and, the year after, Parliament was for the first time opened in English. Simon de Montfort's innovation, endorsed by Edward I, of summoning representative knights of the shire and burgesses of the towns to give assent to taxation was to become a central feature of representative parliamentary democracy. These innovations, not all of them equally wise, were adopted as the law in Ireland. The attempt to control wages and prices in the wake of the Black Death was swimming against the tide. The new mercantile economy had its own demands as the manorial system drew to its end.

Mortimer's grandson, Roger Mortimer 2nd Earl of March, was not only absolved, but came to play an important part in the French wars. About 1380 Chaucer began *The Canterbury Tales* the first major literary work in what passes for modern English. In 1360, the war came to a temporary end with the Treaty of Bretigny. This was so favourable to the English that the French, sooner or later, were bound to challenge it.

The Treaty of Bretigny allowed Edward to focus on Ireland and to try to devise means of making it again profitable to the crown. In 1368, the French felt strong enough again to resume the war. The Black Prince became ill and the war went badly. Edward became senile and

John of Gaunt and his party or supporters at court became the effective rulers. In 1371 the Black Prince died, leaving a two-year old son who was to succeed Edward as Richard II in 1377. In 1376 the court party was overthrown by the 'Good Parliament' and management of the king's affairs was taken from John of Gaunt. In the following year in the 'Bad Parliament' John succeeded in reversing the decisions. The French were preparing an invasion of England, hence the need for subsidies from Parliament. The Bad Parliament introduced a poll tax. In 1377, every lay person over the age of 14 years who was not a beggar had to pay a groat (4 pennies) to the Crown. This was to lead to the Peasants' Revolt in the next reign. John of Gaunt remained in control of the government.

Ireland under Edward III

The second half of the 14th century was one of the worst periods in Irish history though it was once hailed by Irish nationalists as a brilliant period of Gaelic recovery. Plagues swept the island, and the climate deteriorated. Deaths by disease, famine and murder caused a sharp fall in the population. Law and order broke down so that Ireland resembled a modern failed state like Somalia. Local chiefs and lords acted like local brigands and were engaged in petty warfare and wasting raids. The countryside became unsafe, farms, houses and whole villages were deserted. Kernes, when not employed by one warlord or another simply became bandits and cattle-rustlers. Church-building, architecture and stone sculpture came to an end. Religion, even in monasteries, became deplorable.

One of the first signs of the changes in the times was the revival of the MacMurroughs in Leinster. They had kept their ancestral lands of *Ui Chennselaig* (Hy Kinsella) in Wexford and lived harmoniously with the Norman barons and knights. But when the family of Bigods, Lords of Carlow, died out they reasserted their claimed rights as overlords of Idrone as well as Hy Kinsella. (Idrone survives as the name of two baronies in Carlow to this day. The *Ui Drona* had been conquered by a branch of the *Ui Chennselaig* around 800 A.D., so the claim of overlordship was ancient (Ó Corráin, 108)). The MacMurrough Kavanaghs were the chiefs and by the time of the visit of Richard II they were a formidable secondary force straddling the road to the South. They revived the title of king of Leinster, though it is not clear if this was intended as a declaration of independence of the justiciar rather than a claim of rank.

In 1329 Roger Mortimer, before his downfall, got himself created Earl of March and had Maurice *fitz* Thomas Fitzgerald created Earl of Desmond and James *fitz* Edmund Butler made Earl of Ormond. These promotions seem to have been rewards for support given to Mortimer in his struggle against the Despensers. The wisdom of appointing John *fitz* Thomas Fitzgerald as Earl of Kildare after the defeat of the Bruces is dubious for he was very much a loose cannon. These earldoms were later given palatinate jurisdiction, in effect withdrawing their lands from the control of the sheriffs of the counties. Normal writs of the king's courts were not served in palatine jurisdictions. This later caused a misapprehension when it was stated that the king's writ did not run outside The Pale. The palatine counties were always under the jurisdiction of the justiciar, and cases from them could always be reviewed in the Court of King's Bench in Dublin. The earls always knew that what the king granted he could take away. Edward was not happy with the Mortimer grants and tried to resume them thus provoking the hostility of the grantees (Curtis, 102-4). As the war with France occupied his mind more he became more concerned about getting revenue from Ireland than with trying to enforce submission. The power and prestige of the Earl of Desmond increased as the de Burgh family declined. But Clanrickard remained quite powerful locally until defeated by the Earl of Kildare in 1504. In fact, after the murder of the Brown Earl, the Clanrickard branch became the principal one of the de Burgh line.

The title Lord of Connaught was apparently last claimed by Edmund *Albanach* de Burgh (d. 1375). Edmund's son Sir Thomas de Burgh was 'keeper of Connaught and deputy of the justiciar' under Robert de Vere about 1390. (The Earls of Mayo and Marquesses of Sligo are descended from this branch.)

William *Donn* de Burgh, 6th Lord of Connaught and 3rd Earl of Ulster (1326-33), the 'Brown Earl', was murdered in 1333 and left an infant daughter, who eventually married Lionel of Antwerp, Duke of Clarence, 3rd son of Edward III, who thus inherited the earldom. Without a strong local ruler the earldom gradually wasted away. Henry O'Neill was quick to take advantage. In Connaught, two sons of William *Liath* de Burgh seized the Connaught lands of the young heiress; Ulick seized the lands in Galway and founded the Clanrickard Burkes (Upper MacWilliam), while Edmund *Albanach* got the Mayo lands and founded the Mayo Burkes (Lower MacWilliam). A third relative took the lands in Limerick and Tipperary, the Clanwilliam Burkes. This division meant that none of them was strong enough to act as an effective Lord of Connaught, so the local chiefs, the O'Connors, the O'Kellys, the O'Dowds, the MacDermotts, the O'Malleys, the O'Flahertys, just asserted their independence of him. O'Connor Sligo seized Sligo town which became a tempting target for the O'Donnells. Maurice *fitz* Thomas, the Earl of Desmond, became the most powerful lord in Ireland. Assisting the justiciar he subdued the O'Nolans and O'Murroughs in Wicklow, recovered the castle of Ley from the O'Dempseys, and inflicted a crushing defeat on the MacCarthys.

Apart from this, but allied with this, was the strengthening of the minor Gaelic lordships. The Normans had been in Ireland for over 150 years and had intermarried with the Gaelic clans. Inevitably, the Gaelic chiefs learned a lot from the Normans. They too looked, not for the independence of Ireland, but for their own independence. As they grew in strength and numbers they needed more land and seized it from those near to them regardless of who had owned it originally. On the other hand it is not quite clear why the grip of the local Anglo-Norman barons and knights weakened. In some places they held steady; in others they did not. The original lands of the Butlers of Ormond around Nenagh in County Tipperary proved impossible to hold. Conquest by the Irish was not in pitched battles, though that helped when they were won, but by constant wasting raids. The barons and knights could have used the same tactics and frequently did, but still ground was lost. Minor branches of the O'Briens, the O'Mulryans and the O'Kennedys, crossed the Shannon and occupied lands abandoned by the Earls of Ormond. These marchlands became the haunts of criminal gangs of outlaws under no one's control. Much of the land in those areas must have been depopulated. The population of Ireland probably fell faster than that of England. Those who survived in the border areas began to pay 'black rents' to the bandit clans to buy them off. This was the name that came to be given to the protection money exacted, mostly by Gaelic lords, from local communities and even from the Government.

Art MacMurrough levied it in Leinster from the 1370s. In the 15th and early 16th centuries it became widespread. It had a parallel in the 'blackmail' (in modern terms, protection racket) collected on the Anglo-Scottish borders. Other chiefs, like the MacMahons, O'Hanlons, and Maguires though subject to their overlords, the O'Neills and O'Donnells, became secondary powers in their own right and became in Tudor times 'great captains of their nations'.

The dynamics of Irish society seem to have changed. Regularly between 1000 AD and 1170 the most important of the Gaelic provincial chiefs was able to exert his authority and exact tribute from all the other chiefs. Within a province there were three grades of chiefs, corresponding to chiefs of baronies (cantreds, *tuatha*), chiefs of counties, and chiefs of the province. Each ruled his own territory and exacted tribute from those below him, the mesne or county chiefs from the cantred chiefs, and the provincial chiefs from the mesne chiefs. Each summoned his inferiors to his hosting so a successful provincial chief could end up by exacting tribute and obedience to his call to his hosting from the whole of Ireland, the so-call high king *ard ri*. For some reason this no longer worked. For one thing the lowest ranks in Gaelic society seem to have lost their lands and their status to the chiefs. A holding of land about the size of a parish could support an *oglaech* or knight or squire and these lands were constantly grabbed by members of the greater clans whose sons, often very numerous, who had to be supported. Whether for this reason or some other clans of lowest rank, that of the chief of a *tuath*, like the *Loigse* and *Ui Failge* (O'Mores and O'Connors of Offaly/Faly) became locally quite strong and set about expanding their territories. They constantly attacked Ley castle, a Fitzgerald strongpoint near Portarlington in Co. Laois. The O'Dempseys were of the same stock as the O'Connors of Offaly and were a powerful minor sept in the territory lying on the borders of Leix and Offaly known as Clanmalier (approximately the barony of Geashill). The O'Molloys of the Southern *Ui Neill* seem also to have come under the O'Connors. The fact was that the lesser clans had never been subdued except by force and brutality systematically applied by the greater chiefs. Throughout the later Middle Ages these minor local chiefs seem to have acted independently of any overlord at least most of the time.

By 1340 with massive debt and the Treasury empty Edward had to return to England to try to raise more money. This sparked off a crisis in Ireland. The revenue of Ireland was rapidly falling, and Edward blamed officials in Ireland. He tried to insist that all judges at least should be men of English background with property in England. (This latter proviso would allow the king to seize their property if they were remiss in their accounts.) The widespread corruption prevalent in the Middle Ages meant that the king had reasonable grounds for his suspicions. Edward inflamed opinion further by withdrawing all grants made since 1307 until they were examined. Until this was done all income from such grants would be paid into the Exchequer. (It should be noted that the Black Prince had equal difficulties in collecting money for his wars in France from his extensive lands in Cheshire and Cornwall. Gascony provided a modest surplus to the Exchequer in times of peace, but could not support a war—Barry, 106-8, 112.) A parliament was summoned to meet in Dublin in 1341. It met there and then resumed in Kilkenny. They rejected the royal ordinances and sent envoys to London to the king. Their protest was written in French. The king backed down. He was about to renew the campaign in France, the most victorious and glorious in British medieval history, but with expenses controlled (Frame, 'English policies', 86-100; Otway-Ruthven, 259).

The Earl of Desmond called on the support of the Gaelic chiefs in Munster in pursuit of his own aggrandisement, and followed the example of Sir Edmund Butler by imposing coyne on his own people. He carried out wasting raids against various people, Gaelic and Norman. He joined with the Gaelic chiefs when it suited himself, and it was said he was trying to make himself king of Ireland. The conduct of the Earl of Desmond may be taken as fairly typical of Norman and Gaelic lords in the Middle Ages, often acting within the law of the time and place or stretching or breaking the law. If they did this they always had the backing of their own priests, lawyers and historians to show that their claims were just. Lords were like captains of ships, sometimes trading lawfully, sometimes supporting the king in his wars and at times acting as pirates. The law codes existed, as it were, to provide some equity in the distribution of plunder in a pirate fleet, or to resolve disputes with the chief of the pirates or between pirate captains. Ordinary pirates on ships, like ordinary slaves on slave plantations, were subject only to the arbitrary will of the captain or the slave-owner.

There was this difference however between Anglo-Norman Ireland and Gaelic Ireland. Most kings of England, some effectively and others less so, were trying throughout the Middles Ages to establish some form of royal control based on clear, if possible, rational written laws, and to control the arbitrary actions of the lords. Ranulf de Glanvill, Henry

II's justiciar and Bracton were the great authorities on English law. There was also a wish to involve taxpayers down to the level of knights in the royal councils. Many of the kings may have been no better than the lords but the tendency was there. Lawyers were constantly trying to develop equitable law for all the king's subjects. Books on the law of the land were written for the instruction of gentlemen as well as lawyers. Country gentlemen were made justices of the peace or unpaid magistrates and had to acquire some knowledge of the law. The principle was established that everyone, no matter how high his rank, could be called before the king to account for his actions. (There was always the danger of royal tyranny as the barons clearly saw but it was not a major problem before Tudor times. By that time the wealth and power of the crown had increased so as to be almost irresistible. The conflict was resumed in Stuart times.) Progress was slow and in some ways had not advanced very far by 1500. In 1170 however England was a feudal state based on fiefdoms and vassalage. By 1470, despite the Wars of the Roses, it was a recognisably modern state based on counties and circuits of royal courts enforcing a common law without serfdom or villeinage. The direction was right. More and more people got the status of freemen especially after the Black Death and the economic decline of the 14th century. A similar improvement was not visible on the Gaelic side.

Gaelic and Norman families were closely related by marriage. As French ceased to be spoken, the Anglo-Norman lords adopted the local vernacular as they did in England. As in Wales accepted law in the liberties became to some extent an amalgam of Feudal Law, Common Law, the enactments of the feudal overlord and Brehon Law. The Hiberno-English of the towns and eastern counties who more or less kept up with developments in England regarded them as 'degenerate English'. The lords, Norman and Gaelic, began to keep small standing forces of mercenaries as did their opposite numbers in England. The mailed mercenaries of the Gaelic lords were called gallowglasses.

The Norman lords were described as *Hiberniores Hibernicis ipsis,* which in the context should be translated as 'Greater thieves and cattle rustlers than the native Gaelic chiefs themselves'. It was actually a fair description. Matters were to come to a head at the Parliament held in Kilkenny in 1366.

Sir Ralph d'Ufford, who had married Maud Plantagenet, the widow of the William *Donn* de Burgh, the Brown Earl, was made justiciar in 1344. He took strong action against the Earl of Desmond (Lydon, *Ireland,* 76). D'Ufford was a capable justiciar but the Anglo-Norman lords were suspicious of him. The Earl of Desmond was accused of harbouring Dermot MacCarthy of Muskerry and others, the king's enemies and outlaws. Any dealings, even of trade, with a Gaelic lord in temporary rebellion, could be construed as dealing with the king's enemies. (The Statute of Treasons or Treason Act was passed in 1351 to clarify the concept of treason. It was extended to Ireland specifically in 1495). The Middle Ages were notoriously litigious for those who could afford it, and bishops and abbots spent a lot of their time in courts defending their lands or taking action against those who invaded their lands. (In ecclesiastical courts it was observed that the air became black with excommunications as each side excommunicated the other.) The earl led a great army of 1,000 men against the king's town of Youghal, Co. Cork, a valuable port at the mouth of the River Blackwater. D'Ufford called a parliament, and Desmond called a rival parliament. D'Ufford called out the royal service into which the feudal service had developed and managed to gather a large force, took Desmond's castles and forced him to flee to the MacCarthys (Otway-Ruthven, 262). The economy of Ireland was still in reasonable shape and the revenue Edward III was able to draw from Ireland was so far quite good.

Many believe that Maurice *fitz* Thomas Fitzgerald had ambitions to become king of an independent Ireland (Lydon, *Ireland in the Later Middle Ages,* 56). Robert the Bruce had succeeded in Scotland. Ireland and Scotland closely resembled each other. In both cases the fertile lowlands were occupied by the descendants of Anglo-Norman knights. The highlands and bog lands were occupied by warring Gaelic-speaking clans. In both cases the barons could not agree on who should be the king. In both countries there was a dislike of English intervention. Bruce, a skilful and determined soldier first conquered his enemies in Scotland and then turned his attention to expelling the English army. He was lucky because he got an alliance with France, 'the auld alliance', and the English king was both incompetent and was anxious to spend his money on other things. The chances of the Earl of Desmond achieving the same thing were much less. He would have to succeed in a civil war against the other Anglo-Irish barons and knights and the forces the justiciar could summon. Edward III was a very different king from his father and was determined not to lose Ireland also. There was not the same confusion in the Irish Government that had been displayed during the Bruce invasion. In any case he decided not to risk an all-out attempt and made his peace with the crown.

Then D'Ufford unexpectedly died. He had successfully intervened among the O'Neills where his wife's (de Burgh) interests lay, and took hostages from MacMurrough. He also arrested the Earl of Kildare and took that earldom back into the king's hands. The Earl of Desmond surrendered when given guarantees that he should be free to plead his case before the king. He got all his lands restored and was even made justiciar in 1355.

At this point (1348) the Black Death swept over Ireland. As usual, mortality was worst in the towns where people were crowded together. We must however remember that what were virtually small towns surrounded the halls of chiefs and monasteries. All trades from cooking to blacksmithing had to be carried on there, not to mention the household, the domestic troops, and the servants. Religious houses were badly hit. The scarcity of agricultural labour and rising wages tempted many Irish workers to go to England where they were also in less danger of death from marauding tribes. Edward's Statute of

Labourers was passed in 1351 to control wages. Justices of Labourers, who became justices of the peace, were appointed to enforce the statute. The deterioration of the climate became more marked. About this time the Butlers abandoned their early grant of Nenagh in north Tipperary and it was 150 years before the Butlers were strong enough to get it back. The hold of the earldom of Ulster on lands west of the Bann loosed, and similarly they were not recovered for 250 years. Though pilgrimages and processions and lighted candles abounded nobody bothered to stop the fighting. Especially not in England where the English were having their best ever campaign in France. The plague was to return several times in the course of the next half century and then disappeared.

Sir Thomas Rokeby, an experienced soldier, was appointed justiciar in 1349. He was noted for trying to restrain the extortions of officials. Such extortion was common everywhere in the Middle Ages. He also tried to conciliate those local Gaelic chiefs he was no longer able to conquer with the small force of hobelars and archers, about 100 of each, he was able to maintain. In 1353 Edward passed the Statute of the Staple which appointed 8 towns in England and 4 in Ireland, Dublin, Waterford, Cork, and Drogheda, through which all wool, hides, woolfells and tin must be exported. All foreign traders had to come to the appointed ports; at the same time the foreign traders were given a monopoly of export. Free export of all Irish cloth and frieze was allowed. The Statute also established dedicated courts, known as the Courts of Staple, where disputes relating to commercial matters could be heard, in preference to the courts of Common Law. The aim of these statues was to increase the royal revenue from customs duties. In 1360 the Treaty of Bretigny allowed Edward to focus his attention on Ireland. The peace lasted 9 years with the French resuming the war in 1369.

Lionel of Antwerp 1338-68, Earl of Ulster, Duke of Clarence, was the 2nd son of Edward III. In 1347 Lionel was made Earl of Ulster and in 1352 married the daughter and heiress of William *Donn* de Burgh, 3rd Earl of Ulster (the Brown Earl) Elizabeth de Burgh, 4th Countess of Ulster (d. 1363). He was married to her in 1352, but before this date he had entered into possession of her great Irish inheritance. He was called Earl of Ulster *iure uxoris* from 1347 to 1368. In 1361 he was sent by the king to subdue his domains in Ireland.

He was appointed Lord Lieutenant and in 1361 led the first of five expeditions to Ireland (Connolly, 104-121). In 1362 he was created Duke of Clarence and so is often confusingly referred to as Clarence. Absentee lords in England to the number of 64 were ordered by the king to accompany him. (Absentee lords and landlords were to become a national grievance in Ireland.) These lords managed their estates through seneschals but this was no substitute for a lord on the spot when dealing with land-grabbing local clans. Nowhere was this to be made clearer than in the earldom of Ulster after Lionel's departure. Statutes of Absentees were passed but with little result. A large army of 1,500 men accompanied him. (The Duke of Clarence incidentally never recovered his lands in Connaught which had been seized by the de Burghs.)

One of the great problems for the Government in Dublin at this time was the revival in strength of the Gaelic clans in Leinster, or south Leinster as we would call in nowadays. The fertile strip down the middle, down the valley of the Barrow from Kildare to Wexford was always held by the crown. But the mountainous, hilly or boggy areas on either side of the Barrow valley were held by increasingly hostile Gaelic clans who kept their herds of cattle and cultivated less fertile lands, probably on the long fallow system. By constant raiding, farms in the lowland cultivated areas were rendered uninhabitable, and then were used by the Gaelic chiefs for more grazing for their herds. When attacked they just drove their own herds into the mountains. However it would seem that the aim of many of the small Gaelic clans in Leinster was not to conquer land, but like their Scottish counterparts north of the Highland Line to exact an annual tribute. You either paid a black rent or your cattle were driven off. (In Scotland, the cattle might be sold back to the original owners at the next fair!) Expeditions against them could only be wasting raids in which some buildings or crops were destroyed. This never bothered the Gaelic chiefs for if their house was burned they just took someone else's. The first real attempt to solve the problem was to be made in the reign of Mary Tudor when 'plantations', in essence re-colonisation was seriously attempted. It was not until the ferocious and well-financed campaigns of Lord Mountjoy in the 1590s that the evil was rooted out. (The Government of Elizabeth I made the money available after the defeat of the Spanish Armada in 1588 because of the danger of an independent Catholic Ireland controlled by Spain determined to restore England to Catholicism.) Medieval monarchs mostly lacked both the capacity and the interest and were content with small punitive expeditions. Nevertheless these were taken seriously in the reign of Edward III though the English Parliament regarded Ireland as a royal problem and not for it to finance. The local Anglo-Irish were not anxious for war *a l'outrance* against the Gaelic neighbours who were often their kin.

An attempt was made to impose a tax and Lionel was granted 4 shillings on every ploughland (townland) and a tenth from the clergy but this was not repeated, for the co-operation of the Anglo-Norman lords was essential. To increase revenue an attempt was made to replace inefficient or corrupt officials by more efficient Englishmen, and this caused resentment. It was also decreed the sheriffs of counties must in future be elected not appointed. The cash returns of the sheriffs and seneschals increased. (Connolly, 108-110). Lionel's military success was limited. His wife Elizabeth de Burgh died in 1363.

Lionel summoned a parliament to meet in Kilkenny, a more central city than Dublin in 1366-7. It passed what became known to history as the Statutes of Kilkenny which received notoriety among Irish nationalists as an attack by the English on Gaelic culture. The Burkes were to most notorious example as Edmund **Albanach** de Burgh survived as a pirate until granted a royal pardon. It was of course no such thing. The statutes were directed at the descendants of colonists of the English race who were lowering themselves to the standards of the Gaelic warlords and imitating their manners. England had been a single united country for 450 years. Periodically wars had broken out between the earls and barons, but they were the exception rather than the rule. The last great wasting of England had been done by William the Conqueror 300 years earlier. England had benefited through trade, towns and manufactures and the arts of peace. The English settlers in Ireland had also benefited and they were dismayed to see Ireland visibly degenerating into lawlessness and anarchy, war-making by every lord, Gaelic and Norman, and the wasting and devastation of the country.

They forbade the intermarriage between the native Irish and the native English, the English fostering of Irish children, the English adoption of Irish children and use of Irish names and dress. Those English colonists who did not know how to speak English were required to learn the language (on pain of losing their land and belongings), along with many other English customs. The Irish pastimes of horling and coiting were to be dropped and pursuits such as archery and lancing to be taken up, so that the English colonists would be more able to defend against Irish aggression, using English military tactics. (Hurling and quoits? were forbidden. This particular statute seems to have been adapted from an English statute prohibiting football and similar games for a similar reason.) Other statutes required that the English in Ireland be governed by English Common Law, instead of the Irish March Law or Brehon Law, and ensured the separation of the Gaelic and English churches by requiring that 'no Irishman of the nations of the Irish be admitted into any cathedral or collegiate church . . . amongst the English of the land'. In other words, clerics who were Gaelic-speakers were to be confined to the churches in their own areas. They were not to entertain Irish minstrels, poets or story tellers. This latter was not aimed at Gaelic culture but understood the role of that class in the warlike society of the Gaelic clans. This was to provide justification for any conflict, record victories and defeats in song and to promote warlike valour and emulation. They must use English surnames, speak English, dress in the current English fashion, and observe English customs. Four keepers of the peace were to be appointed in every county and liberty in 'the land of peace' namely the counties or liberties of Louth, Meath, Trim, Dublin, Kildare, Kilkenny, Wexford, Waterford and Tipperary. (A Justices of the Peace Act was passed in England in 1361.) Only in the Marches were kernes and hired mercenaries to be retained.

There was good practical sense in these enactments if peace and prosperity were to be maintained. But they were largely preaching to the converted. Many of the Anglo-Norman lords whose only interest was their own lands had no difficulty in adapting themselves to Gaelic practices. This was especially true of younger sons, excluded by primogeniture, or of relatives when a land-holder left only daughters. These could claim right under Brehon Law and seize the land by force. Some have regretted that a true melding of Gaelic and Norman cultures was not allowed to proceed. But that could only have been done at the time on the basis of accepting anarchy and incessant warfare as the basis of Irish culture. In the event the division of modern Ireland became based on religion not race and remains so to this day. The melding of Ireland which eventually took place was on the basis of the Statutes and this was deplored by romantic racist nationalists.

Lionel was recalled in 1367 to marry an Italian princess. He died in Italy. His only child, Philippa Plantagenet, in 1368 married Edmund Mortimer, 3rd Earl of March (1351-1381) who became, *iure uxoris,* by right of his wife, 4th Earl of Ulster. The earldom remained in royal hands and slowly declined, much of it becoming occupied by the Clandeboy O'Neills now excluded from the chieftainship of the *Cenel Eogain.*

William of Windsor married (c. 1376) Alice Ferrers, the notorious court beauty and mistress of Edward III. William was King's Lieutenant in Ireland 1368-1371/2 and again 1373-1376, and is remembered as the true founder of the Irish Parliament. He held Dungarvan and Black Castle (c.1367) in Ireland. In 1376 he was allowed to buy goods in Ireland to provision his castles in Wales. The title King's Lieutenant rather than justiciar may have derived from his relationship with Alice Ferrers. The English Council was still prepared to invest considerable sums to restore order in Ireland (Connolly, 111; S. Harbison, 155). The difficulties in raising further cash in Ireland itself are described by Connolly, 113). Nor was Windsor successful in dealing with the Gaelic or Norman lords. Indeed he seems to have been hampered by intrigues in the English court as Edward lost his mental grasp (S. Harbison *op. cit.*). Though relatively successful, Windsor was twice recalled to face charges in London where John of Gaunt, Duke of Lancaster, was trying to get control of the government as the Black Prince, the king's eldest son, lay dying. (From John of Gaunt's son, Henry IV came the Lancastrian claim to the throne.) The constant changing of lieutenants (the term justiciar going out of fashion) and the failure to agree adequate financing ensured that as soon as one lieutenant was withdrawn outbursts occurred among the Gaelic chiefs. Edmund Mortimer 3rd Earl of March and grandson of the 1st earl executed in 1330, one of the greater landowners in England and Ireland, came of age in 1373 and headed the opposition to the Lancastrian faction of John of Gaunt which included Alice Ferrers and William of Windsor. Disputes in England usually had repercussions in Ireland.

Ireland was simply too impoverished to provide money. It was at this time too that the manner of holding parliaments became fixed with the lords called by name, and representatives of the commons of the counties and towns and the clergy being summoned, the latter two especially to agree taxation. Bishops and abbots sat in the House of Lords as their assembly came to be called. It was not called taxation but subsidies. Medieval kings were always looking for subsidies.

Chapter 12

Richard II 1377-1422

England under Richard II

Richard was a ten-year old boy when he succeeded his grandfather, with his mother, Joan 'the Fair Maid of Kent' who had married the Black Prince, and a council being in charge. Edmund Mortimer, Earl of March and Ulster, who had married Phillipa Plantagenet *suo iure* 5th Countess of Ulster, daughter of Lionel of Antwerp and Elizabeth de Burgh, the heiress of Ulster, Connaught, and the liberty of Trim was also on this council. (Their son became the heir presumptive to the childless Richard II and through him the Yorkist claim to the throne. Their granddaughter and eventual heiress, Anne Mortimer, married into the Yorkist branch of the English Royal family. The House of York based its claim to the throne on this line of descent.) This arrangement was preferred to a regency under John of Gaunt, but the latter still remained powerful.

The English were now on the defensive in the Hundred Years War and an attack on England was feared. The poll or head tax was levied three times, in 1377, 1379 and 1381, leading to the Peasants' Revolt in 1381. The rebels were defeated. Like Edward II he began to depend on favourites like Robert de Vere, Earl of Oxford and Michael de la Pole whom he created Earl of Suffolk. This led to a revolt of some of the nobility led by Thomas of Woodstock, Duke of Gloucester, the king's uncle with a view to placing limits on the royal power (1386-9). A royalist army led by de Vere was defeated. A parliament, known as the 'Merciless Parliament' led by Thomas of Woodstock and Henry Bolingbroke, John of Gaunt's son, condemned the king's favourites, including Michael de la Pole and Robert de Vere to death but they fled overseas. Others of the king's supporters were banished to Ireland. Later Richard was able to take his revenge on them. He banished the Lancastrians and confiscated the vast Lancastrian estates in 1398 leading directly to his own deposition.

In 1386 John of Gaunt left England to claim the throne of Castile having married the daughter of a deposed king of Castile. However, crisis ensued almost immediately, and in 1387, Richard's misrule brought England to the brink of civil war. Only John, on his return to England in 1389, was able to persuade the Lords Appellant, a group of powerful barons who came together during the 1380s to seize political control of England from the king, and King Richard to compromise, ushering in a period of relative stability.

Richard was now of age and took control into his own hands, and blamed past conduct on the advice of his ministers. A truce was patched up with the nobles and with France, so Richard was able to turn his attention to Ireland. While he was on his second visit to Ireland Henry Bolingbroke returned. Richard was seized on his return and died in mysterious circumstances.

Richard and Ireland

The Mortimers made vigorous attempts to recover their lands in Ireland, in particular the earldom of Ulster, Edmund in 1380 and his son Roger in 1396. In both cases premature deaths ended their efforts. Edmund Mortimer, finding himself obstructed by John of Gaunt accepted the Lord Lieutenancy of Ireland in 1379 and recovered lands in the earldom east of the Bann. The local chiefs submitted to him. He then returned to Meath where he recovered his lands there. He was preparing an expedition against the O'Briens when he died suddenly. A greater problem was building up in Leinster where Art MacMurrough of the Kavanagh branch seemed to be set on turning the clock back to 1169 and styled himself King of Leinster in 1376. Some minor local chiefs agreed to be his urraghs. There was great difficulty in finding a replacement for Mortimer, neither the earls of Desmond or Ormond being willing to undertake the office for they would have to fund the wars from their own revenues.

In 1385 Robert de Vere the Earl of Oxford was made Marquis of Dublin and he agreed to undertake the office. (The title Marquis was a new one intended to be equal in status to the German *markgraf* earl of the march. It was midway between and earl and a duke. de Vere was later made Duke of Ireland.) He was given 500 archers and 1,000 men with expenses for the first two years to be borne by the English Treasury. This appointment coincided with the Lancastrian plot against the king and the Merciless Parliament which caused de Vere to flee abroad. Alexander Petit, (also known as Alexander de Balscot) the bishop of Meath acted as de Vere's justiciar. (John Colton, Dean of St. Patrick's and later Archbishop of Armagh had also acted as an interim justiciar. Like a cleric from a former age he gathered a force which included 26 knights against the O'Mores.)

Art MacMurrough Kavanagh raised black rent from the towns of Castledermot and New Ross, and sought an annual fee from Dublin, together with recognition as 'captain of his nation'. His marriage to the Anglo-Irish heiress Elizabeth Calf (Elizabeth *de Veele*) brought a claim to the important barony of Norragh by right of his wife who had inherited the barony *suo iure* in 1374. The marriage between Art and Elizabeth violated the Statutes of Kilkenny which prohibited intermarriage between the English and the Irish. When the barony was forfeited to the English crown in 1391, Art declared war against the English.

Richard II decided to take matters into his own hands and to come to Ireland in person, the first English king to do so since King John. An ordinance in 1393 ordered all absentee landowners and all Irish craftsmen, artisan and labourers to return to Ireland. Emigration to England was already a problem. He gathered a large army, mainly from his own lands, and his force was estimated at 6,000 men to which other troops could be added from Ireland itself (Lydon, *Ireland in the Later Middle Ages*, 112). Richard arrived in Waterford on 2nd October 1394. He first advanced against MacMurrough, wasted his country and drove off his cattle. MacMurrough quickly submitted with his leading urraghs O'Byrne, O'Toole and O'Nolan. The first two chiefs were in Wicklow, the third in Carlow. In 1395, after defeating MacMurrough, Richard conceded his fee and his wife's barony, in return for a promise to vacate the lands he had conquered and earn compensation through military service against other Irish. MacMurrough promised to quit Leinster, but with the right to conquer and hold any other lands in Ireland he could recover from the king's enemies. The king would pay their armies. Their own lands he proceeded to allocate to English lords. However MacMurrough had no intention of carrying out his part of the bargain and it came to nothing. Art resisted Richard successfully in 1399, retaining to the end his power among the Leinster Irish and his ambivalent relationship with the crown. There was no reason of course why Art could not have been given the barony if he submitted to the king and acquired a knighthood and promised to observe the laws of the barony. As one of the Five Bloods he already had access to the royal courts. But in Gaelic areas it was a backward-looking age when the supposed glories of the past were sung by the rhymers and poets. Like his ancestors Dermot MacMurrough and Dermot mac Mael *na mBo* he could seek to be lord of Leinster with many urraghs paying him tribute, and eventually seek to be king of Ireland. He was accounted a formidable warrior but that day had passed

In the meantime, while Richard was present with his army, the other Gaelic chiefs came to him and made their submission. Part of the reason for this was that they expected protection from the king against the powerful Anglo-Norman lords. Knighthoods were conferred on four Irish chiefs including Niall *Óg* O'Neill. These lords also promised to come to parliament when summoned. (From this time onwards, the chief of the leading branch of the O'Neills was called *O Neill Mór*—the Great O'Neill. Similarly the chief of the leading branch of the MacCarthys was called MacCarthy *Mór* or MacCarthy More. However Niall *Mór*—the big—O'Neill as opposed to his son Niall *Óg*—the young—O'Neill is a personal description. The adjective follows the noun it qualifies.) As Otway-Ruthven observed, the king had established a framework within which local disputes could be resolved. Unfortunately he left the 21-year old Roger Mortimer, 4th Earl of March, in charge, and he was more concerned with recovering the earldom of Ulster as O'Neill had feared. One should not have sympathy for any party for they were all more or less crooks, but some form of arbitration should exist to settle disputes, as even pirates recognised. Roger was killed in a local dispute in 1398 and was succeeded by his 6 year old son Edmund Mortimer, 5th Earl of March, who was now heir presumptive to the throne through his descent from Lionel of Antwerp.

Dorothy Johnston places the failure of Richard's settlement on the Anglo-Irish lords, in particular Mortimer, in their eagerness to reclaim lands recently lost to the Gaelic lords. They were putting personal interest before that of the king or the country (Johnston, 181). Conditions deteriorated so that Richard felt that another personal visit was required. John of Gaunt died on the 3rd February 1399. His son Henry Bolingbroke had been banished, but Richard took his son, the future Henry V, with him to Ireland as a hostage in 1399. Though well equipped he marched his army through MacMurrough's country where they were deprived of supplies, and stragglers were picked of by the local Irish. MacMurrough wished to negotiate. Shortly after he reached Dublin, word was brought to Richard that Henry Bolingbroke was back in England. Richard hastily returned and was captured by Bolingbroke's men.

As Lydon points out, this was to be the last major intervention from England for more than a century. During that century the power of the great Anglo-Norman lords grew ((Lydon, *Ireland in the later Middle Ages*, 124). The death and murder of Richard II was a major disaster for Ireland. The great Gaelic chiefs wanted to deal directly with the king so as to secure the lands they actually held against incursions from Anglo-Irish lords. These latter normally had legally valid grants to their lands, mostly made in the 12th century. The Gaelic lords rarely had any right to lands other than those concocted for them by historians and poets and which were valid only in their own courts. Though normally they would have a clear title recognisable in Brehon Law for the core lands of their *derb fine* dating back for several centuries. There would have to be a great amount of negotiation and arbitration but pragmatic solutions could have been found if Richard had reigned for a further 20 years and did not suffer the distractions of foreign wars. He made a blunder, but not an irremediable one, of appointing Roger Mortimer as Lord Lieutenant who immediately set about recovering lost lands of the earldom as the O'Neills had feared. It was to be 130 years before there was another king who was also interested and had the opportunity.

Irish Society around 1400

This is the period when historians speak of the Gaelic revival and draw a line around Dublin called The Pale to which it was alleged that the rule of the English Government was confined while everywhere else was controlled either by Gaelic lords or Gaelicized Norman lords. This was very far from being the fact. There was indeed an area called The

Pale, and at one time it was proposed to put a pale or fence around it to prevent incursions from the Gaelic tribes. It consisted of the counties of Louth, Dublin, Kildare, and the eastern half of Meath. The Pale was supposed to stretch from Dundalk to Ardee and Collon in Co. Louth, and then to Kells and on to Naas in Kildare and then back to Dublin. This line would be the last backstop for defence. Within this area medieval county government continued regularly. The sheriffs held their courts, the judges made their circuits, the renders from the counties, boroughs and ports were paid into the exchequer, English law and manorial law prevailed, representatives were regularly sent to Parliament, and English was spoken by a majority of the people. The liberty of Trim in Co. Meath and the earldom of Kildare were outside The Pale. Several parliaments were held in Trim in the course of the 15th century. Dublin. The only places the inhabitants of The Pale were in direct contact with the Gaelic clans were in the north of Co. Louth and the south of Co. Dublin.

In the Co. Louth section there were recognised divisions of march and marghery, (*macaire*) the two meaning much the same, but the march was in English hands and the margery in Irish. The distinction was important with regard to coign and livery (O'Sullivan, 57). (The term marghery seems to be derived from two divisions of a plain on the Louth-Monaghan border **macaire Connaille** and **macaire Rois** from the two **tuatha** who occupied it. The name survives in Carrickmacross, Co. Monaghan.) The margery was usually infested by bandits and kerne not under the control of the MacMahons of Oriel. But even in the 15th century the gentlemen of The Pale in north Louth were extending their influence in the Gaelic marghery in Monaghan and south Armagh despite the raids by Gaelic bands which periodically drove the mainly Gaelic-speaking farm workers from their fields (O'Sullivan, 60). (Some parts of north Louth within 3 or 4 miles from Dundalk remained Gaelic-speaking until the end of the 19th century.)

The influence of the Irish Government in Dublin extended far beyond The Pale. Large parts of Munster came under the two great liberties or palatine jurisdictions of Ormond, Desmond, Kildare and Meath who between them covered north Munster from coast to coast and large parts of Leinster and Meath. These had their own courts and collected their own revenues. Some of the earls might speak Irish as well as English and entertain Gaelic harpers. March law might make some concessions to the Brehon Code but very little. The laws of the liberty which closely followed Feudal and Common Law prevailed, and likewise the customs of the manors in the local manors. The towns too followed English law, custom and language. Even in the far west, the towns of Galway and Athenry were connected with Dublin. The road from Dublin to the south was never cut though between Carlow and Kilkenny which was held strongly by the Earl of Ormond the passage was less than 10 miles wide. Even if the local Gaelic chiefs managed to cut the road at its narrowest part they would just have extracted tolls from travellers 'for safe conduct'. The earldom of Ulster was finally reduced to a thin strip along the coast but was never wiped out.

Nationalist historians with their ideas of racial cultures and racial purity chose very narrow criteria to determine what pure Gaelic culture was, in particular the Gaelic language and Brehon Law which they assumed was widely revered and observed. Yet it would be far truer to say that Gaelic areas were largely Normanized in the Middle Ages. In architecture and warfare Normanization was widespread (Ellis, *Tudor Ireland*, 46). Chiefs depended on mercenaries with chain mail to dominate battles. Gaelic chiefs were everywhere building castles to live in. Every effort was being made to procure the right of succession of the eldest son to the chiefdom. Where possible money was used where larger sums were involved, and much of this could come from exports and taxes on merchants. Intermarriage between Gael and Norman was the rule rather than the exception and a woman could pass from one society to the other easily. Brehon Law was gradually adopting concepts of Feudal and Common Law. A common but very Anglicized culture was developing which brought what many in the urbanised areas of the east saw as a loss of their precious gains over the previous 200 years in terms of trade, settled life, the procedures of Common Law and representation in the king's parliament. Some of the worst abuses of Gaelic life, too, like coyne and livery were being imported into the lordships. The state of religion was bad but it was far worse in the Gaelic lordships.

The early part of the 15th century saw Ireland largely reverted to the Dark Ages. Local defence became paramount with each chief and lord extorting as much cash and support from his own territory and engaging in alliances with neighbours. Little cash came from England to support the justiciar. A great problem arose from the inability of the Butlers to hold the manor of Nenagh in north Tipperary. This part of Ireland seems to have been impoverished and poorly inhabited. It had in the past attracted the attention of *Eoganacht* of Cashel, of the O'Briens, and of the O'Mellaghlins. It was the intention of King John to place strong manors and castles there to control the area. These manors failed so all the minor clans around rushed to grab land regardless of who had owned it originally. The *Loigse* (O'Mores) and *Ui Failge*, (O'Connor *Faly*) made some progress in this direction but not to the extent that the modern counties which are artificial constructions would indicate. None of the big chiefs attempted to fill the vacuum, though some of the offshoots of the O'Briens, the O'Mulryans and the O'Kennedys, did cross the Shannon. Chiefly there seems to have been a revival of local chiefs like the O'Molloys and the O'Carrolls of *Eile*. None of these were very particular who lands they occupied, their own or someone else's.

If one looks at a map of Ireland such as that given by Ellis for 1534 (*Tudor Ireland,* 345) we see that the boundaries between Gaelic and Norman lords had scarcely changed from 1334. The big loser was the earldom of Ulster. Part in the north had gone to Scottish mercenaries, a small bit to the Gaelic chiefs of Iveagh, and quite a large part to the

O'Neills of Clandeboy. In Leinster the MacMurroughs had thrown off their allegiance and controlled territories in Wexford and Carlow. In Cork, the boundaries of the MacCarthys had been extended a little, but internally they had seized control over the whole area. In Ulster, the O'Neills had succeeded in grabbing much of the lands of the *Oirgialla* except those of the MacMahons. Connaught is often written off as being completely Gaelicized. The MacWilliam and Clanwilliam Burkes (de Burgh) are considered to have gone native. The Burkes were illegally holding the Connaught territories belonging to the de Burgh and Mortimer Earls of Ulster and had no intention of submitting to the government. Still less paying any money to it. They still however continued to deal with the Government and the Government with them. They probably all spoke Irish but it is unlikely that Brehon Law had supplanted manorial law on their estates. (Ulick Burke was created Earl of Clanrickard by Henry VII in 1543.) Two royal boroughs, Galway and Athenry remained in the Clanrickard domains, and one of the family was regularly appointed sheriff of Connaught. (The crown did not dare to appoint anyone else.) The Clanrickard Burkes opposed the advances of the O'Donnells into Connaught (Ellis, *Tudor Ireland*, 90-91).

It is noteworthy that the great chiefdoms of the 'Five Bloods', the provincial chiefs of Ulster, Meath, Leinster, Munster, and Connaught made little progress even when the Lordship of Ireland was at its most vulnerable. The great Gaelic lordships were themselves riven with divisions, and none was able to build up military or political power. Had they been able to build up their strength they would have been more able to resist the conquest in Elizabethan times when the Government finally made a determined, sustained and well-financed effort to suppress all rebellions no matter by whom. They were still strong locally in 1500 as they were in 1200, yet none developed the power to challenge for domination even in their own province

There can be little doubt that there was a direct connection between the deterioration in climate, and the plagues and famines which plagued Ireland in the 14th century and the revival of local power in this area. Central Ireland is not densely populated today and probably never was. Ireland is at the limit for the cultivation of cereals and probably only oats was grown in many parts as the climate deteriorated. Since Neolithic times the bulk of the food of the lower classes was formed by cereals, so even in cattle-rearing country enough land had to be tilled to provide oat cakes. (As the poor had no cooking pots the alternative porridge was not feasible.) The chiefs were accumulating most of the cattle which were useful not only for meat and milk products but also for hides which were exportable. The density of population in the re-occupied regions must have fallen quite drastically.

By this time all the great lords in the British Isles were maintaining their private armies, in England and Scotland as well as Ireland. In England the names associated with these armies are livery and maintenance, but in Ireland coyne and livery. Livery was more correctly called livery and retaining. Livery was the dispensing of food and clothing to servants. It was also the provision of provender for horses. Those retained by the lord, (or the livery companies in towns) his retainers, wore his livery or uniform and were expected to fight in his battles. They were also given maintenance, namely the action of wrongfully aiding or abetting by the lord in any lawsuit. This assumed a cash economy. In a non-cash economy there were other ways for lords to gather a body of retainers. They could be paid in cows. Mercenary chiefs could be given pieces of land on which to support themselves and their followers, the petty lords owning those lands being evicted for the purpose. In coyne, a superior chief billeted soldiers, perhaps one to a townland or ploughland on inferior clans or subject clans. This was later known as free quarters. Coyne and livery was also called **bonnacht.** The most famous of these was the Bonnacht of Ulster which the Earls of Ulster in their heyday imposed on the O'Neills. It amounted to 345 soldiers. With the decline of the earldom the O'Neill chiefs wished to retain the bonnacht for themselves. When the Earl of Desmond adopted the plan he was just following well-established precedents.

The justiciar was allowed a small annual sum to keep a small body of troops. At first the main body of armed man at the government's disposal was supposed to come from the great feudal tenants. But gradually the local defence of The Pale came from a short-term call out of able-bodied men, an early militia, to repel what were mostly local incursions of adjacent marauding clans. Coyne and livery meant that the great earls could gather large forces more easily and swiftly than the Lord Lieutenant so the policy was gradually adopted of making one or other of them Lord Lieutenant or Lord Deputy.

The Church Around 1400

There is a problem with this section and that is deciding what standard religious observance should be judged by. Catholic nationalist historians in the 19th century based their moral stand on the puritanical standards of contemporary Britain and the north eastern states in America. By those standards the clergy in Latin American countries did not come up to the mark. It was well known that Latin American priests had wives or mistresses and that the whole village colluded to cover this up when the bishop or dean arrived. Without going into the matter whether this was a true or false picture it was one that many rural parishes in the British Isles would have understood. The nationalist historians, while admitting these irregularities, blamed everything on the British Government, which is what nationalists do. And if it was not the Government at fault it was lay patrons, another 19th century obsession, but here MacCaffrey may be on stronger ground (MacCaffrey, passim). Yet puritanical observances in both Catholic and Protestant churches were largely the result of intense social pressures rather than grace. However that was never what the Christian religion in either East or West was supposed to be about.

Though it was a sore point among Irish nationalist historians the exclusion of Gaelic-speakers from offices and benefices in English-speaking areas was not necessarily a cause of decline. On the contrary the prohibition seems to have been the result, not the cause, of dissentions in monasteries and churches. Nor does royal influence on the election of bishops seem to have been a factor in causing the decline. The king might try to obtain beneficed dignities for some of the clerics who had served him faithfully. These then would have been capable, learned and experienced clerics, who nationalist feeling aside, who could only benefit the Irish Church. Nor, up to the 20th century at least, did the Holy See object to indications of the mind of the Government, even when that Government was Protestant. The Holy See always preferred to work along with Governments than against them, though some purists deplored that.

A much greater problem was papal provision to the benefices, dignities, or offices. The matter was made worse when there were two rival Popes whose chanceries were only too anxious to make money by taking appeals directly. This abuse was already in existence in the 12th century when Saint Bernard expressly warned pope Eugenius III of the dangers in by-passing the normal stages of appeal, first to the bishop's court, then to the metropolitan court, and then only to the papal court. One common way was for an ambitious cleric to go to Rome or Avignon and there denounce an incumbent as an unworthy man, and suggest himself as more suitable.

'This extravagant application of patronage and reservations to ecclesiastical appointments produced results in Ireland similar to those it produced in other countries. It tended to kill learning and zeal amongst the clergy, to make them careless about their personal conduct, the proper observance of the canons, and the due discharge of their duties as pastors and teachers. Some of them were openly immoral, and many of them had not sufficient learning to enable them to preach or to instruct their flocks. It ought to be remembered also that in these days there were no special seminaries for the education of the clergy. Candidates for the priesthood received whatever training they got from some member of the cathedral chapter, or in the schools of the mendicant friars, or possibly from some of those learned ecclesiastics, whose deaths are recorded specially in our Annals. Before ordination they were subjected to an examination, but the severity of the test depended on many extrinsic considerations' (MacCaffrey). There were often several parishes on monastic lands and the superior of the monastery was responsible for providing vicars while the monastery took the tithes. Mellifont had seven parish churches (Columcille, 172).

That many of the parish clergy were ignorant and had just memorised the Latin services, or most of them, and had little instruction in doctrine and were unable to preach is not denied. The wage of such a rural priest was three marks a year and might be even less in Gaelic districts (Corish, 42). Such priests were almost certainly surreptitiously married like many of the beneficed priests. The wealth of the Church was concentrated in the upper classes. Nor is it denied that preaching was largely left to the friars. Whether all friars had university degrees is not clear, but priests among them would have received a certain amount of training. Their preaching was based on the common stock of sermon material found all over the Continent (Corish, 44). For the rest, it seems that a lot of the decline in religious observance was just a return to the old practices of the Irish Church before the 12th century reformers tried to impose the new Hildebrandine standards. This reversion occurred even in Cistercian monasteries. What was new was the felt need to apply for a papal dispensation where the son of a priest wanted to follow his father into the profession in the time-honoured way. (All trades and professions were family businesses handed on from father to son.)

As Corish points out this may have been a rural problem. Towns often had better educated clergy and it was in the towns that the friars were based. It is interesting to note that the Franciscans had friaries in Cavan and Armagh in Gaelic areas which would indicate that towns of sorts existed there. Similarly the Dominicans had a house in Derry. As many of the friars were Gaelic-speakers there is no doubt that they preached in Gaelic at least in the areas surrounding the towns.

No new monastic houses were founded after the Black Death and it may well be that unsuitable applicants were accepted. A report from the Cistercian abbot of Mellifont stated that in only two Cistercian houses was the Rule observed or the habit worn. Acceptance by a monastery meant food on the table for life. Even an observant house like Mellifont was subjected to coyne and livery by the lords of The Pale (Columcille, 148). However Mellifont in the preceding century was not so edifying. Having been re-populated with French monks in 1228, by 1300 Gaelic monks were again in the majority and contended for the abbacy with men-at-arms. Though it is surprising that there still were Gaelic-speaking monks at all for most of Louth and Meath had been granted to Anglo-Norman lords (Columcille, 97). Novices were drawn largely from local families. Monastic houses were often reduced to near poverty by constant demands for money by the king, the pope, and foreign superiors so that the Statutes of Westminster of 1275 had to be extended to Ireland: common right to be done to all, as well poor as rich, without respect of persons, elections were to be free, and no man is by force, malice or menace, to disturb them; excessive amercements, abuses of wardship, irregular demands for feudal aids, to be forbidden. However regular visitations and inspections of Cistercian houses became impossible because of numerous local wars. This became more of a problem when Mellifont became English-speaking and many of its daughter houses were in Gaelic areas (Columcille, 109f). Corish points out that the decay in religion was more marked in the Gaelic areas than in the Norman-English areas (Corish 55).

An effort was made by Archbishop Fulk of Sandford, archbishop of Dublin (1256-71) to introduce English canonical rules on the conduct of the clergy into Ireland. These rules for clerical conduct were to be taken up more widely in 15th century synods (Watt, *The Church in Medieval Ireland*, 158).

Though an age of religion it was not an age of morality. Local chiefs could attack their neighbours for any cause. The priests and poets were there to declare the war just. Wars meant murders, burning, stealing, rapes and wasting and these were by no means confined to the kerne. The observation of the Church's marriage laws, so desired by the 12th century reformers, was largely ignored especially by the chiefs who much preferred the scope accorded to them by Brehon Law. One O'Donnell chief had 18 sons by 10 different women, an O'Reilly chief had 58 grandsons, and a Maguire had 20 sons by 8 mothers and at least 50 grandsons. All these had to be provided with at least one townland, so the existing occupiers had to be evicted or reduced in status. The brehon judges would ensure this. It is doubtful that any working class girl in Gaelic areas remained a virgin whether she wanted to or not. It is not clear when the bourgeois morality of sexual continence for women at least until they married arose. Matrimony and property were tied together. If a girl has earning potential a bride price is demanded. If she has not then a dowry to support her at least partially must be provided. Men object to rearing other men's children so 'damaged goods' are likely to be returned. It is most likely that this stricter morality arose in the towns and in rural areas influenced by the towns. It would be an additional reason why English-speakers wanted the Statutes of Kilkenny.

Chapter 13

The Lancastrians, Henry IV, Henry V and Henry VI 1399-1461

The low point in Ireland, Britain and most of Europe was probably reached about 1400. From that date onwards there were signs of recovery. The most spectacular recovery was in Italy where the great era of the renaissance of art and learning was commencing. In England there was a switch from exporting wool to exporting cloth. In the aftermath of the Black Death and other plagues the population had shrunk and marginal and less profitable land was abandoned with regard to tillage. The acreage under tillage in the 13th century was not reached again until the 19th century. Farm sizes grew larger and the peasants more prosperous. Serfdom disappeared. The Lancastrians were not very interested in Ireland. During the reigns of Henry V and Henry VI the eyes of all Englishmen were on France, and any money available was spent there.

Henry IV

Henry IV and Henry V are well known from familiar plays of Shakespeare. Henry Bolingbroke was named after Bolingbroke castle where he was born. Though a usurper he was accepted as king in 1399.

Much of his reign was spent in quelling uprisings, including the revolt of Owen Glendower who declared himself Prince of Wales in 1400, and the rebellion of Henry Percy, 1st Earl of Northumberland. The king's success in putting down these rebellions was due partly to the military ability of his eldest son, Henry of Monmouth, who would later become king (though the son managed to seize much effective power from his father in 1410).

Henry V

Called Henry of Monmouth from the place he was born, he pursued a policy of conciliation. There was little opposition apart from a plot in favour of Mortimer so he was able to turn his attention to the English claim to the kingdom of France. In 1415 he won the battle of Agincourt, again with the help of archers. He successfully conquered the northern French provinces. He married Catherine de Valois and they had an infant son, Henry VI. The king died of dysentery in 1422. The English held the North of France until the siege of Orleans in 1428 when Joan of Arc came to the rescue of the French army. It was the decisive turning point in the Hundred Years War though the claim to the throne of France was not given up until A.D. 1800.

Roger Mortimer, 4th Earl of March and 6th Earl of Ulster, was the heir presumptive to the throne when he died in 1398 leaving two sons, Edmund and Roger, and a daughter Anne Mortimer who married Richard Plantagenet of Conisburgh, 3rd Earl of Cambridge. Lady Anne was born on 27 December 1390 in New Forest, Westmeath, one of her parents' Irish estates. Their uncle Sir Edmund Mortimer and Henry Percy were leaders of the opposition to Henry IV. Henry IV kept the children in custody but treated them honourably. The son Roger died in 1409. Edmund was restored to his estates by Henry V and he joined Henry in the wars in France and was made Lord Lieutenant of Ireland in 1423. Edmund Mortimer died in Ireland of the plague in 1425 leaving no issue. The Earldom of March, the Earldom of Ulster, and his estates therefore passed to his nephew, Anne Mortimer's son, Richard Plantagenet (later restored as 3rd Duke of York, who was nevertheless styled Earl of March, as was his son). On Richard's son Edward's accession to the throne in 1461 as King Edward IV, the earldoms merged into the Crown.

John Beaufort, 1st Earl of Somerset (1373-16 March 1410) was the first of the four illegitimate children of John *of Gaunt*, 1st Duke of Lancaster, and his mistress Katherine Swynford, later his wife. In 1396, after his parents' marriage, John and his siblings were legitimated by a papal bull. Early the next year, their legitimation was recognized by an act of Parliament, and then, a few days later, John was created Earl of Somerset (10 February 1397). The children however were not accorded succession rights to the throne. The Beauforts were the great supporters of the House of Lancaster while the Mortimers were supporters of the House of York.

Henry VI

Henry became king when he was one year old. His mother, Catherine de Valois, as a Frenchwoman was not trusted with the regency which was formed by a council headed by Henry V's brothers, John, Duke of Bedford, Humphrey, Duke of Gloucester, and Cardinal Henry Beaufort. Bedford was largely in charge of the war in France, while Gloucester remained in England. Catherine de Valois entered a relationship with a Welsh gentleman named Owen Tudor. Their sons, Edmund and Jasper Tudor, were made earls by their half-brother Henry VI.

The Duke of Bedford in alliance with the Burgundians was successfully carrying on the war in France until Joan of Arc forced him to raise the siege of Orleans in 1429 and then recaptured Rheims where the kings of France were traditionally crowned. In reaction to Charles VII Valois's coronation as French King in Rheims cathedral on July

17, 1429[, Henry was soon crowned King of England at Westminster Abbey on 6 November 1429, followed by his own coronation as King of France in the cathedral Notre Dame in Paris on 16 December 1431. Bedford died in 1435 and in the same year the Duke of Burgundy concluded a treaty with France. A month before his sixteenth birthday on 13 November 1437 Henry obtained some measure of independent authority before he finally assumed full royal powers when he came of age. The peace party at the English court gained the upper hand and Henry VI was married to Margaret of Anjou in 1445. Later the war was re-started but the Hundred Years War came to an end with a French victory in 1453, leaving only Calais in English hands. During this period guns and artillery were being developed rapidly in France.

In 1453 came the fall of Constantinople a date which is often used to mark the beginning of the Renaissance and the revival of the study of Greek in Western Europe. (The Renaissance was a multi-faceted affair noted for the extraordinary development of art and architecture in Italy and particularly in Florence, but 1453 remains a convenient marker date for its origin. John Argyrophoulos, a refugee from Byzantium began to teach Greek in Florence in 1456). In 1453, nearer home the battle of Castillon in which the English army was defeated and John Talbot the Earl of Shrewsbury the English commander was slain marked the virtual end of the Hundred Years War and the loss of all English possessions on the Continent except Calais. In 1453 Ormond was appointed Lord Lieutenant displacing York who was being marginalized at court. In 1454-5, Gutenberg printed the Gutenberg Bible an edition of the Latin Vulgate.

In 1453, Henry VI suffered his first bout of insanity. Richard of York was made Lord Protector. Richard gained the powerful support of Richard Neville, 16th Earl of Warwick and 6th Earl of Salisbury, known as Warwick the Kingmaker. When the king recovered in 1454 a faction around Margaret of Anjou forced York out of the court and this led directly to the Wars of the Roses 1455-85. Margaret above all wanted to protect the interest of her son Edward of Westminster. Henry restored the Beauforts under Edmund Duke of Somerset. York and Warwick took up arms. Richard and his ally defeated the Lancastrians under Edmund, Duke of Somerset, who was killed at the Battle of St Albans 22 May 1455. York also captured Henry VI and had himself appointed Constable of England and Lord Protector. At a battle called the rout of Ludlow, or Ludford Bridge, in 1459 the Yorkist army retreated and York fled briefly to his supporters in Ireland. During the king's second bout of insanity in 1460 Richard claimed the throne. He was killed at the battle of Wakefield in December 1460 but his son Edward routed the Lancastrians at Towton in March 1461 and claimed the throne. Though Henry survived until 1471 his reign was virtually at an end in 1461 when Edward of York, son of Richard of York seized the throne for the Yorkist faction. (Edward of Westminster was killed at the Battle of Tewkesbury 1471.)

Ireland

In the period from 1399 to 1483 the English court had little time or money to spend on Ireland. Yet the process of Gaelicization came to an end as three powerful earldoms emerged. The Great Earl of Kildare finally succeeded in doing what no Gaelic ruler since Rory O'Connor had achieved, namely subduing every chief and lord in Ireland. The earldom of Ulster was in terminal decline from which it never recovered. The earl was an absentee and the earldom lacked the constant presence of someone with the authority to settle disputes among his own followers. Ellis points out that the Gaelicization process was not caused by any great accession of power by the Gaelic chiefs but by divisions, rivalries, and royal neglect and mismanagement within the Lordship itself. This allowed minor local Gaelic chiefs to reassert themselves locally. These could normally do no more than inflict constant irritation in the form of cattle raids on the margins of The Pale and the great earldoms without substantially altering the borders. A temporary decline in the power of the earls of Kildare allowed the advance of the MacMurrough Kavanaghs which was quickly reversed in the second half of the 15th century (Ellis *Tudor Ireland*, 29, 65).

James Butler, 3rd Earl of Ormond died in 1405. When Nenagh was no longer tenable he built Gowran castle in Co. Kilkenny in 1385 and bought Kilkenny castle from Thomas le Despencer, 1st Earl of Gloucester in 1391. This became the principal residence of the earls of Ormond. Kilkenny is about 40 miles from Nenagh though probably 50 miles by road. His son, James Butler, the 4th earl, called the White Earl, was earl from 1405 to 1452. Most of his life was spent in disputes with the Talbots. His daughter however was to marry Talbot's son.

John Fitzgerald (called *Cam*, the humpback), 6th Earl of Kildare (1410-27) strengthened and enlarged the castle of Maynooth in Kildare, making it the principal residence of the earls of Kildare. His son was Thomas, 7th Earl of Kildare (1427-77). He was succeeded in 1477 by his son Gerald, 8th Earl of Kildare, famous in Irish history as Geroit or *Gearoid Mór* (Garret or Gerald the Great, or the Great Earl of Kildare) 1477-1513. The earls of Ormond were most influential in the first half of the century and the earls of Kildare in the second half.

Though the largest landowners in Ireland, the Earls of Desmond were never as powerful in most of this century as the earls of Ormond or Kildare. They were estimated to control 500,000 acres of land and had 20 great houses and castles. They adopted many Gaelic customs, and like all the great rulers in Ireland their only concern was for the advancement of their own house. They were notorious for 'coign and livery, cartings, carriages, lodgings, cosherings, bonnacht and such like' (Curtis, 143). In other words they exacted everything they could think of or get away with from those subject to them. They were not alone in Ireland in doing this, but it was considered wrong for an Anglo-Norman family to do them. Their lands stretched across central Munster from

Kerry and Limerick to Cork and Waterford. The earls were Thomas Fitzgerald, 5th Earl of Desmond (c. 1386-1420); James Fitzgerald, 6th Earl of Desmond (d. 1463); Thomas Fitzgerald, 7th Earl of Desmond (d. 1468); James Fitzgerald, 8th Earl of Desmond (1459-1487); and Maurice Fitzgerald, 9th Earl of Desmond (d. 1520). There was habitual feuding with the earls of Ormond.

The history of Ireland for the next century was to revolve around these three great families. The Government in London might intervene from time to time, but rarely had enough money to do much. The families allied themselves to the fortunes of the houses of York and Lancaster. But it was not until the 1530s when Silken Thomas Fitzgerald, the 10th Earl of Kildare, overplayed his hand that royal rule again became effective. Numerous letters were sent at this period describing the evils the Lordship of Ireland suffered at the hands of the king's enemies and asking for support. Yet the remedy lay in the suppliants' own hands. If they all put aside their petty squabbles with each other and all agreed to unite their forces and wealth behind the justiciar or Lord Deputy the whole of Ireland could have been brought under control. (Nationalist writers used to deplore the fact that the Gaelic chiefs could never unite under a single chief and drive the invaders into the sea. But that was not how society worked in the Middle Ages.)

At this time too there began to emerge in The Pale families who were to play an increasing role in the government of Ireland, often filling the chief offices. Among these were the Prestons (Barons Gormanston), the St Lawrences (Barons Howth), the Fitzeustaces, the Plunketts (Barons Killeen and Earls of Fingal), the Talbots of Malahide (not Shrewsbury), the Barnewalls (Barons Trimleston), the Nettervilles (Viscounts), the Bellews (baronets and later barons), and the Cusacks. Many of these families dated back to the earliest Norman subinfeudation and rose, not in power but in influence, largely through the law and administration. Their titles of nobility often came much later. They were repeatedly detested by reforming English administrators who wished to reduce the number of official positions they had created for themselves with no visible increase in efficient and economic administration. The detestation was mutual. It is not clear if these gentlemen were included among the *nobiles* of the diocese and province of Armagh who were wasting the lands of Mellifont Abbey on the borders of Louth and Meath and imposing coyne and livery on those lands (Columcille, 148. *Nobilis* had wide meaning in the Middle Ages.)

Because of a shortage of cash an expedient was developed of paying with tallies not cash. These tallies were then presented to the Exchequer in Dublin who paid them (or did not as the case might be) from the revenues it received from various sources in Ireland. Under William of Windsor (1368-71) the revenue of Ireland had been raised to £3,600 a year (Ellis, 25) but it was to fall at times to £1,000 (Lydon, *Ireland in the Late Middle Ages*, 130). Henry IV had some good intentions regarding Ireland for he appointed his second son, Thomas of Lancaster, later Duke of Clarence, as Lord Lieutenant. The king promised a subsidy of £12,000 a year but had no money to pay it. Thomas did his best and ran up debts, and his tallies were not honoured. Thomas of Lancaster was no more successful than other chief governors. He led attacks on various minor chiefs surrounding Leinster, but did not dare intervene in the war between the earls of Ormond and Desmond, with the MacWilliam Burkes assisting the Earl of Ormond. Despite, or perhaps because of, Mortimer claims Sir William de Burgh of Clanrickard was made Keeper of Connaught. Lancaster came twice to Ireland and then departed for France. The only option was to make either the Earl of Ormond or the Earl of Kildare Lord Deputy to manage from their own resources as best they could. The justiciar had another method of raising funds for campaigns and this was called purveyance. Purveyance was the right of the Crown to requisition goods and services for royal use. The main problem with the system was that it was open to abuse from corrupt officials. The official set the price he was prepared to pay and it was always below the market price.

In 1414 Henry V sent over Sir John Talbot, deputy constable of Montgomery castle in Wales who had re-captured Harlech castle from the Welsh. (He was made Baron Talbot in 1421 and Earl of Shrewsbury in 1442 and Earl of Waterford and Lord High Steward of Ireland on 17 July 1446. The Earls of Shrewsbury, Earls of Waterford in the Peerage of Ireland have held the office since the 15th century. The Lord High Steward of Ireland is a hereditary Great Officer of State in Ireland, sometimes known as the Hereditary Great Seneschal. The earls remained Catholic after the Reformation and were closely involved in the campaign for Catholic Emancipation. John Talbot, the 16th earl was a great patron of Augustus Welby Pugin.) Talbot had Irish connections for his wife was one of the de Verdon heiresses who retained interests in Westmeath and the lordship of Wexford.

Talbot's instructions were to treat rebel Gaelic chiefs with severity. This was directly contrary to the policy of the Earl of Ormond. The great desire of the O'Neills at this stage was to hold their lands as tenants-in-chief from the crown and not through the earldom of Ulster. The chief of the O'Neills at this point was Dónal O'Neill (1404-32, a son of Henry *Aimhreidh*, (Avery, the Confused) and nephew of Dónal Óg. (Harry Avery's castle is regarded as the first attempt by the O'Neills to build a habitable castle.) Dónal was succeeded by Eogain (1432-5) the son of Niall *Óg*.

Talbot departed for France where he achieved fame as a general. He left his brother, Richard Talbot, Archbishop of Dublin as Lord Deputy. Richard Talbot (d.1449), archbishop of Dublin 1418-49 was a younger brother of John Talbot and previously had been dean of Chichester. Richard Talbot was more prominent in royal government in Ireland than any other late medieval archbishop of Dublin. He served three deputy lieutenancies (1419-20, 1435-7, 1447-8), five justiciarships (1420, 1422-3, 1430-1, 1437-8, 1445-6), and was twice Chancellor (1423-6, 1427-31). James Butler, the White Earl of Ormond attended Henry V in the wars in France. He had the reputation of being one of the most learned men in Ireland at the time. In 1417 Talbot confiscated Ormond's lands in Ireland for non-payment of debts at the Dublin Exchequer. On obtaining the lieutenancy himself in 1420, Ormond purged Talbot appointees from the Irish administration. Thereafter there was fierce competition to control or influence the power and patronage of the chief offices and numerous charges and counter charges of misgovernment. The White Earl spent the rest of his life until his death in 1453 combating the influence of Talbot and his family. Ormond's policy of conciliation was the only practical one. Archbishop Talbot died in 1449. Thirty years were wasted in this futile dispute in which the only beneficiaries were the local Gaelic chiefs who could raid and plunder virtually at will.

A curiosity of this period was the interventions of the Knights Hospitallers under Thomas *le Bottiler* (Butler) Ormond's illegitimate half-brother who was prior of Kilmainham the chief house of the Hospitallers in Dublin. Kilmainham was to become the capital of County Dublin for administrative purposes and the county gaol was built there. The site of their priory is now occupied by the Royal Hospital Kilmainham built in the time of Charles II for old or disabled soldiers. Part of their lands was later acquired to form the Phoenix Park. By this time war against the Turks was largely abandoned and their armed men were used in local wars. In 1418 Prior Thomas took 18 score men with red shields and 18 score men with white shields to Henry V in France in 1418 and he died in France the following year (Otway-Ruthven, 355). (We can safely assume that these were hired mercenaries and not members of the Order.)

On the death of Henry V the regency appointed Edmund Mortimer, Earl of March and Ulster as Lord Lieutenant though his right to the throne had been brushed aside by Henry Bolingbrook. He appointed the White Earl as his Lord Deputy. Ormond believed in engaging with the Gaelic chiefs while fomenting factions among them. The pressure on the earldom of Ulster was coming from the Clandeboy O'Neills so

Ormond supported the Great O'Neill who opposed them. A resident Earl of Ulster was now essential not only from the pressure of the Clandeboy O'Neills while both the MacGuinnesses and MacCartans of Iveagh were also inching forward. At the same time in the very north of Antrim the MacQuillan gallowglasses of the Route (approximately the barony of Dunluce) had entrenched themselves. In 1399 John MacDonald (usually MacDonnell in Ireland) of the Scottish Isles married the heiress of the lands of the Bisset family in the earldom and established a Scottish presence. (The Bissets or Bysets were originally Scottish and had received grants of land from Hugh de Lacy. They always retained links with Scotland and had sided with Edward the Bruce.) He submitted to Richard II in 1395. (The MacDonnells were later to build up their possessions in the Glens of Antrim and as Earls of Antrim still occupy Glenarm castle. The Glens are largely Catholic to this day). Ormond did his best to protect the earldom though he had no lands in Ulster. Allowing the earldom to be over-run would allow the raiding clans easier access to The Pale.

It is strange to us how careful people in the Middle Ages respected the received order. They always justified themselves whenever they departed from their obligations and they had priests and poets to provide the justification. The O'Neills were not demanding independence but the right for they themselves to hold from the crown while the other clans in Ulster would be their urraghs: the same right as Rory O'Connor. This despite the fact that the English monarchs had abolished subinfeudation so that every feudal tenant held directly from the crown. (A dispute over former urraghs led to the Flight of the Earls in 1607.) The right of overlordship of the king of England was never questioned in the Middle Ages.

Edmund Mortimer was appointed Lord Lieutenant in May of 1423 (a post also held by his father and grandfather). As Earl of Ulster he was the recognised overlord of most of the clans in Ulster in 1425, and received their submission at Trim castle in Co. Meath. Simms remarked that the early deaths of the Mortimers resulted in their failure to restore and hold their earldom unlike the other three, or four if one includes the MacWilliam Burkes (Simms, 'The King's Friend, O'Neill', 218). He worked through a deputy at first, but in February 1424 he took ship for Ireland. Mortimer died in Ireland of the plague in 1425. He married Anne Stafford, daughter of the, 5th Earl of Stafford, but he left no issue. The Earldom of March, the Earldom of Ulster and his estates therefore passed to his nephew, Anne Mortimer's son, Richard Plantagenet (later restored as 3rd Duke of York). On Richard's son Edward's accession to the throne in 1461 as King Edward IV, the earldoms merged into the Crown. As Simms notes the O'Neills then held directly from the crown (*op.cit.* 234).

A strange fact in the following century was that the Gaelic lords who for two centuries resisted building castles or tower houses now began to construct them in large numbers. These were often more adapted for display than for defensive purposes. They were usually built by minor local lords, not by the great chiefs. They are evidence too of the growing wealth of the minor lords which resulted from the switch in exports to cattle hides, wool and sheepskins. There is little doubt however that their principal role was to provide a secure and temporary defence for an individual family of sufficient means against the incessant cattle raiding and skirmishing. Their popularity may have been stimulated by a royal grant to gentlemen of The Pale in 1429 to build defensive houses, but they spread among the minor Gaelic lords. The Midlands and North Munster have by far the greatest concentrations. They are rare in the North West (Barry, *Archaeology*, 186-7).

In many ways the 15th century was a glorious period for many of the lesser Gaelic chiefs. The government of the Lordship was weak and faction-ridden and the powers of the great provincial chiefs were restricted. In pre-Norman times they would never have dared to disregard a king like Murtagh O'Brien, Turlough O'Connor or Murtagh MacLoughlin for any disrespect would be met with a devastation of their lands that it would take a generation to repair. Now the power of the great chiefs was reduced, their own little territories were in more easily defensible places, cash from tributes, black rents, and the export of hides together with coyne and livery enabled them to maintain small professional forces at all times. Even the great chiefs like the MacCarthys in Cork occupied the upper stretches of the great river valleys, while the Anglo-Normans had the broader, more fertile and less easily defensible lower reaches of the same rivers. Within their more limited spheres of power the provincial chiefs extorted the utmost from those under them and from the peasantry or betaghs. The welfare of the common people in peace or war was never a concern of the chiefs. In particular lesser landowners were systematically deprived of their lands and holdings to provide for the numerous sons of the chiefs. Warfare was not necessarily profitable but it provided an occupation, a blood sport for the young men who got either death or glory. (The same was true on the Anglo-Norman side, but these could go to France with the king.)

As in England, the great earls and great chiefs were able to build up substantial private armies which they used to fight each other or the Government. Had the great earls been willing to combine with the justiciar or Lord Deputy the whole of Ireland could have been swiftly brought under central control. The Lord Deputy frequently was not paid. Sources of royal revenue were often given away as gifts or became impossible to collect. (The same conditions were found also in England leaving the kings permanently short of money.) Even when collected the revenue was often spent locally on local defence. The Lord Deputy could call a hosting to the royal service and gather a force of up to 1,000 armed men with some military skills. The fighting quality of those sent to the Lord Deputy was not necessarily high when the best fighters were retained for local defence. But the hosting lasted only 40 days at a time and only a handful of the most obnoxious of the raiders could be dealt with in any given year. Those exposed to the raids of the Gaelic chiefs often found it easier and better to pay a black rent or protection money to the nearest chief. This could not be a long-term solution as the young men and the kernes wanted the excitement of the raid with its opportunities for looting, raping and killing.

There is little point in recalling all the moves and counter moves in this period of domestic squabbling (Otway-Ruthven, 339-376). It was brought to an end with the appointment of Richard Mortimer, Duke of York as Lord Lieutenant in 1447 and with the death of Archbishop Talbot in 1449 and the White Earl of Ormond in 1453.

The death of Humphrey Duke of Gloucester in 1447 made Richard of York the first Prince of the Blood though he made no attempt as yet to claim the throne. In 1448 he was appointed Lord Lieutenant of Ireland, a convenient means of keeping him out of England which was being controlled by the Beaufort (Duke of Somerset) faction. The Earl of Ormond allied himself with the Beaufort/Lancaster faction when he married his son James to a sister of the Duke of Somerset. Nearly all the other Anglo-Norman lords backed the Mortimers whose head was now Richard Plantagenet, the 3rd Duke of York and 8th Earl of Ulster. The Yorkists remained the dominant power in Ireland until the execution of Silken Thomas, 10th Earl of Kildare, best remembered for his name, by Henry VIII in 1537. The next 90 years were to see the rise to dominance of the Geraldines of Kildare while the earldom of Ulster went into decline. However in the short term Richard of York got the submission of the Earl of Ormond.

The O'Neills too were anxious to meet the new Earl of Ulster, now a prince of the blood with vast estates in the Welsh Marches. Every Gaelic chief in Ulster knew that if the Earl of Ulster, with his own wealth and the wealth of the crown behind him, kept an adequate armed force of several hundred men with at least half of them horsed he could subdue and keep in subjection all the clans in Ulster even if they combined against him. O'Neill's chief aim was to be subject to the king of England in equality with the Earl of Ulster and not subject to him (Simms, 'The King's Friend', 217). This was to be their policy until the fatal 'Flight of the Earls' in 1607 signalled the end of their dreams. They wished to retain the right that Rory O'Connor had obtained from Henry II, that the other chiefs in Ulster whom they regarded as their urraghs should pay their tribute through them. The English monarchs had however abandoned the policy of subinfeudation and insisted that every nobleman and knight was directly subject to the crown. (The problems of Gaelic chiefs holding fiefs of the crown was to come to the fore under the Tudors.)

As the siege of Orleans marked the turning point in the Hundred Years War and the battle of Castillon in 1453 marked its end so the coming of the Duke of York marked a turning point in medieval Irish history. After the battle of Castillon English kings and nobles were no longer very concerned with events in France. Events in Ireland loomed larger. By the same token the great Irish noblemen became more deeply involved in English affairs. They formerly had attended the king in his hostings; now they attended his court. An ability to read and write became essential. Grammar schools like Eton and Winchester were founded, primarily to provide a basic education for future clerics by teaching Latin but also to provide an education for the sons of gentlemen.

In itself the short visit of the Duke of York was not different from any other visit by a Lord Lieutenant. He arrived in Ireland in June 1449 and was warmly welcomed not least by Eogan O'Neill and his son Henry (1455-83) who was later to send an armed force to England in 1460 and was to receive 48 yards of scarlet cloth and a collar of gold from Edward IV. O'Neill was to assist the Lord Lieutenant with 500 men-at-arms and 500 foot-soldiers (presumably including the Bonnacht of Ulster) armed with axes, lances and bows. The agreement with Henry O'Neill lasted until the latter's death (Burke, **Peerage**, 2028; Simms, 'The King's Friend', 223). The Duke of York had to return to England in 1450 leaving the aged Earl of Ormond as his Deputy. (Archbishop Talbot had died the previous year while John Talbot, the Earl of Shrewsbury was to be killed by the new French artillery in 1453.) Ormond died in 1452 and his son, James Butler, 5th Earl of Ormond and 1st Earl of Wiltshire succeeded him in the earldom and the deputyship.

The Wars of the Roses broke out in 1453 and the supporters of each faction were closely involved though no fighting occurred in Ireland. Both factions sent troops to fight in England. Thomas Fitzgerald the 7th Earl of Kildare was made Lord Deputy to Richard, Duke of York, and from this point the rise of the earls of Kildare commences. After the Rout of Ludlow Richard of York came to Ireland and held a parliament which opened in Drogheda on 4 February 1460 and then adjourned to Dublin (Otway-Ruthven, 387; Cosgrove, 'Parliament and the Anglo-Irish Community'). The parliament in Dublin gave its full support to the duke against the king. One of its declarations seemed to say that English statutes did not bind Ireland and this claim was being repeated in 18th century Irish parliaments. Nevertheless historians were sharply divided regarding what the 1460 parliament intended. It is clear that English parliaments had no right to tax Ireland, nor any right to summon lords, knights or burgesses to vote such taxes. But English laws, whether or not passed with the consent of Parliament (which was in itself a novelty) did bind Ireland. The Declaration of 1460 had no basis in history, but it seems clear that if Richard of York had declared himself king of Ireland, the Irish Parliament was prepared to back him to the hilt. (Whether this would have resulted in a situation like that of the short-lived independent Irish Parliament from 1782-1800 is another matter entirely.) As Cosgrove concludes, the Anglo-Irish simply could not afford to press their claims to separateness too strongly (*loc. cit*). Ellis notes that from 1460 onwards parliaments were held frequently in Ireland (Ellis, 'Parliament and Community', 45). They passed little legislation being content with English statutes. Their concerns were administrative and judicial, this because of the decline of the Courts of King's Bench and Common Pleas to be largely debt-collecting agencies (*op. cit.*, 46).

Richard, Duke of York was slain at Wakefield in 1460. The 5th Earl of Ormond was actively engaged in the Wars of the Roses and was defeated at Mortimer's Cross in 1461 and was executed as a traitor after the battle of Towton in the same year. Richard's son Edward was crowned king as Edward IV. John Butler, the 6th Earl of Ormond was pardoned by Edward IV.

Chapter 14

The Yorkists and Tudors
1461-1509

Edward IV

After his father was killed in 1461, Edward was crowned as king largely through the influence of his cousin Richard Neville, the Earl of Warwick, who hoped to take over the management of the king from the Beauforts. Edward had a mind of his own and insisted on making a marriage alliance with Elizabeth Woodville of a Lancastrian family. Warwick changed sides and Edward was deposed in 1470, and Warwick had Henry restored, hence his name the kingmaker. Edward fled to his sister Margaret in Burgundy but returned the following year and defeated and killed Warwick and most of the leading Lancastrians at the battle of Barnet outside London in 1471. Henry VI was captured and died shortly afterwards. Edward, or alternatively his brother Richard, was suspected of his murder, but Edward remained secure at home for the next 20 years. He led an army to France but was bought off by the French king. His eldest daughter, Elizabeth of York, was to marry Henry Tudor the remaining Lancastrian claimant and ended the Wars of the Roses. England in his reign became peaceful and increasingly prosperous. He died in 1483 leaving his brother Richard protector of his infant sons.

Richard III

Richard of York was the youngest son of Richard, 3rd Duke of York and Cecily Neville. He was made Duke of Gloucester by his older brother Edward IV. He went into exile with his brother and returned with him in 1471. He seized the throne himself claiming that his brother's marriage to Elizabeth Woodville was invalid and that their children were therefore bastards. He confined the young princes to the Tower of London where they died, allegedly murdered by their uncle. He was defeated and killed at the battle of Bosworth in 1485, the last battle in the Wars of the Roses, by a Lancastrian with a slender claim to the throne, Henry Tudor. (Shakespeare's play *Richard III* is not regarded as reliable evidence.)

Henry VII

After the defeat of Owen Glendower and the Percys of Northumberland by Henry IV Welsh resistance to English claims died down. One Owen Tudor of Anglesey joined Henry V in France and he was attached to the household of Catherine of Valois, Henry's French wife. After Henry's death she settled in England and Owen Tudor became Keeper of the Queen's Wardrobe. Tudor historians always insisted that they were legally married. One of their sons was called Edmund Tudor, 1st Earl of Richmond, who married Margaret Beaufort. Their son was Henry Tudor, 2nd Earl of Richmond. Henry's tenuous claim to the throne was through his mother who was a Beaufort. After the victory of the Yorkists in 1471 he fled to Brittany. By 1485 he was the Lancastrian with the best claim to the throne. Elizabeth Woodville and Margaret Beaufort came to an agreement that Henry Tudor should marry Elizabeth of York and depose Richard III. He returned to England and was aided by the defection of the Earl of Northumberland and William and Thomas Stanley from Richard III. He was a prudent and cautious king who made peace with France, Scotland and the Netherlands. He reduced the power of the great nobles by various devices such as laws against livery and maintenance. The dynasty or ruling family was no longer called Plantagenet but Tudor. As a sign of changing times John Cabot sailed from Bristol in the *Matthew*, a small ship of 50 tons and reached Newfoundland in 1497. Henry made strategic alliances. He married his son Henry to Catherine of Aragon and his daughter Margaret to James IV of Scotland.

Ireland

In 1462 Thomas Fitzgerald, 8th Earl of Desmond, succeeded to the earldom. In 1463 he was made Deputy to George, Duke of Clarence, the brother of Edward IV. (Clarence is chiefly famous for being drowned in a butt of Mamsley wine by his brother Richard.) Desmond built castles around The Pale and carried on the hereditary feud with the Butlers. He was strong in Munster but could not prevent attacks on The Pale by local chiefs. An Act was passed establishing a university at Drogheda but nothing came of it. At this stage there were various notices about the great earls commending their learning. Clearly the day of the illiterate knight and baron was passing. The learning was not the new learning of the Renaissance—it was too early in Ireland for that—but an ability to read and write English and Latin. John Butler, the 6th Earl or Ormond, spoke several European languages and was sent by Edward IV as ambassador to various European courts.

In 1466 Desmond suffered a defeat in Offaly and was replaced in 1467 as Lord Deputy by John Tiptoft, Earl of Worcester. A parliament was called at Drogheda in February 1468, where the earls of Desmond and Kildare and Edward Plunket of Balrath, Co. Meath a son of

Sir Christopher Plunket, a former Lord Deputy, were attainted as supporters of the Earl of Warwick who had opposed the king's marriage to Elizabeth Woodville. This was allegedly for alliances, fosterage with the Irish, for furnishing them with horses and arms, and supporting them against the King's subjects. The Earl of Desmond was beheaded, 15th February 1467, at Drogheda, and was there buried in St. Peter's Church. In 1468 the Munster Geraldines invaded The Pale. Though Thomas Fitzgerald, 7th Earl of Kildare, was attainted along with Earl of Desmond the revolt of the southern Geraldines made the Government anxious to avoid a similar simultaneous uprising in Leinster. The archbishop of Dublin and others became his securities, and in 1468 his attainder was repealed. Ormond, who supported the Lancastrians was in exile but was also still attainted. *Gearoid Mór* (meaning *Big Garret*), the son of Thomas Fitzgerald, 7th Earl of Kildare and Jane Fitzgerald, the daughter of James Fitzgerald, 6th Earl of Desmond, succeeded his father in 1477. He was only 22 years old and King Edward was unwilling to appoint him Lord Deputy but finally had to give way.

In the brief interlude of the restoration of Henry VI in 1470 Tiptof was recalled to England and was executed by the Lancastrians. Kildare was elected justiciar by the Irish Council. He was made Lord Deputy by Edward who had returned and decisively defeated the Lancastrians at Barnet and Tewkesbury. John Butler, 6th Earl of Ormond had his attainder removed and was restored to his lands in Ireland but not in Wiltshire. He died in 1478 on a pilgrimage to the Holy Land and was succeeded by his younger brother Thomas Butler, the 7th earl. Besides being in the possession of major lands in the Irish counties of Kilkenny and Tipperary, he owned 72 manors in England, making him one of the richest subjects in the realm. In 1509, he was appointed Lord Chamberlain to Catherine of Aragon. He held this post until 1512. Anne Boleyn was a granddaughter of his.

Richard III appointed his own eldest son Edward as Lord Lieutenant and persuaded the Earl of Kildare to continue as Lord Deputy, but with appointments in the king's hands. Kildare was to use his influence with his brother-in-law Henry O'Neill who was married to Lady Eleanor Fitzgerald, daughter of the Earl of Kildare to get the O'Neills to withdraw from Richard's earldom of Ulster. (Two generations of O'Neills married into the Earl of Kildare's family.)

The authorised bodyguard of the Lord Deputy of 20 men-at-arms was increased to 80 archers and 40 horsemen with an increased salary. The men of the Lordship gained experience from the wars in France and in England, while the soldiers in the Gaelic areas did not (Ellis, 'The Tudors', 118). These formed the nucleus to which the hostings for service to the king were added. Feudal tenants were still asked to pay scutage for the hire of additional troops. (No doubt the prior of Kilmainham would assist with a quota.) A number of gentlemen of The Pale in 1474 established the Brotherhood of Saint George. To their captain, who was to be chosen for one year on their anniversary, were assigned as his train 120 archers on horseback, and 40 other horsemen with one attendant to each. The archers were to receive sixpence daily pay, the others, for themselves and their attendants, five pence, with an annual stipend of four marks. Thus was the defence of The Pale entrusted to 200 men and 13 officers, with such levies as might be raised on any sudden emergency. To support this armament the fraternity was empowered to demand 12 pence in the pound out of all merchandises sold in Ireland. At this time patents of nobility were being issued to gentlemen of The Pale, Viscount Gormanston (Preston) 1478; and Barons Trimleston (Barnewall) 1462, Portlester (Fitzeustace) 1462, and Ratowth (Bold) 1468, and Viscount Barry (Barry) 1461.

In 1485 when Richard was slain at the Battle of Bosworth field Henry Tudor who had slender Lancastrian claims seized the throne. This caused a problem for the strongly Yorkist Earl of Kildare and all the other Irish lords who supported the Yorkist cause. Their support for the two Yorkist pretenders Lambert Simnel and Perkin Warbeck should have led to their ruin but Henry Tudor could find no plausible alternative Lord Deputy and was forced to come to terms with Kildare. Henry when told that all Ireland cannot control this man was reported to have replied, 'Then this man shall control all Ireland'. The king had no choice but to select one of the three great earls.

But first there was the pretension of Lambert Simnel. A priest named Richard Simon conceived the idea of passing him off as one of the princes murdered in the Tower. The Yorkist leaders may have been involved in the imposture. Simon took Lambert to Oxford to educate him for the part, but in 1486 there was a rumour that the Edward, Earl of Warwick, son of George of Clarence, had escaped from the Tower so Simon took him to Ireland in 1487 and claimed he was the Earl of Warwick. The Earl of Kildare, the Lord Chancellor Sir Thomas Fitzgerald, and the archbishop of Dublin, Walter Fitzsimons, were persuaded. The archbishop of Armagh, Octavian *de Palatio* was sceptical. Margaret of Burgundy, sister of Edward IV, recognised him and persuaded her son-in-law to dispatch 1,500 German mercenaries to Ireland under Martin Schwartz who landed in Ireland 5th May 1487. Schwarz is said to have brought the first firearms to Ireland. Schwartz's army was joined by a contingent of Irish under Thomas Fitzgerald. Though Henry paraded the real earl it made no difference. On 24 May Simnel was crowned in Dublin as Edward VI, John Payne, bishop of Meath, preaching the sermon. On 4 June 1487 the Yorkist forces invaded England, landed in Lancashire and were joined by other Yorkists. They were defeated by Henry's forces at Stoke near Newark. Simon was imprisoned for life while Simnel was said to have been sent to the king's kitchens. The king exacted oaths of allegiance from Kildare and the other Yorkist leaders and left Kildare as Lord Deputy. Furthermore Kildare was able to use the king's artillery to demolish the castles of those who opposed him. A parliament in 1488 prohibited coign and livery within the marches, and within the maghery it could only be imposed by landlords on their own tenants.

A Flemish impostor named Perkin Warbeck through his impersonation of Richard, Duke of York, got some acceptance on the Continent, especially from Margaret of Burgundy, but received little support in Ireland in 1494 though he approached the Earls of Kildare and Desmond. However Henry decided to send an English Lord Deputy to Ireland, Sir Edward Poynings. Poynings became notorious among Irish nationalist historians for one particular law passed by the parliament he called in Ireland, always called Poynings' Law. In fact there was little unusual in the Acts passed by this Parliament. Poyning's Law required that the heads of every bill about to be presented to the Irish Parliament should be shown to and approved beforehand by the king and his Council in England. It was intended to prevent any legislation favourable to the Yorkists being passed by an Irish Parliament. Parliaments in any case could not enact legislation independently of the king, and every Act had to receive the signature either of the king, the Lord Lieutenant, or the Lord Deputy. Various other acts like the resumption to the crown of appointments, and extending English laws to Ireland were commonplace at the time. The abolition of the private army of the Brotherhood of St George was in line with royal policy in England. The Earl of Kildare was arrested and charged with treason. The Earl of Desmond thereupon backed Perkin Warbeck. Poynings with the help of the royal artillery broke the opposition and the various lords, including the Earl of Desmond, submitted. Only Lord Barry and John Water, the mayor of Cork, were excluded from the pardon.

In 1496, after the departure of Poynings, Garret *Mór,* the Great Earl of Kildare was re-appointed Lord Deputy and in a few short years established a control over Ireland that had not been seen since the days of Rory O'Connor. This culminated in 1504 in that rarity in Irish history a full-scale day-long battle. Kings and chiefs in the Middle Ages tended to avoid battles, preferring raiding and harassing and prudent retreat to the hazard of battle. These usually occurred in succession disputes where both parties wished for a quick and decisive result. The Earl of Kildare gathered a force to attack his son-in-law Ulick Burke, lord of Clanrickard Burkes, for rather obscure reasons. The ostensible reason was that Burke was maintaining a private army and making war without royal permission. Both sides gathered their supporters and the armies met at Knockdoe. It was distinguished by two fact of the presence of large numbers of the mercenary gallowglasses with their battleaxes and mailed armour, and on the other hand the use of guns in a major battle against infantry. Kildare gathered his forces from The Pale and the liberties and towns, and also from the great Gaelic chiefs like the O'Neills and O'Donnells. The gentlemen and lords of The Pale gathered their forces of billmen and bowmen, the preferred weapons of the English armies at this period. Burke was supported by the O'Briens and other Gaelic chiefs from the West. The battle was won by the billmen and bowmen over the kernes and gallowglasses (Hayes-McCoy, 48-67.) Nobody dare contend with the Earl of Kildare until his death.

In fact by this time the worst period of attacks on The Pale was over and the English-speaking residents were extending their influence and control over the marches (Ellis, *Tudor Ireland*, 59). The Ormond Butlers recovered Nenagh by 1505, Tullow by 1515, and Arklow by 1525. The Earl of Desmond had difficulty holding his own against the O'Briens. On the other hand the junior MacCarthy branches, MacCarthy **Reagh** (**Riabhach** or swarthy) and MacCarthy of Muskerry consistently sought alliance with the crown (Ellis, 'Tudor Ireland', 91-2). Hugh Duff (*dubh*, black) O'Donnell made a pilgrimage to Rome and was knighted by Henry VIII on his way back, presumably for services to the Lord Deputy (Ellis, *op. cit.* 100). To the north and west of Co. Louth local landowners in The Pale were gradually recovering lands in Monaghan and south Armagh granted in the 12th century which had passed into Gaelic control. These were often marginal lands which the MacMahons of Monaghan had not been able to control either, and which were infested with bandits, landless men, and kerne, who were probably all the same. The merchant families of The Pale were to the front in this penetration of Gaelic lands. On the other hand, the O'Neill chiefs loved to come to the town of Dundalk. In return the merchants paid the O'Neill chief protection money (O'Sullivan, H., 60-62).

The Church in the Fifteenth Century

There always were some clerics of irreproachable life who tried to maintain the highest standards of the twelfth century reform. But nowhere in Europe could high standards be generally attained and maintained. It is a boast of the Carthusians that their Order was never reformed because it never needed reform (*Nunquam reformata quia nunquam deformata*). The general chapters of most Orders, like the Cistercians, tried to maintain a measure of discipline. Life was made easier, and where Cistercian monasteries survived, particularly in Germany, their lifestyle came to closely resemble that of the Benedictines. (The Cistercians of the Strict Observance or Trappists come from a 17th century reform in the monastery of La Trappe in France.) Similar attempts at reform were made in the Dominican and Franciscan Orders for example. Two observances developed among the Franciscans, the more relaxed Conventuals and the stricter Observance. Relaxed did not imply anything morally wrong but the use of dispensations with regard to fasts and such things from the original Rule. Reform therefore could mean two things, rooting out abuses and immorality, or returning to a stricter interpretation of the Rule. Thomas Merton gives an example of Cistercian monks manning river barges shipping cargoes of wine from the Moselle valley down the Rhine into Holland (*Catholic Encyclopaedia*; Merton *Waters of Siloe*, 31).

Corish notes that the decline in religious observance was more marked in Gaelic-speaking areas than in English-speaking areas. This may be because they were more remote from their superiors general and general chapters, or because the old habits from the Dark Ages persisted more strongly. The 'Observant Reform' spread to Ireland. New convents were formed in the 15th century, 14 of them Conventual and 10 Observant. The Observants were allowed by the Council of Constance to have their own vicar general in every province of the Order. There were similar observant reforms among the Dominicans and Augustinians (Watt, *Church in Medieval Ireland*, 193-198). At last the mendicant friars began to move into Gaelic areas where there were no towns in the conventional sense. But there were assemblages of buildings as large as towns alongside every monastery and castle. As the spread of castle-building indicates, many local lords were getting richer and could maintain greater households, and consequently there had to be large numbers of craftsman and labourers. As Watt also observes, building a monastery could be a status symbol and also a means of buying one's way out of Purgatory. Nor was any great wealth necessary to establish a friary. There was the initial cost of building a small wooden house, leaving the construction of larger houses and churches until later. The only other ongoing cost was to provide sufficient food each day for the community.

There was a great development of the Franciscan Third Order Regular especially in the western, Gaelic-speaking dioceses. The connection, if any, of this movement with the Franciscan Third Order on the Continent is obscure. It seems to have had a connection with or been inspired by the chantry movement in England. Basically a gentleman endowed with land one or more clerics who would chant masses or offices for his intentions, in particular for the souls of deceased relatives in Purgatory and for himself after his death. They would also undertake to teach Latin to the sons of the local gentry or those who wished to be priests. The Third Order, which eventually numbered 40 convents, all founded in the 15th century, were also particularly concerned with education. They did not survive the Reformation (Corish, 57). The

Cistercian Order failed to effect any reformation, though some efforts were made. Reforming abbots from Dublin and Mellifont were often met with violence when they approached houses in Gaelic-speaking areas (*Ibernici silvestres*, Wild Irish, or Irish of the woods. The Latin suggests that wild was connected with the German *Wald* a wood; see *O.E.D*). Most of the monasteries had been seized by monks or their relatives, or by laymen solely to gain their revenues. Indeed in 1496 many abbots in Gaelic-speaking areas were not even summoned to a reforming chapter, suggesting that they no longer had contact with their motherhouses in English-speaking areas (Columcille, 153-4). A provincial synod of the province of Armagh held by Primate Octavian in Drogheda on the 6th July 1495 denounced the extortions including coyne and livery on the lands of Mellifont by the local lords. These would have been lords of The Pale. (These same lords rushed to benefit from the dissolution of the monasteries half a century later to get grants of lands.) The fact that Primate Octavian was holding a synod shows that some churchmen were attempting reform.

Another example of the revival of religion in the 15th century was the construction of churches. After a hiatus in the 14th century church building recommenced on a small scale. Much of this was the result of the expansion of the friars (Harbison, *Irish Art and Architecture*, 95). Two Cistercian houses in Tipperary, Holy Cross and Kilcooley underwent considerable reconstruction. Additions were made to some cathedrals and parish churches. There were a large number of small very plain parish churches built between 1400 and 1600 presumably often replacing wooden structures. They were little more than rectangular barns. (Ireland has nothing like the wealth of tiny medieval parish churches such as can be found in England, but they must have existed.) Some lords of The Pale built their own churches (*op. cit.* 100). Ecclesiastical art showed a revival as well, though manuscript illumination showed a sad decline (*op. cit.* 108-115).

Chapter 15

The Provinces

In the roughly 300 years covered by the term Middle Ages the political scene in Ireland did not change to a large extent. But there were some significant changes. Before the arrival of the Normans there were four provinces, represented by the ecclesiastical provinces. In each there was a hierarchy of chiefdoms with one dominant family which exacted tribute and military service from the others. Usually there were mesne chiefs who resisted the paramount chiefs (to borrow a phrase from the 19th century) whenever they could. (The Irish spoke of the 'Five Provinces' which seemed to indicate that Meath was counted as a separate province, but in the 12th century when the ecclesiastical provinces were established it was not.) Though the territorial expansion of the provincial chiefs was restricted by the Normans they still managed to expand the power and wealth of the ruling family by seizing the lands of the lesser chiefs within their domains. Against this was set the fact that a ruling family could only consist of 4 generations the *derb fine*, so at each death of the head of a family the outer layers were spun off to found chiefdoms of their own if they could. In this way MacCarthy **Reagh** and MacCarthy of Muskerry became more or less independent of MacCarthy **Mór** and the O'Neills became ridden with factions.

The greatest change was in the east where the great opposing chiefdoms of Meath and Leinster were merged to form present-day Leinster. The centuries-long struggle between these powers on either side of the Bog of Allen was over, and a capital founded on land between them in Norse Dublin. Louth was detached from Ulster politically but not ecclesiastically to form part of Leinster. The new power in Leinster still had to contend with unruly small clans at its edges, so there was no change there. There was little alteration except at the margins. Munster comprised the territory of its later six counties, and Connaught the territories of its later five counties. The Tudors were later to form 'presidencies' in Munster and Connaught which recognised the fact that each required its own provincial ruler.

In general it can be said that a great many of the European developments of the Middle Ages passed the Gaelic chiefdoms by. The great exception was warfare where warring chiefs were always anxious to have the latest equipment. (This remained common in the more backward parts of the world up to the 21st century.) Traditional lore was pursued in the traditional learned families but little attempt was made to bring it up to date. Annals remained annals, in 1500 AD as in 500 AD. No attempt was made to develop the writing of history. Poets remained traditional poets with traditional roles. Genealogists remained genealogists. All worked in their own local areas. Some members of the brehon class made attempts to modernise law but never could come together to develop a modern code or incorporate more recent decisions. Trade continued in the old ways and may even have increased, but there were no attempts to develop or promote mercantile towns, to clear roads, to build bridges, or to develop an international mercantile code. In the preceding period the Norwegians and Danes spread across the North Atlantic. In the Medieval period the Portuguese became world leaders in deep sea fishing, exploration and colonisation. Though the Gaelic chiefs had similar rocky coasts indented with deep harbours no attempt was made to develop large-scale fishing, to develop ocean-going vessels, or to establish companies engaged in foreign trade. No attempt was made to emulate the statute law of England. Statutes in Anglo-Norman Ireland were made to promote trade, or to strengthen the system of royal courts. Appeals to a higher court, fundamental in canon law (and indeed excessively abused) were developed in the royal courts so that a case from any local court could be removed to a royal court. There could be abuses in this system too but on the whole it proved beneficial. Local officials like sheriffs could be elected by the local gentlemen and then approved by the crown giving some kind of balance. All these developments passed the Gaelic lordships by.

There is little point in pursuing the destinies of the little local clans who were significant only locally. K.W. Nichols gives brief summary accounts of the leading families in each province which is useful for identifying the chief players (Nichols, *Gaelic and Gaelicized Ireland*).

Ulster

Ulster was peculiar in that there were two branches of the dominant family: the Northern *Ui Neill* (O'Neills) in present-day Ulster and the southern *Ui Neill* (O'Mellaghlins) in present-day Meath and Westmeath. There was no great change in Ulster in 1500 compared with 1200. The great protagonists remained much as they were. In the course of the Middle Ages, the *Ulaid*, now under Norman domination had thrown off the overlordship of the O'Neills and re-established their own former overlordship of Ulster. The other chiefdoms were still in a state of vassalage but as usual feudal dues were only paid as long as they could be enforced. As the earldom of Ulster passed to the crown, the Ulster chiefs dealt directly with the Lord Deputy and not with the Earl of Ulster or his seneschal. More important perhaps was the internal colonisation by the O'Neills whose clans and sub-clans grabbed more and more lands of the *Oirgialla* in mid-Ulster. But there were limits to their expansion.

The O'Donnells in Donegal made themselves virtually independent of everyone and became again almost the power they had been in the 8th and 9th centuries. The O'Donnells had succeeded in imposing a chief of their own called Maguire as an urragh in the western part of the MacMahon territory. The *Oirgialla* in south Ulster under the MacMahons became too strong to be absorbed. Other minor chiefs like the MacGuinnesses and O'Hanlons had securely established themselves. As elsewhere in the Middle Ages, internal colonisation, where relatives of the ruling chiefs were imposed on lands, was more important than external expansion which was restricted by the power of the Anglo-Norman lords and the crown. Breifne of the O'Rourkes split into two, one controlled by the O'Rourkes and the other by their cousins the O'Reillys.

The unending succession disputes among the O'Neills of *Cenel Eogain* from the death of Ardgar MacLoughlin in 1064 to the family feuds and disputes in Elizabethan times ensured that the Northern *Ui Neill* remained largely ineffective except locally in mid-Ulster. They were never in a position to have effective overlordship even in Ulster. Nominal overlordship was useless unless it could be enforced. The lesser chiefs in Ulster were as likely as not to be allied to the justiciar or Lord Deputy in Dublin. (The same was of course true for the leading families in the other provinces.)

Brian O'Neill's claim to be king of Ireland it is said was recognised, at least verbally, by O'Connor, O'Mellaghlin, and O'Brien chiefs in 1241 after he had eliminated the MacLoughlins. But after Brian O'Neill's death in 1260 the O'Neills gave up any pretensions to the highkingship (*ri na hEireann*) which had been nursed by Brian. This was not necessarily a challenge to the overlordship of Henry III but a claim to the position of Rory O'Connor under the Treaty of Windsor. (It is probable that the other four leading families gave up their pretensions to the highkingship about the same time, conceding they were no longer realistic). His son Dónal O'Neill was described merely as King of Ulster and *tanaiste* of Ireland (Burke, *Peerage*, O'Neill.)

In Meath/Westmeath in the 12th century the O'Mellaghlins were in a state of disintegration. The surrounding chiefs were intent on partitioning their territories between themselves, so Henry II granted it as a single fiefdom to Hugh de Lacy. It survived virtually intact until the end of the Middle Ages with it boundaries defended by the powerful subinfeudated families who were placed there for that purpose. The O'Mellaghlins remained in the far west of their territory, in the west of present day Co. Offaly. (The present Co. Offaly is a Tudor formation and bears little relation to the territory controlled by the medieval *Ui Failge*.) This part of south west medieval Meath became a cockpit of struggles between minor local clans trying to survive and local invading families when the greater provincial powers dwindled in strength and could no longer enforce control. This state of affairs was the result of the rivalry of the great Norman lords who exhausted their strength in struggles against each other. It was not a situation likely to last very long.

Leinster

Leinster was quite small, extending from Dublin to Wexford, and then westward as far as the Slieve Bloom Mountains. In the 12th century it was ruled by the *Ui Chennselaig* (MacMurroughs) and the *Ui Dunlainge* (O'Mores, O'Tooles etc) who were normally overlords of the *Osraige* (Fitzpatricks). The fertile lands in Leinster occupied an hourglass shape with the *Ui Chennselaig* in Wexford and the *Ui Dunlainge* in Kildare joined by a narrow strip of fertile land in the valley of the Barrow, Co. Carlow. Historically the chiefs of the northern fertile area were the dominant chiefs in Leinster. But in the 12th century the *Ui Chennselaig* became the dominant family. Remnants of the *Ui Dunlainge* contested this overlordship throughout the Middle Ages. The MacMurrough Kavanaghs sided with the Normans and retained their ancestral lands, intermarrying with the Normans. Later in the

Middle Ages, possibly out of pique at not being allowed to inherit a wife's fiefdom, they turned against the crown.

The MacMurroughs ensured that grants to the Normans were made chiefly from the lands of the *Ui Dunlainge* and *Osraige*. Ironically, by the end of the Middle Ages the centre of power had again returned to the north with the earls of Kildare taking the place of the *Ui Dunlainge*. The earls of Ormond in Kilkenny replaced the *Osraige*. The displaced chiefs moved into the less fertile areas and displaced the local chiefs. With internal colonisation the strong minor chiefdoms, like the O'Hanlons and MacGuinnesses further north, formed nuisances which were hard to eradicate even if the will to do so were present. (No attempt was made to do so before the reign of Mary Tudor.) As in Meath a concerted effort by the great Norman lords to eradicate them would have been successful but the will was lacking for they were often useful as allies. Linguistically, socially and economically there were great changes however.

Munster

Though the boundaries of the province did not change the political structure changed greatly. By the 12th century the O'Briens had succeeded in dislodging the *Eoganacht Caisil* (MacCarthys) from their lands in north Munster (Thomond) so they took refuge in south Munster (Desmond). Neither was able on a permanent basis to control the area between them. To forestall them and to prevent either party gaining control King John made feudal grants of lands belonging to lesser chiefs in a wide belt across the centre of Munster from Waterford to the furthest point in Kerry. The O'Briens were confined to Co. Clare, and lands they had seized in north Munster on the eastern side of the Shannon in Tipperary were taken from them. (These lands in Tipperary were then called east Munster, Ormond, while Thomond was restricted to Co. Clare as it is to this day.) The Earl of Desmond came to control most of the territory in central Munster and replaced the other two as the dominant power in Munster. It was the largest earldom and in many ways the richest and should have been the most powerful. But the earls of Desmond got involved in perpetual feuds with the earls of Ormond.

The O'Briens and MacCarthys consolidated themselves by internal conquest, eliminating local chiefs and replacing them with their relatives. They became quite powerful in defence but rarely successful when advancing to attack. The MacCarthys occupied the upper reaches of the rivers while the Anglo-Normans occupied the rich fertile lower reaches. As in Meath, subinfeudation to local knights formed a stable barrier defending the earldom of Desmond from penetration by Gaelic chiefs though these had some local successes. For some reason the northern part of Tipperary where the Butlers of Ormond had their chief manor proved untenable. There was nothing new in that for their predecessors had not been able to control it either. It seems that insufficient English colonists were attracted to form a chain of mutually supporting manors and much of the land, as in the earldom of Ulster where there was a similar problem, was simply farmed out to Gaelic cultivators. In both cases this meant that the manors of the English colonists were vulnerable. (The manor of Nenagh was no different from the *tuatha* of the petty Gaelic chiefs, which were wasted by annual raids until they were no longer viable.) Offshoots of the O'Briens, the O'Mulryans and the O'Kennedys occupied the deserted lands. The Butlers purchased new manors in Kilkenny and by the end of the Middle Ages had re-taken Nenagh. The external boundaries of the province remained largely unchanged.

Connaught

In this province there was the least change. Two members of the Burke family seized the Connaught lands of the de Burgh earls and went native to some extent at least. They kept the best lands in central Connaught, but as they split into three families they had no hope or desire to control Connaught. The just replaced the O'Connors as the dominant chiefs but because they were divided they could not control Connaught. Of the three families Clanrickard emerged as the most important. The displaced Gaelic families followed the usual pattern of displacing lesser families. The former rulers, the O'Connors, split into competing families. None of the families in Connaught could have resisted a strong attack from outside. Even combined with the O'Briens and their offshoot families, and employing numerous gallowglasses, the Clanrickard family was unable to resist the Lord Deputy at Knockdoe. In a battle reminiscent of the time of Dermot MacMurrough the Leinster chief beat the Connaught chief. Nevertheless they managed to hold off the attacks by the O'Donnells who were themselves riven by factions. Two English-speaking towns, Galway and Athenry survived.

Postscript

Henry VII died in 1509 and was succeeded by his son Henry VIII. There was no Yorkist challenge. Garret *Mór* was killed by a bullet in a minor local skirmish in 1513 and was succeeded by his son Garret *Óg*. There were no immediate changes. The young Henry returned to the old preoccupation with France until England was again virtually bankrupted and did not immediately intervene in Ireland. But he was a very different man from his father and with different preoccupations as Ireland was soon to learn.

The raising of the siege of Orleans in 1429 by Joan of Arc proved not only to be the turning point in the Hundred Years' War but also a turning point in world history. The power of France was to increase over the next 500 years and led French arms to the four quarters of the globe. Similarly in England, the ending of the Hundred Years' War and the Wars of the Roses in 1485 resulted in a strong monarchy and a dynasty of capable monarchs. England too though more hesitantly than France began its advance towards the formation of the British

Empire. Modern Spain commenced in 1479 when Ferdinand of Aragon married Isabella of Castile and Leon, uniting the two kingdoms. In 1492 Columbus reached the Americas from Spain, and in 1497 the Portuguese found the sea route to the Indies. Spain and Portugal went on to found rich overseas empires and Spain became the most powerful country in Europe. The Portuguese reached the coasts of China going east and the Spanish the Philippines going west. Italy and Germany remained fragmented until the 19th century.

The Middle Ages in Europe was a ferment of local wars out of which four major kingdoms emerged having finally overcome internal strife. Ireland had its full share of this domestic turmoil and seemed to have emerged finally as united under a strong ruler. The appearance was deceptive because when in 1535 the revolt of Silken Thomas collapsed the whole country again fell into disorder. Unlike Portugal, and to a lesser extent Denmark, Ireland was unable to build up industries and an overseas trade. Its trade remained in the hands of foreigners.

Though the numerous petty wars did not significantly alter the political balance of power in Ireland, the country, or at least its eastern parts was very different from what it had been 400 years earlier. The great developments in Europe in these centuries had trickled into Ireland, and all the great institutions of state and religion, of government and war were in place.

In many ways the Middle Ages did not end in Ireland until the overthrow of Silken Thomas. But the reign of Henry VIII indicates a new era was beginning. The commencement of France's Italian wars in 1494 marked France's new status in Europe. Spain and Portugal were beginning to develop overseas empire which became the sources of great wealth. The nature of warfare was changing with the development of artillery and hand guns, and with it the means of making war, guns, lead shot, and gunpowder, all of which had to be purchased from manufacturers.

The End

Bibliography

Alder, K., *The Measure of All Things*, London, 2002.

Allmand, C., 'War and the Non-combatant in the Middle Ages', in Keen, *Medieval Warfare*, 253-272.

Arnold, B., *Concise History of Irish Art*, London, 1977.

Ayton, A., 'Arms, Armour, and Horsemen', in Keen, *Medieval Warfare*, 186-208.

Barber, R., *The Black Prince*, Stroud, 2003

Barnett, C., *Britain and her Army 1509-1570*, Penguin, 1974.

Barnie, J., *War in Medieval Society*, London, 1974.

Barraclough, G., *The Origins of Modern Germany*, Oxford, 1952.

Barry, T. B., *The Archaeology of Medieval Ireland*, London, 1988.

Barry, T., 'Manorialism', in Duffy, *Medieval Ireland*.

Bartlett, T and Jeffery, K., *A Military History of Ireland*, Cambridge, 1996.

Bellamy, D., *The Wild Boglands*, London, 1986.

Benedict, St., trans Dysinger, L., *The Rule of St. Benedict*, Valyermo, CA, 1996.

Bible, New Jerusalem, London, 1971.

Bible, Vulgate, Ultra Bible, CD-Rom, Oklahoma City, 2001.

Bolton, W., ed., *History of Literature in the English Language*, London, 1970.

Bowe, P., 'Horticultural and Garden Design', in de Breffney, *Ireland: A Cultural Encyclopaedia*.

Bowlt, E. M., *Harrow Past*, London 2000.

Boylan, K., *Medieval Irish (1300-1487)* www.fanaticus.org/DBA/armies/IV58.html.

Brady, C., 'Sixteenth-century Ulster and the Failure of Tudor Reform', in Brady, O'Dowd and Walker, 77-103.

Brady, C. & Gillespie, R. *Natives and Newcomers*, Dublin 1986.

Brady, C., O'Dowd, M., & Walker, B., *Ulster an Illustrated History*, London, 1989.

Brady, C., 'Court, Castle, and Country: the Framework of Government in Tudor Ireland' in Brady and Gillespie, 22-49.

Brand, P. 'Courts' in Duffy, *Medieval Ireland*.

Brand, P. 'March Law', in Duffy, *Medieval Ireland*.

Braun, Hugh, *English Abbeys*. London, 1971.

Briggs, M. and Jordan, P., *Economic History of England*, London, 1970.

Brooke, I., *English Costume in the Early Middle Ages*, London, 1956.

Brooke, I., *English Costume in the Later Middle Ages*, London, 1963.

Brown, R.A., *The Origins of English Feudalism*, London, 1973.

Burke, J. B., *Burke's Peerage, Baronetage & Knightage*, London, 1970.

Burke, J.F., *Outlines of the Industrial History of Ireland*, Dublin, n. d.

Canavan, T., *Frontier Town*, Belfast 1989.

Catholic Encyclopaedia, 1913, New Advent, www.newadvent.org.

Charles-Edwards, T.M., 'Irish Warfare before 1100', in Bartlett and Jeffrey, *Military History*, 26-51.

Chrimes, S. B., *An Introduction to the Administrative History of Medieval England*, Oxford 1966.

Clarke, H.B., 'The Vikings', in Bartlett and Jeffrey, *Military History*, 36-58.

Clarke, H.B., 'Population', in Duffy, *Medieval Ireland*.

Coldstream, N., 'The Visual Arts', in Saul, *Medieval England*, 207-244.

Columcille, Rev. Fr., *The Story of Mellifont*, Dublin, 1958.

Connolly, P., 'The Financing of English Expeditions to Ireland', in Lydon, *England and Ireland*, 1361-1376.

Copplestone, T., *World Architecture*, Feltham, Middx. 1963.

Corish, P., *The Irish Catholic Experience*, Dublin, 1985.

Cosgrove, A., 'Parliament and the Anglo-Irish Community: the Declaration of 1460', in Cosgrove and McGuire, 25-42.

Cosgrove, A., and McGuire, J.I., *Parliament and Community*, Belfast, 1983.

Cunningham, B., 'Native Culture and Political Change 1580-1640', in Brady and Gillespie, 148-170.

Curtis, E., *A History of Ireland*, London, 1968.

Daly, M. D., *Traditional Irish Laws*, Belfast 1997.

Davies, N. A., *History of Europe*, Oxford, 1997.

de Breffney, B. ed., *Ireland: a Cultural Encyclopaedia*, London, 1983.

de Breffney, B., 'Architecture', in de Breffney, *Ireland: a Cultural Encyclopaedia*, London, 1983.

de Breffney, B. and ffolliott, R., *The Houses of Ireland*, London, 1984.

de Paor, Liam, *Saint Patrick's World*, Dublin, 1993.

de Paor, Liam, *The Peoples of Ireland*, London 1986.

Dictionary of National Biography, cdrom edition, Oxford, 1996.

Dolley, M., *Anglo-Norman Ireland*, Dublin, 1972.

Duffy, P.J., 'Geographical Perspectives on the Borderlands', in Gillespie and Sullivan, 5-22.

Duffy, S., ed., *Medieval Ireland, an Encyclopaedia*, Abingdon, 2005.

Dunbabin, J., France *in the Making 843-1180,* Oxford, 2000.

Dyer, C., 'The Economy and Society', in Saul, *Medieval England,* 137-173.

Edwards, N., *The Archaeology of Early Medieval Ireland,* London, 2004.

Ellis S.G., 'Parliament and Community in Yorkist and Tudor Ireland' in Cosgrove and Maguire, 43-68.

Ellis, S. G., 'The Tudors and the Origins of the Modern Irish States', in Bartlett and Jeffery, *Military History,* 116-135.

Ellis, S. G., 'Henry VII and Ireland 1491-1496', in Lydon, *England and Ireland,* 237-254.

Ellis, S. G., *Tudor Ireland,* London, 1985.

Elton, G. R., 'The English Parliament in the sixteenth century: estates and Statutes', in Cosgrove and Maguire, 69-96.

Empey, C.A., 'The Settlement of the Kingdom of Limerick', in Lydon, *England and Ireland,* 1-25.

Evans, G., *Land of my Fathers,* Talybont, 1992.

Fernandez-Armesto, F., 'Naval Warfare after the Viking Age 1100-1500', in Keen, *Medieval Warfare,* 230-252.

Fitzgerald, M., 'Clothing' in Duffy, *Medieval Ireland.*

Flanagan, M. T., 'Irish and Anglo-Norman warfare in twelfth-century Ireland', in Bartlett and Jeffrey, *Military History,* 52-75.

Ford, A., 'The Protestant Reformation in Ireland', in Brady and Gillespie, 50-74.

Fox-Davies, A. C., *A Complete Guide to Heraldry,* London, 1985.

Frame, R., 'The Defence of the English lordship 1250-1450', in Bartlett and Jeffrey, *Military History,* 76-98.

Frame, R., 'English Policies and Anglo Irish Attitudes in the Crisis of 1341-42', in Lydon, *England and Ireland,* 86-103.

Fraser, D., *Wales in History,* Cardiff 1967.

Freeman, T.W., *Ireland, a General and Regional Geography,* London, 1960.

Furlong, N., *Dermot King of Leinster and the Foreigners*, Tralee, 1973.

Garnett, G., 'Conquered England 1066-1215', in Saul *Medieval England*, 61-101.

Gillespie, R. and O'Sullivan, H., *The Borderlands*, Belfast, 1989.

Gillespie, R., 'Transformation of the Borderlands', in Gillespie and Sullivan, 75-92.

Gillingham, J., 'An Age of Expansion 1020-1204', in Keen, *Medieval Warfare*, 59-88.

Given-Wilson, C., 'Late Medieval England 1215-1485', in Saul *Medieval England*, 102-136.

Gregory of Tours, trans. L. Thorpe, *The History of the Franks*, Penguin, London, 1974. Gwynn, A., and Handcock R.N, *Medieval Religious Houses in Ireland*, Dublin 1988.

Halpin, A., 'Coinage', in Duffy, *Medieval Ireland*, New York, 2005.

Harbison, P., Potterton, H., and Sheehy, J., eds., *Irish Art and Architecture*, London, 1978,

Harbison, P., 'From Pre-history to 1600', in Harbison, *Irish Art and Architecture*, 1-118.

Harbison, S., 'William of Windsor, the Court Party, and the Administration of Ireland', in Lydon, *England and Ireland*, 153-77.

Harthan, J., *The Book of Hours*, New York, 1977.

Hawkins, D., *Avalon and Sedgemoor*, Newton Abbot, 1973.

Hayes-McCoy, G.A., *Irish Battles, a Military History of Ireland*, Belfast 1990.

Henson, E., *Rare Breeds in History*, printed privately in Cheltenham, 1982.

Hinde, T., *The Domesday Book*, London, 1985.

Hindley, G., *England in the Age of Caxton*, London, 1979.

Housley, N., 'European Warfare 1200-1320', in Keen, *Medieval Warfare*, 113-135.

Hyland, A., *The Medieval Warhorse*, Stroud, 1994.

James, L., *Warrior Race*, London, 2001.

Jarman, T.L., *Landmarks in the History of Education*, London, 1963.

Johnston, D., 'The Interim Years: Richard II and Ireland, 1395-1399', in Lydon, England and Ireland, 175-195.

Jones, E., *The English Nation, the Great Myth*, Stroud, 2000.

Jones, G. R. J., The *Pattern of Settlement on the Welsh Border*, www.bahs.org.uk/08n2a2.pdf.

Jones, R.L., 'Fortifications and Sieges in Western Europe 800-1450', in Keen, *Medieval Warfare*, 163-185.

Jordan of Saxony, *The Life of the Brethren*, Villanova PA, 1993.

Kearney, H., The *British Isles, a History of Four Nations*, Cambridge, 1989.

Keen, M., 'The Changing Scene', in Keen, *Medieval Warfare*, 273-292.

Keen, M., (ed), *Medieval Warfare a History*, Oxford, 1999.

Keenan, D., *The True Origins of Irish Society*, Xlibris, Philadelphia, 2003.

Keenan, D., *Pre-Famine Ireland, Social Structure*, Xlibris, Philadelphia, 2000.

Keenan, D., *Ireland 1800-1850*, Xlibris, Philadelphia, 2001.

Kenny, C., *King's Inns and the Kingdom of Ireland*, Dublin, 1992.

Kidson, P., The Medieval World', in Myers and Copplestone, 279-438.

Killanin, Ld and Duignan, M., *The Shell Guide to Ireland*, London, 1967.

King, C.A.M., *Physical Geography*, Oxford, 1980.

Knowles, D., *Thomas Becket*, London 1970.

Lennon, C., 'The Counter Reformation', in Brady and Gillespie, 75-92.

Leyser, H., 'Piety, Religion, and the Church', in Saul, *Medieval England*, 174-206.

Leyser, H., *Medieval Women*, London, 1995.

Lydon J., 'Edward I, Ireland, and the War in Scotland, 1303-04', in Lydon, *England and Ireland*, 43-61.

Lydon, J., *Ireland in the Later Middle Ages*, Dublin, 1973.

Lydon, J., ed., *England and Ireland in the Later Middle Ages*, Dublin and Towota. 1981.

MacCaffrey, Rev. J. S.J., *History of the Catholic Church*, London, 1914.

MacCurtain, M., *Tudor and Stewart Ireland*, Dublin, 1979.

MacNiocaill, G., *Ireland before the Vikings*, Dublin, 1972.

Malcolm, E., 'Medicine' in Duffy, *Medieval Ireland*.

Mallet, M., 'Mercenaries', in Keen, *Medieval Warfare*, 209-230.

Mason, P., *A Matter of Honour*, London, 1974.

McEvedy, C., *Penguin Atlas of Medieval History*, Penguin, 1971.

McNeill, T.E., 'Lordships and Invasions: Ulster 1177-1500', in Brady, O'Dowd and Walker, 44-76.

McNeill, T.E., *Anglo Norman Ulster*, Edinburgh, 1980.

Merton, T., *The Seven Storey Mountain*, London, 1990.

Merton, T., *The Waters of Siloe*, London, 1976.

Mitchell, F., *Readings the Irish Landscape*, London, 1986.

M'Kenna, J. E., *Diocese of Clogher Parochial Records, Monaghan*, Enniskillen 1920.

Moody, T. W., Martin, F. X., Byrne, F. J., eds., *New History of Ireland* Vol. IX, Oxford, 1984.

Morrison, A., *Early Man in Britain and Ireland*, London, 1980.

Mullin T.H. and Mullan J.E., *The Ulster Clans*, Limavady, 1984.

Murphy, M., 'Chief Governors', in Duffy, *Medieval Ireland*.

Myers, B. and Copplestone, T., *Landmarks of Western Art*, Feltham, Middx., 1985.

Nelson, J., 'Anglo-Saxon England 500-1066', in Saul, *Medieval England*, 25-60.

Nicholls, K.W., *Gaelic and Gaelicized Ireland in the Middle Ages*, Dublin, 2003.

Nikomodius, St., trans. Palmer, G. et al, *The Philokalia*, Vol. II, London, 1990.

Ó Corráin, D., *Ireland Before the Normans*, Dublin, 1972.

Ó Gráda, C., *Ireland, a New Economic History, 1789-1939*, Oxford, 1995.

O'Dowd, M., 'Gaelic Economy and Society', in Brady and Gillespie, 120-147.

O'Loan, J., 'Livestock in the Brehon Laws', www.bahs.org.uk/07n2a1. pdf.

Ordnance Survey Publications, *Field Archaeology in Britain*, Southampton, 1973.

Ordnance Survey, *Atlas of Great Britain*, London, 1982.

O'Sullivan, A., 'Fishing', in Duffy, *Medieval Ireland*.

O'Sullivan, A., 'Diet and Food', in Duffy, *Medieval Ireland*.

O'Sullivan, A., 'Houses', in Duffy, *Medieval Ireland*.

O'Sullivan, H., 'The March of South East Ulster in the Fifteenth and Sixteenth Centuries', in Gillespie and Sullivan, 55-74.

Otway-Ruthven, A.J., *History of Medieval Ireland*, New York, 1993.

Oxford English Dictionary, Compact edition, Oxford, 1987.

Painter, S., *The Reign of King John*, Baltimore, 1966.

Partridge, M., *Farm Tools through the Ages*, Reading, 1973.

Pearsall, D., 'Language and Literature', in Saul, *Medieval England*, 245-276.

Penn, S. A. C., *Female Wage-Earners in Late Fourteenth-Century England*, www.bahs.org.uk/35n1a1.pdf.

Philips, J.R.S., 'The Mission of John de Hothum to Ireland 1315-1316', in Lydon, *England and Ireland*, 62-85.

Pounds, N.J.G., *The Medieval City*, Westport Ct. 2005.

Power, E., M.M. Postan ed., *Medieval Women*, Cambridge, 1975.

Preece, D. and Wood, H., *The British Isles*, London, 1977.

Prestwich, M., 'Parliament and the Community of the Realm in Fourteenth-Century England' in Cosgrove and Maguire, 5-24.

Pretty, J. N., *Sustainable Agriculture in the Middle Ages: The English Manor*, www.bahs.org.uk

Reed, M., *The Age of Exuberance 1500-1700*, London 1987.

Reuter, T., 'Carolingian and Ottonian Warfare' in Keen, *Medieval Warfare*, 13-35.

Rice, D.T., 'Medieval Architecture', in Copplestone, 13-35.

Rodgers, N., *Roman Empire*, London 2006.

Rogers, C. J., 'The Age of the Hundred Years War', in Keen, *Medieval Warfare*, 136-162.

Rowan, A., *The Buildings of Ireland; North West Ulster*, Penguin, 1979.

Rowse, A.L., *The Expansion of Elizabethan England*, Basingstoke, 2003.

Salzman, L.F., *Edward I*, London 1968.

Saul, N., *Oxford Illustrated History of Medieval England*, Oxford 1997.

Saul, N., 'Medieval England: Identity, Politics, and Society', in Saul, *Medieval England*, 1-24.

Sayles G.O., Modus Tenendi Parliamentum, Irish or English?', in Lydon, *England and Ireland*, 122-152.

Severin, T., *The Brendan Voyage*, London, 1975.

Shahar S., *Growing Old in the Middle Ages*, London, 2004, http://books.google.co.uk/books.

Sheehan, A., 'Irish Towns in a Period of Change', in Brady and Gillespie, 93-119.

Simms, K., 'Women', in Duffy, *Medieval Ireland*.

Simms, K., 'The King's Friend: O'Neill, the Crown and the Earldom of Ulster', in Lydon, England and Ireland, 214-236.

Simms, K., 'Gaelic warfare in the Middle Ages', in Bartlett and Jeffery, *Military History*, 99-115.

Smith, B., 'The Medieval Border', in Gillespie and O'Sullivan, 41-54.

Thomas, W.S.K., *Brecon 1093-1660*, Llandysul, 1991.

Thornbury, W., *Old and New London*, 1985, www.british-history.ac.uk.

Underhill, N., *The Lord Chancellor*, Lavenham, 1978.

Van Bavel, T. and Canning, R., (trans), *The Rule of St Augustine*, London, 1996.

Ward, B., *The Sayings of the Desert Fathers*, London, 1983.

Warren, W.L., *Church and State in Angevin Ireland*, http://www. Ucc.Ie/Chronicon/Warrfra.Htm Chronicon 1 (1997) 6: 1-17.

Warren, W. L., *Henry II*, London 1991.

Warren. W.L., King John and Ireland, in Lydon, England and Ireland, 26-42.

Watt, J.A., 'John Colton, Justiciar of Ireland (1382 and Archbishop of Armagh' in Lydon, England and Ireland, 196-213.

Watt, J., The *Church in Medieval Ireland*, Dublin, 1983.

The following books contain monographs or entries by various authors and are referred to as follows.

Bartlett, T and Jeffery, K., *A Military History of Ireland*, Cambridge, 1996: (Bartlett and Jeffrey, *Military History.)*

Brady, C. & Gillespie, R. *Natives and Newcomers*, Dublin 1986: (Brady and Gillespie.)

Brady, C., O'Dowd, M., & Walker, B., *Ulster an Illustrated History*, London, 1989: (Brady, O'Dowd and Walker.)

Copplestone, T., *World Architecture*, Feltham, Middx. 1963: (Copplestone.)

Cosgrove, A., and McGuire, J.I., *Parliament and Community*, Belfast, 1983: (Cosgrove and McGuire.)

de Breffney, B. ed., *Ireland: a Cultural Encyclopaedia*, London, 1983: (de Breffney, *Ireland: A Cultural Encyclopaedia*.)

D.N.B, Dictionary of National Biography

Duffy, S., ed., *Medieval Ireland, an Encyclopaedia*, Abingdon, 2005: (Duffy, *Medieval Ireland*.)

Gillespie, R. and O'Sullivan, H., *The Borderlands*, Belfast, 1989: (Gillespie and Sullivan.)

Harbison, P., Potterton, H., and Sheehy, J., eds., *Irish Art and Architecture*, London, 1978: (Harbison, *Irish Art and Architecture.)*

Keen, M., (ed), *Medieval Warfare a History*, Oxford, 1999: (Keen, *Medieval Warfare)*

Lydon, J., ed., *England and Ireland in the Later Middle Ages*, Dublin and Towota. 1981: (Lydon, *England and Ireland.)*

Myers, B. and Copplestone, T., *Landmarks of Western Art*, Feltham, Middx., 1985: (Myers and Copplestone.)

O.E.D, Oxford English Dictionary

Saul, N., *Oxford Illustrated History of Medieval England*, Oxford 1997: (Saul, *Medieval England.)*

References to internet sites are normally given in the text.

Reference is made to the following books of the Bible: Exodus, Deuteronomy, Psalms, Proverbs, Daniel, Maccabees, Luke, Revelation.

Gaelic terms

Aonach (ane-ach), the assembly of a chief, a fair

Ard ri (ard ree), high king of Ireland.

Baile (balleh) a town or townland, bally.

Barony, a division of a county, a hundred.

Biatach (betta), betagh, a client farmer reduced to serfdom or quasi serfdom in Middle Ages.

Boaire Bo aire (bow arra), a freeman or independent farmer.

Bonnacht (bonn ocht), a compulsory levy of soldiers.

Botach (bow tach), cottier, herdsman.

Brehon (breh on), a judge or adjudicator, an expert in law.

Buidhe, (bwee) yellow-haired.

Cantred, a division of land smaller than a county, like a barony.

Coarb (co arb), successor in rights.

de, from.

Derb fine (derb finneh) a four-generation family

Eraic (eric), pecuniary compensation, blood money

erenagh (eren ach), hereditary stewards of church property.

Fine (finne), a kindred group.

fitz, son of.

Gael (gale), one who spoke the Gaelic language.

Gaelic, (gale-ic), a branch of the Celtic languages spoken in Ireland.

Galloglach (*gall*, foreigner + *oglaech*, soldier) gallowglass, a heavily armed foreign mercenary.

In capite (in cap-it-ay), the head tenant holding directly from the king

Iure suo (Yuray soo-o), in his own right.

Iure uxoris (Yuray ux-oar-iss), by right of his wife.

Kerne (kern), lightly armed troops.

Hobelar, a lightly-armed horseman.

Lios (liss), a fenced enclosure around dwellings.

Mac, (mock) son of, followed by father's name in the genitive.

Mór (more), great of big.

Ó or *Ua*, pl. *Ui* (ee) grandson of. As surnames became increasingly fixed from the 12th century onwards Fitz, de Mac, and O' became permanent parts of the surname and lost their original meaning.

Óg (rhymes with rogue), young.

Oglaech (ogue lake), a young warrior, a warrior.

Rath (rath), a fenced enclosure around dwellings.

Ri (ree) a chief.

Ri ruirech (ree roorreck), chief of a province.

Ri tuaithe, (ree too-a), local chief.

Ruiri (rooeeree), mesne chief, chief of a county

Saertach (sayer tock), free farmer or landowner.

Socage (sockage), tenure by money not service, i.e. by rent.

Tain (toyn), a cattle raid.

*Tanaiste (*tawniste*)*, designated successor.

Trivium and *quadrivium*, the lower and higher parts of Roman education.

Tuath, (too-a) pl. *tuatha*. (tootha), gen. *tuaithe* (tooee-heh), cantred, district, barony

The genitive of nouns often have an added i inserted, or a added to the end. They are easy to recognise.

Urragh, Oir ri, a subordinate chief with military and other obligations to his superior chief.

Names

Historians commonly assign numbers to various kings and popes, though these numbers were not used by themselves or their contemporaries. The numbering of English kings commences with William I 'the Conqueror' though the earlier habit of using nicknames did not die out. Among the Gaelic chiefs nicknames were common. Parliaments were often given nicknames like the Long Parliament and the Short Parliament.

Permanent surnames were just beginning to be adopted. I normally in this book adopt the permanent surnames as they were known throughout the Middle Ages, like O'Briens or MacCarthys, whether or not they were in contemporary usage. Some surnames were just beginning to be adopted, so I have used *fitz* or *mac* without a capital when clearly referring to a man's own father. Men were distinguished by their father's name, or by the place they came from, de Lacy, by their occupation, the butler, or by some characteristic, the fat, which subsequently stuck to the family.

As far as possible I have used the Anglicized version of personal and place names for most general readers outside Ireland have no idea how to pronounce Gaelic words. The received Gaelic pronunciation is, in any case, the modern Gaelic version not the medieval one. To give one example Rory O'Connor was often written in the past as Roderick O'Connor, the writer assuming that the consonants were not aspirated at the time. But for the most part, before the 12th century there was no Anglicized equivalent.It is presumed that serious students of Irish history would make some attempt to acquaint themselves with the Gaelic language. It is unreasonable to expect that anyone else would bother.

Index

A

B

F

G

Lightning Source UK Ltd.
Milton Keynes UK
UKHW041503081121
393608UK00001B/235